60 0077561 9

TELEPEN

Collective bargaining
in industrialised market economies

Collective bargaining in industrialised market economies

International Labour Office   Geneva

ISBN 92-2-101050-3 (limp cover)
ISBN 92-2-101065-1 (hard cover)

First published 1973
Third impression 1978

Printed by "ATAR S.A.", Geneva, Switzerland

Contents

Collective bargaining

II. Recent Trends in Selected Countries

Preface

In all the countries covered in the present volume, collective bargaining has traditionally been regarded as a desirable method of laying down wage rates and other conditions of work, and of regulating labour-management relations. There are national differences in collective bargaining methods and practices, institutions and procedures, and countries endeavouring to improve their own methods and practices have long been aware of the usefulness of understanding and benefiting from the experience of other countries with similar problems. This volume is an ILO contribution to such an understanding.

The flexibility and adaptability of collective bargaining have been repeatedly demonstrated in the past. The ILO is committed by its Constitution and by the will of its constituents, i.e. the representatives of governments, workers and employers, to promoting that form of decision making, and it is ready to help its constituents to show that collective bargaining procedures and results are capable of reflecting not only the vital interests of the immediate parties and their members but also the fundamental interests of the community as a whole. The publication of the present volume is part of a series of activities that include studies and research, meetings, and the provision of information and advice, at their request, to governments, trade unions and employers' organisations.

The last comprehensive ILO study on collective agreements was published as far back as 1936 [1], and is now obviously out of date. Since the Second World War comparative information on collective bargaining has been published in various reports submitted to the International Labour Conference in connection with the discussion and adoption of international instruments on collective bargaining [2], as well as in various reports submitted to sessions of ILO regional conferences and Industrial Committees or to other ILO meetings [3], and in a

---

[1] ILO: *Collective agreements,* Studies and Reports, Series A (Industrial Relations), No. 39 (Geneva, 1936).

[2] In particular, the Right to Organise and Collective Bargaining Convention, 1949 (No. 98), and the Collective Agreements Recommendation, 1951 (No. 91); in preparation for the adoption of those two instruments, reports on industrial relations were submitted to the International Labour Conference from the 30th to the 34th Session (1947-51).

[3] The texts of international standards and guiding principles on labour relations, including collective bargaining, adopted between 1944 and 1968 have been published in ILO: *International standards and guiding principles, 1944-1968,* Labour-Management Relations Series, No. 34 (Geneva, 1969). A number of papers submitted to ILO meetings and dealing with industrial relations, particularly with regard to meetings of a more recent date, have been reproduced in other issues of the Series.

number of other ILO publications.[1] The most important items of national legislation on labour relations, particularly on collective bargaining, are published regularly in the ILO *Legislative Series.*

The study in Part I of the present volume is a systematic comparative survey of recent developments and present trends in methods and practices of collective bargaining in industrialised countries with a market economy. This group of countries has been chosen for two reasons: first because of the similarity, and hence ready comparability, of the problems, concepts, institutions and procedures involved, and secondly in order to demonstrate the ILO's interest in and concern with labour relations problems in the highly industrialised societies of Western Europe, North America, Japan and Australia. The study is not exhaustive: examples are given primarily to illustrate certain developments or trends, and no attempt is made to include references to all the countries or industries in which a similar evolution is taking place. Part of the information used was taken from ten articles that were originally published in the *International Labour Review* and which have been reproduced as Part II of the volume.[2]

For the purposes of the present study the term "collective bargaining" has been used in a wide sense: it refers not only to the negotiation of formal collective agreements as defined and regulated by law but to the whole range of collective dealings, in as far as they contain an element of negotiation, between employers and workers and their representatives. The emphasis is on the methods and practices of collective bargaining; this means that questions of substance, i.e. the contents of collective agreements, are considered only in as far as they have a bearing on bargaining methods and practices. Further omissions of importance include the means of dealing with industrial disputes and the increasingly important subject of collective bargaining in the public service.[3]

It is almost superfluous to point out that the great diversity of institutions in the various countries covered make it next to impossible to formulate observations of all-inclusive validity. In a study such as the present one, close approximation is usually the most that one can aim for, and even then a margin must be granted for inevitable exceptions, deviations, variations, and of course inadvertent errors.

---

[1] See for instance *Collective bargaining,* A workers' education manual (Geneva, 1960). A list of ILO publications on labour relations in general and collective bargaining in particular is contained in *International standards and guiding principles, 1944-1968,* op. cit.

[2] These articles describe trends in collective bargaining in the early 70s in Australia, Belgium, France, the Federal Republic of Germany, Italy, Japan, the Netherlands, Sweden, the United Kingdom and the United States.

[3] For a recent comparative analysis of the law and practice of labour relations in the public service see ILO: *Freedom of association and procedures for staff participation in determining conditions of employment in the public service,* Report II, Joint Committee on the Public Service, First Session, Geneva, 1970.

Because the basic unit of analysis in this study is of necessity an entire country—and because the comparisons are therefore inter-country in scope—the full measure of diversity does not always emerge as clearly as it undoubtedly would, had it been possible to call more attention to the wide spectrum of collective bargaining practices which exist within the various industries and enterprises of any single country. On the other hand the diversity in the main practices followed in different countries, industries and enterprises is already so great that it is impossible to draw conclusions on the basis of a summary applying to all the countries in question; however, in the course of the study an attempt is made to point to certain general trends and to explain, from a comparative point of view, differences and similarities between collective bargaining structures and procedures of different countries, industries and undertakings.

In working out the present study the ILO had the benefit of the co-operation of Professor John P. Windmuller of the New York State School of Industrial and Labor Relations at Cornell University, who prepared the basic draft.

I. Comparative Study of Methods and Practices

1. Origins and Nature of Collective Bargaining

Collective bargaining is a process of decision making. Its overriding purpose is the negotiation of an agreed set of rules to govern the substantive and procedural terms of the employment relationship, as well as the relationship between the bargaining parties themselves. Although institutional arrangements in the countries covered in the present study are quite diverse, there are enough common elements of fundamental importance to allow a comparative examination of contemporary methods and practices of collective bargaining. It is of course true, as Allan Flanders has noted, that "many of the problems likely to dominate the future of collective bargaining can only be sensibly discussed in their specific national context".[1] However, although the accuracy of that remark may not be open to question, there is nevertheless a strong case for the proposition that certain insights into the operation and the potential of collective bargaining can best be gained by comparative analyses—with due regard to their unique features—of the ways in which different systems respond to the relentless challenges generated by modern societies.

The superiority of collective bargaining over other decision-making procedures as a form of joint industrial government, as a way of managing complex organisations and as a means of setting wage rates and other terms of employment and of regulating labour-management relations needs constant demonstration; and the degree of public support which it can continue to command, if perhaps not its very survival, ultimately depends on its adaptability to the ever-changing character of its environment.

This is not the place to trace the history of collective bargaining. That important task has been undertaken with much success elsewhere, although it should be recognised that for several countries the historical

---

[1] Allan Flanders: "The changing character of collective bargaining", in *Employment and Productivity Gazette*, Dec. 1969, p. 1103. Richard Lester made the same point when he wrote: "The noteworthy fact about collective bargaining is how the institution differs in its various aspects from one country to another and in the same country from one period to another" (Richard A. Lester: "Reflections on collective bargaining in Britain and Sweden", in *Industrial and Labor Relations Review*, Vol. 10, No. 3, Apr. 1957, p. 401).

record is still incomplete. Only a few quite general comments on the subject will be made here.

The emergence of collective bargaining is intimately linked to the economic and social consequences of that complex constellation of technological, demographic, ideological and other developments which took place in the last century. The insecurities and disturbances ensuing from the profound changes occurring during that period had a particularly unsettling effect on the traditional relations of employers and workers. First in Great Britain, but not much later in other countries, working men sought to protect themselves against the harsh effects of new machines, new methods of production, new divisions of labour and new intensities of competition by forming organisations capable of representing their interests as a group vis-à-vis employers and the State. At the outset, the only organisations that were able to survive the vicissitudes of the business cycle, the adamant resistance of employers and the hostile policies of the State were the ones set up by the skilled workers, the craftsmen; they alone had the material and administrative resources and the leadership to build solid institutions. Viable organisations among less skilled and unskilled employees came into existence only later. It is worth pointing out that it took longer to narrow the organisational gap between skilled and unskilled workers in Great Britain and North America than in many other countries. This fact may help to explain the continuing importance of craft unions and of bargaining structures originally based on craft unionism in Canada, Great Britain and the United States.

Craftsmen organised for various purposes: some emphasised restriction of entry to the trade to avoid the market disabilities resulting from an over-supply of qualified workmen, while others sought to build up mutual benefit societies to provide rudimentary protection against loss of income due to unemployment, old age, ill health or industrial disputes; of course, these purposes were not mutually exclusive. Regulation of wages and other key terms of employment was usually an important object, but there was no single pattern, no common channel through which such regulation developed. Some early organisations merely tried to determine unilaterally the wage scales (or job rates) under which their members would work, while other organisations sought to reach agreement with employers on a satisfactory schedule. On the employer side, reactions varied, depending on the circumstances, from the defensive formation of employers' associations to an outright refusal to deal with workers except on an individual basis.

Thus collective bargaining had no single, uniform origin. Sometimes it was the employers who sought to establish it in place of union-imposed "price-lists"; sometimes the unions strove to establish joint wage determination in the face of employer opposition; and sometimes, though perhaps more rarely, the impetus came from both sides. As

Allan Flanders and others have rightly pointed out [1], it would certainly be unjustified to overlook the role of employers and their associations in the initial development of collective bargaining; but the main burden eventually came to rest on workers and their unions, especially in the industries where the bulk of the labour force consisted of unskilled and semi-skilled workers, for there the employers were often extremely reluctant to abandon the advantages of unilateral rule making.

The resistance of many employers to engaging in joint dealings with their workers was powerfully reinforced by public policy, which in several countries derived its philosophical justification from the anti-combination principles of economic liberalism. Restrictive legislation and the disabling judgements of courts, seeking to uphold the sanctity of the individual contract of employment, tended to weaken the unions, especially outside the crafts, and to retard the development of collective bargaining. However, in some countries by the turn of the century, and in most of the rest during the 1920s and 1930s, public policy had swung around to at least a benevolent tolerance of collective bargaining, and increasingly even to its active promotion. To be sure, the development was not an even one in all countries. In some, employer resistance was deeply entrenched; in others, severe weaknesses and divisions among the unions slowed down the pace of development. On the whole, however, a major report on collective agreements prepared by the International Labour Office in the mid-1930s could justifiably take notice of—

... the increasing importance of the collective agreement as an element in the social and economic structure of the modern industrial community. The growth of the movement for regulating conditions of work by means of collective agreements has been particularly marked since the war [i.e. the First World War], and in many countries the collective agreement is now a recognised method of determining working conditions. The movement is primarily based on the desire of employers and workers to settle for themselves the conditions in their industries, but it has proved to be not inconsistent with various forms of the co-operation, the regulation or the control of the State. Although the collective agreement has become widely established in a large number of countries as an integral part of the industrial system, it has discharged its important functions on the whole so smoothly and efficiently that the full extent of its influence on national life is often overlooked.[2]

At the time when these observations were made the expression "collective bargaining" was already well recognised. The practice itself had, of course, existed well before the name came into existence, some

---

[1] "Today, with advantage of hindsight, it is easy to appreciate the inadequacy of any theory of either the nature or the growth of collective bargaining which sees it only as a method of trade unionism and overlooks in its development the role of employers and their associations" (Allan Flanders: "Collective bargaining: A theoretical analysis", in *British Journal of Industrial Relations,* Vol. 6, No. 1, Mar. 1968, p. 3).

[2] ILO: *Collective agreements,* op. cit., p. 265.

early forms of collective bargaining being known as arbitration or conciliation even though no neutral third parties took part in the proceedings.[1] The credit for coining the expression belongs to Beatrice Webb, who first used it in 1891 in her study on *The co-operative movement in Great Britain.*[2] It took some time for the term to be absorbed into the everyday language of Great Britain, the United States and other English-speaking countries. As late as 1902, the final report of the Industrial Commission in the United States still observed:

This term, collective bargaining, is not often employed in common speech in the United States, but is gradually coming into use among employers and employees in Great Britain. It evidently describes quite accurately the practice by which employers and employees in conference, from time to time, agree upon the terms under which labour shall be performed.[3]

In non-English-speaking countries, particularly on the European continent, where the process of collective bargaining has an equally long history, the emphasis was placed on the term "collective agreement" because during the early period the workers aimed not so much at establishing the procedure of bargaining itself as at having such agreements recognised and enforced as legally binding contracts.

In most of the countries covered by the present study, collective bargaining has become a pre-eminent method of industrial rule making. This is the case even where the proportion of workers covered by the terms of collective agreements falls short of a majority of the total number of wage and salary earners. The reason is that the terms of employment negotiated under collective bargaining tend to set a pattern in relevant fields of comparison, i.e. an industry, a region, or some combination of the two. Often this happens informally, as when enterprises not represented at the bargaining table decide to incorporate newly negotiated provisions into their own wage scales, working conditions, personnel policies or shop rules, as the case may be. Not infrequently, too, such action stems from efforts to demonstrate to workers that there is no need to be represented by a union.

In a number of countries, however, the pattern-setting aspect of collective bargaining has become a matter of public policy and has received a legal foundation of its own. One expression of such public policy is the requirement encountered in certain countries that an employer who is a party to a collective agreement must apply its terms without discrimination to all categories of workers whom the agreement

---

[1] Vernon H. Jensen: "Notes on the beginnings of collective bargaining", in *Industrial and Labor Relations Review,* Vol. 9, No. 2, Jan. 1956, pp. 230-232.

[2] For a reference to the origin of the expression see Sidney and Beatrice Webb: *Industrial democracy* (London, Longmans, Green, 1902 ed.), p. 173, note 1.

[3] *Final Report of the Industrial Commission,* Vol. 19 (1902), p. 834, as quoted in Neil W. Chamberlain and James W. Kuhn: *Collective bargaining* (New York, McGraw-Hill, 2nd ed., 1965), pp. 1-2.

covers, whether or not they are union members. In the United States
and Canada a comparable obligation is imposed by law on the union
certified as the exclusive bargaining agent to represent fairly the
interests of all employees in the bargaining unit, whether or not they are
union members.

A different form of recognition of collective bargaining as a setter
of socially useful patterns is the legislation encountered in a substantial
number of countries, which provides, often with the prior support of the
parties themselves, for the the possibility of "extending" the scope of an
agreement: in such countries collective agreements can under certain
conditions be declared to be generally binding on all employers and
workers within a given industry or region.

The administrative details of the "extension" procedure vary
considerably from country to country [1], and need not be described here.
It should be noted, however, that the practice appears to have lost some
of the support which it enjoyed in the past, especially from trade
unions.[2] Apparently unions in some countries have come to realise that
the advantages of "extension" have counterbalancing disadvantages:
while it is true that the proclaimed purpose of "extension" is to prevent
non-organised employers from operating at a competitive advantage, it
is also evident that workers who benefit from it have that much less
incentive to become union members.

Collective bargaining is by no means the only method of determining conditions of employment or regulating labour relations, and
even where it predominates it always exists side by side with other
methods. The main other methods are individual bargaining between
employer and worker, regulation by the government or another third
party, imposition of wages and working conditions by management, and
imposition of terms by a trade union. The latter two methods, which
amount to unilateral determination, are now relatively rare but by no
means non-existent, especially in industries where management or the
trade unions are particularly powerful. Of greater importance,
however, are individual bargaining and third-party regulation. In view
of the customarily prevailing disparity of bargaining power, individual
bargaining will often be tantamount to unilateral imposition of the
terms of employment by the employer.

Regulation by the government or by another third party as an
alternative to collective bargaining cannot be readily distinguished from
regulation as a supplement to it: there are no countries in which the
State abstains completely from legislating in the area of working conditions. However, the scope of such legislation varies enormously

---

[1] See Otto Kahn-Freund (ed.): *Labour relations and the law* (London, Stevens, 1965), p. 12.

[2] For a comprehensive review of the origins of extension see L. Hamburger: "The extension
of collective agreements to cover entire trades and industries", in *International Labour Review*,
Vol. 40, No. 2, Aug. 1939, pp. 153-194.

between countries, as does its effect: whereas the North American countries have generally adopted only a minimum of legislation on substantive working conditions, social legislation in many European countries covers a broad spectrum of issues which might also be subjects for collective bargaining. The general consequence of large-scale regulation of terms of employment on the part of the State tends to be a narrowing of the scope for collective bargaining, although the parties normally still have the possibility of using standard-setting legislation as a starting point for the negotiation of better terms through collective bargaining.

Compulsory arbitration, as practised in Australia at the federal level and at the level of the individual states, represents a special case of third-party regulation. There the process of collective bargaining is linked to compulsory arbitration in an intricate way which enables bipartite negotiations to go on simultaneously with the argument of a case before a disputes tribunal. The relationship between the two processes has been described as an "intertwining of negotiations and arbitration [which] is essentially a process of legislation in which the parties participate as far as they can, shaping the outcome as closely as possible to their objectives".[1]

There can be little question about the broad acceptance which collective bargaining has gained in most industrialised countries. Speaking quite generally, one might say that collective bargaining has become so firmly established in the past three to four decades that it is sometimes regarded as synonymous with, or as constituting the essence of, the prevailing system of industrial relations. Nothing could be more revealing of the virtual identity between collective bargaining and the industrial relations system in certain countries than the comprehensive report of the Canadian Task Force on Labour Relations: the report is entitled *Canadian industrial relations,* but its contents are devoted almost entirely to collective bargaining and its key institutional components.[2]

In any attempt to explain the vitality of collective bargaining, it must be recognised at the outset that collective bargaining is a complex institution which draws its strength from a variety of sources. It is, in the first place, a highly flexible method of decision making, far more so than legislative, judicial or public administrative processes could be expected to be. Not only does collective bargaining allow for substantial inter-

---

[1] Kenneth F. Walker: *Australian industrial relations systems* (Cambridge, Massachusetts, Harvard University Press, 1970), p. 91.

[2] *Canadian industrial relations,* The report of the Task Force on Labour Relations (Ottawa, Privy Council Office, 1968). In this connection, see also United Kingdom, Royal Commission on Trade Unions and Employers' Associations, 1965-1968 (Chairman: Lord Donovan): *Report,* Cmnd. 3623 (London, HM Stationery Office, 1968), cited subsequently as the "Donovan Report".

country variations, which shows that it can be adapted to a broad range of economic and political systems, but within a given national context it can be adjusted to cope with the exacting requirements of many different industrial and occupational sectors, of private as well as public undertakings, of single-plant as well as industry-wide units, and of unskilled manual operatives as well as of employees performing the most highly skilled tasks.

This flexibility is reflected in the diversity of agreements that can emerge from collective bargaining negotiations. They may range from a purely oral understanding or the simplest and briefest document, containing barely more than an agreed wage scale, to the most complex agreement not only covering a wide spectrum of issues but also allowing for the addition of supplementary agreements. General agreements, with their customary provisions covering wages, hours, and working conditions, can be amended by highly specialised agreements, as for example on the integration of a private retirement plan with a publicly administered pension scheme or on the retraining of workers whose jobs are being eliminated by the introduction of technological improvements. Supplementary agreements may also take the form of shop-level agreements specifying rules of conduct and dealing with other issues that arise in the shop and cannot be readily settled at a higher level.

A second reason that accounts for the prevalence of collective bargaining is its use as an instrument for applying widely held notions of equity or social justice to the industrial setting or the labour market. In proportion to the growth of the conviction that the individual worker could not be adequately protected against exploitation through individual dealings with his employer, there gradually developed a readiness in many societies to entrust the requisite protective function to a process that allowed the combined strength of workers to offset the initially superior bargaining power of the employer. Reinforced by public policies increasingly favourable to collective bargaining, workers' organisations assumed a share of responsibility for the proper operation of a joint rule-making system. Fear of more radical solutions to the complaints about exploitation, or distaste for the excessive paternalism of state regulation and private employer benevolence, may well have played a role in helping to secure public acceptance of collective bargaining. The fact remains that bargaining became a major means of achieving social justice and fair treatment on the job.

Besides its advantage of flexibility and the contribution it can make to the adoption of equitable terms of employment, collective bargaining is a means of ensuring workers' participation in decision making. The notion that workers are entitled to participate in setting the terms under which they are to work is inherent in collective bargaining: even the

13

most rudimentary form of collective bargaining involves a transfer of certain issues, be it only wages, from the area of unilateral to the area of bilateral decision making. Clearly, the scope of collective bargaining is broadening very rapidly, and an increasing number of questions are coming within its range. In this sense, collective bargaining represents a diminution of absolute management power in fields which employers in the past considered to be exclusively within their own domain. In this sense, too, collective bargaining introduces democratic practices into paid employment, virtually all forms of which used to be organised along authoritarian lines. It is worth pointing out that the scope of collective bargaining has been enlarged, admittedly not without disagreements and conflict, to follow the shift of opinion about the proper range of issues that are legitimately subject to joint decision making.

Conflicting and joint interests are simultaneously inherent in an employment relationship. Collective bargaining cannot negate the conflict in the relationship, since the conflict is based on the existence of different goals, needs and aspirations; but it does provide an opportunity for the exchange of information tending to enhance the understanding of the parties for each other's problems and objectives, both where they differ and where they are identical. Moreover—and this is very important—it provides an orderly procedure by which each side can seek to present to the other the best possible case for the satisfaction of its particular demands. There is no guarantee of an agreed outcome, but the process of negotiation creates at least the possibility that each side may move closer to the attainment of its own separate objectives while contributing to the attainment of those that are shared with the other side.

Another significant source of strength underlying collective bargaining lies in the fact that it elicits the consent of those who will have to live under the terms of any agreement derived from the bargaining process. Stability is an important element in employment, and "consent assures stability because parties who have accepted an agreement will live by its terms".[1] To the extent to which notions of democracy can be applied to employment, as indeed they have been on an increasing scale, collective bargaining helps to substitute freely given consent for grudging or blind obedience.

Finally, and without trying to give an exhaustive list of the advantages of collective bargaining, mention should be made of its potential usefulness for solving problems. The conventional view of collective bargaining emphasises its function as a means of resolving

---

[1] Vernon H. Jensen: "The process of collective bargaining and the question of its obsolescence", in *Industrial and Labor Relations Review,* Vol. 16, No. 4, July 1963, p. 556.

conflicts of interest in situations characterised essentially by scarce resources. In purely distributive bargaining, what one party gains, the other loses; however, another view of the possibilities inherent in collective bargaining emphasises its use as an "integrative" or "creative" process from which both parties can derive benefit.[1]

---

[1] Richard E. Walton and Robert B. McKersie: *A behavioral theory of labor negotiations* (New York, McGraw-Hill, 1965), p. 11 ff.

2. Structure and Organisation of the Parties

B asic to collective bargaining is the capacity of the "parties of interest", as the Canadian Task Force on Labour Relations calls them, to develop internal structures suited to the bargaining process and to adapt those structures when necessary to current changes in bargaining patterns. Moreover, the relative position of workers and employers in their mutual dealings can be significantly affected by the ability of each of the parties to organise for concerted action.

The principal forms of organisation on the worker and employer sides will be analysed in this chapter, but only in as far as they relate to collective bargaining. The emphasis will be on such major questions as the basis and extent of organisation, the ways in which the parties seek to mobilise their forces, the challenges to their cohesiveness and solidity, the locus of decision making within the various structures, the relationship between bodies at different levels in workers' and management organisations, and the presence of any trend towards centralisation or decentralisation.

Workers

In all the countries covered in this study trade unions are the most important organisations representing the workers' interests in collective bargaining. However, they are not the only organisations performing that function, and some attention will be devoted to works councils and analogous bodies whose dealings with employers can increasingly be described as collective bargaining.

The first observation which needs to be made on the subject of trade unions is that of all the varied activities in which trade unions engage in the political, educational, cultural, social and other fields, collective bargaining is by far the most important. Trade union structure reflects that fact by conferring particular prominence and authority on the organs that bear the main responsibility for collective dealings with employers. This helps to explain why in countries in which industry-wide bargaining is prevalent the national unions, as the appropriate counterparts of national organisations on the employer side, concentrate most of their power at the national level, whereas in countries with a substantial amount of local or enterprise bargaining local trade union organisations have retained a good deal of independence from central direction.

Local unions

As a rule, the lowest administrative unit of trade union organisation is the local union or branch, hereafter simply referred to as the local union, i.e. an organisation of workers usually covering a given enterprise or plant or, in some cases, a locality. To highlight the existence of significant inter-country and intra-country differences as regards the local union's place in collective bargaining, at least three important distinctions should be drawn.

The first relates to the constitutional position of the local union within the larger entity to which most local unions belong, i.e. usually a national union, the regional or district branch of a national union or a federation of (local) unions. In some countries, notably in North America and Japan, where collective bargaining takes place mainly at the enterprise level, the local union (or the enterprise union in Japan) often enjoys a high degree of autonomy. This means that within certain limits, set by constitutional mandate or custom, local unions can take independent action concerning the employment relationship between their members and the employers in the local unions' territorial jurisdiction. Frequently such independent action includes the negotiation and administration of collective agreements. The precise degree of local autonomy will vary from country to country, from union to union, and over time; the main point is the existence of a substantial amount of independent local decision making.

An important consequence of local autonomy is the amount of influence which individual union members can exercise on the bargaining policies of their unions because of their proximity to the policy-making process. In fact, there is a close correspondence between local union autonomy and a decentralised bargaining structure.

In other countries, including many of the European ones, where collective bargaining is normally industry-wide, the local union tends to have less autonomy: it operates more as an administrative arm of the larger organisation of which it forms a part, with more emphasis given to its administrative and service functions than to collective bargaining; local unions fitting this description tend to play a more subordinate and distant role in collective bargaining. As indicated, there is clearly a fairly close relationship between administratively dependent local unions and a substantial degree of centralisation of collective bargaining.

The Australian union branch exemplifies the relationship between the degree of centralisation of bargaining and the autonomy of the local union. Branches which operate under the jurisdiction of a state industrial tribunal, that is whose sphere of activity relates to an industry that comes under the authority of one of the state industrial tribunals, are usually free to follow their own policy in negotiations; on the other hand branches which function in industries that are subject to the authority of the federal industrial tribunal are required to co-ordinate their negotiations under the direction of the national officers of the union.[1]

The second distinction among different kinds of local unions relates to their organisational base. In many countries, particularly in Europe, local unions tend to be geographical entities: their territory covers a given city, town, county, department, or similar unit of government and administration. In these circumstances union membership is almost always a function of a person's place of residence and is not limited to employees of a particular enterprise, so that members of local unions based on geographical subdivisions will probably be working for many different employers.

The alternative base of organisation is, of course, the plant and enterprise. Where all members of a local union work in the same enterprise, the activities of the organisation will naturally be focused on the problems of that enterprise to a greater extent than in cases where the union members work for different employers.

Local unions based on territorial criteria predominate in European countries, including Great Britain. They also exist in North America, especially in certain skilled occupations, but they are less characteristic of the North American union structure than local unions based on employment in a given plant or workplace. In Japan, almost all local-level organisations are formed on the basis of attachment to a particular enterprise.

The third distinction relates to the occupational composition of local unions. At the extreme ends of the range, local unions can consist either of members in a single occupational category (teachers, bricklayers, locomotive engineers) or of all employees attached to an enterprise or industry in a given locality regardless of occupation. In countries where industrial unionism predominates, as for example in Austria, in the Federal Republic of Germany and in Sweden, local unions uniformly reflect the all-inclusive occupational structure of their parent organisations. In Japan too the enterprise union is all-inclusive. On the other hand, in countries where the structure of unionism is mixed rather than uniform, with industrial, craft, general and other forms of unionism co-existing, local unions will tend to present a mixed appearance. In such countries, notably Canada, Great Britain and the

---

[1] Walker, op. cit., p. 51.

United States, purely craft unions exist side by side with occupationally mixed local unions, and it is entirely possible for a national union to accommodate within its ranks local unions of the most varied composition.

In countries where local unions have some degree of autonomy and have secured a firm foothold in the workplace, they represent the vital link between the collective bargaining process and the individual worker. Where the union is not directly represented in the workplace, however, other ways must be found to establish the link. This is especially urgent where companies or unions are large and the individual must cope with forces that must sometimes seem far beyond his control.

In general there are three ways in which unions can deal with situations in which they lack a secure and manifest position at the workplace: they can leave workplace tasks to other organisations; they can try to transform the membership bases of their local organisations so that each represents workers in a particular workplace; or they can seek to establish outposts in the workplace, but leave the local union structure more or less intact.

The first solution is the traditional one in many countries in continental Europe, where works councils and analogous bodies exist that are distinct, at least in law, from the trade union organisations. A separate section of this chapter will deal with the functions of works councils and their relationship to unions as far as collective bargaining is concerned.

The second solution has so far proved unattractive or excessively difficult, though developments in Sweden come close to it. There the principal national confederation, the Swedish Confederation of Trade Unions [1], has encouraged its affiliates to consolidate their local unions into larger and administratively better equipped bodies, while simultaneously fostering the growth of sub-local organisations at plant and shop level.[2] Whereas in 1948 there were 8,950 local unions in national unions affiliated with the Confederation, the figure has now been brought back to 3,500 and may be reduced even further in the future. At the same time the number of active sub-organisations in places of work has grown substantially. The result appears to be a combination of territorially oriented local unions with attached subsidiary plant-based units. The process of consolidation may have been facilitated by the concentration of industry in particular areas.

The third solution, or a variant of it, appears to be at present the most widely favoured. In the Netherlands, for example, the three national unions in the metal industry that are affiliated with the major trade union confederations have undertaken a long-term programme to

---

[1] Landsorganisationen i Sverige.

[2] Bo Carlson: *Trade unions in Sweden* (Stockholm, Tiden förlag, 1969), p. 55.

establish separate and specialised organisations at plant level.[1] They are doing this without changing the territorial basis of their local unions, which will continue to operate principally as administrative arms of the national organisations and will thus have relatively little to do with collective bargaining. The new approach of the unions in the metals industry is intended to draw them to the attention of ordinary members who in the past have not always relied on the unions for the solution of job-related problems. If successful, the innovation may require a realignment of responsibilities between unions and works councils, but it is much too early to draw any conclusions about the long-term prospects of the new approach.

Similar efforts are under way among certain unions in the Federal Republic of Germany: they too are seeking to cultivate a plant-level organisation much more elaborate and responsive than it has traditionally been in the past. The union's plant level representatives, the stewards, will be called upon to advise on desirable changes to be sought through collective bargaining, to estimate the degree of rank-and-file support which the union would be likely to obtain if it were to decide to turn to industrial action, and to act in general as a link between the organisation and its members. A number of employers are showing increasing willingness to recognise the status of the union's plant level representatives.[2] In some collective agreements, especially in the metal industry, provisions have already been adopted which relate to the recognition and protection of such representatives.

In France an important aspect of the agreement reached between the Government, unions and employers in May 1968 (the so-called "Grenelle Agreement") was embodied in legislation of December 1968[3] which likewise grants trade unions a position in the enterprise for which they had been pressing for several years but which they had for the most part lacked until that time.

A similar change is taking place in Italy. A "workers' charter" passed into law as Act No. 300, dated 20 May 1970[4], seeks to implement existing constitutional principles which guarantee to workers the right to fair treatment at the workplace, and seek to remove obstacles to trade union action at factory level.[5] However, in requiring that representative trade unions should be granted recognition at the workplace, the charter aims more at the provision of special facilities for the conduct of trade union business in the plant than at recognition for purposes of collective bargaining; the unions themselves have

---

[1] See Albeda, below, pp. 329-330.

[2] See Reichel, below, p. 263.

[3] ILO: *Legislative Series,* 1968—Fr. 1.

[4] Idem, 1970—Italy 2.

[5] See Giugni, below, pp. 283-284.

been opposed to any tight definition of their bargaining powers at plant level on the ground that this would in effect restrict their freedom of action.

A special case is that of Great Britain, where the recent rise to prominence of the shop steward has occurred independently of any deliberate campaign to strengthen the position of unions at shop level. Though shop stewards are almost everywhere a part of the union structure or at least members of the union, their precise relationship to the union is frequently not yet well defined. In the past, as long as the steward's functions related primarily to union administration and to the application of collective agreements concluded at much higher levels, the common lack of precision created no serious problem. In recent years, however, the steward has increasingly become a workplace negotiator. The reasons for this change are complex. Among them are the wider introduction of incentive pay systems that both provide an opportunity and create a need for detailed plant-level bargaining; inadequacies in the staffing patterns of British unions which suffer from a dearth of full-time officials; until quite recently a relative shortage of labour which promoted employer willingness to engage in plant-level supplementary bargaining. In any event, not only has the number of stewards sharply increased to perhaps as many as 200,000, but the stewards' new bargaining functions have helped them to achieve more autonomy within their own unions than they have ever had before.[1]

Because the prevalence of multiple or parallel unionism in British industry commonly leads to situations in which stewards of several different unions engage in plant-level bargaining simultaneously or consecutively, serious problems of inter-union co-ordination have arisen. The new Commission on Industrial Relations has suggested that union policies could stress more clearly than they do at present the need for inter-union co-operation at workplace level, while management could help avoid potentially conflicting claims and negotiations by providing facilities for joint steward committees and by meeting and negotiating with such unified bodies.[2] The recommendation is in line with practice in Australia, where when more than one union is active in a plant—a very common occurrence—a combined shop stewards' committee may act as a bargaining agent with management on internal plant matters.[3]

---

[1] Commission on Industrial Relations: *Facilities afforded to shop stewards,* Report No. 17, Cmnd. 4668 (London, HM Stationery Office. 1971), pp. 4-5. See also Roberts and Rothwell, below, p. 362.

[2] Ibid., p. 16.

[3] Walker, op. cit., p. 51.

Regional union organisations

In most countries local unions (except those choosing to lead an entirely independent existence) are affiliated with, and subordinate to, organisations at national level—the national unions. For a variety of reasons, including effective administration, co-ordination of collective bargaining, and the maintenance of a desired degree of decentralisation, national unions frequently establish regional or district bodies at an intermediate level between themselves and their local unions.[1]

Collective bargaining may be an especially important reason for establishing intermediate union bodies. Two rather different situations ought to be distinguished. The first arises when key collective bargaining negotiations for an industry or occupation take place at the regional level. It then becomes virtually essential that there should be a regional union body to act as bargaining representative opposite the regional organisation on the employer side. An impressive number of bargaining situations in Europe and Australia, and to a lesser extent in North America, reflect this sort of regionalisation.

The establishment of union bodies at the intermediate level can also result from local bargaining: when two or more local unions belonging to the same national organisation operate within the same product or labour market, a co-ordinating body is sometimes required to prevent the local unions from competing with one another. One analyst of intermediate union bodies has observed in this connection that "in unions which have multiple locals in the same branch of industry in the same area, and in which each local is a potential competitor of every other local either for the work or for a share of the employer's wage bill, there must be and there is a strong intermediate body to handle matters of collective bargaining".[2] Such situations are especially common in North America, where the basic bargaining units are often local.

In countries where local unions are too small to support full-time paid officials or where, regardless of size, financial resources are inadequate, the district may be the lowest level at which a full-time paid official is employed. In the Netherlands, which exemplifies this situation, the district official's responsibilities include collective bargaining as well as services to individual members; district officials operate under the direction of the union's central office. In other countries, where

---

[1] Studies of the functions of intermediate union bodies are still extremely rare. For the United States see Herbert J. Lahne: "The intermediate union body in collective bargaining", in *Industrial and Labor Relations Review*, Vol. 6, No. 2, Jan. 1953, pp. 163-179, and Alice H. Cook: "Dual government in unions: A tool for analysis", in idem, Vol. 15, No. 3, Apr. 1962, pp. 323-349. For Great Britain see H. A. Clegg: *The system of industrial relations in Great Britain* (Oxford, Blackwell, 1970), pp. 101-105.

[2] Lahne, op. cit., p. 178.

unions are able to afford a more elaborate regional structure, district officials may be responsible to an elected board chosen from among union members in the region. The question whether in their collective bargaining activities regional officials should be primarily responsive to the wishes of the members at the base of the organisation or should follow policies shaped at national union headquarters has been resolved in many European unions in favour of the latter approach. In North America no clear pattern is discernible, and for the time being not much more can be said than that "the intermediate body must be looked upon as part of the union's search for effective structure".[1]

National unions

In virtually all industrially advanced countries national unions emerge at a certain stage of development as the principal directive bodies for marshalling the collective interests of workers in defined industrial or occupational sectors. This concentration of labour's resources at national level seems to be independent of any parallel formation on the employer side. For example, in the United States, where employers in many sectors of the economy have traditionally preferred to administer their own labour policies on an enterprise basis and to refrain from establishing associations for collective bargaining purposes, national unions have nevertheless become very powerful.[2]

The factors which further the rise of national unions and the speed at which this development occurs have, of course, varied considerably between different countries. In some countries, such as France, localist tendencies among workers were soon so firmly established that for a long time national organisations were to be primarily loose federations of largely autonomous local union groups. (This conception of the national organisation as a relatively weak co-ordinating body was often reflected, in France and other countries, by attaching the term "federation" to the name of a national union.) By contrast, national unions in other countries, for instance the Federal Republic of Germany, established their authority over local bodies at an early stage.

National unions now derive their strength from their command over financial and other resources essential to trade union activities (including strike funds), from the acknowledged need to meet the combined strength of employers at national or regional levels with countervailing union power, from the enlargement of product and labour markets far beyond local boundaries, and from the general escalation of the size of institutions in industrialised societies.

---

[1] Lahne, op. cit., p. 178.

[2] For the most comprehensive analysis of the reasons behind the growth of national unions in the United States see Lloyd Ulman: *The rise of the national union* (Cambridge, Massachusetts, Harvard University Press, 1955).

To some degree, the concentration of authority at national union level and the accompanying centralisation of bargaining structures have been under challenge in recent years, as is indicated, for example, by the fact that the rank-and-file union membership has become increasingly self-assertive and restless. The manifestations of this restlessness and its consequences for the decentralisation of the bargaining structure will be explored in a subsequent chapter.

One important exception to the pre-eminence of the national union in collective bargaining should be noted here. In Japan the enterprise unions, which are the basic organisations, still play the most important role in collective bargaining, and the bargaining structure in most industries is still highly decentralised, enterprise by enterprise. As a consequence, national unions in Japan are for the most part no more than loose federations of enterprise unions.[1] The Japanese worker's continuing close attachment to his enterprise, especially in large manufacturing plants, the recognised role of the enterprise—especially the large enterprise—as a social community and not merely a place of employment, and the reluctance of enterprise management to allow bargaining to develop at levels above the level of the enterprise are factors that account for this exceptional situation.[2] It is far from certain whether the present pattern will remain frozen, and the prospects for vesting more authority in the national unions are a matter of conjecture.

National unions play their crucial role in collective bargaining in many ways. Most importantly, it tends to be their responsibility to define major bargaining objectives and policies and to perform the research required to support the main economic demands. Usually it is the national union that administers the organisation's strike fund. Where a substantial amount of bargaining takes place at local or regional levels, the national union is usually represented by an official responsible for helping local bargainers and simultaneously for seeing to the observance of national bargaining policies. In the Federal Republic of Germany for instance, a decision on whether a collective agreement should be cancelled or renegotiated or not may be made by the national union or by the collective bargaining committee of the union's regional office, depending on whether the union bargains on a national or on a regional scale. If it is the latter, an official of the national union will usually participate in the negotiations.[3]

In bargaining with very large multi-plant employers, national unions may form corporation councils, as the United Automobile

---

[1] See Mitsufuji and Hagisawa, below, pp. 303-305.

[2] Taishirô Shirai: "Prices and wages in Japan: Towards an anti-inflationary policy?", in *International Labour Review*, Vol. 103, No. 3, Mar. 1971, p. 234.

[3] Murray Edelman and R. W. Fleming: *The politics of wage-price decisions* (Urbana, Illinois, University of Illinois Press, 1965), p. 100.

Workers' Union in the United States has done to co-ordinate the bargaining of its local unions with General Motors and other large firms in the industry.

As a rule it is also the national union that assumes the responsibility of dealing with government agencies when the government becomes deeply involved in the bargaining process.

Another important collective bargaining function which national trade unions have in various countries is the negotiation, with the respective employers' organisations, of basic agreements, joint statements or similar agreements setting out procedural principles and guidelines for the conduct of industrial relations.[1]

Special negotiating bodies

In countries where industrial unionism is the prevailing principle of union organisation, where as a rule only one union represents the employees of a particular enterprise and where bargaining units are reasonably homogeneous in composition, the uncomplicated hierarchy of local-regional-national union encompasses the main elements on the union side of collective bargaining. (The possible additional involvement of confederations in collective bargaining will be discussed in the next section.) However, in a sizeable number of countries craft, white-collar and general unionism are to be found alongside industrial unionism, a multiplicity of unions are represented in important industries and enterprises, and the composition of negotiating units is not standardised. Sometimes, therefore, unions have been compelled to evolve new structural forms capable of achieving three objectives simultaneously: providing effective representation for their members in collective bargaining, coping with the problems caused by multiple unionism, and preserving the autonomy of all the unions concerned.

The simplest means of achieving all this is to set up an ad hoc negotiating committee representing two or more unions in a particular industry or enterprise, as is done in France when the unions form a liaison committee and in the United States through the kind of coalition bargaining which has emerged in recent years in large corporations like General Electric. A similar device, though somewhat more formal, has been developed in the United Kingdom by unions associated in joint industrial councils.[2]

Other kinds of inter-union co-operation in collective bargaining which stop short of formal links are often encountered in countries

---

[1] Texts of such agreements and statements have been reproduced in ILO: *Basic agreements and joint statements on labour-management relations,* Labour-Management Relations Series, No. 38 (Geneva, 1971).

[2] Clegg, op. cit., pp. 73-74.

where two or more unions co-exist in a particular industry and share common economic interests, yet are divided from one another by ideological or institutional considerations. Thus, in Australia some of the problems of co-ordination are overcome by the practice of acting through informal federations, as in the metal and building trades, although unions of opposing political views tend to be excluded.[1] In Italy the success of informal co-operation between the several national unions in the metal industry may lead to their unification in the near future.[2]

A more formalised arrangement is the creation of bargaining federations. The purpose of such federations is identical with that of the informal co-operating bodies, namely a co-ordination of objectives, an identification of common interests and a combination of economic strength on the part of several unions that are all involved in bargaining with the same party. A federation is distinguished from looser arrangements by the presence of a governing structure, a formal set of rules, a staff of employed officials and a greater expectation of institutional continuity. Furthermore, a federation is often able to handle joint negotiations in more than one industry. In the United States some of the departments of the American Federation of Labor-Congress of Industrial Organizations (AFL-CIO), particularly the Industrial Union Department, have functioned as bargaining federations, although this was originally not envisaged as one of their main tasks. In Great Britain, where multiple unionism at industrial and enterprise levels is traditional and widespread, 45 formally constituted federations existed in 1968 to co-ordinate the joint collective bargaining efforts of their affiliated unions.

A development pointing to the formation of special trade union structures for eventual bargaining at the international level should be briefly cited here. This is the formation of "corporation" or "company councils" composed of national unions, from different countries, whose membership includes the employees of a multinational enterprise. Corporation councils exist in particular in the automobile industry (General Motors, Ford, etc.); their formation is also well advanced in several other industries. Their long-term objectives include collective negotiations with top corporate management on questions transcending national interests, for example the employment effects of shifts in plant location, the retraining and re-employment rights of employees laid off because of the consolidation of production facilities, and the equalisation of major fringe benefits.

It has often been noted that where multi-industry bargaining prevails or where plural unionism exists within a given industrial sector, as

---

[1] See Yerbury and Isaac, below, p. 193.
[2] See Giugni, below, p. 275.

in France, it is difficult for the unions to remain in touch with each other. In the above review of institutional arrangements, an attempt has been made to indicate the various ways in which unions have tried to deal with the problem.

National confederations

The apex of the trade union structure is the national confederation (or confederations in the case of plural trade unionism). In most industrialised countries the principal responsibilities of such national bodies extend to the conduct of relations with the government, political parties and employers' confederations, the exercise of influence on the legislative process, the dissemination of workers' views on public issues, and, where necessary, the settlement of disputes between unions. Collective bargaining tends to be a peripheral activity, for national unions are usually not keen to share authority over collective bargaining with their national confederations. To be sure, the maintenance of a central strike fund, where it exists, will give national confederations a measure of influence over collective bargaining, but this is not likely to be of decisive importance unless the national unions are heavily dependent on external financial assistance in times of need.

Under certain conditions, however, a confederation can become directly involved in collective bargaining. This is especially the case when governments seek to align the outcome of collective negotiations with key objectives of national economic policy. From a government's point of view, dealing with a single national confederation is administratively preferable to dealing with a large number of individual organisations. At the same time, it is reasonable for a government to expect the leaders of a national confederation to have a greater understanding of macro-economic issues than leaders of local, regional or national unions. It is also conceivable that trade unions will prefer to cede a measure of autonomy to their national confederation if the alternative is direct government intervention in collective bargaining.

In any event, the greater the degree of government intervention —or at least the threat of such intervention—in economic affairs, the stronger is the likelihood that the national confederation will play an active part in collective bargaining.

A substantially different form of participation of national trade union confederations in collective bargaining is involved in the negotiation of so-called basic agreements. Such agreements have been concluded at the national level in a number of countries, including Belgium, Denmark, Finland, France, the Federal Republic of Germany, Italy, Norway and Sweden. They deal with certain substantive issues (e.g. vocational training, dismissal, productivity) or with the relationship between the parties (e.g. shop stewards, works council, procedures for collective bargaining and labour disputes); or they may contain statements of general industrial relations principles, practices and objectives.[1]

If national confederations are to become engaged in collective bargaining for the entire economy or a whole industry, they must have a corresponding measure of authority. Practically speaking, it does not matter very much whether such authority is anchored in constitutional provisions or whether it is simply recognised de facto by affiliated unions, as is usually the case.

Austria probably exemplifies one extreme of a broad range of possibilities. In that country, with its long-standing machinery for the central determination of wage and price policy[2], the national trade union confederation[3] has the exclusive right to sign any of the collective agreements negotiated by the national unions at industry level.[4] This also helps the confederation to ensure that the weaker sectors of the union movement do not fall too far behind in wage settlements. It is also worth noting that in Austria all union dues collected by the national unions are turned over to the trade union confederation, which redistributes a part of the total to affiliates on the basis of need and other criteria, while retaining the major share.

In Norway the General Confederation of Trade Unions[5] "has come increasingly to take command of industry-wide contract negotiations. A collective agreement cannot be terminated, new demands cannot be presented, a strike cannot be called without the approval of the Secretariat".[6] Indeed the Confederation even has the right to reject excessive bargaining demands of affiliates. In certain circumstances the Confederation can decide that all contract demands should be uniform. When this occurs it is the Executive Board that negotiates for all unions with agreements expiring in a given period, though representatives of the unions concerned do participate in the negotiations.[7]

The Swedish Confederation of Trade Unions[8] negotiates basic wage and other agreements with its counterpart on the employer side.[9] Under a government-initiated concentration of decision making by the

---

[1] See ILO: *Basic agreements and joint statements on labour-management relations*, op. cit.

[2] Jack Barbash: "Austrian trade unions and the negotiation of national economic policy", in *British Journal of Industrial Relations*, Vol. 9, No. 3, Nov. 1971, pp. 371-387.

[3] Österreichischer Gewerkschaftsbund.

[4] *Der Österreichischer Gewerkschaftsbund* (Vienna, 1970).

[5] Arbeidernes Faglige Landsorganisasjon (LO).

[6] Herbert Dorfman: *Labour relations in Norway* (Oslo, Norwegian Joint Committee on International Social Policy, rev. ed., 1966), pp. 56-57.

[7] Ibid., p. 76.

[8] Landsorganisationen (LO).

[9] Svenska Arbetsgivareföreningen (SAF).

confederations, which dates back to the 1930s, national agreements constitute a framework within which the constituent organisations of the Confederation of Trade Unions are expected to negotiate agreements at industry and enterprise levels. Representatives of the Confederation have the right to be present at those negotiations.[1]

In the Netherlands the three national trade union confederations were intimately involved in the determination of wage policy at the national level during the period of national wage control from 1945 to about 1963.[2] They also participated in administering the machinery which was designed to ensure that the outcome of collective negotiations at industry level between national unions and their corresponding employers' associations conformed to wage norms laid down for the economy as a whole. However, since the mid-1960s, the participation of the national confederations in collective bargaining in the Netherlands has become more indirect and distant, while at the same time the Government has relinquished a substantial portion of its former control over national wage policy.

As already noted, government economic policy is the most important factor tending to shift authority over collective bargaining to the national confederations. Concern over persistent deficits in the balance of payments tends to be a particularly strong incentive for the imposition of central economic controls; inflationary pressures may also have the same effect. However, the long period of full employment and economic liberalism after the Second World War should not allow one to forget that economic interventionism was already very extensive during the depression of the 1930s. In fact, in some countries such as the Netherlands and Sweden the basis for post-war centralisation of authority in the trade unions was laid at that very time.

Of course, the link between extensive government participation in economic affairs and an enhanced role for the national trade union confederations goes beyond collective bargaining. As Allan Flanders has pointed out, the adoption of economic controls calls for a shift in the emphasis of trade union action from the industrial to the political sphere, and "the representation of the trade union point of view on any proposed legislation or administrative action can best be undertaken by a central body".[3]

The size of the country also seems to bear a relationship to the propensity to centralise authority in trade unions. In terms of size of population, Austria, the Netherlands, Norway and Sweden, where centralisation is very great, are all rather small countries. By contrast,

---

[1] T. L. Johnston: *Collective bargaining in Sweden,* A study of the labour market and its institutions (London, Allen and Unwin, 1962), especially pp. 39-44.

[2] See Albeda, below, p. 320; also John P. Windmuller: *Labor relations in the Netherlands* (Ithaca, New York, Cornell University Press, 1969), pp. 338-364.

[3] Allan Flanders: *Trade unions* (London, Hutchinson, 7th edn., 1968), p. 61.

the countries in which the national confederations have only modest powers over their affiliates—Canada, the Federal Republic of Germany, Great Britain, Japan and the United States—have either relatively large populations or a large territory, or both. The correlation is by no means perfect, but it would seem likely that centralisation comes about more easily in small than in large countries.

Organisational variables and union strength

The ability of trade unions to participate effectively in collective bargaining is determined not only by the appropriateness and adaptability of the structure of the trade union movement but also by such considerations as the extent and solidity of trade union organisation. This means, for example, that a low union membership or a severe division in the labour movement will impair the quality of representation which trade unions can provide for their members.

As regards union membership, precise comparisons are not possible for lack of comparable data. One of the main difficulties is that the base used for the purpose of computing percentages of unionisation is not always the same: it can be the total labour force, the civilian labour force, the non-agricultural labour force, the number of wage and salary earners or other aggregates. But this is by no means the only difficulty. Total membership figures for an entire country hide areas of strength as well as weakness in individual industries or occupations. This is a very important deficiency in the total figures because so much collective bargaining takes place on a sectoral basis. Furthermore, aggregate figures do not reveal anything about the turnover rates of union membership, the difference in unionisation rates for manual and white-collar workers (almost always higher for the former), or the direction of membership trends, that is, whether they are up or down. In addition, it is virtually impossible to obtain data for a common base year.

For all these reasons no effort has been made here to assign specific percentages to union membership in the several countries; to do so would only convey a misleading impression of accuracy. It is also important to note that the growth and strength of the trade union movement are determined by various factors of a quite different nature that cannot be discussed in this study.

Continuing changes everywhere in the composition of the labour force will inevitably have an effect on the aggregate rate of unionisation, and ultimately, therefore, on labour's bargaining strength. The main change is the rise in the proportions of non-manual workers and women in the labour force. In the past these groups were less well organised than male manual workers and therefore tended to lower the average rate of unionisation. In recent years, unions in many countries have tried to strengthen their appeal to those groups, and the sharp increase of collective bargaining in the public sectors of many countries may well be one of the results of those efforts.

Another variable capable of affecting trade union bargaining strength is the presence, or absence, of competing organisations. As a general rule the ability of workers to present a common front to the employer side strengthens labour's bargaining power, whereas a split in labour's ranks tends to weaken it. Divisions based on differences of ideology and philosophy account for the existence of plural unionism especially in Belgium, the Netherlands, Italy, France, Japan and Canada (Quebec). In the first two countries institutionalised or other forms of accommodation have attenuated the divisions; in Italy efforts are at present being made to strengthen co-ordinated action of different union movements; in the other countries attempts to find more common ground have become more frequent and more intense in recent years.

Divisions along major occupational lines, although encountered in a large number of countries, are of special importance in Sweden, the Federal Republic of Germany, and France. They are reflected in the existence of separate national organisations for non-manual employees, those organisations being sometimes further subdivided, as in Sweden, between the public and the private sector. Most of the time national organisations separated along main occupational lines have found ways of co-operating for collective bargaining purposes. Thus, in the Federal Republic of Germany for example, where both the German Confederation of Trade Unions and the separate German Union of Salaried Employees [1] seek the allegiance of white-collar workers, employers are usually able to deal with the two organisations jointly, instead of separately, as far as collective agreements for salaried employees are concerned.[2] However, there have been periods of inter-organisational friction in all three countries.

Attention needs to be called to one other organisational variable which can have an important effect on the bargaining posture of the trade union side, namely the number of national unions among which union members are distributed. Other things being equal, the lower the number the greater the resources available to any one union. A relatively small number of unions with large sectors of industry under their control may also significantly reduce the possibility of jurisdictional disputes. Conversely, a large number of small autonomous unions may entail a significant diminution in the capacity of many or most of them to provide effective representation. Of course, other things are never exactly equal, and one must also take into consideration such factors as

---

[1] Deutsche Angestelltengewerkschaft (DAG).
[2] See Reichel, below, p. 256.

the size of a country, the complexity of its industrial structure, the traditions of the trade union movement, and other factors.

Among the various countries under review here the national confederations of Austria and the Federal Republic of Germany each have only 16 affiliates, most of them industrial in composition. At the other extreme the British Trades Union Congress had 170 affiliates in 1966, while the total number of trade unions in Britain amounted to 574.[1]

Because of the possibility that an excessive number of organisations may damage the interests of union members and of the movement as a whole, the national confederations in a number of countries have deliberately but cautiously steered towards a reduction in the number of unions through amalgamation and other devices. The most sizeable reductions have occurred in Britain, which has also had the most fragmented movement, but consolidations have been undertaken even in situations where the original number of unions was far smaller than in Britain. Thus the Danish national confederation [2] has succeeded in reducing the number of affiliates from 70 in 1950 to 59 at present.[3] In Sweden the same process has resulted in a gradual reduction in the number of affiliates to the national confederation from 44 to 27, while in Norway there are now 41. Important amalgamations are occurring in the several national confederations of the Netherlands. There has also been a modest decline in the number of national unions in the United States, from some 209 in 1949 to 183 in 1969.

Another factor apt to influence the bargaining power of unions is their financial position. There is little doubt that an effective system of collection of union dues will directly enhance a union's position in collective bargaining. In recent years trade unions in several countries have tried to negotiate check-off arrangements with employers.

Works councils

In their capacity as institutions representing employee interests in collective bargaining, trade unions in many continental European countries have traditionally not played a very active part at the workplace. For historical reasons which cannot be explored here [4] spe-

---

[1] Donovan Report, op. cit., p. 7.

[2] Lands Organisationen.

[3] The reduction was made easier by indirect government assistance. Danish unions disburse unemployment insurance to their members, for which they receive government subsidies. Under a new law, the Danish Government will not contribute subsidies to unions having fewer than 1,000 members.

[4] A comprehensive account will be found in Adolf F. Sturmthal: *Workers' councils* (Cambridge, Massachusetts, Harvard University Press, 1964).

cialised institutions have been mainly responsible for representation at the workplace in Belgium, France, the Federal Republic of Germany, Italy, the Netherlands and other countries. The names of those institutions differ from country to country, but the designation "works councils" will be used throughout this study to avoid confusion.

Works councils are usually not within the organisational domain of unions, in the sense that they are not formally trade union branches or organs. They must therefore be distinguished from the shop committees of a union and especially from the North American or British shop stewards, who are an integral part of the union structure even where they appear to be acting rather independently of their organisations. In fact, however, the members of works councils are often active union members, and the councils co-operate closely with the trade unions in several countries. Works councils are virtually always bodies whose establishment in enterprises of a certain size and kind is provided for by law, or by agreements concluded between trade union confederations and employers' organisations.

It must also be emphasised that works councils, again unlike unions in many countries, have an all-inclusive representational responsibility: their constituency is made up of all workers in a given enterprise, whether they are union members or not, and as a rule works councils are bound by law (or agreements) to represent the interests of all the workers without distinction; in this respect they are like unions in the United States, which are legally bound to represent all workers employed in the bargaining unit.

In practice, of course, as mentioned above, there can be, and there are, many links between unions and works councils. Some of these links have achieved legal validation and support. For example, in a number of countries unions have an explicit right to present lists of nominees for election to works councils, but this right is generally not an exclusive one; non-union groups may also present lists of candidates. Still, most works council members tend to be union members, and in many cases trade unions have managed to have their most active members elected to the councils. Moreover, unions often assume responsibility for training works council members so as to help them perform their tasks more effectively. This service, too, helps to strengthen the unions' influence over works council policies.

There is no uniform set of functions for works councils. Quite often their principal concern, as laid down by law, is the promotion of co-operation between management and employees for the good of the enterprise; in some cases they are supposed to have consultative or co-management rights.[1]

---

[1] See for example Blanpain, below, p. 209.

As far as collective bargaining is concerned, works councils have traditionally been relegated to an ambiguous role: on the one hand they have frequently been excluded by law or custom from the negotiation of collective agreements in the formal statutory sense because that task has been considered to be within the exclusive province of the trade unions, while on the other hand the councils have almost always been assigned a specific responsibility for supervising the proper application of collective agreements. In this supervisory and administrative part of councils' work there has in the past been little potential conflict with the trade unions, which often had no plant-level organisation of their own. In a sense, therefore, works councils have been a substitute for a union organisation at plant level.

The balance between trade unions and works councils has never been a perfectly stable one, but until quite recently the existing statutory and de facto division of labour appeared to be the optimum solution to the problem of what in effect amounted to dual representation of employee interests. In the past few years, however, a number of developments have occurred that call into question the continuation of this long maintained equilibrium.

The works councils have increasingly concerned themselves with activities that come exceedingly close to conventional collective bargaining over local conditions. In the Federal Republic of Germany, for example, despite the Act governing the establishment of works councils [1], which limits the extent to which the councils can negotiate with the employer over the terms of employment, the statutory restraints are often disregarded.[2] In fact, there has been a noticeable increase in the number of agreements between individual employers and works councils. Their agreements—for that is what in practice they amount to—are no longer confined, as they once used to be, to such subjects as work schedules, rest periods, and similar matters which could not possibly be regulated in an industry-wide agreement. Instead, they now sometimes cover subjects central to the collective bargaining interests of the unions, such as protection of workers from the consequences of technological change.

Another instance, though possibly one which is more in the nature of an exception, is the leading role which works councils in the Netherlands assumed in the bargaining over a substantial one-time wage payment in the autumn of 1970, when they by-passed the unions.[3]

Among the trade unions a directly opposite tendency has been developing: they have been improving their position at plant level, sometimes simultaneously with the entry of works councils into collec-

---

[1] ILO: *Legislative Series*, 1972—Ger. F.R. 1.

[2] See Reichel, below, p. 262.

[3] See Albeda, below, p. 329.

tive bargaining. For reasons already noted above, the largest unions in the metal industries in the Federal Republic of Germany and in the Netherlands are diligently pursuing policies designed to strengthen their footholds in individual enterprises, while similar developments are under way on an extensive scale in France and Italy.

In Italy, as indicated by Professor Giugni, the growth of the workers' delegate movement may be threatening the functions and possibly even the very existence of the traditional works councils [1], which are said to be fading out of existence.[2] This impression is supported by another observer who notes that the lowering of the level of bargaining to the shop floor has led to the representation of small, homogeneous work groups in plant negotiations by workers' delegates who increasingly take the place of the shop delegates designated by the unions to sit on the works councils.[3] The appearance of the workers' delegates seems to be a response to the high degree of centralisation and division in the trade union movement in Italy, for one of their important qualities is their ability to maintain an ideologically undivided work group constituency.

The present situation may on occasion lead to friction as different institutional interests compete for advantage. Dual loyalty problems can arise in various circumstances. This can occur, for example, when an individual tries to combine the more aggressive role of the new type of plant-level union representative with the traditional co-operative responsibilities of a works council member. Under the system of the Federal Republic of Germany, which in this respect may be taken as exemplifying several others, a works council member should by law refrain from engaging in any militant activities directed against the employer. He is expected, on the contrary, to concentrate on the co-operative aspects of his task. But when he simultaneously tries to fill the role of a union shop steward, as occasionally happens, he may end up in a difficult position, notably in the event of an open dispute between his employer and the union.[4] The problem even arises, though not quite so sharply, in the still more frequently encountered situation in which the works council member has no special union responsibilities but simply tries to be, at one and the same time, a loyal union member and a competent works council member.

It is still too early to forecast whether the works council will ultimately be absorbed or superseded by plant-level union bodies (as may perhaps be occurring in Italy), or whether a new relationship and a

---

[1] Commissioni interne.

[2] See Giugni, below, p. 277, note 3.

[3] François Sellier: "Les transformations de la négociation collective et de l'organisation syndicale en Italie", in *Sociologie du travail,* Apr.-June 1971, p. 154.

[4] See Reichel, below, p. 263.

new division of responsibilities between the two kinds of institutions will emerge, as may be the case in the Federal Republic of Germany and in the Netherlands. Should the latter path be chosen, it may in some countries take the direction which it has in Sweden, where the establishment of the works councils and the demarcation of their activities were the result of an agreement [1], first concluded in 1946 and since revised, between the national confederations of labour and of employers. Because works councils in Sweden were developed as an adjunct to a collective bargaining system in which the strength of unions at all levels was never in doubt, the system has avoided many of the problems found elsewhere.[2]

Whatever the outcome, there can be little question that a structural realignment is now under way in response to the new emphasis on collective bargaining at enterprise and workshop levels.

Employers

The complexities of structural alignment for collective bargaining on the union side have their counterparts on the employer side. Indeed, there the diversity can be even greater: employer interests in collective bargaining may be represented by an individual enterprise acting only on its own behalf, by a group of enterprises acting jointly through an ad hoc body, or by a permanent association of employers. These possibilities, broadly outlined, cover the private as well as the public sector. However, government-operated services and publicly owned industrial enterprises often have their own form of representation for dealing with unions of their employees.

Employers' associations

An outstanding characteristic of the industrial relations systems of Western Europe and Australia is the high degree of organisation and common action among employers in the private sector. In this respect there is a substantial difference with employers in North America and Japan.

Information on membership of employers' associations is not readily available, but some illustrative figures can be provided. Thus, the Federation of Belgian Enterprises is reported to have as affiliates, directly or indirectly, 45,000 out of 79,000 enterprises in Belgium, representing the employers of over 50 per cent of all employed persons.

---

[1] Reproduced in ILO: *Basic agreements and joint statements on labour-management relations,* op. cit., pp. 187-206.

[2] T. L. Johnston, op. cit., pp. 219-232.

Collective bargaining

Most of the enterprises are affiliated indirectly through their membership of one of the 48 associations which belong to the Federation. In the Federal Republic of Germany the Confederation of German Employers' Associations represents employers who employ about 80 per cent of workers in the private sector of the economy.[1] In some industries, for example in metals fabrication, the proportion is likely to be in the neighbourhood of 90 per cent. Figures for Great Britain indicate that in many industries the member firms of employers' associations employ 80 per cent or more of the labour force, although there are a few industries in which the rate is something less than 50 per cent. In the very important engineering industry the Engineering Employers' Federation covers only 4,600 out of 18,000 enterprises, but these employ about 60 per cent of all workers connected with the industry.[2] In France the national association[3] consists of regional and industrial organisations which have a million member enterprises with some 13 million workers. Very few enterprises do not belong to an association.[4] The Swedish Employers' Confederation is composed of 40 affiliated industrial employers' associations with some 25,000 member enterprises, employing about 1.25 million people.[5]

In assessing these figures it ought to be noted that in a number of countries the employers' associations can point to a rate of organisation which is higher than the corresponding rate among trade unions. Moreover, since most of the available data do not cover the employers' associations that are independent, i.e. not affiliated with a national confederation, the actual rate of organisation is sometimes likely to be even higher than the figures indicate.

What, then, accounts for this substantial degree of organisation? No doubt there are elements of a traditional willingness to seek strength in cohesiveness, to transcend the divisive forces of economic competition in the search for a united stand against external challenges, and to submerge a certain portion of enterprise independence in exchange for the strength which flows from common action. In certain countries the

[1] Ernst-Gerhard Erdmann: "The Confederation of German Employers' Associations", in ILO: *Role of employers' organisations in Asian countries,* Record of proceedings of, and documents submitted to, an Asian round table, Tokyo, December 1970, Labour-Management Relations Series, No. 39 (Geneva, 1971), p. 132.

[2] Clegg, op. cit., p. 133 ff.; see also Royal Commission on Trade Unions and Employers' Associations: *Employers' associations,* Research Papers, No. 7 (London, HM Stationery Office, 1967).

[3] Conseil national du patronat français (CNPF).

[4] J. Nousbaum: "France", in Organisation for Economic Co-operation and Development (OECD), Manpower and Social Affairs Directorate: *Recent trends in collective bargaining,* Supplement to the final report, International management seminar, Castelfusano, 21-24 September 1971 (Paris, 1972).

[5] Per G. Holmquist: "The Swedish Employers' Confederation", in ILO: *Role of employers' organisations . . .,* op. cit., p. 308.

existence of a high proportion of small and medium-sized firms seeking protection through coalition may also be a contributing factor. Curiously enough, in a few industries in the United States, where in principle employers are not much inclined to associate, the decisive initiative for the establishment of an employers' association, or at least for some form of multi-employer bargaining, has come from the union side as part of a general effort to achieve industry-wide uniformity of the terms and conditions of employment.

In recent years certain reasons that are not necessarily new have come to the fore. In particular, economic and industrial relations problems are becoming increasingly complex and their handling requires the kind of expert knowledge that many enterprises are too small to acquire economically; there is a need for employers' interests to be effectively represented in dealing with the government; and employers are now faced with strong trade unions as bargaining partners. In Australia the existence of compulsory arbitration at federal level and in most of the constituent states of the federation, and of wage boards in the remainder, increases the utility of employers' associations to their members and hence tends to raise the rate of organisation.[1]

Realising that economic power can be effectively enhanced by concerted action, European and Australian employers have delegated important functions of representation to their associations. Collective bargaining is only one of those functions, though for our purposes the most relevant. In fact, collective action on labour-management relations has not necessarily been the most important factor in the founding of employers' associations in all countries: some were originally formed primarily to deal with public authorities and others were originally established to act chiefly as trade and self-regulatory bodies.

As a result of these varying antecedents, employers' associations typically span a range of functions at least as wide as those of unions: they engage in important representational and lobbying tasks in relation to the legislative and administrative branches of government; their public information and public relations services are designed for the effective dissemination of employers' views; they often maintain research and data-gathering departments, and they may offer their constituents limited specialised legal services; and a number of them also assume responsibility for training and apprenticeship in their economic branches and seek to promote further development in their particular industrial sectors or geographical areas. Closer to the subject of labour-management relations, employers' associations engage in a wide variety of tasks which may include the formulation of common

---

[1] Frank T. de Vyver: "Employers' organisations in the Australian industrial relations system", in *Journal of Industrial Relations,* Vol. 13, No. 1, Mar. 1971, pp. 31-32; see also G. Polites: "The Australian Council of Employers' Federations", in ILO: *Role of employers' organisations . . .,* op. cit., p. 85.

personnel policies for their members, the analysis of the collective bargaining proposals of unions, the research required for the adoption of a uniform employer position on union negotiating demands, and, in Europe and Australia, the actual conduct of collective bargaining on behalf of their members, the administration of collective agreements that are in force and the determination of employer strategy in the event of open industrial conflict.

Given the extraordinary diversity of production and ownership units operating under a market economy in industrialised countries, for example single-plant enterprises, multi-plant enterprises in the same industry, multi-plant enterprises in different industries, vertically integrated enterprises, conglomerates, holding companies and so on, it should not be surprising that a similar variety of structural forms is encountered among employers' associations. Any description of their structure can therefore give only an approximate notion of the kaleidoscopic variety encountered in practice.

Nevertheless, certain features are common to most countries. The first is the simultaneous existence of associational forms based on geographical (or "horizontal") and industrial (or "vertical") principles of organisation. Associations along geographical lines represent the interests of enterprises located in a specified territory, which can be a city, region, province or other specific area. The resulting industrial heterogeneity, which is a characteristic feature of associations with a geographical basis, explains why their attention is focused on issues of only indirect significance to collective bargaining, although they may offer certain ancillary services, such as the collection and distribution of wage statistics, to their member firms. Such associations are therefore only rarely involved in negotiations with unions. Associations along vertical lines seek to group all enterprises in a particular branch of economic activity, which usually comprises an industry, a part of an industry, or a combination of two or more industries. Vertical-type associations occupy a foremost position in collective bargaining, especially in a system of industry-wide bargaining, in which they are the logical negotiating counterparts of unions.

Frequently, though by no means universally, an enterprise belongs in the first instance to a local employers' association covering a defined industrial sector. Where collective bargaining customarily takes place at local level, as for example it often does in the United States in the construction trades of a major city, the local association will be the main spokesman for employers in the negotiations and may also have a continuing responsibility for the subsequent administration of agreements. The local association is also likely to be called upon by its members when difficulties arise over conflicting interpretations of the agreement. In a number of industries the organisations tend to be formed at the regional rather than the local level, though still along industrial lines. This is the case particularly where collective bargaining itself is conducted at the regional level, as is frequently the case in manufacturing industries, certain of the services and mining. In such cases the initial point of contact between an enterprise and an association will be the regional employers' association for the particular branch of economic activity concerned. In many countries local and regional associations in particular industrial sectors are affiliated, in turn, both with a national organisation for their particular sector and also, especially in the larger countries, with a geographically based (horizontal) association. As a rule, only the national organisation for the industry will be concerned in a substantial way with collective bargaining.

National industry associations of employers generally exercise one of two responsibilities. Where the basic collective agreement is industry-wide in scope and covers an entire country, the national association acts directly as the bargaining agent on behalf of its employer members. An example of such a situation is the function of Belgian employers' associations in relation to the more than 80 joint committees that cover individual sectors of industry throughout the country.[1] However, where negotiations are conducted at regional or local levels the national association acts more as a co-ordinating and service-rendering organisation to back up the work of its subsidiary affiliates; in this capacity it will not only supply information to support the bargaining position of its regional groupings but will also seek to avoid excessive differences from arising among the various localities and regions. In other words one of the main tasks of a national industrial employers' association within a setting of regionalised collective bargaining is the development, as far as possible, of national norms and principles. In addition, of course, the association makes a corresponding effort to secure the adherence of its affiliates to its policy.

In trying to devise the optimum structure for the representation of their interests, employers and their associations—just like workers and their unions—must strike a balance between several different considerations, including the potential consequences of concentrating on the strength of membership attachment and on relative bargaining power. In some countries, notably in the Federal Republic of Germany, in Sweden and in the United Kingdom, this weighing of different considerations has led to the emergence in some trades, notably the metal trades, of multi-industry associations which cover, for example, such individually large industries as automobile manufacturing, the production of electrical machinery and equipment, and engineering. Because of the vast economic power represented in their ranks, these multi-industry associations have at times assumed a leading role among employers' associations. As one observer of labour-management

---

[1] See Blanpain, below, pp. 210-211.

relations in the Federal Republic of Germany has pointed out, the employers' association for the metal industries [1] occupies about the same key position inside the national employers' confederation as the very large union of metalworkers [2] does within the trade union confederation.[3]

The peak of the organisational pyramid on the employer side is represented in most countries by a single all-encompassing confederation of employers' associations. Division along ideological or denominational lines, which in the trade union movements of several countries has resulted in the formation of two or more national confederations, is exceedingly uncommon. In Europe such a division among employers exists on a national basis only in the Netherlands, which at present has a non-denominational as well as a denominational (Roman Catholic and Protestant) confederation. In the United States, too, there are two national confederations, the National Association of Manufacturers and the United States Chamber of Commerce, but the division is not the result of ideological considerations.

With exceptions to be noted below, the national confederations are usually not bargaining associations engaged in the direct negotiation of terms and conditions of employment; rather, like their counterparts on the union side, they give authoritative national expression to the views of the members they represent.

In their capacity as peak organisations, they often include not only industry (vertical) associations but also regional (horizontal) associations. For instance, the confederation in the Federal Republic of Germany includes 43 vertical and 14 horizontal organisations. The employers' confederation in Italy [4] contains slightly over 100 industrial and trade associations and approximately the same number of regional groupings. The Japan Federation of Employers' Associations [5] consists of 47 industrial-type associations plus 9 regional and 44 prefectural associations. However, purely vertical and purely horizontal federations also exist. In Australia the member associations of the national employers' confederation are entirely regional in character, thereby reflecting the federal character of the Australian political structure. On the other hand, the employers' confederations in the Scandinavian and Benelux countries consist almost entirely of industry associations, in part no doubt because of the unitary nature of the State and in part also because of the relatively small size of the countries. Occasionally,

---

[1] Gesamtverband der metallindustriellen Arbeitgeberverbände (GESAMTMETALL).

[2] IG METALL.

[3] Pierre Waline: *Cinquante ans de rapports entre patrons et ouvriers en Allemagne, 1918-1968,* Cahiers de la Fondation nationale des sciences politiques, No. 178, Vol. 2: *Depuis 1945: la République fédérale allemande* (Paris, Colin, 1970), p. 193.

[4] Confederazione Generale dell'Industria Italiana (CONFINDUSTRIA).

[5] NIKKEIREN.

national federations and confederations will accept industrial enterprises into direct membership alongside their member associations, but the enterprises are likely to be very large ones in small countries: for example, the Norwegian Employers' Confederation [1] accepts both associations and individual firms into membership, as do the two Confederations in the Netherlands and the one in Denmark.

Just as in the case of unions, the locus of decision making among employers' associations is determined chiefly by the structure of collective bargaining. Since industry-wide bargaining, whether on a regional or on a national basis, is the most prevalent form in Europe and Australia, the industrial employers' associations or their regional subgroupings generally carry the most weight on the employer side. In some countries a substantial amount of decision making in industrial relations occurs on an economy-wide basis, frequently with the active participation of governments. In such cases the national employers' confederation acquires a considerable amount of influence over its affiliates. This is the case, for example, in the Scandinavian countries and the Netherlands. As mentioned above, a centralised form of collective bargaining conducted by national confederations on both sides exists with regard to the conclusion of basic agreements on specific substantive matters or on rules and principles regulating labour relations.

Where there is no precedent for centralised authority in collective bargaining but where, for whatever reason, circumstances arise which dictate the conclusion of a collective agreement between the most representative institutions on the employer and trade union sides to cover the whole economy, difficult internal negotiations may ensue between the confederation and its associated members. The case of France offers a recent example. Yves Delamotte has described the situation in these terms:

A similar problem [to that confronting the unions] faced the National Employers' Council over its links with the employers' federations, and in order to clarify the question it decided to amend its rules. Under the old rules it had no clear right to engage in inter-industry bargaining, since this was considered to be a matter for its member federations, which were entitled to argue that the Council could only represent them with their specific authorisation and if this were not given, they were not bound by the agreement. In the new rules which came into force at the start of 1970, the principle is laid down that "wages are a matter for individual employers and their trade associations". At the same time, however—and this is the new feature—an exception is allowed: "in other fields, the French National Employers' Council may in exceptional cases and with the approval of its Permanent Assembly be empowered to negotiate and sign general agreements for all . . . occupations". On the other hand, each federation is explicitly entitled to opt out of such an agreement before it is signed. A number of them took advantage of this right in the case of the vocational training agreement signed in

---

[1] Norsk Arbeidsgiverforening (NAF).

July 1970. This procedure may reduce the coverage of an agreement, but it also increases the likelihood that it will be something more than a catalogue of minimum standards based on what the least go-ahead industries can afford.[1]

By virtue of joining an association, an employer in many cases delegates to the association the right to enter on his behalf into negotiations with the unions representing his employees. It is in the very nature of an employers' association which bargains for its members that it must seek to preclude its member firms from entering into separate agreements with unions because separate agreements represent a threat to the association's ability to protect adherence to an agreed policy. Some associations have therefore been granted extensive powers over their member firms, such as the power to order a lockout, to grant or to withhold payment in case of a strike, to assess fines for violations of association policy, and ultimately to expel a recalcitrant member.

To be sure, in countries where individual enterprise bargaining is the rule, as in Japan and the United States, associations may have only a very limited amount of authority. It has been noted in this connection that in Japan the employers' associations have even less power over their member firms than labour federations have over their affiliated enterprise unions: "This lack of authority over their members is all the more evident under the present conditions of acute labour shortage, long-term prosperity, and intensifying competition among employers."[2]

There may be an emerging problem of association authority even in countries where employers' associations have traditionally been able to count on a high degree of discipline among their members. Clegg has pointed to a decline of association authority in Great Britain[3], while the following analysis of the Australian situation may be acquiring wider relevance at a time of generally decentralising tendencies in collective bargaining:

... The problem of internal discipline is even more acute in employers' associations than in unions. It has often brought about the dissolution of associations, and this possibility remains an ever-present threat to the solidarity of associations in industries where there is a wide divergence of interests between members. Such divergence is found mainly where the membership is drawn from different industries, or sections of an industry, which operate relatively independently.

The problem of internal discipline arises in two main connections, resistance to union pressure, and competitive bidding for labour when labour is scarce. In both situations, the aim of the association is to "hold the line" and to avoid having the position of the majority weakened by the concessions of a minority. Penalties have been proposed from time to time to bring recalcitrant members into line but few associations have dared to experiment far with these for fear of splitting the association.[4]

---

[1] See Delamotte, below, pp. 250-251.

[2] Shirai, op. cit., p. 235.

[3] Clegg, op. cit., p. 142.

[4] Walker, op. cit., pp. 73-74.

It seems in any event quite likely that by virtue both of the increasing complexity and of the seemingly progressive decentralisation of collective bargaining, employers' associations may be called upon to adjust to their members' increasing need for a wider range of services and for readier accessibility.

Multi-employer bargaining

Bargaining through an employers' association is only one way, though no doubt the most frequently employed, through which employers seek to combine their individual strength in dealing with unions. Where employers prefer not to submit to the discipline inherent in membership in an employers' association, or where for some other reason they do not wish to establish a body with institutional continuity, as is the case in many industries in the United States, some other form of action sometimes needs to be developed for the purpose of enabling employers to prevent unions from undermining a joint employers' stand by bringing concentrated pressure to bear in separate bargaining with individual enterprises (so-called "whipsawing" tactics).

The steel industry in the United States offers an example of a situation in which (since 1955) the major companies have most of the time negotiated as a group through a single bargaining committee but have not sought to transform their ad hoc coalition into a continuous association. This is also a case in which the effective impetus for multi-employer bargaining came initially from the union side as part of a general effort to achieve uniform basic terms of employment.[1]

The ad hoc coalition is a half-way station between enterprise bargaining and association bargaining. It offers employers the advantages of combination without the cost of diminished freedom of decision making in day-to-day labour-management relations. For if it is true that "management is beset by the fear of having its 'right' or 'freedom' to manage taken from it", as the former vice-president for industrial relations of a major American steel company once expressed it[2], then this concern extends not only to the inroad which unions try to make through their collective bargaining demands but also to the accumulation of authority in the hands of an employers' association.

The individual enterprise

Whereas in European countries and in Australia the negotiation of collective agreements has, generally speaking, been regarded as a matter external to the firm, North American and Japanese enterprises

---

[1] William G. Caples: "Development and problems of bargaining structure in the steel industry", in Arnold R. Weber (ed.): *The structure of collective bargaining* (Glencoe, Illinois, Free Press, 1961), pp. 186-187.

[2] Ibid., p. 192.

have by and large chosen to regard collective bargaining as an enterprise affair. The ways in which collective bargaining on an enterprise basis differs from industry-wide collective bargaining will be explored in subsequent chapters. Here attention should be drawn to the almost self-evident proposition that the need for specialised managerial resources to cope with collective bargaining is particularly great in single-enterprise bargaining where firms cannot rely on the expertise of association staffs. Labour-management relations in an enterprise may be improved by appointing trained industrial relations officers instead of relying on external services. The need for trained corporate staff is becoming particularly acute in countries where the current trend towards decentralised bargaining is occurring against a background of traditional industry-wide bargaining and reliance on association expertise.

There are some indications that the size of enterprises has a bearing on the question of individual-enterprise versus association bargaining. In part, this is a matter of cost, for the large enterprise is in a better position than small and medium-sized undertakings to absorb and spread the cost of a specialised industrial relations staff. It is also, in part, a matter of bargaining power, for here again a large multi-plant enterprise is usually better able to match the bargaining power of a national union than a smaller firm. Employer attitudes toward a union presence in the enterprise itself have also played their role. Where employers have insisted on meeting unions only outside the enterprise, an associational form of joint employer representation has evident advantages. Conversely, where the union has succeeded in penetrating into the enterprise itself, the employer may find it to be in his interest to set up administrative machinery of his own to conduct negotiations and handle day-to-day relations with union representatives.

The decision for or against direct dealings at enterprise level may well be a function of national traditions, policies and preferences. The strong competitive element in American business, reinforced by a long-standing national anti-trust policy, forms the background against which the predominance of individual enterprise bargaining in the United States needs to be appraised. By contrast, the sense of shared interests and solidarity among European employers and their willingness to submit to group regulation in trade matters, going back to the guild era, may well help to explain their clear preference for association responsibility in labour-management relations.

The public sector

The importance of the government as an employer of large numbers of civil servants is equalled in many countries nowadays by its importance as the operator of publicly owned industries and services. It is the latter capacity that the role of government is particularly relevant to this chapter (as already mentioned, the public service as such is not covered by this study).

In a few countries collective bargaining in public enterprises is a recent innovation. In France it was only in the late 1960s that collective bargaining became formally recognised as a decision-making process in the nationalised enterprises where wages and working conditions had previously been laid down by statute. These enterprises, which are engaged, for example, in coal mining and the production and distribution of electric power and gas, must be distinguished from nationalised enterprises like Renault and certain banks and insurance companies that have all along been subject to the provisions of the 1950 legislation on collective bargaining.[1]

Publicly owned enterprises do not commonly join associations in the private sector for purposes of collective bargaining, even in industries which consist of a mixture of private and public enterprises. Thus, the publicly owned industries in Italy that are operated by the Institute for the Reconstruction of Industry[2], i.e. all except the petrochemical industry, have their own employers' association. This association[3] was formed simultaneously with a government decision in 1956 against letting publicly owned enterprises be subject to the rules of the national employers' confederation in the private sector.[4] (The publicly owned petrochemical sector, operated by a separate public corporation [5], has a separate association for bargaining purposes.) State-owned enterprises in Sweden also have their bargaining interests represented by an independent body, the Public Enterprise Bargaining Organisation.[6] However, the general rule that government-owned industries do not join private sector associations for bargaining purposes does not necessarily apply to membership of a confederation of employers' associations: the Confederation of British Industry covers not only private industry but also virtually all the nationalised industries, and the employers' confederations in Japan as well as in the Netherlands are also open to public enterprises.

The degree to which the managers of public enterprises in service and industrial sectors are able to take independent decisions in collective bargaining is influenced by so many different variables that no generalisation is feasible. In France the Government has in recent years given nationalised industries in the monopolistic sector substantially

---

[1] See Delamotte, below, pp. 225-226, 235.

[2] IRI.

[3] INTERSIND.

[4] CONFINDUSTRIA.

[5] Ente nazionale idrocarburi (ENI).

[6] Statsföretagens Förhandlingsorganisation (SFO).

greater autonomy to engage in collective bargaining by abandoning an earlier procedure which had left the management little say over final decisions.[1] On the other hand, Belgium has preserved a strong measure of centralised government control over decision making in the industrial relations policies of the public sector. As Blanpain has pointed out—

> Under the cabinet system the Executive, which negotiates, will find the legislature almost automatically willing to implement the decisions or agreements reached through the necessary budgetary measures and other legislative action. The centralised system of fixing wages and conditions of work means that the national Government is the main locus of decision making and the trade unions concentrate their efforts at that level.[2]

As far as Britain is concerned, Clegg has noted that—

> formally the responsible minister has the power to give "directions of a general character as to the exercise and performance by the Board of their functions in relation to matters appearing to the Minister to affect the national interest", but this power has been used only once, in relation to transport charges. Indirectly, however, the minister has great power over the boards whose members he appoints and may decide not to reappoint at the end of their terms.

The same author has also observed:

> Government influence has been felt in many pay settlements in nationalised industries, which normally require the blessing of the cabinet, if not its formal approval. For some years ministers tried to maintain the fiction that labour matters were entirely within the managerial discretion of the boards, and board chairmen were required to support this pretence. Ridiculous subterfuges were employed. Since 1958, however, successive prime ministers have themselves conducted the final discussions with the railway unions at crises in railway negotiations, and the secret is less well kept.[3]

The issue of ministerial intervention has several aspects. One is the complex problem of ultimate political responsibility for the operation of public enterprises; this problem becomes particularly acute in the face of strikes or imminent strike threats involving vital public utilities, but it is always present in the background as a restraint on the freedom of action of managers in the public sector.

A second aspect is the role of treasuries (or ministries of finance) and legislatures whose attitudes and actions are likely to exert significant influence on the bargaining stance of public enterprises. The enterprises that are customarily able to balance their budgets are likely to have somewhat more room for manoeuvre in collective bargaining than industries chronically in need of public subsidies, but are not exempt from high-level direction: "The political importance of pay decisions in

---

[1] See Delamotte, below, pp. 240-241.

[2] See Blanpain, below, pp. 221-222.

[3] Clegg, op. cit., pp. 388-389.

nationalised industries is bound to attract ministerial intervention, and there is no means to protect the boards against their influence."[1]

A third aspect is the effect of an incomes policy. When a government has adopted such a policy, public enterprises become prime objects of ministerial attention, as examples of how the policy should be applied.

-----

[1] Clegg, op. cit., p. 389.

3. Procedures and Machinery

If collective bargaining is to be effective, the parties must address themselves to a number of procedural matters. For instance they must recognise each other as duly authorised representatives of their constituents, be willing to meet at reasonable times and places to negotiate, make careful preparations to support their bargaining demands, decide how much authority is to be vested in their negotiating teams, consider the length of time for which they wish to enter into an agreement, and deal with a host of other questions not directly part of the substance of the negotiations. Several of the more significant of these procedural matters will be discussed in the present chapter, to indicate the range and diversity of possible approaches to the various problems and to suggest alternatives to practices that have proved ineffective or inappropriate.

Recognition

There has rarely been any serious difficulty about union recognition of employers or employers' associations as their appropriate counterparts. In many countries, however, the reverse—namely employers' recognition of unions as the legitimate representatives of their employees or at least of union members—accounted for much of the early struggles for existence of the trade union movement.

With exceptions to be noted shortly, public authorities have generally refrained from adopting, or have not felt the need to adopt, measures that would lead to compulsory employer recognition of unions as duly qualified representatives of the workers for collective bargaining purposes. Therefore the act of recognition, which is after all a prerequisite for bargaining, has depended in most countries either on the economic power of unions to compel such recognition or on the employer's voluntary acceptance of collective bargaining with the union concerned as a desirable process. Both elements have often played a role, but in most countries recognition came about only gradually, painfully, and at varying rates, industry by industry and sometimes enterprise by enterprise. This was certainly the pattern in Great Britain and the Scandinavian countries. Occasionally a major political transformation—as in Germany in 1918 and in France in 1936—led to national negotiations at top level which implied a general recognition of trade unions by employers. Employers' associations at industry level then tended to fall into line. On the whole, once recognition had been extended and collective bargaining had established itself, the situation stabilised in such a way that unions did not need to fight the battle of recognition all over again, though sometimes that, too, became necessary.

It was only seldom that employer recognition came easily to the unions; but violent conflicts over this as a matter of principle occurred chiefly in the United States, where employer resistance was most determined. During the New Deal period, as a consequence of prolonged, repeated and embittered recognition disputes, the public authorities intervened more vigorously than anywhere else in the question of recognition: at first through the National Labor Relations Act of 1935 and subsequently through the 1947 amendments to that Act, the whole question of recognition and the associated question of the duty to bargain came, in this way, under far more detailed regulation in the United States than in other countries, where the public authorities did not refrain entirely from intervening in this aspect of industrial relations.

To shed light on the different approaches adopted in various countries on these matters, a preliminary distinction ought to be drawn between recognition and the duty to bargain, even though in practice these are closely related concepts. "Recognition" in this context means formal acceptance of one party by the other as a bargaining agent for a defined constituency; the parties may be unions, employers or employers' associations. Fulfilment of the duty to bargain requires, as a minimum, a clearly expressed willingness to meet the other party for the purpose of negotiating a mutually acceptable agreement.[1] Recognition can perhaps exist without good faith bargaining, but good faith bargaining without at least implied recognition would be a logical inconsistency.

In Canada and the United States the law provides that the union selected by the majority of the workers in a given bargaining unit shall be the exclusive representative for all the workers in that unit and shall be so recognised by the employer. Four important principles are present here: the decision is made by rule of the majority, whether it be a choice between two or more unions or between union representation and none

---

[1] It will be noted below that in the practice of the United States the concept of good faith bargaining has not only a procedural but also a substantive aspect.

at all; the majority union obtains exclusive representation rights as the bargaining agent; the bargaining agent assumes an obligation to represent all the workers and not only union members; and the employer must recognise the majority union as the bargaining agent for all the workers in the bargaining unit.

It is an important feature of the North American approach that it settles recognition questions without resort to industrial strife. That, indeed, was a major factor behind the adoption of the procedure, and in practice it has met its objective most of the time. One kind of dispute avoided by the procedure arises when two or more unions contend to represent a given group of workers; an election decides the claim. Another occurs when a union asserts that it represents a majority of the workforce in a given bargaining unit, and the employer disbelieves the assertion; here again, an election settles the difference. A third conceivable dispute stems from an employer's refusal to recognise a union in principle; if there is a majority union the law compels him to recognise it, without there being any need for the union to call a strike for the purpose.

There is no identical situation in continental Europe. Instead of the principle of exclusive bargaining rights, pluralistic representation is accepted in many countries. In many the trade union in a legal sense represents only its members, although in practice the employer will almost invariably extend the terms of an agreement to all his employees whether they are union members or not. In addition the employer is usually under no legal obligation to recognise a union of his employees for the purpose of collective bargaining.

A basic reason for the difference lies in the bargaining structure. From a practical point of view, industry-wide bargaining does not lend itself as readily as enterprise-wide bargaining to the application of majority rule and the accompanying determination of a bargaining unit. In addition, the ideological divisions among trade unions in many European countries have traditionally militated against adoption of exclusive bargaining rights for any one organisation since such a procedure might force an ideological minority to have its material interests represented by a politically antagonistic majority.

Belgium and France have developed the notion of the most representative union, which is part of the law of both countries. For all practical purposes, the same concept exists in the Netherlands, but there it is of an extra-legal nature. The most representative unions are organisations deemed by the Government to have met certain criteria which are prerequisites for designation as most representative unions. In law and in practice, organisations having received that designation have the exclusive right to represent the interests of the workers at various bargaining levels (national, industry, and enterprise) as well as on tripartite advisory bodies. It should be noted, however, that several unions often can and in fact do qualify for the designation of "most representative".[1]

In Great Britain until very recently public policy did not concern itself with the recognition issue at all. The nationalised industries were an exception: only they had imposed on them a statutory duty to enter into consultation with any organisation appearing to the management boards of the industries to be appropriate for the purpose of collective bargaining. The new Industrial Relations Act [2], however, lays down a procedure for the selection of an appropriate bargaining agent and requires the employer to deal with him. In order to leave undisturbed the British practice of multiple representation of employees, which logically would conflict with the principle of exclusive bargaining rights, the new British legislation allows for the formation of joint negotiating panels on the union side, to be treated as single bargaining agents.

The duty to bargain

Where recognition is regulated by law, the purpose is, in particular, the peaceful establishment of a bargaining relationship; consequently the regulation of recognition tends to be coupled with rules concerning the duty to bargain; and conversely in countries where no explicit provision is made for recognition the establishment of bargaining also tends to be left to the voluntary efforts of the parties.

The approaches of the United States and of the Federal Republic of Germany represent the two extremes. There is no duty to bargain under the current legislation of the Federal Republic of Germany.[3] The fact that bargaining nevertheless occurs extensively indicates, of course, that non-legal considerations have generally sufficed to bring employers and their organisations to the bargaining table. Yet that achievement must be assessed in the light of the fact that the negotiations have mostly taken place at the level of an entire industry (nationally or regionally), and that they have sought only to set minimum standards which individual enterprises may and do surpass.

In two other European countries the situation is somewhat different in law if not in practice. In Sweden since 1936 the law has conferred a right to negotiate upon associations of employed persons on the one hand, and employers and employers' associations on the other. At the same time the law imposes a corollary duty upon each side to

---

[1] For the Belgian concept of "most representative union" see Blanpain, below, pp. 207-208, 212-213. For the French concept see J. D. Reynaud: *Les syndicats en France* (Paris, Armand Colin, 2nd ed., 1966), p. 13.

[2] ILO: *Legislative Series,* 1971—UK 1.

[3] Hans Reichel: "Zwanzig Jahre Tarifvertragsgesetz", in *Bundesarbeitsblatt,* Vol. 20, No. 4, Apr. 1969, p. 195.

enter into negotiations when asked to do so. The principal purpose of the Act, when passed in 1936, was to give the then still weak organisations of salaried employees a bargaining capacity which manual workers had already achieved for themselves through the use of their economic power.[1] In France, under Section 9 of an Act of 13 July 1971 amending the basic French collective bargaining law of 1950, all representative organisations of employers and workers that have been convened to attend national bargaining meetings are obliged by law to be represented. The other and very recent departure from a highly voluntaristic tradition is the British Industrial Relations Act of 1971 which, in addition to provisions regarding recognition, imposes on the employer a duty to negotiate seriously with a recognised bargaining agent, failure to do so being defined as an "unfair industrial practice".[2]

Principles and practices paralleling this new approach in Great Britain have prevailed for some years in the United States, where under Section 9 *(a)* of the Labor Relations Act, as amended in 1947, both parties are required to bargain in good faith "in respect to rates of pay, wages, hours of employment, or other conditions of employment". In interpreting and applying this provision, particularly as regards the obligations of employers, the administrative agency supervising the application of the legislation (the National Labor Relations Board) has developed criteria of performance in two respects, one procedural and the other substantive.[3]

The procedural provisions require the employer or his representative to meet the workers' bargaining agent at reasonably frequent intervals and at an agreed time and place. The employer must make a genuine effort to reach agreement and may not avoid his obligations by, for example, pretending to engage in bargaining without any intent to reach agreement, taking excessive time, or refusing to present counter-proposals to the union's demands. He may not try to deal directly with his employees over the heads of the union negotiators, nor may he unilaterally change the terms of employment. While he is not under a legal obligation to reach an agreement at all costs, he must be willing to have any agreement reached reduced to writing, and to sign the written text. In sum, the employer's freedom of action is severely limited.

The substantive duty to bargain relates to the subjects which the union may legitimately introduce into the negotiations and which the employer may not declare to be outside the scope of bargaining. The language of the statute itself is specific only up to a point. Basic issues like hours and wages are indisputably bargainable subjects, and an

---

[1] T. L. Johnston, op. cit., pp. 129-130.

[2] Sections 55 (1) *(b)*, 56, 102, and 126-127.

[3] See, for example, Averill G. Marcus: "The employer's duty to bargain", in *Labor Law Journal*, Sep. 1966, pp. 541-558.

employer's refusal to negotiate about them would almost certainly constitute a violation of the duty to bargain, but over the years unions have advanced demands which go well beyond the elementary ones. Employers' resistance to negotiation on questions such as supplementary retirement benefits, subcontracting of work, supplementary unemployment compensation benefits, plans for the purchase of company shares, work rules and many others have led unions to complain to the Board of employer refusals to bargain in good faith. In ruling on these complaints the Board, supported by the courts, has tended to put a broad interpretation on what the law means by "good faith" bargaining, and has thereby contributed to a considerable extension of the range of bargainable issues.[1]

In Canada the Task Force on Labour Relations noted that the United States had "developed an elaborate jurisprudence on the issue of good faith bargaining, revolving largely around what subjects must be bargained, what may be bargained and what a party cannot insist be bargained".[2] Its adverse conclusions regarding the adoption of a similar approach in Canada were couched in these terms:

> We do not think it is useful to industrial relations in Canada to put the issue of good faith bargaining into such an elaborate jurisprudential container. The duty to bargain is not a duty to agree, nor does the right to bargain grant a right to a particular bargain. We see no reason why the subject matter of bargaining should not include anything that is not contrary to law. As to tactics, the highest duty that should reasonably be placed on either party to a bargaining situation, in which each has a claim to preserve its freedom respecting its bargaining position, is to state its position on matters put in issue. But we cannot envisage such a duty being amenable to legal enforcement, except perhaps to the extent of an obligation to meet and exchange positions.[2]

From the diverse practices and views that have just been described the following conclusion seems to emerge. In a system of industry-wide bargaining in which employers' interests are represented by employers' associations, questions of recognition and the duty to bargain are almost necessarily of less importance than in a system of enterprise bargaining. For that reason they are less likely to be regulated by statute. Dealings at industry level normally do not involve the individual enterprise in direct bargaining with a union. The threat to managerial authority at operating level is therefore felt to be much less immediate, and the resistance to industry-wide recognition is correspondingly lower. A good part of the reason why management in the United States held out so adamantly against union recognition was that its established practice

---

[1] There is a continuing sharp divergence of views on whether this policy marks a salutary or unfortunate administrative intervention in the collective bargaining process. For a full discussion of the issue see Philip Ross: *The government as a source of union power: The role of public policy in collective bargaining* (Providence, Rhode Island, Brown University Press, 1965).

[2] *Canadian industrial relations*, op. cit., p. 163.

of direct dealings with the workers was threatened by union claims for recognition. In the absence of an equivalent threat, the recognition issue never acquired the same importance in European countries.

Virtually the same points apply to the duty to bargain, plus the additional one that for an employers' association the activity of bargaining has constituted not an onerous restriction on management prerogatives—as it might be regarded in the case of an individual enterprise—but rather a *raison d'être*. Seen in this light, the basic difference between European and North American experience becomes clearer. Also clearer is the resistance, particularly on the part of employers' organisations, to plant-level bargaining which has recently become a more acute issue in a number of European countries. Of course, the parallel is not perfect, but the essence of the problem is very similar. This explains why a certain amount of legislative intervention is already occurring, as is demonstrated by the new British approach with its legal requirements regarding recognition and good faith bargaining, and as demonstrated further, though not quite so directly, by the already cited French legislation of December 1968, the 1971 amendments to French collective bargaining law of 1950, and the Italian legislation on the so-called "workers' charter". The recent revision of the 1950 Works Council Act in the Netherlands and the even more recent revision of the works council legislation in the Federal Republic of Germany also fit the general proposition, for they all aim, in part, at enabling the union to play a more significant role in the enterprise. Collective bargaining is bound to be a part of that role, whatever be the name given to it.

Permanent bargaining machinery

Both the development of machinery for collective bargaining and the characteristics of that machinery are the outcome of the diverse needs and circumstances existing at country, industry, and enterprise levels. Complete standardisation of the machinery would be unattainable in practice and probably undesirable. Even where governments have legislated on the subject of bargaining machinery, differences between industries are bound to emerge as an inevitable result of the endless variety in such factors as the geographical distribution of industries and enterprises, their size and technology, the nature and extent of organisation among employers and workers and the history of collective dealings. In some respects, however, analytical distinctions can be drawn, provided that they are not rigidly applied. Perhaps the most important distinction is that between permanent (or standing) and ad hoc machinery.

For permanent machinery there is at least a written or unwritten "charter" or "constitution" which designates the parties, defines the main purposes, and probably includes provisions concerning procedures. Where permanent machinery exists, there tend to be regular meetings, and there may be a small full-time staff employed by the parties jointly. Permanent machinery is not limited to any particular bargaining level. Although it is most frequently found at the level of an industry, it can be extended to regional, district and even enterprise levels, or to cover the whole economy. Its origins may be voluntary in the sense that the parties set it up on their own, or it may stem from national legislation.

Great Britain provides a good example of permanent machinery within a voluntary system in which the centre of gravity is at industry level. As a result of a history which goes back as far as the well known Whitley Committee reports of 1916-18, substantial numbers of permanent bargaining groups, mostly known as joint industrial councils, have come into existence, and now total something like 200, covering 3 million workers.[1] Although most are based on a single constitutional model, there is nevertheless a great deal of variety in the structure of the joint industrial councils and in the nature of their activities. While a few concern themselves only with wage negotiations—and while a few others do not conduct any wage negotiations at all—most of them go beyond such negotiations and take on a host of other matters germane to the problems of their industries. There are also variations with regard to the size of councils, the frequency of their meetings, and the existence of subsidiary councils at regional level.[2]

Permanent machinery dealing primarily with the national economy as a whole is fittingly represented by the Foundation of Labour in the Netherlands. The Foundation, which came into existence in 1945, represents the major confederations of trade unions and employers' associations. From the very beginning it had a written constitution (drafted without the knowledge of the occupation authorities during the Second World War), a permanent secretariat, and an agreed set of procedures. While not at first intended to be chiefly a meeting place for centralised national bargaining, that is in fact what it became. Although it has taken on a number of other functions, including a major role in the administration of wage controls between 1945 and 1963, bargaining on issues of nation-wide importance has remained one of its principal tasks. However, since the collapse of the central wage determination

---

[1] The figures are impressive, but it must be borne in mind that the latter does not amount to a majority of British workers covered by collective agreements. W. E. J. McCarthy (ed.): *Industrial relations in Great Britain: A guide for management and unions* (London, Lyon, Grant and Green, 1969), p. 109 ff.

[2] For details see United Kingdom, Ministry of Labour: *Industrial relations handbook,* An account of British institutions and practice relating to the organisation of employers and workers in Great Britain; collective bargaining and joint negotiating machinery; conciliation and arbitration; and statutory regulation of wages in certain industries (London, HM Stationery Office, 3rd ed., 1961), p. 23 ff.

system in about 1963 the importance of the Foundation as a central bargaining instrument has declined substantially, while the importance of bargaining machinery at industry and enterprise levels has correspondingly increased.[1]

Whereas the bargaining machinery in Great Britain and the Netherlands exists at the pleasure of the parties and can be dismantled or modified by them without the consent of the public authorities, the permanent machinery of Belgium functions within a legislative framework for individual industries and for the economy as a whole.[2] At industry or comparable level, some 80 joint committees have been established by royal decree after consultation with representative organisations on both sides.[3] There may be separate committees for manual and white-collar workers, and there may be subcommittees, functioning under the supervision of a national committee, for individual sub-sectors of industry. The committees are composed of equal numbers of representatives from both sides, with an independent chairman and vice-chairman. As is often the case with permanent machinery, the committees have their own secretariat which provides continuity and administrative services. For the economy as a whole the statutory permanent machinery in Belgium takes the form of a bipartite National Labour Council functioning under an independent chairman. While the main function of the Council is to act as a consultative body in relation to the Government, it nevertheless has the authority to conclude collective agreements. Under the 1968 Act on collective agreements this authority, under which a number of agreements have been concluded, extends to economy-wide agreements as well as to agreements for individual industries that are not within the competence of an established joint committee or where an established joint committee does not function.

The cases of Great Britain, the Netherlands and Belgium exemplify various approaches to the operation of permanent bargaining machinery; they represent a minority. In most other countries collective bargaining proceeds on an ad hoc basis: it is not haphazard or disorganised, but the parties have not experienced a sufficiently strong need to go beyond their periodic bargaining negotiations and to create an institution that would confer a greater degree of continuity on their dealings.

One additional situation should be mentioned here. It concerns the Human Relations Committee in the basic steel industry of the United

---

[1] See Albeda, below, pp. 320-326.

[2] See Blanpain, below, pp. 208-212.

[3] For the legislative basis of the Belgian statutory standing machinery see ILO: *Legislative Series,* 1968—Bel. 1.

States.[1] The Committee came into existence in 1959, after the termination of a costly strike. The purpose of the Committee was the continuous examination in depth of problems of mutual concern to the steel companies and the United Steelworkers' Union, free from the pressures of ordinary collective bargaining negotiations. It was anticipated that the Committee would be able to determine facts and make recommendations concerning controversial issues, and that this action could at least constitute a basis for subsequent formal bargaining on expiry of the collective agreement, and might even become the means of altering the traditional deadline situations that are characteristic of the collective bargaining system in the United States. In any event, there was an expectation from the outset that the Committee would improve communication between the parties by establishing a continuous channel between key figures on both sides and by substituting frequent problem-solving and fact-gathering meetings for intermittent crisis bargaining. Although the Committee seemed to fulfil the expectations held out at its start, it fell victim in 1965 to an intra-union dispute in which the victorious group maintained that the union was in danger of forsaking its basic responsibility for the militant representation of its members' interests in return for the dubious advantages of closer association with management.

The question remains whether permanent bargaining machinery has intrinsic advantages. At least in a potential sense the following can be put forward. Permanent machinery offers an opportunity of conducting joint research on the performance and prospects of the economic unit represented by the parties (the economy as a whole, an industry, a sector of an industry, or an enterprise, as the case may be); such research will, or at least can, constitute an agreed basis for collective bargaining, thus making it possible for the parties to proceed from a common factual base. Permanent machinery may also be useful for the joint implementation of agreements. Thirdly, depending on the quality of the relationship which the parties are able to cultivate, permanent machinery originally set up for bargaining purposes may become the foundation for joint arrangements concerning industrial relations in general, so that the parties will endeavour to take a joint approach not only to subjects conventionally included in collective bargaining but also to broader economic and social questions.

It should be emphasised that all these potential advantages can conceivably, although perhaps not quite as readily, be secured by ad hoc arrangements without permanent machinery. Moreover, not all parties to collective bargaining, nor all students of the subject, would

---

[1] For a description see James J. Healey (ed.): *Creative collective bargaining* (Englewood Cliffs, New Jersey, Prentice-Hall, 1965), pp. 194-229. See also: "Labour dispute and settlement in the United States steel industry", in *International Labour Review*, Vol. 82, No. 1, July 1960, pp. 59-69.

necessarily agree unreservedly that the above-mentioned opportunities are advantageous. For example, some might consider the establishment and operation of permanent machinery as a first step towards joint industrial government, which they would think of as a negative development and even as the beginning of a corporatist tendency. Others would regard permanent machinery as an undesirable compromise with their conception of collective bargaining as a process taking place in a situation of conflict; or they might regard it as a possible threat to the role of fixed-term collective agreements. Finally, it may be objected that permanent machinery, whatever its advantages, is usually linked to a system of bargaining on an industry basis and does not fit as readily into a system based on enterprise bargaining.

Elaboration of negotiating positions

One of the neglected subjects in publications on collective bargaining is the mechanics of the bargaining process itself and the systematic preparatory work that customarily precedes bargaining sessions. What Professor Blanpain observed about the situation in his own country— "There has been hardly any research in Belgium on the actual procedure of collective bargaining"[1]—applies to many other countries as well. None the less, this is a subject of considerable importance. It has been pointed out more than once that collective bargaining involves a good deal more than actual negotiations between employers' and workers' representatives. Both sides must prepare for the negotiations well before they begin. This requisite has policy-making and technical aspects which are interrelated but best discussed separately.

By "policy-making" is meant here the achievement by each side of an internal consensus on its basic bargaining position. Two main sets of factors determine the ease (or difficulty) of reaching such a consensus. One is the heterogeneity of constituency interests which the leaders on each side must take into account in order to present a reasonably coherent and unified stance at the bargaining table. The other is the range and complexity of issues that make up the substance of the bargaining. Other things being equal, the greater the heterogeneity of interests and the greater the range and complexity of issues, the more difficult it will be to achieve a consensus. These observations apply fully as much to the employer side as to the union side, though the policy-making problems on the union side may be more difficult to solve.

To take the employer side first, it may be fairly assumed that it will consist either of a single enterprise or of an association, although within these broad categories there is room for considerable variation. In a single enterprise consisting of more than one plant, the plant managers or their representatives will expect to be consulted on the firm's bargaining position, and do need to be. The problems faced by the

---

[1] See Blanpain, below, p. 216.

various plants are likely to be quite different in terms of the organisation of production, the local labour market, the skill mix of the labour force and other major variables, and those differences must be taken into account. Even in the case of a single-plant enterprise, the department heads are often involved in the internal deliberations before bargaining begins, in view of their knowledge of plant affairs and their key role in the future implementation of the agreement. In these deliberations the management official responsible for personnel and industrial relations often plays an active and indeed leading role.

In the case of an employers' association, the problem of achieving a consensus may be aggravated by substantial diversity among member firms in regard to size, market position, efficiency of operations, financial resources, location and other factors. Precisely in order to avoid the problems arising from diversity, employers' associations often strive to conclude collective agreements on minimum terms that can be met by their most marginal members. This preserves the existence of firms that might otherwise be driven out of business (or out of the association) and leaves the better situated enterprises free to offer improved terms to their employees, whether unilaterally or through supplementary bargaining. For an association, this may be the only feasible way of maintaining the adherence of its members. Even then, however, a certain amount of internal bargaining may be necessary before the member firms of an association are able to arrive at a mutually acceptable position. It is also entirely conceivable that after the actual bargaining with the union begins, the agreed position will have to be kept under constant review, and if necessary modified. Understandably enough, the process of reaching internal agreement increases in difficulty as the complexity of the agreement itself increases. This applies particularly to economic questions: for example, when the union demands a supplementary pension scheme, the receptiveness of the member firms of an employers' association towards the principle or the terms of such a demand may well be influenced by the age structure of each firm's labour force. For reasons such as this, employers' associations generally prefer to limit the range of issues in bargaining.

On the union side, the policy-making aspect of preparing for collective bargaining is accentuated by the character of unions as mass-membership organisations. What this means for the authority of union negotiators will be spelled out in a later section of this chapter, but it should be noted here that unions often have particular difficulty in deciding what their demands shall be because of the diverse composition of their membership. It then becomes the responsibility of the leaders to put together a set of demands that meets the expectations of the various sections of the union—young and old, skilled and unskilled, hourly paid and incentive workers, manual and white-collar workers (if covered by the same negotiations), and so on—sufficiently to keep them reasonably satisfied with their organisation. As a rule the task is easier when the bargaining unit is limited to a single enterprise and a single local union (i.e. at the level of the enterprise), as in North America, and easier still if the local union consists of a body of similar people, such as a group of skilled craftsmen. While drawing up the list of demands to be presented to the employer, many local unions ask for suggestions from the membership, either at regular or special meetings open to the entire membership or through close contact between union leaders and shop stewards, who are relied upon to transmit the wishes of the members. A special problem arises when local unions must conform in their single-enterprise bargaining to standards set by the national union with which they are affiliated. Since written instructions from the national union office may not suffice to implement national policy, many national unions are represented in local bargaining by their own officials, who may play a leading role in the bargaining process and will in any event be present in order to ensure that the union's national policy is followed in any settlement to which the local union agrees.

In preparing for bargaining above the enterprise level, it becomes more difficult to elicit membership opinion. Because of the longer lines of communication and the centralisation observable in many unions nowadays, the tendency at regional and national bargaining levels is to rely more heavily on the judgement of union officers and less on the opinions of the rank and file. Of course, the officers must still find ways of discovering the wishes of the membership and to incorporate the various views which reach them into a mutually consistent set of bargaining demands. In the Belgian metal industry, where bargaining takes place on a national basis, the initial formulation of demands occurs at separate regional delegate meetings of the Christian and Socialist metalworkers' unions. At the second stage, proposals from the various regions are collected at national level and combined into a single list of demands. A third step then follows in which the national leaders of the two unions work out a joint programme to be submitted to their counterparts on the employer side.[1] In the United States, unions approaching national negotiations on an industry-wide basis, as in basic steel, or in a major enterprise as in the case of a large automobile manufacturer, may decide on a basic list of demands at a regular convention or at a conference specially called for the purpose. The various local unions with members in the plants of the industry or enterprise concerned are represented at such meetings and have an opportunity to put forward the special wishes of their members.

When they are faced with a profusion of diverse and sometimes conflicting interests, unions have a tendency, more so than employers'

---

[1] See Blanpain, below, p. 216.

associations in similar situations, to pile up a large number of demands rather than risk offending a section of their constituency by weeding out in advance certain clearly unrealistic claims. The impetus toward all-inclusiveness stems from the nature of unionism, and is often justified on the grounds that it is easier for the leadership to minimise the importance of demands having a low priority than to exclude them entirely. The same explanation applies, more or less, to the seemingly excessive nature of certain demands. Here again, it may be a case of the union's having decided for internal political reasons to defer a decision on its preferences and priorities until after the bargaining has got under way. What occurs, in effect, is that the union postpones the difficult and politically hazardous task of reconciling the conflicting interests of its membership. Generally speaking, the size and intractableness of this task increase in proportion to an increase in the diversity and number of members represented at the bargaining table.

There is also a tactical aspect to the preparation for bargaining which is actually not far removed from the policy one. Many union negotiators expect that the higher their demands, the more generous the ultimate settlement. (Employers likewise often anticipate that the lower their initial offer, the more limited the final bargain.) A standard treatise on collective bargaining in the context of the United States has expressed this consideration in the following terms:

> Both [sides] have believed that bargaining meant compromise and that compromise meant receding from an announced position; therefore, in order to play the game, each set its announced position—the proposal or counterproposal—high or low enough to permit plenty of "compromise". Negotiations then involved, in part, the game of discovering what the other party really was after, its irreductible minimum, and its genuine demands.
>
> The role of the proposal in the bargaining process when it is viewed as a horse-trading process is well enough understood by union and company leaders and by the rank-and-file workers. This is perhaps the most prevalent view. Despite such an understanding, the feeling-out operation involved in the initial proposal or counter-proposal has its repercussions. It is not simply a harmless bit of bluffing. For one thing, the tactical use of the bargaining demand has been extended by union leaders because of the political nature of their organisations, with officers seeking re-election and organising new members on the strength of "promises" which are fulfilled by being incorporated in bargaining proposals.[1]

A subsequent section deals with how the policy-making aspect of bargaining preparations may be related to membership support for the negotiators and membership acceptance of agreements. However, it may already be pointed out here that if for policy or tactical reasons the leaders of a union about to engage in collective bargaining decide to put forward a set of unrealistic demands, they will have difficulty in obtaining the support of their ordinary members for the terms of the agreement ultimately reached.

---

[1] Chamberlain and Kuhn, op. cit., pp. 55-56.

Technical preparation of case

It is questioned by some whether the technical preparations of the parties have much effect on the outcome of collective bargaining: there are those who maintain that bargaining is chiefly a contest of economic force, persuasive skills and ability to dissimulate, and that it will remain so because that is the essence of the process. Holders of a contrary opinion maintain that only an agreement based on a realistic and informed appraisal of past economic performance and future prospects, as perceived by both sides, can ensure that collective bargaining fulfils its economic and social possibilities. Walter Reuther, the late leader of the automobile workers' union in the United States, once commented on the future of collective bargaining by expressing the view that—

... we need to recognise that in a free society bargaining decisions should be based upon economic facts and not upon economic power. I hope the day will come in America when, in collective bargaining problems and other problems that bear upon economic interest, decisions can be based upon the power of economic persuasion rather than upon the persuasion of economic power. In the exercise of naked economic power we make arbitrary decisions, which too frequently are in conflict with the basic needs of the whole of our society.[1]

Whether this hope can be realised or not, employers and unions in a significant number of countries spend a substantial amount of time and financial resources building up a plausible and professionally competent case for their bargaining positions. For certain kinds of bargaining, for example productivity bargaining, such preparations are virtually essential. On the other hand there are bargaining situations in which economic research is not essential. As a rule, the negotiation of a national basic agreement on industrial relations principles and procedures[2] requires research along other lines, because agreements of that sort are not normally intended to set specific terms and conditions of employment. They are usually not concerned with the economic performance of an industry nor with the state of the labour market; instead, most of such agreements reflect the joint positions of senior representatives of both sides on certain very basic aspects of labour-management relations. They are intended to create a climate of labour-management relations and a set of procedures through which bargaining over wages and conditions of employment can proceed.

The most extensive research work precedes the negotiation of agreements that are to set basic terms and conditions of employment for an industry or enterprise and that deal with wages, hours and related

---

[1] Walter P. Reuther: "Labor's role in 1975", in Jack Stieber (ed.): *U.S. industrial relations: The next twenty years* (East Lansing, Michigan State University Press, 1958), p. 63.

[2] For examples of such agreements see ILO: *Basic agreements and joint statements on labour-management relations,* op. cit.

issues. To prepare for such negotiations, unions, employers and employers' associations frequently maintain qualified research staff whose main function it is to supply their principals with information to bolster their bargaining arguments. Unions and employers in the United States commonly undertake a substantial amount of economic research as an integral part of their preparations for collective bargaining. Over the years the use of economic analysis has, if anything, been increasing, as has the degree of sophistication of those who prepare and use the data as part of their bargaining material. The introduction of computers in preparation for negotiations is referred to below. In European countries the trend is in the same direction, that is, toward reliance on more quantitative background data than used to be the case in the past. In fact, for certain forms of bargaining, research has become essential. A striking demonstration of the research required for productivity bargaining is the work which preceded one of the earliest and most significant examples of it, namely the Fawley productivity agreements in the United Kingdom.[1]

Where public authorities become involved in bargaining as a third party, the importance of research rises considerably for the evident reason that public authorities aim to form their opinions on the basis of the demonstrated merits of the case. The Australian arbitration system with its intricate combination of direct negotiations and hearings before arbitration tribunals represents a particularly apt example of the weight attributed to research in a situation akin to collective bargaining. In the belief, no doubt borne out by years of experience with the system, that a case apparently based on good research is best designed to command the sympathetic attention of arbitration tribunals, unions and employers' associations have made it a practice to prepare voluminous evidence in support of their arguments.[2] In the Netherlands the importance of research as an integral aspect of bargaining preparations increased substantially during the period of centralised wage determination because both parties were invariably expected to demonstrate to the wage control agencies the economic rationale for a wage change. A contributing factor was the Government's own approach to collective bargaining, with its heavy reliance on the findings of the Central Planning Bureau and other research agencies as a guide to economically defensible wage levels. The research capacity of unions and employers' associations became particularly strained in 1959, during the shift from strict wage controls to a more flexible system, because of the importance attributed at that time to productivity increases, industry by industry, as a justifiable basis for wage changes.

---

[1] See especially the chapter on "The origins of the Blue Book", in Allan Flanders: *The Fawley productivity agreements: A case study of management and collective bargaining* (London, Faber, 1964), pp. 65-102; also Roberts and Rothwell, below, pp. 370, 374-375.

[2] Walker: *Australian industrial relations systems,* op. cit., pp. 88-89.

Although the importance of technical preparations for collective bargaining has been on the increase everywhere in the past few decades, the trend has generally not yet reached a point at which the parties have undertaken to gather the relevant information jointly. In almost all the rare cases in which this has occurred, the interests of employers and unions in relation to the public authorities have coincided. Thus, during the strict phase of wage controls in the Netherlands, when labour was becoming increasingly scarce, employers and unions in certain industries found that they had a common interest in demonstrating to the administrative agencies supervising the wage determination system the need to allow specific wage increases—the employers because they were being squeezed in the labour market and the unions because of the expectations of their members. The general point remains, however, that economic and related research tends to be conducted separately by each party and for the specific purpose of strengthening its bargaining posture. Chamberlain and Kuhn have explained the reasons:

> With few exceptions, [economic data] have been injected into negotiations by one of the parties as an argument to bolster its position; they have seldom been introduced by both parties as the basis for arriving at agreement. After deciding on its bargaining position, each side makes selective use from among available data of whatever will support its demands. There is seldom any consideration given to a procedure whereby each party contributes relevant information which will add up to the total situation in which the joint decision must be made. Facts are regarded as "bargaining cards" to be played or withheld as tactical considerations warrant.[1]

Clearly, a strong case can be made for the proposition that a more objective and sober approach to the use of facts will improve the quality and the results of collective bargaining, but equally clearly there is some way to go before this objective comes within reach. The problem is in large part one of reconciling collective bargaining as process of negotiation, which it is and will surely remain, with collective bargaining as a problem-solving process, which it is as yet to only a limited extent. Among the ways of creating a more objective basis for collective bargaining, and thus of reconciling the two notions, are the joint use of independent experts and the development of bipartite preparatory research. Independent experts could be particularly useful in exploring issues which relate the problems of the "bargaining unit" to the larger economic issues. For example, independent research regarding the effect of prospective labour market changes on labour supply and demand in the particular industry or enterprise about to embark on collective negotiations could establish a framework within which the quality of wage bargaining might improve. To a limited extent, this is already recognised in the sense that the parties will often accept certain data prepared by government agencies (consumer price indices,

---

[1] Chamberlain and Kuhn, op. cit., p. 75.

average wage and earnings data, etc.) as a basis for their bargaining; but the specific application of such data to a particular bargaining situation may be limited. Joint employer-union research teams are sometimes in a better position than either side is singly to draw up relevant wage rate and earnings comparisons, to estimate past and prospective changes in labour productivity or to assess the adequacy of particular incentive systems.

However, neither joint research nor the use of independent outsiders would remove all elements of contentiousness and judgement from collective bargaining. The divergence of interests will remain, as will opposing views over a fair allocation of income.

Employer obligation to furnish information

In connection with the technical preparation for collective bargaining the question frequently arises whether, and if so to what extent, the employer is under an obligation to provide the workers' representatives with background information on matters that are considered to be proper subjects for bargaining. This is particularly relevant in bargaining at the level of enterprises. Unions frequently maintain that in the absence of supporting evidence they are in no position to verify an employer's plea of financial inability to grant a wage increase or meet some other demand. The employer will usually reply that the information sought by the union is confidential, and he may add that if it were divulged he would be at an undue competitive disadvantage.

In the United States litigation on this particular issue has been taken on appeal as far as the Supreme Court, and it has also frequently arisen in union complaints lodged with the National Labor Relations Board. As a rule, the complaints allege that the employer is refusing to bargain in good faith, by withholding information which the union considers vital to the preparation of its case. In a basic decision rendered in 1956 the Supreme Court upheld the principle of an employer obligation to transmit information to the union to prove the employer's plea of inability to meet a claim for a wage increase. Referring to the good faith bargaining requirement of the National Labor Relations Act contained in Section 8 *(a)* (5), the Court held that—

Good-faith bargaining necessarily requires that claims made by either bargainer should be honest claims. This is true about an asserted inability to pay an increase in wages. If such an argument is important enough to permit in the give and take of bargaining, it is important enough to require some sort of proof of its accuracy.[1]

---

[1] *National Labor Relations Board* v. *Truitt Manufacturing Co.*, 315 U.S. 149 at pp. 152-153.

Subsequent decisions of lower courts and of the National Labor Relations Board have expanded on this precedent in both substance and procedure. Procedurally, the obligation to provide explanatory information is no longer linked exclusively to a situation where the employer simply denies a union claim. Under current rulings he is required to furnish any requested information that is reasonably related to the union's preparations for collective bargaining. The requirement also implies a significant substantive expansion of the disclosure obligation: in fact, the range of issues on which employers must on request supply information about items entering into collective bargaining has in recent years become very broad.

A similar approach, with as yet untested implications, is foreshadowed in the new Industrial Relations Act in Great Britain. Section 56 (1) of that Act provides that it shall be—

... the duty of the employer to disclose to those [union] representatives all such information relating to his undertaking as is in the possession of the employer, or of any associated employer, and is both—

(a) information without which the trade union representatives would be to a material extent impeded in carrying on collective bargaining with him, and

(b) information which it would be in accordance with good industrial relations practice that the employer should disclose to them for purposes of collective bargaining.

This provision goes well beyond the law and practice of most other European countries as far as collective dealings with trade unions—as distinct from works councils—are concerned. In most cases there are no explicit statutory requirements at all with regard to the employer's disclosure of information to trade unions for collective bargaining purposes. This absence may be largely explained by the somewhat diminished relevance of detailed information in a system of industry-wide bargaining, which as a rule aims only at the setting of minimum standards.

However, European unions have a number of indirect ways of informing themselves about the economic position of the employers. One of these arises from the presence of union officials on the supervisory boards of corporations, notably in the Federal Republic of Germany but also in the publicly owned enterprises and industries in France, the United Kingdom and other countries.[1] Although the information accumulated by union officials in their capacity as corporate board members is to be treated by them as confidential, it would be unrealistic to assume such a compartmentalisation of mind on their part that such information is relegated to oblivion during union preparations for contract negotiations. Another at least potential

---

[1] For background information see ILO: *Participation of workers in decisions within undertakings,* Documents of a technical meeting, Geneva, 20-29 November 1967, Labour-Management Relations Series, No. 33, esp. at pp. 15-16.

means of obtaining information is through the works councils, which under the law and practice of a substantial number of countries are entitled to receive information at regular intervals about the financial affairs of the enterprise. This type of information can be used in the supplementary bargaining that often takes place at enterprise level. In many cases worker members of works councils have close ties to the union which conducts bargaining, and which may thus have access to certain basic information. Moreover in some countries union representatives are entitled to be present at works council meetings and are thus in a position to obtain financial information directly.

It would be difficult to compare the relative adequacy of information supplied to unions in the United States and in Europe, but unions are rarely completely satisfied with the pre-bargaining information placed at their disposal by employers.

Use of computers [1]

The development of sophisticated methods of information storage and retrieval by means of high-speed computers has led unions and companies in North America to explore their uses for collective bargaining. The existence of multiple bargaining relationships and of many thousands of collective agreements makes the use of computer technology potentially attractive because such technology enables unions and companies to make numerous quick comparisons among contracts whenever comparative conditions of employment are accepted as valid justifications for bargaining demands. Generally speaking, however, the use of computers for bargaining is still in its infancy, and many companies and unions do not yet use them, or not to their fullest extent. Even where they already are in use, it is more in preparations for bargaining than in the course of bargaining proper. The reason, as explained by a former negotiator for management, is that the data produced by one of the parties on computers do not acquire any greater intrinsic credibility for the opposite party. On the contrary: "It is reasonable to assume that data which do not support a bargaining position or objective of one of the parties will be rejected by that party regardless of how they were developed." [2]

Nevertheless a number of unions and companies are already making use of the new technology. The Industrial Union Department of the AFL–CIO, which covers about 60 unions, has fed into its

---

[1] The material on this subject is still extremely sparse. At present the only major work in existence is Abraham J. Siegel (ed.): *The impact of computers on collective bargaining* (Cambridge, Massachusetts Institute of Technology, 1969).

[2] William G. Caples: "The computer's uses and potential in bargaining: A management view", in Siegel, op. cit., p. 87.

computerised records 21 key provisions (for example on holidays with pay) from 208 major agreements, covering at least 5,000 workers each and together more than 3 million workers in 3,000 different plants and workshops. As new contracts are negotiated, the changes are fed into the system to keep the records up to date.

The system is used in several ways. First of all it provides the raw material for general reports from the Industrial Union Department on major developments concerning issues of substance in collective bargaining; by this means the affiliates of the Department can compare the agreements under their jurisdictions with agreements concluded by other unions, and can also draw comparisons with agreements which they have already concluded with different enterprises in their own industry. Secondly, the system can supply special reports for use in preparations for particular negotiations: for example, a union about to enter negotiations with a major enterprise can obtain through the computer specific comparisons between the terms of employment prevailing in that enterprise and in its major competitors. The computer can also price different union demands and provide comparative cost information on terms and conditions of employment prevailing in the industry or in comparable industries. In this way, unions are able to obtain at short notice more accurate estimates of the projected cost of their demands than would be possible through laborious non-mechanical methods, and can compare this information more readily with the information provided by the employer. Use of the computer also enables both sides to carry out quick tests of a large number of possible solutions to their problems, with reasonably precise indications of the probable cost in each case.

Since in European countries unions are generally not responsible for such a large number of agreements under their systems of national or regional industry-wide collective bargaining, their use of computers is still infrequent. In view of the high cost of using computers, lack of money may also be a factor. Employers likewise have not yet made extensive use of computers in European countries because the range of bargaining topics is more limited. However, it would not be surprising to find this technology increasingly resorted to where bargaining becomes more decentralised to the enterprise level.

Negotiating patterns

Nowhere do differences based on national peculiarities, industrial traditions or even personalities show themselves more strikingly than in the varied ways in which the parties periodically seek to reach agreement on future conditions of employment through collective bargaining. Whether to wear the bargaining partner down through long and

71

exhausting night sessions or to blast him into quick concessions, whether to enter the negotiations with inordinately high demands or to begin close to the minimum acceptable settlement level, whether to make an almost public spectacle out of the encounters or to negotiate in strict seclusion—these are questions which labour and management in each country, in each industry, and in certain countries in almost each enterprise, have answered in quite different ways.

Generalisation in the face of this manifest diversity is made even more complex by the fact that the level at which bargaining occurs has a decided effect on the character of the negotiations. To illustrate this proposition by citing extremes, there is a vast difference between negotiations on the spot, such as occur almost daily at the plant level between the shop steward (or the works council) and the foreman or the plant manager, and the highly formalised annual or biennial confrontations between leading representatives of national federations of employers' associations and trade union confederations. Another difference is that between pattern-setting and pattern-following bargaining in systems under which negotiations are highly decentralised. Once a pattern has been established through negotiations involving a leading firm or set of firms in an industry, the ensuing meetings of union and management in the so-called pattern-follower enterprises often involve little more than the routine ratification of terms already hammered out elsewhere.

Since it is not practicable to cover all conceivable kinds of negotiations in this review, the emphasis will be placed on negotiations at the levels where basic bargaining takes place over an agreement to set terms and conditions of employment. For most of the countries covered in this study the following account will therefore cover an industry or a part of one, for a few others (Canada, Japan, the United States) the enterprise, and for one or two (e.g. Sweden) the economy as a whole.[1]

Negotiations always proceed by stages. The number and duration of the stages depend on such factors as the complexity of the matters discussed, the diversity of parties represented, the need for consultations with constituents, the use made of conciliation and mediation services, the resort to industrial action, if any, and the effectiveness of the negotiators. Where a bargaining relationship already exists and an agreement is in force, negotiations are usually started when one party notifies the other of its intention of terminating and renegotiating the existing agreement. (In a new relationship the same purpose is accomplished by notice from one party to the other of its desire to negotiate a first agreement.) As a rule it is the workers' representatives

---

[1] Published descriptions of actual negotiating procedures are relatively rare. The following studies may be cited: Chamberlain and Kuhn, op. cit., pp. 51-73; Johnston, op. cit., pp. 263-275; Benjamin M. Selekman *et al.*: *Problems in labor relations* (New York, McGraw-Hill, 3rd ed., 1964), pp. 359-606; and Lester, op. cit., pp. 375-401.

who open negotiations, but it is conceivable that the first step would be taken by employers, for example in a period of economic decline.

The rules regarding notice may emanate from law, an existing agreement, custom, or some combination of these. Where statutory requirements exist, they are usually intended to allow ample time for negotiations before an existing agreement expires and, more specifically, to alert mediation and conciliation agencies to the possible occurrence of a dispute. For that reason the law in the United States (Section 8 *(d)* (1) and (3) of the National Labor Relations Act) includes as part of the duty to bargain in good faith two requirements relating to notice. Under the first, the initiating party must give 60 days' written notice of its intention to terminate the agreement to the other party; this is intended to provide sufficient time for renegotiating the agreement. If during the first half of the 60-day period no agreement has been reached, the parties must notify the existence of a dispute [1] to the Federal Mediation and Conciliation Service and to any corresponding agencies concerned in the constituent states; this notice opens up a period of 30 days for negotiations with the assistance of impartial outsiders if the mediation and conciliation agencies wish to intervene. A notice requirement is frequently inserted in collective agreements regardless of whether or not it is required by law. In countries where bargaining follows a set cycle, as it generally does in the Netherlands, Sweden and several others, the date of notification has become fairly uniform over the years; thus in Sweden for agreements expiring at the end of December, as many do, the usual time for giving notice is 30 September.

Before or at the actual start of negotiations the parties need to agree on rules of procedure. In established relationships they will be guided mainly by precedent. Questions that need to be settled include whether there is to be a chairman and if so who he is to be, whether or not a verbatim transcript is to be kept, where the meetings are to be held, and similar matters; they are not necessarily of crucial importance to the success of the negotiations, but can influence their course to some extent.

On the question of chairing the negotiations, the main possibilities are having no chairman, appointing a chairman from one of the parties, rotating the chairmanship among the parties, or bringing in an outside chairman. Many negotiations take place without an explicitly designated chairman and proceed without difficulty. It is sometimes considered useful, especially where the negotiating committees are large, to have someone who is responsible for the maintenance of an orderly discussion, knows when to call a recess, can keep tempers under

---

[1] A dispute is thus defined as a situation in which 30 days before the expiry of an existing agreement no new agreement has yet been reached.

control, senses when to stick strictly to the agenda and when to lay it aside, allows digressions if they seem to serve a useful purpose, and yet always tries to steer the talks toward reaching an agreement by however circuitous a route. When the official or unofficial chairman is provided by one of the parties, he must none the less be sufficiently impartial to remain acceptable to the other side. Rotation of chairmen is infrequent and often considered unsatisfactory because it may interrupt the continuity of discourse which a capable chairman knows how to promote. An impartial chairman brought in from the outside has the advantage of not being identified with either party, but he may not be familiar with the issues under discussion, the technology and economics of the industry and the personalities of the negotiators. Besides, to introduce an outsider already at the very beginning of negotiations may evoke prematurely the possible need for third-party assistance, normally by way of conciliation, to reach agreement, and that is something which the parties may not wish to acknowledge at such an early stage.

As a rule, verbatim transcripts of negotiations are not kept, probably in the usually justified belief that they would unduly inhibit the negotiators from expressing themselves freely. Instead, the parties generally keep notes which they can consult if the need arises. Verbatim transcripts do have the advantage of indicating with greater precision any provisional agreement arrived at in the course of the negotiations, and have the additional advantage of constituting a ready-made record to which the parties or an arbitrator can refer in the event of subsequent interpretation disputes, but these advantages do not seem sufficient to outweigh the drawbacks unless it is desired that the proceedings should be very formal.

Selecting a place for negotiations involves a choice between the premises of one of the parties or a neutral location. Where standing bargaining machinery exists with its own premises, they are an obvious choice if adequate for negotiations. Many negotiations, however, take place on the premises of an enterprise, or sometimes of an employers' association, because they offer superior conference facilities. Where the relationship between the parties is less than close or where the union is concerned about adverse rank-and-file reaction to negotiations held on the employers' own ground, a neutral location is clearly indicated. In European countries such a neutral location is sometimes made available in, or by, the ministry of labour. In North America bargaining partners looking for a neutral location seem to prefer hotels. Major negotiations that have reached a critical stage are sometimes shifted under government urging to a place where the negotiators are more readily accessible to the entreaties of high government officials. On the other hand, for certain kinds of long-term negotiations the parties may seek a completely undisturbed environment, as did the Swedish

74

negotiators who in 1938 worked out their basic agreement at Saltsjöbaden, a popular holiday resort.

Other things being equal, publicity may have an adverse effect on negotiations that are under way; for that reason the parties to a mature bargaining relationship often agree in advance to make no unilateral statements to the communications media about the progress or lack of progress of the negotiations. However, the use of publicity as an instrument for exerting pressure on the other side is by no means unheard of.

By the time the negotiations start, the representatives on each side will probably have reached agreement among themselves on how they wish to conduct the negotiations and to make interim decisions as particular points come up. Negotiating committees often designate a single spokesman, almost invariably their senior member, through whom all statements are conveyed to the other side at the bargaining table. Alternatively, there may be different spokesmen, or at least persons helping to present the case, on particular points. In other cases it is agreed that all members of the committee may participate freely in the discussions. Where only a single union or a single employer is involved, it may not be very difficult to reach internal agreement on one spokesman. In multi-union and multi-employer bargaining, however, such an agreement becomes more difficult to arrange because of the presence on the negotiating committee of representatives of autonomous organisations who may wish to remain free to express their particular views. Actually, it is in just such situations that a single spokesman is often considered most useful, so as to conceal as far as possible from the other side the existence of internal disagreements which, if known, could be exploited for the purpose of creating divisions and weaknesses. This danger arises more often on the union than on the employer side, especially in the European countries where several unions affiliated with different national confederations participate jointly in bargaining. In such cases ideological and related divisions frequently preclude agreement on the most effective way of proceeding, not to mention agreement on points of substance. Similar problems can also arise in the context of multi-union bargaining in Great Britain, where there are no institutionalised ideological and related divisions, or in coalition bargaining in the United States. Employers under multi-employer bargaining usually find it easier than unions to keep their disagreements, if any, to themselves and to let a single spokesman express their views, whether he be the chief full-time official of the employers' association or a senior management member of an affiliated enterprise.

Negotiations begin as a rule with the formal presentation of union proposals for changes in the agreement, possibly followed by brief explanatory comments. If the employer side has had no previous information on the union's demands, it may at this point wish to withdraw in order to prepare its initial position. Alternatively, it may place on record its own initial bargaining position, reflecting changes which it wants to see made in the agreement, and it may also indicate a preliminary reaction to the union's claims. The extent to which these initial conditions are removed from, or close to, the minimum settlement terms of the negotiators depends on a wider range of factors than can be fully discussed here. Before the current period of inflation set in, the initial bargaining positions were frequently farther apart in North America than they tended to be in most bargaining situations in Europe. This may have been due in part to intrinsic differences between bargaining for an entire industry or the economy as a whole and enterprise bargaining, since in the first two cases the accent is on the marginal firm's ability to pay and the preservation of the maximum number of jobs. Another possible reason may have been a difference in union attitudes toward their macro-economic responsibilities. It is conceivable that part of the answer might also be found in prevailing relationships between union leaders and their constituents, at least in the sense that where leaders compete for high union office union negotiators may feel under greater pressure to begin their bargaining from a position of exaggerated demands.

The actual bargaining that follows the presentation of starting positions may range from short and simple sessions, with agreement or deadlock quickly reached, to extremely time-consuming and involved endurance contests. There seems to be some variation in national patterns, negotiations in Great Britain and in most of continental Europe being usually of relatively short duration in terms of total time consumed and number of sessions held, whereas in North America and in Sweden bargaining can stretch out long enough to tax the physical stamina of the negotiators.

It is during this period of actual bargaining that the parties seek to test out their respective priorities, potential concessions and flexibility. For certain technical subjects, for example supplementary retirement benefits, technical subcommittees may be formed whose findings are reported back to the full group. As the negotiations progress, it may become useful for the key participants on both sides to agree on private meetings, since departures from positions previously announced to be inflexible are easier to concede in smaller groups. It is also likely that negotiations will have to be interrupted from time to time to allow each negotiating committee to meet on its own. Especially when the bargaining covers a wide range of topics and when many different kinds of workers and employers are represented, there are almost certain to be internal divergences, which need to be reconciled as each particular point arises in the negotiations. There must also be opportunities for each side to reappraise its bargaining objectives and strategy as the position of the other side becomes clearer.

At a certain stage outside assistance may become necessary, but the role of mediation, conciliation, and other forms of dispute settlement will not be dealt with here.

It should be stressed that the possibility of a work stoppage with its attendant costs for both parties is ordinarily the most compelling factor inducing them to seek agreement.[1] In certain cases employees do not work if there is no currently valid agreement. The imminent termination of an expiring agreement therefore gives rise to what is known as "deadline bargaining", in which the parties strain to reach a meeting of minds before tools are downed. In other bargaining situations the pace of negotiations is more leisurely, and although tentative dealines may exist they are subject to change if the parties wish to give themselves more time to explore areas of agreement and disagreement. It would be difficult to be sure whether the certainty of a work stoppage when an existing agreement expires will lead to a more rapid settlement, but it does seem that when deadlines are treated more tentatively there is a somewhat lower incidence of industrial disputes than when unions adhere strictly to the rule of "no contract, no work".

Authority of negotiators

While the aim of collective bargaining is to arrive at an agreement with which both sides can live, the objective of each party's negotiators is to secure the best possible terms for thcir constituents. However, precisely what constitutes the best possible terms is an abstract question to which there is no practical answer, and in practice negotiators will settle for an agreement which they consider acceptable. Yet the acceptability of an agreement is a matter of opinion. In principle either the negotiators themselves have the authority to conclude a binding agreement or that authority rests somewhere among the people whom they represent; in practice, however, the position is not so clear, especially not on the union side where entrenched principles of democracy sometimes conflict with the needs of bargaining efficiency even where the negotiators are supposed to have full powers.

Employers

To begin with the employer side, one should distinguish between association and multi-employer bargaining on one hand and single-

---

[1] See in this connection the section on "The role of the strike", in Donald E. Cullen: *Negotiating labor-management contracts,* Bulletin 56, New York State School of Industrial and Labor Relations, Sep. 1965, pp. 2-5.

enterprise bargaining on the other. Although further distinctions are possible (for example, some enterprises have several plants for which bargaining is carried on separately), the differences between the two major categories referred to above are sufficient to bring out the main points that need to be made.

The simpler case is that of the single enterprise. Among companies with a wide diversity of shareholders, the well known separation between ownership and control precludes stockholders from having any direct influence on collective bargaining, and the stockholders do not normally expect to be consulted on bargaining questions. Boards of directors or supervisory boards may become involved, but even then as a rule only for the purpose of providing operating management with general guidance on the size of an acceptable settlement, or in case of need to consider the pros and cons of a strike. Effective responsibility for negotiations almost always lies with the highest level of management, although the conduct of the bargaining sessions may be delegated to other senior executives, such as in the United States a vice-president for industrial relations. The principal negotiator for the employer side may have full powers to conclude a binding agreement, or he may be little more than a messenger between the negotiating room and the top management. A union invariably considers the latter situation to be highly unsatisfactory, for it prefers to deal face to face with managers who have authority to make decisions on the spot. For its part, however, top management may want to avoid making hasty concessions on questions the full implications of which may not be clear at the time of the transaction, especially if made under pressure of deadline bargaining. For that reason top managers sometimes prefer not to be present at the bargaining table but to let themselves be represented by trusted subordinates. Management negotiators therefore usually have an intermediate range of flexibility, being free to come to terms on some questions or at least to enter into preliminary understanding, but obliged to refer back to their superiors on the more important ones.

The problem of negotiating authority is potentially more complex in the case of association bargaining. Unfortunately, reliable information in the form of in-depth studies about it appears to be extremely scarce. Furthermore, it is highly unlikely that identifiable national patterns exist: it is far more probable that in each country there is a wide range of association practices, with variations from industry to industry and from region to region. Because precise information about them is lacking, only the sketchiest comments are possible.

Since it is usually not feasible for all members of an association to have a place at the bargaining table, associations must make arrangements for setting up negotiating teams. As a rule they will seek to combine the professional and technical talents of their full-time staff with the authority and influence of the leaders among their member firms. Negotiating teams or committees may be led either by the chief official of the professional association or by a respected representative of one of the member firms whose negotiating skills have been recognised. In this respect, practice is as mixed in France as it is elsewhere: in metal fabrication, including the iron and steel industry, negotiations with the unions are as a rule in the hands of officials (i.e. full-time officials of employers' organisations), but the practice has not spread far outside those industries.[1] In the United States employers' associations sometimes entrust the actual negotiations to a lawyer or law firm that is also likely to serve as legal adviser to the association. The representativeness of a negotiating team is an important factor. The various branches and regions expect to be adequately represented, and where there is a mixture of large and small firms due account needs to be taken of that fact too.

Employers' associations tend to confer on their negotiators relatively wide powers to conclude agreements, although sometimes they designate a representative group of member firms to whom the negotiators are expected to turn for guidance and instruction on knotty problems. In the Federal Republic of Germany both practices are followed. Under the first, the leaders of the employers' bargaining team submit the provisional agreement to the competent committee of their association, while under the second either the team itself or the executive committee of the association is fully empowered to act on behalf of the association.[2]

By and large, associations seek to avoid making decisions by means of outright voting. The preferred procedure for deciding what stand to make on a contentious bargaining issue is to seek a consensus. A ballot in which each firm had one vote would not reflect the differences in the size of firms, and its outcome could be easily contested; for that reason some associations that do decide issues by vote seek to assign differential weights to their members in terms of such criteria as number of employees, total payroll or gross output. The following description from a study of British employers' associations illustrates these practices:

Whatever method of consultation is employed, the common aim is to obtain a consensus of opinion rather than to take a vote. The policy has to be generally acceptable and simple majority voting can produce a substantial minority in opposition. The process of consultation therefore tends to involve the moulding and modification of views until they are acceptable as widely as possible. Voting by the membership is,

---

[1] Gérard Adam, Jean-Daniel Reynaud and Jean-Maurice Verdier: *La négociation collective en France* (Paris, Les éditions ouvrières, 1972), p. 74.

[2] Reichel, below, p. 264.

however, sometimes used to obtain a direct expression of views on important issues. The National Federated Electrical Association arranged a series of regional conferences of members before the crucial decision was taken to adopt a policy of uniform wage rates and took a vote on the issue. In the engineering associations voting by the membership is resorted to on national wage claims. Members' votes are weighted in relation to their wage roll so that the result reflects the importance of the decision to each member, and those employing two or three workers have less influence on the result than those employing several hundred. The result of the voting is reported to the Federation Management Board which takes the decision in the light of the support or opposition to the action proposed.[1]

It is interesting to note that in the British engineering associations the Management Board retains the right to determine what policy to adopt, so that the result of a vote provides guidance but does not in itself constitute a final decision.

Unions

While there are important parallels between employers' associations and unions with regard to the authority conferred on negotiators, the problem tends to become more complex on the union side. The main reasons are easy to discover. Like their counterparts, unions need both technical expertise and authority to negotiate. Their representatives must be in a position to judge the proper moment to demand or to concede, to stand firm or to relent, to probe or to extract, and of course to haggle and to bluff; all of this requires judgement and flexibility, and union negotiators who can act only as message bearers between the bargaining chamber and their constituents are under a severe handicap. Yet at the same time unions pride themselves on the democratic character of their institutions. For some of them, representative democracy with its delegation of power is insufficient: they interpret democracy in terms which require direct member participation in decision making. Even where representative democracy is accepted as appropriate, union members may insist that decisions on the acceptance of collective agreements are too important to be left to the discretion of negotiating committees. The weight attached to these and similar considerations will vary not only from country to country but also from union to union; as a result a variety of practices have evolved, in which the stress is sometimes on bargaining efficiency and sometimes on membership participation.

If there are any trends, they are difficult to trace. The following description of the situation in the Netherlands illustrates the diversity:

---

[1] United Kingdom, Royal Commission on Trade Unions and Employers' Associations, *Employers' associations*, op. cit., p. 66.

The unions in manufacturing industries have a highly decentralised structure, within which each industrial sector has its own governing body, representative of the local unions, that can take decisions concerning a new collective agreement. Other unions—for example the building unions—have a more centralised structure and their sector committees have only advisory powers.[1]

A recent review of practice in the Federal Republic of Germany points out that by becoming union members and accepting union rules workers grant full powers to their organisations to negotiate on their behalf. The author also notes, however, that union members can still avail themselves "of the principles of internal democracy in order to state their personal views to the association and perhaps influence the line of conduct followed".[2] As a matter of fact if a union bargaining committee in that country is not certain of membership support for a given agreement or conciliation proposal it may submit the question to a referendum. Proposed agreements are deemed to be accepted unless 75 per cent of the members entitled to vote call for their rejection in a vote by secret ballot.[3]

One of the most interesting cases is that of Sweden. Under one of the rules of the national trade union confederation, each affiliated union must insert in its own by-laws a provision to the effect that the executive board or executive council of that union has the right to make all final decisions concerning collective bargaining, including the termination of agreements, the acceptance or rejection of agreements, and the question of resorting to direct action. Without such a provision, a union may not remain affiliated with the confederation.[4] At the same time, the rules of the confederation state that unions should find ways, in a manner left to their discretion, to consult their members about proposals for collective agreements. They can do this through referenda or through delegate conferences. In their case the voting, if any, may have only an advisory effect, so as to preserve the executive board's final decision-making power.[5]

This brings us close to the end of the spectrum at which greater restrictions are placed on union negotiators. It has been pointed out that in Japan union representatives are not normally authorised to make final decisions in collective bargaining. Their decisions must be reviewed several times by general delegate meetings.[6] In France, like-wise, it was recently observed that a negotiator representing a workers'

---

[1] From the article by Albeda reproduced below, p. 318.

[2] See Reichel, below, pp. 260-261.

[3] Idem, below, p. 264.

[4] Johnston, op. cit., p. 50.

[5] See Carlson, op. cit., pp. 63-65.

[6] Hisashi Kawada: "The Government, industrial relations, and economic development in Japan", in Arthur M. Ross (ed.): *Industrial relations and economic development* (London, Macmillan, 1966), p. 84.

or employers' organisation in fact has no real power, and must constantly draw attention to the terms of his appointment and refer back to those who appointed him.[1] Parallel observations have been made on Belgium, where there is an increasing tendency for the results of negotiations to be submitted for approval to the rank and file, and where "not infrequently bargainers are sent back to the negotiating table".[2] Clearly this practice limits the authority of negotiators to conclude binding agreements.

Frequent restrictions on the authority of union negotiators also exist in the United States. No statistics are available for a comparative survey, but more than one observer has drawn attention to the fact that there is more emphasis in the United States than elsewhere on ultimate control by the membership over collective agreements.[3] Practice in the United States is no doubt partly due to the prevalence of enterprise bargaining, for as Shirley Lerner once pointed out, "the degree of popular participation in determining an agreement to a considerable extent varies inversely with the size of the geographic area for which the bargain is conducted".[4] In part, the practice is also due to strongly held notions about direct membership participation under the system of union democracy obtaining in that country. Moreover, the relative absence from labour-management relations in the United States of multi-union bargaining—in contrast to the situation in several European countries—has lent itself to the existing restrictions on negotiators, for single-union bargaining is better adapted to ultimate membership decision making than multi-union bargaining with its several diverse constituencies.

Ratification of agreements

As we have seen from the discussion in the preceding section, the question of ratification of agreements is intimately linked with that of the authority of negotiators. Where ratification or approval of collective agreements by the workers belonging to the bargaining union is required, several difficult problems arise for union and employer negotiators when a draft agreement is rejected by the workers. Only the main ones will be mentioned here. First, since consultation of the membership on the ratification of a new agreement usually occurs close

[1] Adam, Reynaud and Verdier, op. cit., p. 73.

[2] See Blanpain, below, p. 218.

[3] See for example Owen Fairweather: "Questioning the need for ratification", in Bureau of National Affairs, Inc.: *Collective bargaining today* (Washington, 1970), pp. 126-127.

[4] Shirley W. Lerner: *The impact of technological and economic change on the structure of British trade unions,* paper submitted to the First World Congress of the International Industrial Relations Association, Geneva, 4-8 September 1967 (doc. 1C-67/8-3, mimeographed), p. 3.

to the terminal date of an existing agreement, or even later if by mutual consent the date has been extended, a negative vote in some countries, notably in North America, may signify an immediate cessation of work. Should the rejection be unexpected, both the union and the employer may find themselves in the midst of a strike for which neither side was prepared and which presumably neither side wanted.

Secondly, to renegotiate a rejected agreement on the basis of improved terms creates a presumption that the employer's final bargaining position in the negotiations that have just been concluded was not his final position after all; it implies also that the union negotiators did not obtain the best possible agreement at the first attempt. The generation of such uncertainties may lead to serious complications in future negotiations, once a precedent exists that seems to demonstrate that a refusal to ratify leads to an agreement on better terms; for in that event the employer may be likely to withhold his best offer until after the anticipated first rejection, and the union negotiators may become reluctant to commit themselves to any settlement before having heard from their members.

Thirdly, rejections tend to undermine established relations between employer and union because in certain circumstances they cast doubt on the good faith of union negotiators. The employer may suspect, for example, that as a means of extracting additional concessions union officers have failed to recommend ratification, or he may believe that the union leaders are not representative of the members or not in control of them.

In the United States negative ratification votes have apparently been increasing, though to an extent that is still in dispute, as is its significance. In recent years this trend has given rise to a vigorous discussion of how best to cope with the problem.[1] This discussion holds wider interest since the problem is by no means confined to the United States nor to North America as a whole, even though its recent manifestations have been more acute there.[2] Although a full account of the controversy would go beyond the confines of this survey, some of the most important points should be indicated.

Several considerations are advanced in favour of vesting in the hands of negotiating committees full authority to commit their organisations. It is maintained that ratification votes lend themselves to

---

[1] See, among other contributions, William E. Simkin: "Refusal to ratify contracts", in *Industrial and Labor Relations Review*, Vol. 21, No. 4, July 1968, pp. 518-540; the addresses by John R. Cooke, Joseph A. Beirne and Owen Fairweather in Bureau of National Affairs, op. cit., pp. 109-135; and Clyde W. Summers: "Ratification of agreements", in John T. Dunlop and Neil W. Chamberlain: *Frontiers of collective bargaining* (New York, Harper and Row, 1967), pp. 75-102.

[2] The role of dissatisfied young workers in negative ratification votes in Canada is brought out in Gil Levine: "The coming youth revolt in labour", in *Labour Gazette* (Ottawa), Vol. 71, No. 11, Nov. 1971, pp. 722-737.

abuse in that they can become part of a union's normal negotiating tactics, that defective lines of communications inside unions prevent leaders and members from gaining a realistic appreciation of their respective aspirations and objectives, that only those who actually participate in the bargaining can accurately gauge the economic constraints bearing upon a settlement, and that unions sometimes do not adequately explain and defend the provisions of a proposed agreement to their members before a ratification vote is taken. As against these views a number of countervailing arguments have been brought forward. They hold that workers are more likely to respect and be satisfied with agreements which they have themselves ratified, that the democratic character of unions requires for its preservation a test of membership sentiments about a proposed agreement, and that any device to circumvent such a test would only shift the potential discontent of union members into other channels, whether inside their union or on their jobs.

While the discussion over the principle of ratification continues, there is no disagreement with the proposition that unions can take several measures to lessen the possibility of an adverse ratification vote. The more salient ones have been summarised in these terms:

> In many cases, ratification can more certainly be achieved if enough time is given before the vote to allow the leaders to explain the settlement carefully and advocate its approval effectively. Voting procedures, too, may need examination, since they influence the number and characteristics of the members who actually vote. The results of a ratification vote may be influenced by whether it takes place in open meeting, by secret ballot at a meeting, or by mail; a procedure that produces a light vote may prejudice the legions of satisfied, apathetic members in favor of the aroused and indignant minority. A vote against ratification of a settlement by union members also requires careful assessment, since a higher offer is not always the most appropriate response by management. Some rearrangement in the package settlement, or a new vote, may be all that is needed to settle the dispute.[1]

To these recommendations one should add that the representativeness of a negotiating committee may also have a strong effect on the willingness of union members to ratify an agreement, particularly when unionists are divided in their views. In such instances, however, the indubitable advantages of representativeness must be balanced against the undesirability of having a negotiating committee so large that it prevents rapid progress in negotiations.

The Norwegian approach to the problem is worth special mention.[2] It is founded on the principle, agreed to by all parties concerned, that a ratification vote should be a representative vote. This means that the decision to accept or reject a collective agreement should be made by

[1] Derek C. Bok and John T. Dunlop: *Labor and the American community* (New York, Simon and Schuster, 1970), p. 245.

[2] For a detailed description see Dorfman, op. cit., pp. 112-114.

the largest possible number of eligible voters. The principle has even been incorporated into the basic agreement between the confederations of trade unions and employers' associations, which also lays down detailed procedures for voting by unions, and by employers if they also take a vote.[1] To ensure maximum participation, a new vote may be ordered if the results of the first poll do not adequately reflect the views of a majority of the members.

Duration of agreements

The conclusion and, where customary, the ratification of a collective agreement establish the terms and conditions of employment and the relations between the parties that are to be in force during the effective duration of that agreement, whether it be for a fixed term or not. Two questions are of particular interest in that connection. One is that of fixed-term versus open-ended agreements; the other concerns the length of fixed-term agreements.

In most countries nowadays agreements are negotiated for a fixed duration, but in a few (notably Great Britain) there are still quite a few agreements of indeterminate duration. Yet even in Great Britain fixed-term agreements are becoming more frequent: in October 1965, 27 per cent of employees were covered by agreements concluded for a definite period.[2] Although both parties can cite reasons to support either fixed-term or open-ended agreements, it is widely considered that the net advantage is with agreements of definite duration. This is certainly so for employers in relation to the forward calculation of labour costs, production planning, submitting bids on prospective orders, and others business activities dependent on ascertainable wage and benefit levels. For their part, workers are protected against any sudden and unilateral worsening in their employment conditions that might otherwise result from the employer's cancellation of an agreement. The maintenance of industrial peace for a definite and predictable period, which under the systems in most of the countries concerned is implicit in a fixed-term agreement, is normally thought of as an important advantage for both parties.

Of course, during a particularly volatile stage of industrial relations these advantages may not be operative. As regards recent developments in Italy, for example, a change appears to have occurred "in the significance attached to collective agreements, with the parties no

---

[1] See "Basic agreement of 1969 between NAF and LO", in ILO: *Basic agreements and joint statements on labour-management relations,* op. cit., pp. 137-139.

[2] J. F. B. Goodman and T. G. Whittingham: *Shop stewards in British industry* (London, McGraw-Hill, 1969), pp. 160-161.

longer agreeing to observe a period of truce, and bargaining liable to be reopened at any time during the period of validity of the agreement".[1] This means that collective agreements have for a certain time become in effect open-ended, regardless of their formal provisions, and as usual in such situations the unions are likely to initiate contract changes in midstream. This departure from adherence to agreed provisions reflects the profound changes that are taking place in the Italian system of labour-management relations.

The French situation, too, is in this regard different from most others.[2] While it is normal practice to conclude agreements for a fixed period, usually one year, the parties tend to operate as though the agreements were of indefinite duration. For one thing, it is tacitly understood that expiring agreements will be extended if not renegotiated. Existing legislation supports this understanding by providing that unless otherwise stated, a fixed-term agreement will remain in operation after expiry in the same way as an agreement for an indefinite period.[3] Nor do French unions necessarily recognise the link between agreements of fixed duration and a renunciation of strike action during their effective period. On the other hand, the joint acknowledgement that agreements continue to remain in effect after they formally expire and even in the event of a breakdown of collective bargaining makes the failure of negotiations less serious.

Although fixed-term agreements are on the whole unquestionably more common than open-ended ones, it is difficult to identify trends in the actual length of fixed-term agreements. However, a trend towards two-year and even three-year agreements does appear to have emerged in the past two decades, notably in Belgium, Canada, the Netherlands, Norway, Sweden and the United States. In Canada the average duration of agreements, weighted by the number of workers covered, rose from 18.1 months in 1953 to 28.5 months in the first half of 1966: in 1953 one-year agreements covered 63 per cent of workers and three-year agreements barely more than 1 per cent, whereas in 1965 the corresponding percentages were 15 and 39.[4] In Sweden the Swedish Employers' Confederation and a number of unions of white-collar and supervisory employees concluded an agreement in 1970 which is to be valid for five years; it makes provision for periodic increases in wages and benefits, and leaves open the possibility of a fundamental reassessment in the event of a major economic change. For the United States information is available on 252 agreements covering 5,000 or more

---

[1] See Giugni, below, p. 292.

[2] See Delamotte, below, pp. 228-229.

[3] Idem, below, p. 228.

[4] H. J. Waisglas and Alton W. J. Craig: "Collective bargaining perspectives", in *Labour Gazette* (Ottawa), Vol. 68, No. 10, Oct. 1968, p. 578.

workers each: the figures show that 50 per cent of agreements are for 36 months, 20 per cent for less and 20 per cent for more; it should be stressed, however, that only 4 per cent of these agreements are intended to last for less than 24 months.[1]

On the other hand, one-year agreements still appear to be the rule in France, in the Federal Republic of Germany and in Japan, but in the Federal Republic the master agreements, which customarily do not set actual wage rates, are frequently of longer duration. The necessary qualification with regard to France has already been pointed out. In Japan the effective term is one year for 68 per cent of agreements, two years for 9 per cent and three years for 7 per cent; a term of six months is found in 4 per cent, while no definite term is indicated in 6 per cent; it should also be noted that the Trade Union Law prohibits the conclusion of agreements running for more than three years.[2]

There is nothing irrevocable about the apparent trend toward longer-term agreements, but it would be useful to identify the underlying factors. One is probably the search of both employers and unions for a greater measure of stability in industrial relations. Long-term agreements do not in themselves guarantee stability; in fact under certain conditions, as noted below, they may provoke exactly the opposite result; but if care is exercised they can be an important stabilising element. A second factor is that long-term agreements facilitate longer-term planning. This is an advantage mainly for employers, but not of negligible value for unions. (It must be noted, however, that the planning advantages of long-term agreements depend on a reasonably close correspondence between the nominal provisions of an agreement and the conditions actually in force: if the agreement only sets a floor and if effective conditions are substantially better, for example as a result of supplementary bargaining after an industry-wide agreement has been concluded, then the planning advantages of long-term agreements are proportionately reduced.) A third reason leading to agreements of longer duration is the increasing complexity of agreements and the consequent demands on the time of negotiators: the total amount of time consumed by bargaining preparations and the negotiations themselves may be a compelling factor in lengthening the period of agreements.

Set against these considerations, and notably so in a period of rapidly rising prices, is the reluctance of unions to commit themselves to long-term settlements that do not offer adequate protection or compensations. These could take various forms, among them the possibility of periodically renegotiating specific sections, such as those relating to

---

[1] United States Bureau of Labor Statistics: *Characteristics of agreements covering 5,000 workers or more,* Bulletin 1686 (Washington, 1970), p. 6.

[2] Section 15 (ILO: *Legislative Series,* 1949—Jap. 3).

wages, or the guarantee of automatic increases in wages and benefits, tied perhaps to a cost-of-living or other index. In the absence of such protective devices, or similar ones, unions and employers assume a certain risk of being by-passed by unofficial strike movements, as is shown by developments in the Federal Republic of Germany and in Sweden in 1969 and 1970, even though those countries had previously been relatively free of disputes initiated by the rank and file. The notion that long-term agreements increase the likelihood of anti-inflationary collective bargaining is therefore of doubtful validity. Under conditions of full employment, any substantial changes in the price level, any unexpectedly high increases in the productivity and profits of industry or any generous wage settlements in neighbouring sectors of the economy tend to operate against faithful union adherence to the terms of an existing long-term agreement if the agreement does not have a built-in capacity of adjustment to greatly changed circumstances.

---

4. The Bargaining Structure

One of the more changeable aspects of collective bargaining in contemporary industrialised societies appears to be the bargaining structure. As used here, the expression "bargaining structure" is intended to refer to the entire network of bargaining relationships which extends across a national industrial relations system. It refers in particular to the horizontal and vertical divisions and subdivisions for bargaining purposes in every system, to the resulting sectors or "units", sometimes overlapping, within which bargaining takes place, and to the relationship of those units with each other.

Bargaining structures are not easy to classify. At first reading, the term "structure" conveys an image of logic, symmetry, hierarchy and neatness; in reality, however, the bargaining structure in most countries has usually been adapted to the evolving traditions and ideologies and the changing objectives and strategies of organisations of employers and workers, to technological and market requirements, and where necessary to rules laid down by the authorities; consequently bargaining structures rarely conform to a tidy pattern. Moreover in the contemporary period the rate of structural change has seemingly accelerated: new forms of bargaining are being created, such as coalition bargaining in the United States and enterprise and plant-level bargaining in various European countries. Yet these innovations are not completely upsetting the existing patterns: rather they become additional elements of the structure, thus further complicating the already complex network of bargaining relationships.

In much of the published work on this subject the notions of bargaining level and bargaining unit are used. The level of bargaining refers customarily to the hierarchical and horizontal layering which is characteristic of the bargaining structure in a number of countries. Schematically, and in descending order, the main layers may include an economy as a whole, a given industry, a group of enterprises and an individual enterprise or plant. But these are only the chief categories: between them it may be possible to distinguish additional layers in which bargaining takes place. For example, in many countries where so-called industry-wide bargaining is said to be the rule, bargaining often occurs in what are actually regional subdivisions of an industry. On the other hand what passes in national usage for an "industry" for the purposes of industry-wide bargaining can also turn out to be a good deal more extensive than a single industry in the everyday sense: the British "engineering" industry encompasses what can be regarded as several distinct industries, and certain kinds of bargaining take place in a single forum to cover them all; a similar situation exists in the "fabricated metal products industry" in the United States or in the "metals industry" [1] in the Federal Republic of Germany, for they too would be regarded by most outside observers as being more properly groups of industries. It should also be borne in mind that an enterprise and a plant are not necessarily identical: when an enterprise consists of more than one plant, bargaining may take place at both levels. The breakdown can of course be carried beyond the plant level, into individual departments and even into individual work groups; for practical reasons, however, such distinctions will not be attempted here, and the terms "enterprise" and "plant" will be used synonymously unless otherwise specified.

In an increasing number of countries the terms and conditions of employment applying to a given worker are the cumulative result of two or more agreements concluded at different levels. Minimum standards that are intended to cover very large numbers of workers in an entire industry or perhaps even in an entire economy may be embodied in an industry-wide or economy-wide agreement. Additional and supplementary agreements are then concluded at regional, enterprise or plant levels to deal with issues not suitable for a more general agreement. They may also improve upon agreements concluded at higher levels. The following description of Australian practice well illustrates the point:

Parties often operate, of course, on two or more levels: a formal basic agreement may be reached, for example, on a near industry-wide level, supplemented by informal company and plant agreements made by its signatories, and accompanied by single company agreements made by those employers who prefer to act independently, as is usually the case in the pulp and paper manufacturing industry.[2]

The necessary relationship between two or more levels of bargaining also constitutes an important aspect of the bargaining structure. As new levels of bargaining are added to existing ones or as the relative importance of bargaining at given levels changes, the relationships between the layers of the bargaining structure may be said to change also. Enterprise agreements may overtake industry-wide agreements in importance, while in other cases coalition or multi-employer bargaining may supersede plant-level bargaining as the primary locus of decision making.

The term "bargaining unit" is an expression which originated in the United States, and which having acquired some international currency

---

[1] Metallverarbeitende Industrie.
[2] See Yerbury and Isaac, below, p. 191.

is applied to other systems as well. It comprises the employers and workers who are represented in collective negotiations and who are subject to the terms embodied in the agreement. On both the employers' and the workers' side the coverage of a bargaining unit varies. The employers' side of a bargaining unit may be as small as an individual enterprise (or an even smaller plant, workshop, or department), or it may be as large as a group of enterprises at regional or national level, i.e. an industry or industry group. It may contain a single employer or it may encompass hundreds of separately owned enterprises held together by an employers' association. In terms of the workers covered a bargaining unit may be equally large or small. It may hold no more than a small number of craftsmen sharing a certain skill in a single enterprise or it may comprise the entire workforce attached to an industry. Between these extremes, myriads of different possibilities are conceivable, for the workers concerned can vary in number, occupational status, function and many other respects: for example, there may be joint bargaining units for production and office workers, or those categories may be separate from one another; or there may be joint units for skilled maintenance workers and semi-skilled assembly line operators, or they may be in separate bargaining categories. The following description of several American bargaining units illustrates but by no means exhausts the possible variety of bargaining units:

When negotiating with a large can company, the United Steelworkers union negotiates a master agreement which covers all its members in all the company plants; the International Association of Machinists, on the other hand, prefers to bargain for its members on a plant-by-plant basis in the same industry. In the case of the General Motors Company, each plant local of the UAW is a bargaining unit for certain subjects, such as relief time; but for most matters, including wages, the whole company is one bargaining unit, and representatives of the international union and the company sign a master agreement. This agreement covers several units but only one employer. On the other hand, an employer or a single company may negotiate with a number of unions in many bargaining units. The General Electric Company, for example, has a "company-wide" agreement with the International Union of Electrical Workers which covers the production workers in a number of plants, but it also negotiates agreements with about ninety other unions.[1]

Dispersion and heterogeneity of bargaining units are characteristic of the industrial relations systems not only of the North American countries but also of others: the absence of symmetry and orderliness is not unique to the North American continent. As regards France it has been pointed out that—

... fragmentation is sometimes extremely great. Oddly enough, the extensive metal products sector does not include some very small industries such as the manufacture of toys, children's prams and camping equipment and the repair of agricultural machinery, all of which have their own collective agreements. These are all very small industries, the largest employing fewer than 10,000 people. In the extensive clothing sector

---

[1] Chamberlain and Kuhn, op. cit., pp. 235-236.

fragmentation seems to be almost the norm: apart from the agreements for the two major industries producing civilian clothing and administrative and military uniforms, there are others for—to take trades at random—the manufacture of tulle, lace, hats (two agreements), belts and braces, and buttons, the reting of flax and the making of shirts to measure. Yet even in this apparently close network there are gaps: there is nothing to cover cloth gloves, which fall between leather gloves and knitted gloves (part of the hosiery trade).[1]

Determining factors

The structure of collective bargaining that becomes identified with a given national industrial relations system (e.g. enterprise bargaining in Japan) is the result not so much of a series of coincidences or historical accidents as of the aggregate effect of identifiable forces. Behind every bargaining unit there lies a prior decision to establish that unit, whether the decision be agreed upon by the parties, imposed by a government or dictated in other ways. Sometimes the shape of a particular unit is the outcome of a vigorous struggle over new arrangements; sometimes it comes into existence because both parties have recognised it from the outset as being best suited to the development of their relationship. Thus the prevalence of industry-type bargaining units in most European countries is historically traceable to union and employer preferences for such units rather than to any accidental set of circumstances. The emergence of plant-level bargaining in Great Britain in the period since 1945 stems in large measure from the difficulties encountered in the plant-level application of industry-wide settlements and from the pressures of shop stewards on plant managers to establish informal bargaining units at plant level as supplements to national and industry-wide bargaining. The creation of coalition bargaining in the United States is the result of an effort by several unions in a number of major companies to create new bargaining units better suited than the old-established ones to equalising the bargaining power of employers and workers.

The bargaining unit is determined by the parties themselves, together with the public authorities in certain countries. That the specific configuration of a bargaining unit is of vital interest to the parties potentially constituting that unit goes almost without saying: it is they, after all, who have to conduct their bargaining within the framework of the bargaining unit. Different kinds of units impose different kinds of constraints; to put it another way, bargaining power may be significantly affected by the shape of the bargaining unit. This is as valid for employers and their organisations as it is for workers and their organisations: it has been pointed out that "the selection of the bargain-

---

[1] Adam, Reynaud and Verdier, op. cit., p. 60.

ing unit is bound to be of concern to all, since quite apart from its influence on the relative strength of the parties and the determination of wage rates it completely modifies the nature of the powers in the undertaking, and the freedom of the employer and therefore of his workers."[1] It is natural, therefore, that the parties should evolve policies specifically designed to shape the bargaining unit in line with their own interests and objectives.

A number of questions arise at this point. How does one explain the general differences in bargaining structure between national industrial relations systems? Why do some countries have a structure that is predominantly composed of industry-wide bargaining units (in some form or other), while others seemingly prefer a more decentralised structure? And how does one account for the specific contours of any given bargaining unit? Although definitive answers to these questions are beyond the scope of this work, the following analysis of several relevant factors should provide a better understanding of the main reasons.

Early bargaining patterns

In most European countries and in most cases collective bargaining originally took place in a group of enterprises engaged in identical or very similar operations within a particular region or district. In the smaller countries the bargaining might not be confined to a particular region, and an entire industry across the nation might then constitute a single bargaining area. In the larger countries, however, regional or district bargaining, or at least bargaining to cover a group of related enterprises within a single city, usually preceded the emergence of national bargaining. The really important point here is not whether bargaining began as a regional or national practice but rather that bargaining virtually from the very first involved a group of enterprises instead of individual firms or plants.

In Great Britain district bargaining dates back to the early part of the nineteenth century, possibly even before that time in some trades. In any case, it was firmly established by 1860. For the employers multi-employer bargaining had several advantages as compared with single-employer bargaining. It reinforced their individual bargaining power as long as group solidarity was maintained, prevented cut-throat competition by pegging wages at levels commonly bearable by the marginal firms, and diverted the unions from direct interference with what nowadays would be called managerial prerogatives. Employer preferences for district bargaining have been vividly described in the following terms:

---

[1] François Sellier and André Tiano: *Economie du travail* (Paris, Presses universitaires de France, 2nd ed., 1970), p. 585.

If the employers had begun by feeling that the wider the combination was, the greater the threat to them, they soon found it was really the other way round: except where they were pinned down by foreign competition they might have little to fear from a wage settlement if only it was enforced on all of them alike, and a strong union was their guarantee that it would be. Not a few reached the conclusion that it was a positive advantage to them to have a floor put under price competition in this way. Those who had little love for the union were still willing to meet it to negotiate a rate, because of all union activities this interfered with them least. They could resent hotly any encroachment on their prerogatives as managers of their own businesses, but collective bargaining only meant that they were paying the same price as their competitors for one factor of production, just as they did when they bought a raw material in the same market.[1]

Employers on the continent of Europe were motivated by similar considerations. If bargaining per se was unavoidable, then they too preferred multi-employer bargaining at district or higher levels to direct dealings with unions in their plants, and they were usually strong enough to defeat union efforts to penetrate into the individual enterprise for bargaining purposes.

On the whole, unions were willing to settle for regional or national bargaining, even if some of them might have preferred to move closer to the level of the job itself. Regional or national bargaining helped to set a floor under wages, kept the members from competing with one another for available work by offering to work for less, and generally was a substitute for protective labour legislation in establishing a body of rules of general application. There was also an ideological side to the preference for industry-wide bargaining. Many unions regarded themselves as merely part of a broader working-class movement struggling for a fundamental reconstruction of society. From that point of view, enterprise-by-enterprise bargaining or any other kind of highly segmented representation of interests in relation to employers had little appeal. Regarding workers and employers as the embodiment of distinct and basically conflicting forces, the unions emphasised the importance of dealing with employers through massive class action in which an industry as a whole, or a territorial subdivision of it, constituted the appropriate arena.

In Canada, and especially in the United States, developments took a rather different turn. To be sure, district or regional bargaining was by no means unknown in certain economic sectors such as coal mining or the manufacture of men's and women's clothing; on the whole, however, the trend was against it, for reasons to be found mainly on the employer side. The spirit of competition and the belief in individual initiative were often too strong to tolerate the restraint necessary for co-operation and compromise within an employers' association. Anti-trust legislation also seemed to hinder at least certain kinds of employer

---

[1] E. H. Phelps Brown: *The growth of British industrial relations* (London, Macmillan, 1959), pp. 123-124.

combinations. In some industries the size of the individual firm was more than ample to allow full self-sufficiency in dealings with unions. Finally, collective bargaining in the mass production industries made headway only after receiving explicit government support in the mid-1930s, and the rules introduced by legislation at that time (election procedures, bargaining units, majority choice, exclusive bargaining agency, etc.) placed a premium on the establishment of bargaining relationships plant by plant and enterprise by enterprise.

Employer preferences for restricted rather than extensive bargaining units were frequently shared by unions. The latter found that by concentrating their resources it was possible to organise in individual enterprises even where others in the same industry successfully resisted demands for collective bargaining. Moreover, the prevailing philosophical orientation of most unions directed their attention not to distant social goals or sweeping reforms but to practical step-by-step improvements of actual working conditions. These aims were best achieved by organisations that held secure positions inside the enterprise, and unlike their European counterparts the unions in North America insisted on establishing their presence in the plant itself and not merely outside it.

Community of interest

Bargaining patterns established at an early stage have, of course, been of great importance in determining the contemporary bargaining structure, but traditions and custom provide only a partial explanation. Among other factors, due weight must be given to a sense of shared interests, or what one might call a community of interest. A variety of factors can stimulate the emergence of a community of interest strong enough to result, ultimately, in the formation of a particular bargaining unit. On the workers' side, it may be the fact of common employment in a particular enterprise, of being attached to the same industry, of exercising the same skill or trade, of working in an office as distinguished from the shop, or some other relevant factor. For employers various questions arise, such as whether the common interests that link one enterprise to others in the same industry are strong enough to warrant the formation of an employer coalition for bargaining purposes or whether the unique and distinct interests of a particular enterprise are sufficiently important for it to preserve its identity in collective bargaining.

The influence of any particular factor varies. White-collar workers represent a striking example of the possibilities. In some countries, of which Sweden is one, white-collar workers tend to be strongly attached to their occupational status. Collective bargaining on their behalf is therefore conducted as a rule by their own unions in bargaining units separate from those of manual workers. In Japan, however, where the prevailing bargaining unit is the individual enterprise, manual and white-collar workers are frequently represented without distinction by the same enterprise union. Thus in Japan the community of interest created by the fact of common employment in a given enterprise is often a stronger factor in the formation of the bargaining unit than occupational or status distinctions, whereas in Sweden occupational identification overrides the shared attachment to a particular industry. Contrasting examples of this sort could be multiplied almost indefinitely. In most continental European countries bargaining units in the construction industry, though limited to a particular locality, are comprehensive in the sense of taking in all or almost all construction workers in that locality regardless of their specific craft. For European construction workers, the fact of being engaged in the construction industry is more significant than the particular skill to which they have been apprenticed. Quite the contrary situation exists in the United States and Canada, where collective bargaining in construction proceeds in bargaining units that are finely divided by craft. In their case the community of interest arising from the exercise of a certain skill is a stronger force in determining what shall be the basic bargaining unit than the fact of common employment in the industry.

In practice no factor has yet emerged as permanently more significant than any of the others, and for that reason the bargaining structure everywhere, seen as a whole, is in reality not stable but subject to change. This is the case even in the continental countries of Western Europe with their apparently firmly established industry-wide bargaining units. In their case too, issues have arisen in recent years which it has not been possible to settle in a fully satisfactory manner with the existing structure. As a result, bargaining units of a formal or informal character have arisen at plant and company levels to supplement the decisions emerging from traditional industry-wide bargaining. In a sense, this development reflects the manifestation of an enterprise community of interest which transcends the traditional industrial orientation of the workforce and of the labour organisations.

A rather contrasting development has occurred in North America, where the widening of product and labour markets has generally had the effect of raising the level of bargaining from the individual plant or enterprise (or a small and highly particularised group of craftsmen) to a higher level corresponding more closely to the actual extent of the market. The following account indicates the rationale for this development:

If the common terms of an agreement are to be effective in reducing competitive pressures, they must operate over the area within which workers are potential threats to one another. They must also cover that area within which employers threaten one another by competitively cutting labor (or, more generally, production) costs. The threat to workers is direct, affecting their wages and working conditions, while the threat to employers' profit margins is indirect. Willingness on the part of any group of workers to accept a lower wage endangers the wages of all workers; pressure by any competitive company to secure a lower wage also potentially endangers the profits of all other companies. Both union and companies have reason, therefore, to expand and maintain the coverage of the agreement to all competitors.[1]

The development of the bargaining structure in Great Britain fits into this scheme. Before the First World War collective bargaining was still conducted largely on a district-wide basis, but the desire of unions and employers to eliminate competition from low-wage districts tended to widen the area of collective bargaining until it approached national scope. The tendency accelerated during the war as a result of national wage awards, and continued into the 1920s and 1930s, when the implementation of the recommendations put forward by the Whitley Committee led to the formation of the national joint industrial councils.[2]

Of course, one should not conclude that all bargaining units are becoming steadily larger; there are countervailing forces which act in the opposite direction. The fact remains, however, that competitive market pressures tend to exert a widening effect on the scope of the bargaining unit.

Vested interests

As a general rule, the parties to collective bargaining tend to acquire a vested interest in the preservation of the existing bargaining structure, at least in as far as it contributes to the perpetuation of their own institutional existence. This fact must be recognised, for otherwise it would not be possible to understand the reasons for certain kinds of conflict within and between organisations over what constitutes an appropriate unit for collective bargaining. This occurs just as much among employers as among workers, although it may be more striking among the latter. An employers' association whose central purpose includes the conduct of collective bargaining with unions is not very likely to view with indifference an effort by one of its members to leave the association for the purpose of establishing a bargaining relationship based on a single enterprise: any large-scale exodus of members would obviously call into question the need for the continued existence of the association.

Similar considerations enter into union attitudes about appropriate bargaining units. Established craft unions will normally oppose with vigour the establishment of bargaining units based on broader member-

---

[1] Chamberlain and Kuhn, op. cit., pp. 246-247.

[2] Shirley W. Lerner: *The impact of technological and economic change...*, op. cit., p. 3.

ship qualifications. Unions of the industrial type that have established themselves in comprehensive bargaining units are likely to resist the carving out of separate units for specific groups of workers, whether they be craftsmen, white-collar workers or others; such unions will seek to avoid a situation such that the multiplication of fractional bargaining units results in a weakening of their bargaining power and a diminution of their membership. Of course, such resistance is not always successful: bargaining units catering to the special needs of distinct groups of workers do come into existence in place of more comprehensive units. Alternatively, industrial unions may be willing to make special concessions to certain groups among their members in order to preserve the integrity of an established unit. One of the best known instances of such a special arrangement occurred a few years ago in the United States when a large industrial union, the United Automobile Workers, was faced with intense dissatisfaction and a threat of secession by a large portion of its skilled membership over alleged neglect of the interests of that minority of the union. Seeking to avoid the creation of a separate bargaining unit for skilled craftsmen in the various companies of the automobile industry, the union agreed to give its skilled members special veto rights in ratification votes over the acceptance of the collective agreement. This arrangement preserved both the comprehensive bargaining unit and the union's institutional interests, but not without a significant increase in the relative power of the union's skilled members.

Response to change

Major innovations can have a substantial effect on the bargaining structure. Such innovations may involve the emergence of new subjects for collective bargaining, technological developments, or the creation of new forms of business or union organisation.

Developments in France after the events of May-June 1968 indicate strikingly how the pressure of new problems requiring attention affected the existing bargaining structure. Professor Delamotte has shown that many of the new developments in collective bargaining occurred at levels other than those—

traditionally used for collective bargaining, i.e. the industry. The employment agreement (February 1969) and the vocational training agreement (July 1970) are nationwide instruments negotiated by the National Employers' Council and the five nationally representative trade union organisations. They cover between 8 and 9 million wage earners. The question of salaried status also led to meetings at the top (e.g. the joint declaration of April 1970 and the recommendation on maternity benefits issued in July 1970). Simultaneously, profit-sharing agreements at the level of the undertaking became far more common, and it seems likely that plant-level agreements were negotiated more frequently. Everything suggests, therefore, that the mere fact of tackling a question separately and on its own made it possible to break out of the

98

traditional framework (industry-wide bargaining) and to decide the question of coverage on its merits.[1]

The examples given by Professor Delamotte also show that the nature of the new problems helps to determine the most appropriate level for dealing with them through collective bargaining. Their effect could be to shift collective bargaining to either a lower or a higher level; there must be a reasonable degree of correspondence between the substance of the problem and the level at which the parties seek to deal with it. The application of incentive wages to specific jobs can hardly be attempted at industry-wide bargaining levels, and effective bargaining over individual incentive rates or over job classification is usually possible only at shop floor level. On the other hand, collective bargaining over pension schemes to supplement existing social insurance schemes is usually undertaken more suitably at multi-company level (or perhaps at corporate level in the case of very large firms), for obvious actuarial reasons.

As originally conceived, articulated bargaining in the metal industry of Italy represented a deliberate effort to establish a logical relationship between the substance and the level of collective bargaining. It has been described in the following terms:

First comes the national (or "general") agreement for the whole industry, which covers points not regulated at the other levels. Next, the industry is subdivided into six sectors (iron and steel, electrical engineering, shipbuilding, smelting, motor cars, and general engineering). Each has different regulations for minimum wages rates, the classification of workers in the categories fixed by the general agreement, and working hours. Lastly comes plant-level bargaining for piece-rates, job evaluation, productivity bonuses, and new jobs not evaluated in the national agreement (this point concerns only the privately owned undertakings). But plant-level bargaining must conform to the principles established at the national level; this may occasionally (as in the matter of piece-work rates) greatly restrict their scope. It should also be noted that the agreements for the individual sectors were concluded at the same time as the general agreement and terminate with it. So they seem rather to be part of the national agreement than to have an independent identity of their own.[2]

Technological developments can exert concentrating or deconcentrating influences on the bargaining structure, although on the whole they tend toward the former. Improvements in transport and communications widen the effective area of competition in labour and product markets and exert pressure on unions and employers to align their bargaining units correspondingly. Where technological improvements entail potentially adverse employment effects unions or employers, or both, may seek to negotiate protective agreements at higher levels than usual. The metal industry of the Federal Republic of

---

[1] Delamotte, below, p. 234.

[2] Gino Giugni: "Recent developments in collective bargaining in Italy", in *International Labour Review,* Vol. 91, No. 4, Apr. 1965, p. 286.

Germany exemplifies this point. In that country collective agreements are traditionally negotiated at regional[1] levels. When it became apparent in the second half of the 1960s that technological changes were creating hardship for workers in certain parts of the industry, the national union[2] and the employers' association[3] agreed to negotiate at national level instead of at the customary regional level on the major problems created by industrial reorganisation and reductions in working hours. After overcoming an initial deadlock an agreement of nation-wide application emerged from these negotiations in May 1968.[4] Sooner or later, structural changes in management or among unions are likely to produce corresponding changes in bargaining units. Especially in a system of predominantly enterprise bargaining, such as those of Japan, Canada and the United States, a merger of two or more companies tends to result, perhaps after a certain interval, in a parallel merger of bargaining units. The amalgamation of unions is likely to have the same consequence, especially if the amalgamation involves two organisations operating in the same industry and covering identical groups of employees.

Role of public authorities

Up to this point the discussion has proceeded on the assumption that only the parties to collective bargaining are involved in the process of deciding what is the appropriate bargaining unit, and that governments do not concern themselves with the question. In most countries that is indeed the case most of the time. The policy of not intervening follows, of course, from a more general attitude of letting the parties decide the procedural questions arising in their relationship, except where compelling reasons dictate otherwise. In certain circumstances, however, some governments will assume an active role in shaping the bargaining structure. Such circumstances tend to arise especially in the context of widespread industrial unrest, particularly if its causes seem related to structural problems; they also arise in the context of sustained government efforts to master adverse economic developments.

In Canada and the United States applicable legislation entrusts specialised administrative agencies with authority to determine the appropriate unit for collective bargaining. In the past the main reason for the assumption of public responsibility for the bargaining structure has been the need to eliminate or avert industrial conflict arising over procedural and structural issues. The assertion of government authority

---

[1] I.e. Länder.

[2] IG Metall.

[3] Gesamtmetall.

[4] See ILO: *Collective bargaining and the challenge of new technology* (Geneva, 1972), pp. 59-60.

occurred at a time of widespread industrial unrest, in the 1930s. Behind that unrest was not only an ardent struggle between unions and employers over the large-scale introduction of collective bargaining as a major decision-making process in industry but also a protracted dispute between advocates of industrial and craft unionism with their divergent ideas about the proper scope of bargaining units. For the past several decades, therefore, the public authorities in North America have been directly and intimately involved in decisions affecting the bargaining structure of the two countries. Controversies over the boundaries of a given bargaining unit, whether they involve contending unions and employers or two rival sets of unions, are decided by the relevant public agencies. Since it is the practice of these agencies to respect the wishes of the parties whenever the parties are in agreement, as they are in most cases, the parties themselves do in practice have a great deal of influence over the bargaining structure. Even in disputed cases one of the main criteria applied by the public authorities is the history of bargaining arrangements in the sector where a bargaining unit determination needs to be made. Generally speaking, the agencies have not sought to impose any particular philosophy regarding the bargaining structure. In the United States at certain times, notably in the early phases of government intervention, a trend favouring industry-wide negotiating patterns seemed to emerge, but subsequently, especially after passage of the 1947 amendments to the National Labor Relations Act of 1935, the opportunity for relatively small bargaining units to establish and maintain themselves became significantly greater.

Another instance of public involvement in structural problems arising at least in part from concern over an excessive amount of industrial conflict is the case of Great Britain. The Royal Commission on Trade Unions and Employers' Associations focused its examination on the perceived gap between the formal system of industry-wide bargaining and the informal system of workplace bargaining.[1] On the basis of that analysis, the Commission recommended a considerable strengthening of workplace bargaining and its integration with traditional bargaining at industry level. The Industrial Relations Act of 1971, which is in part patterned on the recommendations of the Commission, does not go so far as to grant public agencies the power to determine the boundaries of appropriate bargaining units, but several of its provisions do accord explicit recognition to at least the concept of the bargaining unit[2] and thereby ease the way for the formal introduc-

---

[1] See Donovan Report, op. cit., p. 262, paragraph 1019.

[2] Under section 44 *(a)* of the Act a "bargaining unit" means "those employees or descriptions of employees of an employer, or of two or more associated employers, in relation to whom collective bargaining, in respect of such matters as are not dealt with under more extensive bargaining arrangements, is, or could appropriately be, carried on by an organisation of workers or a joint negotiating panel, or partly by an organisation of workers and partly by a joint negotiating panel".

tion of bargaining at enterprise and subsidiary levels without necessarily eliminating traditional bargaining at the industry level.

While experience does not warrant any generalisation about the precise effect of government involvement in the bargaining structure when such involvement is motivated by concern over the stability of labour-management relations, things are quite different when the impetus stems from economic considerations. In such circumstances the intent and the effect of government intervention is to move the level of bargaining upward. Sometimes this entails bringing representatives of trade union confederations and employers' associations together for the anticipated purpose of obtaining a national agreement in connection with the implementation of a national wage policy. Wage moderation or wage restraint as a factor raising the level of bargaining and modifying the bargaining structure in a centralising direction has at various times played an important role in such countries as Austria, the Netherlands and Norway. In those countries, the bargaining structure has in effect been heightened with government participation or encouragement so as to take in the centralised negotiations at the top levels of employers and trade union organisations. In promoting the upward extension of the structure it is of course the expectation of governments that wage bargains concluded at top level will have a moderating influence on the subsequent bargaining which takes place at the more conventional industry and enterprise levels.

This aspect of the bargaining structure will be further explored in the concluding section of this chapter. At this point it will be useful to explore in some detail the arrangements for bargaining that have evolved in a number of countries and to call attention to recent or impending changes.

Current trends

Australia

The system of compulsory arbitration in Australia does not encourage collective bargaining, but does not entirely preclude it either. While collective agreements may be negotiated independently of the arbitration system, much of the bargaining that does take place is carried out within the framework of the system. The parties may negotiate collective agreements before or during arbitration proceedings, as well as after awards have been issued, and such agreements may form the bases of "consent awards" or may acquire statutory force in some other way. The last 20 years have witnessed a significant movement in the direction of collective bargaining, and while there are no statistics to show the number of workers affected by this development, it appears that collective agreements and consent awards tend to set the pace and pattern of the awards made by the arbitration tribunals.

Bargaining on substantive economic issues for the whole of Australia is very rare, although tripartite consultation takes place on a number of issues. Industry-wide or nearly industry-wide bargaining has taken place at times and even regularly in some cases, in such industries as dock work, shipping, oil, and pulp and paper manufacturing. Agreements reached at these levels are often supplemented by informal company or plant agreements. Also common is regional multi-employer bargaining on an industry-wide basis, usually but not always at the level of the constituent states, such as occurs in parts of the printing, mining and building industries amongst others. Bargaining at the level of a government department or a local government unit is common in the public employment sector, as is company-level bargaining in all areas of private industry.[1]

Plant-level negotiations now frequently take place in all industries, particularly with respect to over-award and supplementary agreements. The growth of over-award plant-level bargaining has been particularly rapid in recent years, and appears to be modifying the character of industrial relations and the arbitration system in Australia. While a combination of factors has contributed to this development, it may be largely explained by the fact that Australia has practically attained full employment, and this has profoundly affected the relative power of workers and employers. Trade unions have been quick to realise the capacity of employers in certain industries to concede wages and conditions of work better than those laid down in arbitration awards. The strategy of trade unions has been to obtain as high over-award benefits as possible by negotiations and strike pressure, and to persuade arbitration tribunals to incorporate such higher standards in awards. On the other hand the employers themselves have become increasingly aware of the narrow limits within which they can now rely on arbitration tribunals to make and enforce awards as the main source of regulations governing employment conditions. This realisation has encouraged an increasing number of employers to see collective bargaining as at least providing an opportunity for securing reasonable compensation from the unions in the form of a no-strike clause applicable during the life of an agreement or consent award.

Belgium

The Belgian bargaining structure consists of three main levels.[2] At the highest level representatives of the national confederations of

---

[1] See Yerbury and Isaac, below, p. 192.
[2] See especially Blanpain, below, pp. 208-212.

employers' associations and of trade unions meet under an independent chairman in a 22-member National Labour Council. Although collective bargaining is not its primary function, under legislation of 1968 the Council may and does conclude two types of collective agreements: economy-wide agreements and agreements to cover industries without a functioning bargaining organisation of their own. Collective agreements already concluded in the National Labour Council have covered the following subjects: a non-competition clause which imposes some restrictions on a worker concerning his future employment by another employer in the same field of activity; a guaranteed monthly income for manual workers and certain white-collar employees in the event of disablement; and the employer's obligation to furnish information to the works council and to consult it on questions of employment and the general outlook for the enterprise.[1] More recent agreements of this kind deal with the role and function of trade union representatives in the enterprise and with the role of works councils. National agreements may also be concluded outside the Council.

Below the top level, there are currently in existence some 80 joint labour-management committees [2], most of them with jurisdiction that is industry-wide. On the other hand only 14 of the 80 cover both manual and white-collar workers: most of the joint committees (some 50) include only manual workers on the worker side, while 16 others cover only white-collar workers. This indicates that the traditional status distinctions are still strong enough to result in many cases in separate bargaining machinery for white-collar workers, even though it is the prevailing practice for such workers to be organised in separate departments of mixed unions rather than in unions of their own.

Most of the basic industry-wide bargaining occurs within the joint committees, and the outcome is embodied in collective agreements applicable to the entire industry. There are, however, some important exceptions. In the metals industry the dominant employers' association[3] and the three major unions bargain outside the joint committee framework, while in the chemical industry collective bargaining is traditionally carried on in the individual plant or enterprise rather than at industry level. Where industry-wide bargaining prevails, there is in most cases additional bargaining in the enterprise or plant; it is thus possible to treat the terms of the agreement concluded at a higher level as a minimum which can be improved upon through local supplementary bargaining, depending on the profitability of the enterprise concerned. In some industry-wide agreements, however, the unions

[1] See Blanpain, below, p. 212.
[2] Commissions paritaires.
[3] Fabrimétal.

have pledged themselves to make no additional general demands at plant level. Nevertheless, such pledges are not always as decisive as the situation in the local labour market, which the enterprise must take into account and which may compel it to make additional concessions if the market is particularly tight.

However, the centre of gravity of the Belgian bargaining structure is at the industry level: most of the time the key bargains are concluded at that level, and to the extent that employers and trade union leaders seek to influence prevailing trends their preferences reinforce the importance of the industry level.[1] On the employer side the reasons are said to include pressure from marginal firms which would be hard put to it by themselves to bargain on equal terms with unions (or to accept terms set by the more efficient firms), a disinclination to reveal more about the affairs of a particular enterprise than is absolutely necessary, and a preference for the relative impersonality of bargaining conducted through the professional experts of employers' associations. Union leaders know that they can exercise more control over bargaining at industry than at plant level. In some cases, moreover, the strength and cohesiveness of local organisations may not be sufficient for effective plant-level bargaining.

Canada

In Canada most bargaining occurs at the levels of the enterprise and the plant. The report of the Canadian Task Force on Labour Relations has described the existing structure as "fragmented and decentralized".[2] The recent trend has reinforced the traditional emphasis on the local level of bargaining. This appears quite clearly from a statistical comparison of the distribution of negotiating (or bargaining) units and the distribution of employees contained within such units in 1953 and 1966 (tables 1A and 1B). While the proportion of negotiating units in the three principal categories has remained stable, the number of employees actually covered has shifted perceptibly. The largest increase occurred in single-company units. A more moderate increase took place in the employers' association category, but both increases came about at the expense of multi-company bargaining arrangements so that the net outcome of the redistribution was clearly a shift towards decentralisation.

Present indications give little cause, perhaps even none at all, to anticipate a change towards centralisation, nor do the recommendations of the Task Force suggest the need for a deliberate effort to bring

---

[1] Guy Spitaels: "Changes in union organization and collective bargaining in Belgium", in B. C. Roberts (ed.): *Industrial relations: Contemporary issues* (London, Macmillan, 1968), pp. 195-196.

[2] *Canadian industrial relations*, op. cit., p. 60.

Collective bargaining

TABLE 1A. PERCENTAGE DISTRIBUTION OF NEGOTIATING UNITS
BY TYPE IN CANADA, 1953-66

Unit	1953	1966
Single company	81.8	81.3
Multi-company	5.3	6.0
Employers' association	12.9	12.6
	100.0	100.0

TABLE 1B. PERCENTAGE DISTRIBUTION OF EMPLOYEES BY TYPE
OF NEGOTIATING UNIT IN CANADA, 1953-66

Unit	1953	1966
Single company	53.1	70.9
Multi-company	31.2	7.9
Employers' association	15.6	21.1
	100.0	100.0

Source: Waisglas and Craig, op. cit., p. 580.

about substantial modification. In fact, the Task Force went on record as favouring "the general principle of freedom for the bargaining structure to find its own form, subject to the exercise of influence by the state where the public interest is high".[1] Since this statement is accompanied by a warning against both excessive centralisation and decentralisation, it would appear that the public interest does not at present require action to bring about any major change in the established structure.

France

Most collective bargaining in France has been carried out in the industry (or branch), either at national or in certain cases at regional level. Under the basic legislation of 1950, "a network of nation-wide collective agreements covering a large part of the economy was somewhat laboriously built up. By 1966 there were 189 national collective agreements in force".[2] This level of bargaining corresponded most closely to the inclinations of the employers' associations, and in part also to those of the unions. The predominant position of industrial affiliates in collective bargaining is explicitly recognised in the constitution of the employers' confederation, the CNPF, which claimed for itself only a liaison and co-ordinating function: "It is not for the CNPF to negotiate collective agreements, but for the competent employers'

---

[1] *Canadian industrial relations,* op. cit., p. 164.

[2] See Delamotte, below, p. 230.

TABLE 2. COLLECTIVE AGREEMENTS SIGNED BETWEEN 11 FEBRUARY 1950 AND 31 JULY 1969 IN THE NON-AGRICULTURAL SECTOR IN FRANCE

Type of agreement [1]	Registered but not extended	Extended	Total
National industry-wide	183	64	247
Regional	147	27	174
Local	442	31	473
Plant	653	—	653
Total	1 425	122	1 547

[1] The table does not take into account the numerous supplementary agreements (avenants) signed during the same period to amend existing agreements.

Source: Jean Pélissier: *Documents de droit du travail* (Paris, Montchrestien, 1971), p. 293.

organisations for each branch." [1] The unions were somewhat more flexible, or perhaps more opportunistic [2], about the choice of bargaining units, and for many years they made few sustained efforts to transfer negotiations to either a higher or a lower level. During the past few years, however, the relative stability of the structure has begun to weaken, and an increasing amount of bargaining has been taking place at levels above and below that of the industry. While most basic agreements are still concluded at that level, both plant-level agreements and economy-wide agreements are assuming increasing importance. Table 2 gives indications of the relative proportion of different types of agreements concluded from 1950 to 1969.

Various factors have contributed to this diversification, not least among them the encouragement of the public authorities. For instance, in August 1967 the then Prime Minister, Mr. Pompidou, took the initiative of inviting the parties at economy-wide level to consider jointly certain important questions related to employment security. Intermittent but continuing contacts at that level have resulted in the conclusion of several economy-wide agreements between the central bodies on the employer and trade union sides on such important subjects as supplementary pension benefits, unemployment insurance and employment security, and most recently vocational training, further training and the extension of salaried status and accompanying emoluments to manual workers who have traditionally been paid on an hourly basis. Although these arrangements are not considered to be collective agreements as defined by the collective bargaining law of

---

[1] Yves Delamotte: *The social partners face the problems of productivity and employment,* A study in comparative industrial relations (Paris, OECD, 1971), p. 129.

[2] Sellier and Tiano, op. cit., p. 587.

1950 [1], the economy-wide level of bargaining has recently received a measure of official recognition. By virtue of amendments of 1971 to the Act of 1950, economy-wide agreements have been declared eligible for extension to enterprises not affiliated, directly or indirectly, with the central organisations of employers.[2]

At the opposite end of the bargaining structure, that is at the level of the individual enterprise, several developments have contributed to making possible an expansion of bargaining, although it is not yet entirely clear whether in the future the principal bargaining agent on the workers' side will be the works councils or the plant sections of the several trade unions. The obligatory employer recognition of trade union plant delegates under the Act of 7 December 1968 tends to favour the trade union sections, but in practice much bargaining in individual enterprises is still conducted by works councils. An additional impetus to bargaining at enterprise level has been provided by the 1971 amendments. Whereas the Act of 1950 viewed the industry at national or regional level as the proper forum for collective bargaining and accorded to enterprise agreements only the somewhat inferior status of wage agreements[3], under the 1971 amendments enterprise agreements received the same statutory recognition as the law has traditionally extended to industry-wide agreements, provided only that there are no national, regional or local agreements already applicable to the enterprise. Where such territorial agreements do exist, the enterprise agreement will be deemed to be a supplementary agreement, suitable for adapting the provisions of agreements concluded at higher levels to the specific conditions of the enterprise.[4] Furthermore, the new amendments require the enterprise to provide the works council with copies of all collective agreements applicable to the enterprise, and also require the works council to make these agreements available to all employees.[5]

These innovations tend to support the views of observers who believe that the enterprise will be moving to the forefront of the French bargaining structure.[6] At the same time, however, the significance of other developments should not be overlooked. In addition to the already mentioned multiplication of contacts at the economy-wide level, which have often taken on the character of bargaining sessions, it should be noted that in some industries, foremost among them the highly significant metals sector, bargaining that was previously carried

---

[1] ILO: *Legislative Series*, 1950—Fr. 6 A.

[2] Act No. 71-561 of 13 July 1971, section 11 (6). ILO: *Legislative Series,* 1971—Fr. 3.

[3] Accords de salaire.

[4] Sections 2 and 3.

[5] Section 15.

[6] Adam, Reynaud and Verdier, op. cit., p. 67 ff.

on predominantly at regional level has been raised at union insistence to the national level (except for minimum wage rates which continue to be set at the regional level). For the time being, a cautious assessment of the evidence as a whole mainly indicates a significant multiplication of bargaining levels, accompanied by a corresponding development of much more complex inter-related bargaining patterns, rather than a pronounced shift towards any particular level.

Federal Republic of Germany

The industry, or more usually the regional subdivision of an industry, is the main bargaining unit in the Federal Republic of Germany; however, bargaining also takes place at the economy-wide level and especially at the level of the plant, where it may become significantly more common in the years to come.

At the end of 1968 there were 18,630 collective agreements in effect in the Federal Republic.[1] Of this number, 2,317 applied to an entire industry or industry sector throughout the country; 9,695 covered an industry or sector in one or several of the provinces; and the remaining 6,618 consisted of individual enterprise agreements.[2] Only a few among the enterprise agreements are of significance for the economy as a whole, for example the agreement between IG Metall and the Volkswagen Company; most of them involve relatively small firms that do not belong to an employers' association and are therefore not bound to accept the provisions negotiated by the association.[3] This is the case, in particular, in industries that are less well organised, among them the food processing, textiles, clothing, leather and wood industries as well as certain service and commercial sectors. It is important to keep this point in mind because the individual enterprise agreements here referred to need to be distinguished from the kind of plant-level agreements described further on.

Agreements of genuinely national scope are found mainly in such economic sectors as printing, paper manufacturing, shoe manufacturing, building construction, banking and insurance. In most other sectors regional agreements predominate, although certain new issues may be subject to special agreements concluded exceptionally at national level, e.g. the agreement on employment security in the metals industry which was cited earlier.

---

[1] Waline, op. cit., p. 258.

[2] For a useful description of the several types of collective agreements that exist, see Claus Noe: *Gebändigter Klassenkampf: Tarifautonomie in der Bundesrepublik Deutschland* (Berlin, Duncker und Humblot, 1970), pp. 148-149.

[3] Accession of non-signatory enterprises to an agreement could be brought about, of course, if the public authorities made use of the "extension" procedure described earlier on (see Chapter 1, p. 11). By the end of 1968 a total of 173 agreements had been extended.

For the economy as a whole the confederations of employers and trade unions have not negotiated collective agreements in the sense in which such agreements have been concluded in the Scandinavian countries and the Netherlands. On neither side would the constituent industrial organisations approve of any relationship between the confederations on the two sides which could develop into conventional bargaining or which could be interpreted as detracting from their exclusive right to engage in negotiations over the conclusion of collective agreements. Nevertheless the confederations have often consulted one another on issues of importance to the whole economy, and some of their deliberations have had tangible results. For example, the two sides have concluded a model agreement on conciliation procedures intended for implementation and adaptation by the parties at industry level.[1] Moreover, the Act on dismissals of 1951 was based on a text which had previously been agreed upon between the two confederations.[2] It is also entirely possible, even if difficult to demonstrate, that the top-level meetings have influenced the climate of opinion within which bargaining at industry levels has taken place. In any event, the confederations remain continuously in touch with their affiliated member associations so as to try to "create and maintain a uniform general position in the negotiation of agreements involving comparable territorial, occupational and individual circumstances".[3]

Collective bargaining at plant level has two quite distinct aspects. There is, in the first place, the well established relationship between the statutory works councils and the managements of individual enterprises. The recently amended law on the relationship of works councils to the enterprise[4] is too extensive and complex to be reviewed here, but it should be pointed out that the law grants the works councils significant rights, which in effect can be implemented only by bargaining and by continuing consultation with management. These rights explicitly include the making of plant agreements.[5] However, at the insistence of the unions the law provides that decisions on wages and other conditions of employment which already have been, or customarily are, settled by collective agreement may not be included in the plant agreement. Nevertheless it frequently does happen that works councils obtain concessions from management, including concessions on wages, which do not properly fall within the sphere allotted to them by law.

---

[1] See ILO: *Basic agreements and joint statements on labour-management relations,* op. cit., pp. 63-65.

[2] "Dismissal procedures—IV: Federal Republic of Germany", in *International Labour Review,* Vol. 80, No. 3, Sep. 1959, p. 263.

[3] See Reichel, below, p. 255.

[4] Works Constitution Act dated 15 January 1972 (ILO: *Legislative Series,* 1972—Ger. F.R. 1).

[5] Betriebsvereinbarungen.

The second category of plant-level agreements is of more recent vintage. It consists of full-fledged collective agreements concluded at enterprise rather than at industry level between a union and an individual employer. The origins of this development, which at the time of writing is not yet very far advanced, are traceable to the efforts of certain unions to secure for themselves a stronger position inside the enterprise than they have traditionally occupied. One of the important aims of the unions engaged in this venture is the closing of the gap between the minimum wage rates laid down by industry-wide agreements and the effectively much higher rates which employers often concede unilaterally. Such a gap, as the unions have realised, tends to undermine the prestige of the union in the eyes of its members and potential members. Employers have on the whole resisted the introduction of plant-level agreements of this second type: they perceive in them a threat to the solidarity of their associations. Furthermore, the stronger firms much prefer to retain the flexibility which they currently enjoy because of the essentially minimal character of the terms of the industry-wide agreements. Employers have also pointed out that trade unions that have concluded national or regional agreements with employers' organisations could not support demands for supplementary enterprise agreements by strikes since such a stoppage would be in violation of the industrial peace obligation inherent in the national or regional agreement covering the enterprise or enterprises concerned.

Not all of the unions are persuaded of the desirability of increasing the number of plant-level agreements. Some at least fear them as a threat to their internal unity and cohesiveness, and are uncertain whether they have the necessary negotiators to engage in effective bargaining at the local level. In addition, there is the by no means small problem of potential conflict which could arise when works council and local union both wish to engage in bargaining. In these circumstances it would be premature to conclude that a major realignment is already taking place in the bargaining structure of the Federal Republic.

Great Britain

In a relatively short time changes of substantial importance have modified the bargaining structure in Great Britain. The change of the greatest significance has been the expansion of bargaining at the level of the company and the plant. Of less importance has been a certain increase in the authority and power of the confederation of trade unions, the Trades Union Congress, not so much by actual participation in bargaining as by more frequent intervention in disputes and by modest efforts to co-ordinate on certain occasions the bargaining activities of its affiliates.[1] Of the two opposite trends currently affecting the British bargaining structure, the decentralising changes are having a much greater effect than the centralising ones. Indeed, one long-time observer of British industrial relations has seen in the large-scale expansion of company or workplace bargaining a spontaneous movement which is largely outside the control of trade unions and employers' associations and which may even threaten the stability of the system of external job regulation.[2]

In the past the industry-wide agreement has been at the centre of bargaining. In evidence given before the Royal Commission on Trade Unions and Employers' Associations, the Ministry of Labour listed some 500 separate pieces of industry-wide negotiating machinery for manual workers (including wages councils) and estimated that the machinery in question covered some 14 million out of a total of 16 million workers. For non-manual workers the Ministry estimated that collective agreements covered somewhat less than 4 million out of 7 million, and that most of those covered were in the public sector.[3] Industry-wide agreements are negotiated by an employers' association (occasionally more than one association) and one or more unions or federations of unions. These agreements may be of either the procedural or the substantive type; occasionally a clear distinction cannot be made because both aspects are covered in a single agreement.

Some of the larger companies which do not belong to an employers' association bargain directly with a union or several unions. The company agreements that emerge from those negotiations come very close to being industry-wide agreements because they represent a basic settlement rather than a supplementary settlement of outstanding issues. In fact, where a single large enterprise is coterminous with an entire industry, as is the case with the national coal and railway boards, the single-company agreement is at the same time an industry-wide agreement. Most of the growing number of company (and plant) agreements are supplementary rather than basic agreements. Precisely how many such agreements are now in existence is almost impossible to say. A register of productivity agreements maintained by the Department of Employment and Productivity showed that between 1 January 1967 and 31 December 1969, 5,185 productivity agreements were registered, though this figure also included some agreements which may not have been productivity agreements in the strict sense. On the other hand there are likely to be a substantial number of plant agreements

---

[1] This does not preclude agreements between the Congress and the Confederation of British Industries; in fact in 1972 those organisations signed an agreement on conciliation procedures.

[2] Allan Flanders: *Management and unions: The theory and reform of industrial relations* (London, Faber, 1970), "What is wrong with the system?", p. 108 ff.

[3] Royal Commission on Trade Unions and Employers' Associations: *Written evidence of the Ministry of Labour* (London, HM Stationery Office, 1965), p. 19. See also below, p. 353.

which never find their way onto a register and thus remain uncounted. The problem of quantifying such agreements has been described as follows:

The greatest difficulty in analysing the growth and development of plant and company agreements arises from the fact that a large proportion of the agreements made at these levels are not negotiated as entirely new and clearly distinguishable contracts. They are supplements and additions that are added to previous agreements in an almost continuous process of bargaining that has no finite boundaries or terms.[1]

In any event there is no doubt about the increasing decentralisation of the structure, but it is unlikely that the advent of company and plant bargaining has already had a significantly diminishing effect on the sheer amount of basic industry-wide bargaining. With agreements being concluded simultaneously at both levels, the net result is more likely to be an increase in the complexity of the structure. A possible exception may be developing in the engineering industry, where in January 1972 19 unions, joined together in the Confederation of Shipbuilding and Engineering Unions, broke off industry-wide negotiations with the Engineering Employers' Federation and announced that henceforth they would seek to negotiate directly with individual employers on all questions of pay and conditions of employment.[2] This decision by the executive of the Confederation came after the collapse of negotiations lasting three years over a new national disputes procedure to supersede that established under an agreement that was almost 50 years old, and after failure of parallel negotiations on substantive conditions of employment.

In the public sector, including the nationalised industries, prospects are good for the continued pre-eminence of national agreements and industry-wide bargaining structures. In some cases (e.g. the national health services) the key negotiations may be conducted at sectoral rather than at over-all national level, but as some commentators have argued, present evidence suggests that the industry-wide national agreement in the public sector will retain its importance.[3]

To the extent that the shift toward more company bargaining in the private sector is the result of a general set of factors operating in a number of countries, the matter will be explored in a subsequent section of this chapter; in the present section attention needs to be drawn only to certain points that are peculiar to the British situation. One of these is the growth, with strong official backing, of productivity bargaining.[4]

---

[1] B. C. Roberts and John Gennard: "Trends in plant and company bargaining", in *Scottish Journal of Political Economy*, Vol. 17, No. 2, June 1970, p. 148.

[2] *The Times* (London), 14 Jan. 1972, p. 1, and 9 Feb. 1972, p. 15.

[3] Roberts and Gennard, op. cit., pp. 164-165.

[4] A recent review of bargaining trends suggests that "productivity bargaining is no longer a major factor in the British industrial relations system" (T. G. Whittingham and B. Towers: "Bargaining for change", in *Industrial Relations Journal*, Vol. 3, No. 1, Spring 1972, p. 64).

Collective bargaining

Not every productivity agreement has been an individual company or plant agreement, but this has certainly been the case for the large majority. As pointed out in an OECD report, in Britain productivity bargaining is "essentially a negotiation within the framework of the firm or the establishment".[1] A second specifically British factor has been the effect of the report of the Royal Commission on Trade Unions and Employers' Associations (the Donovan Commission), especially through its strongly expressed doubts about the sufficiency of the established industry-wide bargaining structure. In its recommendations the Commission explicitly urged an expansion of the bargaining structure through factory agreements for the purpose of bringing more orderliness into relations at workshop and company levels.[2]

In addition, many of the joint consultative relationships at plant level that were originally established during and shortly after the Second World War as part of a general movement toward greater efficiency in industry have turned, with the passage of time, into bargaining relationships. Already in 1964 an observant student of British industrial relations pointed out that "any decision taken jointly by the representatives of management and the shop stewards is a collective agreement. Therefore there is no obvious de facto distinction between consultation and negotiation when the employees' side of a joint consultative committee is composed of shop stewards (a common practice) and when both sides feel a moral obligation to carry out the committee's decision".[3] In the intervening years the distinction has become, if anything, even more blurred, and the view has developed "that consultation and negotiations are part of a single process of involvement of workers and their representatives in decisions affecting their working lives, and that both should be handled by a single committee in which managers meet shop stewards. This development has been hastened by productivity bargaining".[4]

Italy

In Italy a once rather simple bargaining structure has in recent years become complex, with interconnected but not always closely co-ordinated bargaining being carried out at various levels.

During the 1950s the structure still reflected essentially the continental European tradition of primarily industry-wide bargaining

[1] Delamotte: *The social partners face the problems of productivity and employment*, op. cit., p. 30.

[2] Donovan Report, op. cit., especially sections 1019-1021.

[3] Shirley W. Lerner: "Factory agreements and national bargaining in the British engineering industry", in *International Labour Review*, Vol. 89, No. 1, Jan. 1964, p. 9.

[4] Clegg, op. cit., p. 192.

designed to do no more than set minimum wage rates and a few basic working conditions. Since there was almost no bargaining at the level of the enterprise, it was left to individual employers to apply or unilaterally to improve upon the industry minima. In addition to industry-wide negotiations, economy-wide negotiations between the employers' confederation and the three major trade union confederations also took place from time to time. Mention may be made, for example, of the agreements on works councils[1] and on procedures to be followed in the event of dismissals and reduction of personnel.

In the late 1950s a certain amount of disconnected plant-level bargaining got under way, sometimes led by unions and sometimes, but more rarely, by works councils.[2] Spurred on by economic and technological developments, Italian unions began to press in a more organised fashion for an extension of plant-level bargaining, and achieved major successes in the early 1960s. Between 1960 and 1963, agreements were reached in several major industries, notably in the manufacture of electrical products and in the metal-working industries. Those agreements included a recognition of the right of unions to bargain at plant level. The most influential document was the "protocol of intentions" signed in July 1962 by two state-controlled corporations, IRI and ENI, in which they accepted the notion of agreements at plant level to supplement agreements applying to a whole industry. The protocol set an important precedent for other industries, including those in the private sector. Items particularly suitable for plant-level agreements were deemed to be incentive wages, job evaluation, production bonuses, and wage rates for job classifications not dealt with at industry level.

The system which evolved from these agreements was called "articulated bargaining" because it envisaged that there would be a well co-ordinated relationship (or articulation) between industry-wide and plant-level bargaining, or in a different perspective, between multi-employer and single-employer bargaining.[3] Actually, in certain industry groups an additional bargaining level was inserted between the industry group and the plant. Thus in the metal-working group of industries the intermediate level was occupied by the six main industries concerned—iron and steel, electrical engineering, shipbuilding, smelting, automobile manufacturing and general engineering. In practice,

---

[1] Commissioni interne.

[2] For a more detailed review of developments see two articles by Gino Giugni: "Recent developments in collective bargaining in Italy", in *International Labour Review*, Vol. 91, No. 4, Apr. 1965, pp. 273-291, and "Recent trends in collective bargaining in Italy", ibid., Vol. 104, No. 4, Oct. 1971, pp. 307-328 (the latter reprinted below, pp. 273-294). Cf. François Sellier: "Les transformations de la négociation collective et de l'organisation syndicale en Italie", in *Sociologie du travail*, Apr.-June 1971, pp. 141-158.

[3] See p. 99 above for Professor Giugni's description of articulated bargaining.

however, the negotiations at industry level within industry groups have lagged behind the development of bargaining at the plant level.[1]

Since the mid-1960s there has been further movement toward plant-level bargaining. Under several industry-wide agreements unions have been granted extensive bargaining power at plant level and the plant sections of unions have received at least implicit recognition, with the result that in 1971 there were perhaps as many as 4,400 plant-level agreements in force covering more than 1.5 million workers. The metal-working group of industries is still the outstanding case of the shift in the centre of gravity of collective bargaining to a lower level. Subjects for negotiation now include not only the already established ones of piece rates and bonuses but also in some instances the implementation of nationally negotiated reductions in working hours, production standards and job security.

Alongside the decentralising trend toward more plant-level bargaining there has also been a certain amount of top-level negotiation in which all the main confederations have participated. From these meetings have emerged two economy-wide agreements on dismissals and a large-scale revision of the 1953 agreement on works councils. The first two were concluded in 1965, and the third in 1966.[2] At present the bargaining structure is still in a state of flux. As Professor Giugni has observed, "the present situation is characterised by bargaining conducted at a number of levels (national, plant and sometimes company) without any co-ordination and therefore leaving the unions free to lodge claims at one level after they have been settled at another".[3] It remains to be seen whether the primary process of decentralisation will continue or whether there will now begin a period of consolidation.

Japan

The Japanese bargaining structure exemplifies the notion that a high degree of diversity is not necessarily characteristic of a highly decentralised system of bargaining. By far the most important level of bargaining in Japan in terms of the number of workers covered and the number of agreements concluded is the individual enterprise. In fact, in this sense the Japanese bargaining structure shows a remarkable degree of uniformity.

The bargaining structure is, of course, closely linked to the structure of employers' and workers' organisations. Enterprise unions do not operate as subordinate units of national organisations but

---

[1] Sellier, op. cit., p. 142.

[2] For the texts see ILO: *Basic agreements and joint statements on labour-management relations*, op. cit., pp. 84-109.

[3] See below, p. 292.

instead as autonomous and self-governing bodies, even though many are loosely affiliated with a national union in their particular industry. Since enterprise unions are self-directed and set their own policies without co-ordination from above, they conduct their negotiations free from supervision and control by their national union. However, a certain amount of policy guidance is offered by the national organisations in connection with the spring wage offensive.[1] The same relationships apply to the employer side. Management does not usually expect its employers' association to participate in collective bargaining, except perhaps for an exchange of information and some loose co-ordination of employer policies. The Japan Federation of Employers' Associations [2] has been following the practice of issuing a white paper on wages in December or January of each year, analysing the general economic situation and indicating a general policy to be followed in the forthcoming spring negotiations.

There are, however, a few exceptions to the prevalence of enterprise bargaining. In the maritime industry, where collective bargaining existed already before the Second World War, the seamen's union engages in genuinely industry-wide bargaining over wages, hours and working conditions with employers' associations; this helps to explain why the seamen's union is organised on the pattern of a powerful national union with considerable authority over its affiliated sections. In the coalmining industry there used to be a form of multi-employer bargaining in which the coalminers' union negotiated basic wage rates with a group of major coalmining companies; on other matters negotiations then took place at enterprise level. In recent years, however, since coal has ceased to be one of the main sources of energy and after an unsuccessful strike of major dimensions, multi-employer bargaining in that industry has fallen into disuse. In the textile industry the national textile workers' union negotiates separately with employers' associations for several branches of the industry (cotton spinning, wool, etc.) over common starting wage rates. On the private railways, most of which are commuter lines in highly urbanised areas, there has been intermittent multi-employer bargaining. In the public sector the public corporations (the national railways, the telegraph and telephone services and the Japan Monopoly Corporation which runs the salt and tobacco industries) conduct bargaining at three levels, national, regional and local. Basic issues are decided at national level, while "negotiations at the regional or local level deal with the detailed regulation of the agreements concluded at the national level or with problems specific to the region or locality concerned".[3]

---

[1] Or drive *(shunto).*

[2] Nikkeiren.

[3] See Mitsufuji and Hagisawa, below, p. 307.

An exception of a different kind arises in the enterprises and industries where white-collar workers have formed separate unions. Although comprehensive enterprise unions are the rule, there are a considerable number of enterprises with their own unions of white-collar employees. A sample survey conducted by the Ministry of Labour in 1967 found that 32 per cent of all 1,200 enterprise unions included in the sample were separate unions of white-collar employees.[1] White-collar employees also maintain their own unions in the mining industries (coal and ore).

There are no strong indications that the Japanese bargaining structure will become more centralised or that there will be more industry-wide bargaining. Employers who have in the past insisted on bargaining at the level of the enterprise will most probably continue to do so in the future, and the enterprise unions themselves do not seem eager to exchange their present unquestioned autonomy for a subordinate role in a scheme of industry-wide bargaining. It is conceivable that the national unions should seek to assume more responsibility for the formulation of demands and the co-ordination of bargaining strategy in connection with the annual bargaining sessions, particularly during the spring wage drives, but a more fundamental structural change does not seem to be in the offing.

Netherlands

Recent trends in the bargaining structure in the Netherlands must be viewed against the background of earlier developments. In the past most of the bargaining was industry-wide, which meant in practice that the national unions negotiated basic terms of employment with their counterparts, the various employers' associations. Owing to the strength of ideological and religious divisions in the labour movement and in society in general, there were (and still are) three unions in most industries or sectors of the economy. This complicated the bargaining process. In contrast to the situation in other countries the employers' associations were also divided along denominational lines. Supplementary negotiations at enterprise level were highly unusual since the unions were not strong enough at that level and since employers normally refused to engage in such bargaining. However, a substantial amount of bargaining did occur at local level between unions and independent employers, so that in 1940, for example, there were 1,159 individual company agreements in existence.[2]

The need for rapid economic recovery after the Second World War in the face of great scarcity of resources and pent-up consumer demand

---

[1] *Japan Labor Bulletin*, Nov. 1969, p. 8.
[2] See Albeda, below, p. 317.

resulted in the adoption of highly centralised economic controls, including controls over prices and wages. In industrial relations the centralisation of decision making led to an important change in the bargaining structure. Henceforth the key negotiations no longer took place between the parties in each industry—i.e. the national unions and various employers' associations—but instead between representatives of the confederations on both sides.[1] In their joint forum, the Foundation of Labor, the three confederations of trade unions and the corresponding confederations on the employer side periodically sought to reach agreement on major changes in the basic terms of employment, usually in close consultation with the government agencies concerned. The implementation of agreements reached at that level was left to the unions and employers' associations in each industry, whose task it became to adjust the agreed national pattern to the needs and peculiarities of the various industrial sectors.

During its early years the centralised system made an important contribution to the attainment of national economic and social objectives, but inevitably it became exposed to severe stresses which made it virtually inoperative by 1963. Since then industry-wide negotiations have once again become the principal element in the bargaining structure, though the parties occasionally try to settle an issue through economy-wide bargaining. Most industry-wide agreements, of which there were some 270 in 1968, are negotiated for the entire country, but about 100 are regional or local. In addition to industry-wide agreements, there are some 400 enterprise agreements, most of which cover either very large companies (e.g. Philips and Hoogovens) which because of their size do not readily fit into an employers' association composed mainly of small and medium-sized firms, or smaller companies in industries in which product differences and diversities of other kinds prevent the effective co-ordination of negotiations through an employers' association.

Since most workers are still covered by an industry-wide rather than an enterprise agreement, the question arises whether there is any supplementary bargaining at plant level. In general there is no bargaining in the sense of formal negotiations between local management and union representatives at that level. As in other continental European countries the unions in the Netherlands have traditionally neglected the development of a plant-centred apparatus and have instead concentrated on bargaining at industry-wide and even economy-wide levels. The resulting weaknesses at their base led the three unions in the metals industry to decide some years ago to improve their organisations at plant level. Although this scheme has not yet spread very far, partly because of employer resistance, Professor Albeda has raised the

---

[1] See Windmuller, op. cit., pp. 118, 282.

possibility that "the new trade union presence in the firm may encourage the unions to start official bargaining at that level, for it may open their eyes to the special needs of individual firms".[1]

At plant level workers are represented mainly through the works councils, which were established as statutory bodies under legislation enacted in 1950. The prescribed tasks of a works council include advice to the employer (who is chairman) on the social policy of the enterprise, co-operation with the employer in promoting the well-being of the enterprise and representation of workers' interests in practical matters such as arranging holiday and shift work rosters. Although bargaining does not fit into any of these categories, works councils in fact frequently do negotiate with the employer on matters of concern to the workforce. At times the negotiations may even cover wage and salary questions, although the unions do not usually encourage works councils to trespass in fields such as collective bargaining that are reserved for union activity.

Recent revisions of the works council legislation have given the unions greater opportunities to influence the activities of the works councils, and it is likely that they will use these opportunities to try to exert more control over management policies in the enterprise, but it is as yet not at all clear whether the unions will ultimately choose to bargain at plant level through the works councils or through their own plant organisations, assuming they succeed in establishing them widely.

Sweden

Over the years Sweden has maintained the essentially centralised character of its collective bargaining machinery. This does not mean that there are no decentralising forces at work in the system and that no changes are taking place, but it does mean that in essence the authority of the national confederations has remained unimpaired. Of course, centralisation should not be confused with simplicity; on the contrary, the Swedish bargaining structure is so complex that a brief description cannot do it full justice.

The bargaining structure for manual workers is distinct from that of others. For manual workers agreements are of three main kinds: those for the economy as a whole, those for particular industries or groups of industries and those for individual enterprises and establishments. Economy-wide agreements are concluded between the Swedish Confederation of Trade Unions[2] and the Swedish Employers' Confederation.[3] Two types of agreements can be reached at that level. There are, to begin with, agreements that are concluded at more or less

---

[1] See Albeda, below, p. 330.
[2] Landsorganisationen (LO).
[3] Svenska Arbetsgivareföreningen (SAF).

regular intervals, and in which the parties agree on certain major changes in wages and basic conditions of employment; for a specified period, usually but not always two years, those agreements are in effect intended to provide authoritative guidance for negotiations in individual industries or groups of industries. The other type of agreement concluded for the economy as a whole is of a different nature. It represents the outcome of intermittent negotiations over issues somewhat broader and requiring a longer-term solution than wages, hours and other employment conditions. The initial agreement of the latter type, defining in particular the basic nature of the relationship between the "social partners", dates back to 1938; it is the well-known Saltsjöbaden agreement, which has since been revised.[1] Additional agreements dealing with particular subjects have subsequently been negotiated, among them agreements on industrial safety, vocational training, works councils and time and motion studies.

Bargaining for an entire industry or industry group is expected to be guided by the terms of any agreement already concluded for the whole economy.[2] According to one source, "the central model agreements have become increasingly detailed over the years, and there is now very little scope for deviation in the industry-wide agreements; they are nothing more than adaptations of the model".[3] Industrial agreements are mutually exclusive and hence do not overlap or supplement each other. It is noteworthy that while of the industry-wide agreements applicable to members of the Swedish Confederation of Trade Unions only some 330—1.3 per cent of the total—are national agreements, those none the less cover 77 per cent of the total membership of the Confederation, the average national industry-wide agreement covering some 3,000 workers.[4]

A considerable amount of formal and informal supplementary bargaining is conducted between local unions and plant managements over local issues, especially wages and incentive rates. The great

---

[1] For the text of that agreement, as well as of several other top-level Swedish agreements, see ILO: *Basic agreements and joint statements on labour-management relations*, op. cit.

[2] Although it is logical for the bargaining sequence to move from economy-wide to industry-wide bargaining, and from there perhaps to lower levels, this has not always been the case: "Thus in certain years bargaining at the central level has preceded the industry-wide and plant-wide negotiations. In other years, industry-wide bargaining has preceded the SAF-LO negotiations. And in several rounds, claims have been put forward at all three levels simultaneously. Choice of timing and level of negotiation have tended to become important tactics in the bargaining process, inevitably resulting in a strong element of unpredictability in the sequence of negotiations at different levels in any one round" (Steven D. Anderman: "Central wage negotiation in Sweden: Recent problems and developments", in *British Journal of Industrial Relations,* Nov. 1967, p. 323).

[3] Gösta Edgren: "Trends of bargaining for remuneration", in OECD, Manpower and Social Affairs Directorate: *New perspectives in collective bargaining,* Papers prepared for a regional trade union seminar, Paris, 4-7 November 1969, p. 58.

[4] See Carlson, op. cit., p. 12 (figures for the late 1960s).

significance of this bargaining, for which no exact figures are available, can be gauged from an estimate which holds that about half of any wage increase is the result of "wage drift", of which a large proportion, in turn, is traceable to supplementary bargaining at the level of the company and the plant.[1] (As in other countries, there are in Sweden individual enterprises not belonging to an employers' association that conclude their own local agreements; such agreements should be kept distinguished from other company agreements, which in most cases supplement an industry agreement.)

Alongside the bargaining structure for manual workers there are separate and to some extent parallel structures for white-collar workers in the private and public sectors. In the private sector the national agreement for white-collar workers—like its counterpart for manual workers—is expected to lay down general principles governing changes in remuneration and basic working conditions. The specific distribution and allocation of the new benefits are then decided either at industry or at local level. In the public sector the procedure is similar but if anything even more centralised.

In maintaining their predominant position in the bargaining structure, the aim of the confederations of trade unions and of employers' associations continues to be above all to minimise the role of the Government in the determination of procedural and substantive bargaining issues. The will to keep basic decision making in the hands of the parties themselves accounts in large measure for the readiness of individual unions and industrial employers' associations to delegate a great deal of bargaining authority to their own confederations.

United States

The bargaining structure in the United States is marked by a high degree of decentralisation accompanied by noticeable tendencies toward a moderate amount of consolidation and concentration.[2] There are no industry-wide agreements establishing a framework for supplementary plant-level agreements, nor is there any general economy-wide bargaining between representatives of confederations of employers and trade unions. Nevertheless, a certain amount of industry-wide bargaining does occur nationally and regionally in a limited number of industries. Agreements negotiated at the enterprise level are also frequently supplemented by additional plant-level agreements that regulate matters more suitable for local decision. A development of fairly recent origin is coalition bargaining, through which

---

[1] Edgren, op. cit., p. 13.

[2] For a concise discussion of the United States bargaining structure see Cullen, below, pp. 383-406.

unions have tried for their own protection to centralise the dispersed and unconnected bargaining that goes on inside a few large companies.

A relatively recent authoritative estimate put the total number of collective agreements in the United States at about 155,000. These cover some 21.2 million workers.[1] Such aggregate figures conceal many different kinds of bargaining arrangements for which statistical break-downs are not available. However, a recent breakdown does exist for 252 agreements, each of which covered at least 5,000 workers.[2] The total number of workers covered by the 252 agreements was 4.1 million; it is apparent, therefore, that a very small fraction of all agreements in the United States (0.16 per cent) covered about 20 per cent of all workers employed under negotiated terms. This in itself indicates a rather high degree of concentration. Almost half of the 252 agreements (123) were concluded with a single employer and accounted for 2,275,000 workers, while the 129 other agreements were negotiated on a multi-employer basis (through employers' associations or otherwise) and accounted for 1,828,000 workers. Thus in respect of agreements covering large numbers of workers, 55 per cent of workers were in single-employer units and 45 per cent in multi-employer units.[3]

An interesting reversal of proportions between single-employer and multi-employer agreements emerged from a comparison of the figures for the manufacturing and non-manufacturing sectors. The study included 126 agreements in each of the two sectors, with manufacturing accounting for 2,362,000 workers and non-manufacturing for 1,741,000. In the manufacturing sector 87 of the 126 agreements (covering 1,781,000 workers) applied to single-employer bargaining units, while 39 agreements (covering 581,000 workers) applied to multi-employer units. In non-manufacturing, by contrast, only 36 agreements (with 494,000 workers) applied to single-employer units, while 90 agreements (with 1,274,000 workers) applied to multi-employer units. In other words, as far as large bargaining units (5,000 workers or more) were concerned, single-employer bargaining was considerably more prevalent in manufacturing industries, whereas multi-employer bargaining was very much predominant in the non-manufacturing sectors.

---

[1] United States Bureau of Labor Statistics: *Directory of national and international labor unions in the United States, 1969* (Washington, 1970), p. 79.

[2] Idem: *Characteristics of agreements covering 5,000 workers or more,* Bulletin 1686 (Washington, 1970); see especially table 7 on p. 8.

[3] See also Bok and Dunlop, op. cit., p. 208. The 45 per cent figure given above for workers in multi-employer units is somewhat higher than the 40 per cent figure given by Bok and Dunlop, but the difference is probably the result of the fact that the higher estimate was based on a study of agreements covering at least 5,000 workers while the lower estimate refers to the proportion of all agreements, irrespective of the number of workers covered.

Multi-employer bargaining in the United States is also associated with certain other characteristics. It tends to exist in substantial measure in industries where the nature of the work leads workers to change jobs frequently, the number of individual establishments is relatively large, the average number of workers per establishment is relatively small, there is significant geographical concentration (as there would be, for example, in a metropolitan area), competition among establishments in product and labour markets is vigorous, and the rate of unionisation is above average. In those circumstances, which apply in most respects to such manufacturing industries as clothing, printing, furniture and food processing and to such non-manufacturing sectors as mining, wholesale and retail trade, hotels and restaurants, construction and road haulage, the prevalence of multi-employer bargaining is likely to be considerable, even in as decentralised a bargaining structure as that of the United States.[1]

Although a decisive and irreversible trend would be difficult to demonstrate, there are indications that the bargaining structure in the United States is becoming somewhat less decentralised. One of these indications is the emergence in recent years of coalition bargaining.[2] Such bargaining represents an effort by unions to solve the problems of bargaining with multi-plant corporations in which the workers of each plant are represented by different local unions which in turn may belong to different national unions. In coalition bargaining the various unions try to agree on common bargaining objectives and a unified corporation-centred bargaining strategy, very much in the same way as British unions have formed bargaining federations and confederations for industry-wide bargaining. The purpose is to neutralise the corporation's advantage drawn from individual plant bargaining with a divided or at least not co-ordinated group of unions. In this sense, therefore, coalition bargaining represents a union effort to overcome internal weaknesses and to match the employers' bargaining power by extending the workers' community of interests from the plant to the company.

The Industrial Union Department of the AFL-CIO has been particularly active in helping unions to cope with new problems arising out of bargaining with widely diversified corporations. For this purpose it has opened files on individual companies which—

provide detailed records of finances, product lines, plant locations, key officers of the companies and their interlocking relationships with other companies, records of

---

[1] See David H. Greenberg: "The structure of collective bargaining and some of its determinants", in *Proceedings of the Industrial Relations Research Association*, 1966, pp. 343-353, and Robert M. Macdonald: "Collective bargaining in the postwar period", in *Industrial and Labor Relations Review*, Vol. 20, No. 4, July 1967, pp. 553-577.

[2] William N. Chernish: *Coalition bargaining: A study of union tactics and public policy* (Philadelphia, University of Pennsylvania Press, 1969).

divisions of the company which are profitable and those which are not, a history of mergers and acquisitions, and so on. There are files that provide, for each of the company's agreements, records with respect to the agreement expiration date, vacation provisions, and plantwide wage information—in short, all of the relevant information which negotiators would need in their efforts at co-ordinated negotiation. The patterning of these company economic profiles permits union negotiators not only to use the information they have more effectively but to spot gaps in that information and to remedy the gaps by doing additional research.[1]

Other developments tending toward more concentration in the bargaining structure include continued expansion of business organisations, especially through company mergers and the formation of conglomerate companies as well as through normal growth; the introduction of new subjects of bargaining, such as negotiated employee benefit programmes, which cannot be dealt with economically at plant level; and progressive consolidation of decision making in unions and companies, with reciprocal effects on both sides.

If on the other hand the trend becomes too pronounced and changes are too rapid, there may be a reaction, which should not be too surprising in a system that has traditionally been highly decentralised. For example, while economic considerations may dictate the negotiation of benefit plans at levels above that of the individual plant so as to reap the advantages of size and the spreading of risks, the resulting standardisation of benefits may create difficult problems of administration and worker acceptance at the local level. In a number of cases members have been dissatisfied with so-called "over-centralisation" of bargaining, and at least one observer of the United States bargaining structure believes that unions and employers will seek to avoid the dilemma of too much or too little centralisation by evolving "more complex negotiation procedures" rather than by "major balance-of-power shifts from centralised to decentralised systems or the reverse".[2]

A comparative assessment

It is not claimed that the foregoing review of trends in bargaining arrangements in individual countries is comprehensive, but the information it provides is enough, in conjunction with information on countries not separately examined here, to allow a number of general observations to be made. The first is that the basic features of the national bargaining structure, once firmly in place, tend to persist over a long time; changes do occur, but they are usually gradual and additive rather than sudden and revolutionary.

---

[1] Siegel, op. cit., p. 11.

[2] E. Robert Livernash: "Special and local negotiations", in Dunlop and Chamberlain, op. cit., p. 49.

Collective bargaining

There is ample evidence on this point. Industry-wide bargaining, whether at the national or the regional level, has maintained its predominant position in most European countries and in Australia since its introduction some 50 years ago or even earlier, while enterprise bargaining or plant-level bargaining has retained its predominance in North America and in Japan. Genuine challenges to the pre-eminence of a particular kind of bargaining, and thus to the basic configuration of the structure itself, have been few, and really successful challenges even fewer. The centralised bargaining structures of the Scandinavian countries and Austria, marked by the prominent role of the confederations of trade unions and employers' associations, can hardly be considered as exceptions since they are of relatively long standing (in Norway almost since the very beginning of the industrial relations system) and thus represent no major change. In any event, industry-wide bargaining still constitutes a vital element in the systems of all these countries. In the Netherlands the highly centralised bargaining structure of the period immediately after the Second World War was destroyed in the mid-1960s by powerful centrifugal forces, and industry-wide bargaining once again became the norm. In none of the other European countries has the basic bargaining structure been drastically altered from above or from below, though in Italy, France and Great Britain exceedingly strong pressures from the base have led to some significant decentralising modifications. Finally, there has been just as much stability in the systems under which collective bargaining takes place primarily in the enterprise and the plant (Canada, the United States and Japan). The adjustment of such systems to new conditions (corporate mergers, shifts in bargaining power, emergence of new bargaining issues) has been equally gradual and piecemeal.

Relative stability, then, is the outstanding characteristic of the bargaining structure. An aspect of virtually equal importance is the ease with which it can be adjusted to changes made necessary by shifts in markets and technology, government policies, industrial organisation, the composition of the labour force and other factors. Some of these factors have already been examined in earlier sections of this chapter, but certain tendencies deserve renewed mention, especially those that are likely to be of continuing importance. In most countries the dominant trends at present are towards decentralisation, especially in the countries of Western Europe where industry-wide bargaining has been the general rule. With few exceptions, the trend is toward more local decision making, more plant-level bargaining, more company agreements, and generally more participation in collective bargaining by unions and by the management of individual enterprises. Some of the reasons for this development are quite evident, others are more difficult to identify.

126

The effect of full employment or nearly full employment over a substantial number of years should not be underestimated. Under industry-wide bargaining it had traditionally been understood that nationally negotiated terms were minima which could be improved upon at enterprise level, depending on the state of the labour market, the individual firm's ability to pay and other relevant circumstances. In fact, the rationale of the system hinged on an agreement that the national or regional minimum would keep the marginal firms in existence and thus preserve needed jobs while the more efficient firms would offer superior terms of employment corresponding to their economic position. However, owing to union weaknesses and the absence of bargaining machinery at plant level the determination of effective wage rates and of other benefits exceeding the nationally or industry-wide negotiated minimum fell almost by default to the employers. This situation was modified by the effects of sustained full employment, which instilled confidence in workers and their representatives on the job (shop stewards, works council members, local union officials, etc.) that efforts on their part to transform previously one-sided management decisions into negotiated supplementary agreements could be undertaken with a reasonable expectation of co-operation on the part of management. Indeed, plant management for its part increasingly recognised the advantages of negotiated supplementary agreements during periods of acute labour shortages, where employers had to compete for labour, and often actually preferred to deal at plant level with workers' representatives who knew the problems of the enterprise from first-hand experience. Needless to add, this development is also related to the well known factor of wage drift.

In themselves, attempts to link wages and earnings to performance have usually had a decentralising effect. In Great Britain the development of productivity bargaining under government encouragement greatly enhanced the importance of the individual firm and plant as a de facto bargaining unit because of the stipulated linkage between cost savings and the workers' remuneration. A similar development occurred in the Netherlands in 1959-63, when permissible wage changes were also tied to productivity changes, though in this case the downward shift in the bargaining level was mostly from the economy as a whole to the individual industry rather than to the enterprise. Even in Sweden, where collective bargaining has remained basically centralised, the widespread reliance on incentive wages has conferred substantial importance on locally negotiated wage rates, and therefore on enterprise negotiations in themselves.

Economic factors are not the only ones to have had a decentralising effect. Rising levels of education among workers have contributed to a desire for participation in decision making which cannot be readily satisfied by industry-wide bargaining. Although the search for greater

127

workers' participation in decision making is not necessarily identical with demands for improved bargaining in the enterprise, there does seem to be a relationship between the notion of worker participation in decisions at the enterprise and an extension of bargaining to that level. Thus, writing of Italian experience, Professor Giugni points out that—

At shop level the pattern of claims has undergone a remarkable change. Hitherto, industrial organisation has been the prerogative of management and the unions' task has been to bargain over the consequences of any changes in industrial conditions, especially as regards wages. Nowadays, however, they question the whole organisation of work within industry.[1]

Less certain and less obvious is the contribution which recent developments in industrial organisation and management have had on the decentralisation of the bargaining structure. The general trend in ownership has been toward the creation of larger business units, both through mergers and through natural growth of the most efficient ones. In itself, this would seem to have a centralising effect within the company. On the other hand, there has also been a deliberate effort, at least among the more advanced firms, to decentralise responsibility among a company's various establishments, including the delegation of authority to plant managers for local bargaining with unions, works councils or similar bodies. At the same time, the development of more decentralised dealings with unions, works councils or analogous bodies has led to an increasing demand for management specialists in industrial relations, since employers' associations are often not equipped to provide adequate services as far down the line as the individual plant or shop. Whether the net effect of these changes is towards more centralisation or more decentralisation is not yet clear.

Will the spread of multinational enterprises have significant effects on the bargaining structure? A distinction needs to be drawn first between the current effect of the multinational enterprise on established national bargaining structures and the possible emergence in the future of supranational or transnational collective bargaining involving multinational firms and appropriate international organisations of trade unions. As to the latter, one cannot go much beyond speculation, for there have hardly been any significant experiences with supranational collective bargaining. It is possible, however, to envisage the development of an additional level of bargaining, either world-wide or regional, which could serve as a forum for the negotiated solution of problems common to all or most employees of a given multinational enterprise. (An example of a problem of common concern would be the introduction of new methods of production and its effects on plant location, employment, and job security.) Complex problems of "articulation" could then arise, especially if the branch of a

---

[1] See Giugni, below, p. 290.

multinational enterprise belongs to an employers' association that negotiates an industry-wide agreement binding on its members. If there are conflicting provisions, the branch establishment would have to find a way of reconciling the two sets of agreements. Needless to say, this situation is less likely to be an obstacle to supranational bargaining in countries where enterprise bargaining is the rule.

In any event, these are all problems for the future. Up to the present the effects of multinational enterprises on bargaining structures have been either negligible or decentralising. They have been negligible where the multinational enterprises have made no attempt to operate their branches outside the framework of established collective bargaining systems but instead have sought to fit themselves into existing practices and procedures. On the other hand, they have had a decentralising effect where the policies followed by multinational enterprises with respect to collective bargaining have been independent of those of the employers' associations in the industry in the host countries of their subsidiaries: in a substantial number of firms, especially those with headquarters in the United States, the European subsidiaries have followed their own course, including the conclusion of their own collective agreements with trade unions, instead of sub-scribing to the obligations inherent in membership in an employers' association. To this extent, multinational enterprises have in certain countries contributed to the general movement towards a more decentralised bargaining structure.

Not all of the current trends point in the direction of greater decentralisation. There are also countervailing forces, and their strength is particularly compelling in systems which have traditionally emphasised bargaining at the level of the enterprise. Probably this should be expected: after all, if there is any significant change in a decentralised system, it is more likely than not to be in the direction of greater concentration, just as the reverse would be expected in a centralised system. No convergence theory is being suggested here, merely the thought that the search for solutions to structural problems often turns into an exploration of alternative principles of organisation.

Most observers of current trends in the bargaining structure of North America perceive "a drift toward increased consolidation and centralisation".[1] They attribute it to several long-term developments. One of these is the continuing growth in enterprise size, through fusion, diversification and other changes, creating enhanced bargaining power which unions will sooner or later try to match by corresponding adjust-ments, including an extension of the bargaining structure. A second is the development, under union impetus, of coalition and co-ordinated

---

[1] Arnold R. Weber (ed.): *The structure of collective bargaining: Problems and perspectives* (Glencoe, Illinois, Free Press, 1961), p. xx. Cf. Macdonald, op. cit., p. 516 ff.

bargaining, which itself represents a particularised attempt to equalise uneven bargaining strengths. A third stems from the emergence of new substantive bargaining issues (such as adjustment measures in the event of workforce reductions in an enterprise or industry and various types of pension, unemployment and similar benefit schemes) that can be more easily dealt with through negotiations at enterprise or industry level than at the level of the individual plant. A fourth is the result of the efforts of unions and their leaders to maximise their bargaining effectiveness through concentration of power and to protect past gains from being undermined by concessions extracted from their weakest affiliates; more often than not, this strategy requires the placing of limits on the freedom of subordinate units to negotiate their own agreements. Employer responses to the consolidation and co-ordination of union bargaining strategy may include the reinforcement of central corporate authority over outlying plants or the initiation of multi-employer bargaining.

It should be emphasised that these centralising forces can evoke certain reactions, as noted in the following comments on developments in Canada and the United States:

One of the factors of growing rank and file restiveness may be the upward movement of the locus of decisions in large organisations. . . .Such remoteness may result from the role played by employer associations, from the employment of consultants, or from the internal workings of either unions or employers as, for example, in the case of foreign-based corporations and unions.[1]

As the structure of collective bargaining has evolved in the United States, the dominant problem is the need to reconcile pressures for market control and tactical striking power with the demand for the effective representation of special interest groups.[2]

Thus it should not be assumed that the present North American trend toward greater centralisation is either irresistible or irreversible. In fact, it is a very slow development, which shows no signs of leading at an early date to industry-wide bargaining along European lines: the focus of greater centralisation is the company rather than the industry, and so far there has been ample room for supplementary bargaining at plant level and even for ensuring the representation of special interests through various structural devices.

Japanese enterprise bargaining has not yet been as significantly affected by centralising forces, although their potential importance has been acknowledged by competent observers.[3] They call attention

---

[1] Canada, Task Force on Labour Relations, op. cit., p. 165.

[2] Arnold R. Weber: "Stability and change in the structure of collective bargaining", in Lloyd Ulman (ed.): *Challenges to collective bargaining* (Englewood Cliffs, New Jersey, Prentice-Hall, 1967), p. 32.

[3] See especially Taishiro Shirai: "The changing pattern of collective bargaining in Japan", in Japan Institute of Labour: *The changing pattern of industrial relations,* Proceedings of the international conference on industrial relations, Tokyo, . . . 1965, pp. 185-193.

especially to the unifying impact of the annual spring wage drive in which many unions participate; the existence of national bargaining in several industries, notably in the public sector, such as railways and communications; and the spread of unionisation to firms of small and medium size in which enterprise unions have neither the resources nor the experience to provide adequate representation for their constituents without assistance from national unions. On the other hand, forces of at least equal strength stand in the way of any major restructuring, not least among them the complex institution of lifetime employment and the practice of workers' training within the enterprise. Both greatly reinforce employee identification with the enterprise as the essential community of interest.

Of more general importance as a centralising influence has been the increased involvement of governments in labour-management relations, or the threat of increased involvement. In proportion to the growth of their responsibility for the management of the economy, some governments thought it necessary to assume a corresponding responsibility for the supervision of the industrial relations system. Their concern has been particularly acute in relation to questions that connect industrial relations with the functioning of the economy, particularly wages or incomes policies and major labour disputes capable of causing economic dislocation. Although some of the less stringent kinds of incomes policies have had little effect on the bargaining structure, the more strict varieties have had a distinctly centralising effect, partly because governments generally endeavour to obtain the co-operation of employers and trade unions for policy formulation and implementation, and the most effective way of obtaining such co-operation is to work through the confederations of employers' associations and trade unions and their affiliates.

In some cases, of which Sweden and Norway are notable examples, centralisation of the bargaining structure has been associated with the pursuit of negotiated industrial relations procedures rather than with government regulation. In fact, the high measure of authority delegated to the central bodies of Swedish employers' associations and trade unions by their constituents is designed for the purpose of keeping government involvement to an absolute minimum.

Where unions and employers lend their support to the maintenance of centralised bargaining structures, they do so for essentially similar reasons. Both are concerned about maintaining cohesion in their ranks and protecting their weaker associates from the sometimes fatal consequences of fractional bargaining. On the employer side this implies concern about the survival of marginal firms, while on the union side the concern is chiefly centred on the employment security of members in exposed sectors. In the case of Swedish unions the long-standing policy of wage solidarity, designed to reduce earnings differentials as much as possible, has contributed significantly to union support for centralised bargaining, in spite of opposition from younger workers and from those with specialised education and skills. Employers' associations and unions in certain countries also take the view that their ability to influence government policies on social and economic issues depends on the degree of centralised authority which they can muster.

From the preceding review of contemporary changes in the structure of collective bargaining it should be evident that the varied traditions and values peculiar to each country and its institutions have helped to determine the basic structure, while the emergence of new bargaining issues, new technologies, new economic problems and many other kinds of innovations and challenges compels a continual reassessment of the adequacy of that structure. The notion that certain subjects are best dealt with at certain levels in the structure has gained considerable acceptance in recent years. It presupposes that the industrial relations system is sufficiently flexible to allow substantive issues to be negotiated at the levels most suitable for effective results. As stated by Allan Flanders—

One of the clues to the future of collective bargaining is surely to be found in making a clear distinction among the appropriate levels of its regulative influence. In this as in many other aspects of economic organization, we have to decide what is the concern of society as a whole, what should be settled on an industrial scale, and what is the affair of the employees in a single enterprise or a smaller group within it.[1]

In the years ahead, it is conceivable that quite a number of industrial relations systems will acquire a multi-tiered structure.

---

[1] Flanders: *Management and unions,* op. cit., p. 116.

5. The Role of the State

In preceding chapters attention has been called in various places to the important role which public authorities play in the collective bargaining process. That role is more active in some countries than in others, and everywhere it tends to become even more so in times of stress or economic crisis. In one capacity or another the public authorities have been concerned with issues related to collective bargaining from the very beginning of its development.

In this chapter an effort will be made to examine the role of the State as a whole more systematically. A certain amount of duplication with the contents of previous chapters is unavoidable, but will be kept to a minimum. For example, a number of references were made in the last chapter to the influence of the State on the bargaining structure. Since this influence is one of several factors that contribute to an understanding of the over-all role of the State in collective bargaining, a concise repetition of what was said on the subject will be necessary in the proper section of the present chapter. It should also be noted that this chapter deals only with the direct role of the State, not with its indirect role. A plausible case could be made out for the proposition that fiscal and monetary policies, and especially employment policy, have just as much effect—if not more—on the functioning of collective bargaining as, for example, possible rules on negotiating in good faith; but an examination of the general environment in which collective bargaining proceeds would go well beyond the intentions of this study.

There are numerous indications that the proper place of the State in the collective bargaining process has been undergoing a searching re-examination in a number of countries. This re-examination is not always as explicit as in Canada and Great Britain, where national review bodies have probed deeply into the general operation of the entire industrial relations system; nor is it necessarily followed by the kind of extensive legislation which, as in Great Britain, is laying the groundwork for an entirely new and considerably expanded set of government functions; but even in countries where such fundamental changes, clearly intended to be lasting, are not being contemplated at present, a less visible reassessment is going on none the less, perhaps because the acceleration of technological and economic change in industrial societies is everywhere creating problems of labour-management relations that are not entirely amenable to solution within the framework of traditional collective bargaining. This is not to suggest that all the established relationships between the State and the collective bargaining partners are in process of making way for new ones: no doubt many long-assumed government responsibilities will survive because they have proved to be useful and indeed essential; but alongside conventional responsibilities that are bound to endure, from the current period of review and experimentation new ones may well emerge through which the public authorities can better exercise their recognised obligation of ensuring steady economic growth within a framework that still allows for meaningful collective bargaining.

A distinction needs to be made at the outset between the two roles of the State as a third party and as an employer respectively (the State is the employer for the civil service, the publicly owned essential services, and enterprises in the public sector). That both roles are of increasing importance is hardly open to question, but the emphasis in this chapter will properly be on the role of the State as a third party. The ILO has on previous occasions examined the role of the State as an employer of civil servants and the special problems of collective bargaining which arise in that respect. In as far as they differ substantially from those of enterprises in the private sector, some of the problems of public utilities and public sector enterprises have been dealt with in various preceding sections of this study.[1]

Evolution of public policy

References to the "conventional role" of the State in contemporary collective bargaining (distinguishing traditional from newly emerging responsibilities), really refer to the state of affairs resulting from previous innovations, for over the years the role of the State has changed constantly in response to changes in public attitudes both towards collective bargaining itself and towards the economic and social forces which the parties represent. No doubt this process will continue.

Historically speaking, as long as the organs of the State regarded their primary responsibility as being the protection of the freedom of the market, and as long as they considered trade unions to be an impediment to that freedom, the purpose of intervention by public authorities in the relations between employers and workers was, in general, the suppression or tight containment of labour organisations. Under such conditions collective bargaining had neither public sanction nor a legal foundation on which to develop. Where it was nevertheless possible for collective bargaining to establish itself, as in Great Britain already well

---

[1] See Chapter 2, p. 46 ff. above. For a recent and comprehensive review of issues involved in public sector bargaining see Johannes Schregle: "Industrial relations in the public sector: An international viewpoint", in Japan Institute of Labour: *The changing patterns of industrial relations in Asian countries,* Proceedings of the Asian regional conference on industrial relations, Tokyo . . ., 1969, pp. 61-89.

before the middle of the nineteenth century, it had to do so outside the law and usually as a suspiciously regarded alternative to the individual contract of employment which in most countries was the only socially approved and legally recognised agreement between employer and worker. During this early period the courts in a number of countries played a particularly prominent part as instruments of public control by enforcing the rules of statutory or common law against efforts by unions to organise and to obtain recognition from employers for bargaining purposes.

A decided change in attitude, in the direction of at least a limited tolerance of unions and therefore of collective bargaining, became relatively widespread in the last quarter of the nineteenth century, when many of the legal obstacles to trade union organisation were removed. As a result the number of collective agreements then increased substantially, even though in many countries severe restrictions on certain expressions of industrial conflict, such as strikes, remained in being.

Governments generally began to welcome collective bargaining only after the turn of the century, and in a number of countries only during or after the First World War. During that period a substantial body of legislation designed to promote collective bargaining as the most effective form of industrial self-government first found its way onto the statute book. Frequently included in such legislation were provisions defining the rights and mutual obligations of the parties to collective bargaining and the legal status of collective agreements, and in some countries rules concerning the procedure and substance of the negotiations. Other legislation, often also enacted during that period, dealt with the establishment of publicly provided disputes settlement machinery to help the parties to negotiate their agreements with a minimum of friction.

Of the period as a whole it might be said that in most countries the organs of the State—apart from providing for the enforceability of collective agreements under the law and through state action—conceived their role in collective bargaining to be a limited one, centred on the maintenance of industrial peace, the facilitation of the establishment of bargaining machinery, and the protection of workers in the exercise of their freedom of association. The principal responsibility for making collective bargaining work was expected to fall on the parties; apart from providing routine conciliation and other services, the public authorities were to refrain from intervening, except of course in the event of a major breakdown, when the protection of the public interest against serious economic damage became a paramount consideration. On the whole, however, it was to be the responsibility of the parties to reach agreement on their own.

In the United States and Australia rather different conceptions were gaining acceptance; this is not the place to describe them in detail but merely to indicate the essential difference. Public policy in the United States, as expressed in the National Labor Relations Act of 1935, assigned to the public authorities the duty of actively promoting collective bargaining as a socially desirable form of industrial decision making and as a means of reducing industrial conflict. A special administrative structure was created for the purpose of applying the detailed provisions of the law to the continuing relations between trade unions and employers, and in a few years the collective bargaining system in the United States became surrounded by a far more complex network of statutory rules than existed in any other industrialised country. This point will be referred to again. In the case of Australia as early as 1904 a government-operated arbitration system became a major instrument for setting the terms and conditions of employment in cases in which conventional collective bargaining had failed to produce agreement. By contrast with the United States, the Australian approach emphasised the State's role in the adjudication of substantive issues, but it should be stressed that the arbitration system was not intended to become, and in fact did not become, a complete substitute for private collective bargaining.

Given the upsurge of collective bargaining in the period between the two world wars, it was only natural that the ILO should itself embark on a study of the subject. It published its first major review of collective agreements in 1936. After a detailed examination of then current trends, the report included in its concluding section a perceptive comment foreshadowing the direction which future developments were to take:

> If, as seems likely, collective agreements are destined to play an increasingly important part in the future, and if industrial self-government is still to be more firmly established, it is clear that the State will allow the collective agreement to play an increasingly large part in the regulation of conditions of work. Such a development could not fail to have important consequences for the establishment and enforcement of international labour legislation.[1]

Although it could hardly have been foreseen in 1936, a series of international instruments contributed to the continued development of collective bargaining after the Second World War, and did so generally along lines established already before that war broke out. The main instruments were the Freedom of Association and Protection of the Right to Organise Convention, 1948 (No. 87), and the Right to Organise and Collective Bargaining Convention, 1949 (No. 98). In addition, the International Labour Conference adopted a substantial number of Recommendations and numerous resolutions on the subject. To these must be added the resolutions, conclusions and other texts emanating from ILO regional conferences, meetings of Industrial Com-

---

[1] ILO: *Collective agreements,* op. cit., p. 268.

mittees and other meetings.[1] They are mentioned here not so much for their substance as for the general influence which they had on the attitudes of governments toward collective bargaining in the post-war period. For the protective, regulatory and mediating roles of the State underwent further expansion in most countries after the war within a general context of attitudes highly favourable to collective bargaining.

At the same time, however, it came to be thought that the State could not fully discharge its responsibilities to the public interest if it limited its presence in the field of collective bargaining to the roles of impartial outsider, keeper of the peace and purveyor of auxiliary services. According to this line of thought, the proper subjects for state attention also included matters which in most countries had not been regarded as such except in times of national crisis. The espousers of the new ideas, stimulated by a greatly expanded role of state organs in the management of increasingly interdependent economic systems, by the steady pressure of inflationary forces and by the emergence of powerful bargaining units in key economic sectors, maintained that a public concern merely for the smooth functioning of bargaining machinery no longer corresponded to the needs of the times. In future, it was held, the substance of collective bargaining, or at least the part of it relating to wages and more broadly to labour costs, would require at least as much attention from the State as the procedural problems.

Negotiating procedures

As already indicated, the degree to which the State has been prepared to exercise its sovereign powers to define the ground rules for collective bargaining varies significantly between different countries, even within the limited sample covered in this study. In addition, the passage of time can give rise to fundamentally different approaches: thus it would hardly have been considered likely, as recently as a decade ago, that a Government of the United Kingdom would ever make a major departure from its policy of minimal involvement in the procedural aspects of collective negotiations; and the Industrial Relations Act, 1971, marked a distinct break with the traditional stance of public policy in that country. This development suggests that one should be cautious about making far-reaching generalisations on the basis merely of established practice. However, one generalisation does seem widely applicable: this is that whenever changes occur in the degree of state intervention in collective bargaining, or at least in the procedural aspects of bargaining, they more often than not take the direction of more regulation. Ground once occupied by the State is not easily given

---

[1] For the texts of these various documents, up to 1969, see ILO: *International standards and guiding principles, 1944-1968*, op. cit.

up, unless it is understood from the outset that a specific situation, deemed to be temporary, creates a need for temporary arrangements. Times of war, national mobilisation, severe economic dislocation or the threat of it constitute exceptions to the rule; they are considered here only to the extent that the arrangements made at such times hold out the possibility of becoming permanent features of the industrial relations system or of affecting that system in a major and continuing way. In any event, the passing phase of wartime bargaining controls will not be considered.

An additional point that should be noted is that, precisely in order to avoid state intervention in collective bargaining, the national organisations of employers and workers in a number of countries, such as Sweden, Switzerland, the Federal Republic of Germany and more recently the United Kingdom, have agreed on procedural arrangements in the conduct of their labour relations, particularly as regards procedures relating to the settlement of disputes.

With due allowance for the proposition that each country is ultimately unique and can be understood only in terms of its own history, a reasonably persuasive case can be established to show that there are basically two types of government approaches toward the procedural questions in collective bargaining. The first one favours self-restraint and confines itself to a few basic rules, leaving it mainly to the parties to fashion whatever rules are needed, whereas the second relies on detailed regulation. By and large, the first approach is characteristic of the continental countries of Western Europe, though they are often considered to be relatively favourable to legislation regarding conditions of work and the solution of labour problems, while the second one has been espoused by the North American countries, where private decision making is believed to have more free play than almost anywhere else. It should also be noted again that in Great Britain, as mentioned above, there has recently been a switch from non-interference to detailed procedural regulation by statute. No longer will it be possible to write of Great Britain that "in a country in which collective bargaining is so highly developed and of such comparatively ancient origin, the bulk of collective bargaining and collective agreements continues to exist outside the law and without any development of a 'collective labour law' of any major proportions".[1]

There are, of course, explanations and qualifications to be attached to the foregoing description of the European situation. It should be recognised that there can be public regulation without legislation. Nor should one overlook the fact that a limited amount of legislation on procedural questions has indeed been adopted in some European coun-

---

[1] Kahn-Freund: "Report on the legal status of collective bargaining and collective agreements in Great Britain", in his *Labour relations and the law,* op. cit., p. 23.

tries, as indicated for example by the French statutory notion of the "most representative" organisations, under which such organisations are granted certain privileges in collective bargaining, including the right to conclude collective agreements eligible for "extension" by the Minister of Labour to an entire industry or industry branch. However, the fact remains that the largest amount of procedural rule making in industrial relations occurs in North America.

Although the exact provisions of the rules need not concern us at this stage since many of them have already been brought out in an earlier chapter [1], the reasons for the basic difference of approach between Western Europe on the one hand and Canada and the United States on the other are of more than passing interest, for they could help to indicate future trends. It may be useful briefly to recall that the questions under consideration here relate to the determination of bargaining agents, the delimitation of appropriate bargaining units, the handling of union recognition issues and the closely related questions of the duty to bargain, the obligation of employers to furnish information essential to effective negotiations, and other non-substantive but sometimes highly controversial matters. All of them relate essentially to problems which tend to arise either in the pre-negotiation phase or in the course of negotiations themselves. No special significance should be attributed to the order in which those points are discussed below.

The first point might well be that systems of collective bargaining which like the European ones aim chiefly at industry-wide negotiation of minimum wages and other minimum terms of employment are less likely to produce serious procedural disputes than systems of enterprise bargaining from which quite specific and detailed conditions of employment are expected to emerge. The confrontation of an employers' association and a union (or set of unions) for the purpose of seeking agreement on a limited number of general issues would appear to management to present less of a possible encroachment on what it considers to be its established prerogatives that the detailed item-by-item bargaining characteristic of industrial relations in the United States and Canada, especially since in the latter countries it is intended to determine actual wages and other aspects of the employment relationship and not merely minimum conditions as under most European collective bargaining systems.

In this light it is easier to understand why, by and large, employers in North America offered stronger resistance to unions than European employers did, why this resistance extended to every step of the collective bargaining process and why the ensuing conflict brought forth a more interventionist attitude on the part of the State. It would not be too far fetched to expect that a significant decentralisation of collective

---

[1] Chapter 3.

bargaining in Western European countries might well bring with it a significantly greater amount of procedural regulation through state action so as to ensure as far as possible a peaceful settlement of such contentious procedural questions as recognition, the right of the workers' representatives to information, and similar matters.

The British Industrial Relations Act of 1971 provides a good illustration of such a trend, for it establishes for the first time in the United Kingdom a network of statutory rules regarding the duty to bargain, the employers' obligation to furnish certain information, and other procedural questions. It should be kept in mind that to a significant degree the Act was a response to the findings of the Donovan Commission, which had urged the integration of informal plant-level bargaining with the formal industry-level bargaining system. Of direct relevance, too, is the French legislation of December 1968 which, though not immediately or explicitly concerned with plant-level collective bargaining, could provide the groundwork for the development of such bargaining in as much as it specifies among other things that "every representative trade union which has established a trade union section in the undertaking shall designate . . . one or more trade union delegates to represent it in dealings with the head of the undertaking".[1] The Italian legislation of May 1970, known as "the Workers' Charter", should also be mentioned in this connection, for like its French counterpart it establishes detailed rules for the establishment and protection of trade union organisations at plant and enterprise level.[2]

Attention should also be drawn to the relatively detailed regulation of the procedural relations between management and works councils which is found in the legislation of such countries as the Federal Republic of Germany and the Netherlands. Not only do the laws on relations within the plant in those countries exhibit striking contrasts with the legislation on collective bargaining as regards the specificity of prescribed conduct for the parties, but in some respects they even resemble the statutory and administrative rules of collective bargaining which prevail in the North American countries. The employer's duty to furnish certain kinds of information to the workers' representatives exemplifies the similarity.

The general proposition that emerges from the preceding comparison is that the degree of state regulation of the procedural aspects of collective bargaining tends to increase as the prevailing level of negotiations moves closer to the workplace.

To a certain extent, differences in union organisation may also contribute to the differences in the legislation and the exercise of administrative controls in procedural matters: in systems under which

---

[1] ILO: *Legislative Series*, 1968—Fr. 1, section 8.
[2] Ibid., 1970—It. 2.

the main emphasis is on industrial unionism the potential for conflict between unions has been rather less than in systems under which, as in North America, competition between unions has been increased by the uneasy coexistence of industrial, craft, and mixed or general unionism. In this regard Great Britain is only a partial exception, for while it is true that certain features of British unionism (such as plant level representation and the coexistence of craft and general unions) have been closer to the North American than to the continental European pattern, the readiness of British unions to enter into schemes of joint representation in collective bargaining (a form of representation officially recognised by the Industrial Relations Act) has obviated the need to take administrative decisions on the selection of exclusive bargaining agents.

To the extent that unions are able to determine among themselves which one of them may legitimately represent the workers in a given industry or occupation, and to the extent that they can do so without causing jurisdictional strife, there is no pressure on the public authorities to settle such questions by legislation and administrative action; but by the time unions in North America had evolved internal procedures to settle their competitive claims among themselves, the authorities were already firmly established as the arbiters of such issues. To be sure, many conflicts are now kept within the unions, but the principle of state intervention has remained in being and can be invoked whenever a solution is not found through the union machinery. This not only explains the role of the public authorities in the settlement of inter-union disputes in North America but also throws some light on the function of the authorities in deciding which union shall be recognised as representing the workers in a given situation. As Professor Kahn-Freund has pointed out, the need for the "statutory bargaining representative" in the United States, and to large degree in Canada as well—

must be understood against the background of a society in which union practice is hardly influenced by the idea of working class solidarity and in which the intense competition between unions extends into the field of collective bargaining in a way unknown even in those countries (such as Belgium, France, Italy and the Netherlands) whose unions are divided by political and religious differences. In America the law had to create a union monopoly of representation in each bargaining unit.[1]

Since the trend of European unionism is generally towards consolidation rather than dispersion and competition (a trend which, incidentally, is now also present in North America), the structure of unions cannot account for state regulation of bargaining procedures on that continent. Admittedly, the historical division of European trade unions along ideological lines persists in a number of countries. Largely as a consequence of industry-wide bargaining, however, the effects of

---

[1] Kahn-Freund, op. cit., p. 8.

this division on the bargaining process have not been such as to lead to demands for rules and controls imposed by the State. If anything, current developments point more toward the possible unification of competing wings of the labour movement than toward greater internal strife. Inter-union differences do come to the surface rather sharply over the bargaining representation of white-collar employees in industry whenever there are separate unions of such employees that contend with industrial unions over representational rights, but normally such disputes are resolved through mutual accommodation. In this respect, the German experience is fairly representative: since the German Union of Salaried Employees, an independent organisation, covers all salaried employees in every branch of private enterprise and the public service, it is entitled to sit at the bargaining table alongside the other unions concerned, and in particular those affiliated to the German Confederation of Trade Unions. It is common, particularly in the public service, for both of these central organisations to be signatories to a collective agreement, although separate agreements also exist.[1]

To repeat, then, it is unlikely that the structural aspects of European unionism will by themselves lead to any significant increase in the role of the State in industrial rule making. However, it would not be prudent to claim universal validity for a correlation between decentralised bargaining and a considerable degree of regulation of bargaining exercised by the State. The experience of Japan indicates the possibility of combining a preponderance of bargaining at enterprise level with only a moderate degree of state involvement. In the past few decades, the emphasis of Japanese government policy has been on the development of voluntary collective bargaining in which the role of the State is by and large limited to the prevention of unfair labour practices and the adjustment of labour disputes.[2] There has been little effort by the public authorities to lay down rules for negotiations with any degree of specificity, and except in the presence of conflict or the threat of conflict affecting the public welfare it has been left largely to the parties themselves to settle contentious procedural issues.

Substantive issues

To what extent does the State seek to determine the subject matter of collective bargaining? The question is not intended to introduce a

---

[1] See Reichel, below, p. 256.

[2] See Mitsufuji and Hagisawa, below, p. 309; also Teruo Minemura: "The role of the Government in industrial relations: An outline", in Japan Institute of Labour: *The changing patterns of industrial conflict* (Tokyo, 1965), pp. 261-268.

comparative examination of substantive provisions in collective agreements. The aim is rather to show that the relationship of government to collective bargaining is not confined to the latter's procedural side, but that in certain circumstances it also reaches deep into the substance of the bargaining itself.

Through a process of give and take collective bargaining, apart from settling questions of relations between the bargaining parties themselves, enables its participants to attempt to settle for a given but sometimes unspecified time the conditions of employment which in their common judgement are appropriate subjects for joint regulation. To be sure, collective bargaining does not preclude the simultaneous determination of conditions of employment by other means: in many countries where collective bargaining is practised, social and labour legislation plays a very important role in defining workers' benefits and rights, as when statutory provisions are considered to establish a universal minimum on which improvements can be made through collective bargaining. It might be added here parenthetically that certain kinds of labour standards, particularly those of a protective nature (e.g. measures relating to occupational health and safety, the protection of women and young workers, and maternity protection), are considered to be primarily a subject for legislation, rather than for collective bargaining, though they can constitute a vital aspect of the terms and conditions of employment; and just as legislation may sometimes serve as a minimum base for later improvements through collective bargaining, so collective agreements, particularly those concluded at the national or industry-wide level, serve in a number of countries as a definition of minimum terms which may be improved upon through individual arrangements.

The reasons for general acceptance of the principle that the bargaining parties should themselves determine the subjects suitable for collective bargaining are not hard to determine. From a legal point of view the parties have freedom of contract, provided only that they do not violate the mandatory provisions of applicable legislation. From the point of view of practical labour relations, the parties are acknowledged to be in a better position than outsiders to assess their respective needs and capabilities and to let that assessment be reflected in the subjects on which they negotiate. Should a conflict arise over the attempted introduction of a new item into the bargaining, most governments would treat it in the same way as they would treat any other conflict between the parties. Depending on the circumstances, they may attempt to intervene by means of existing conciliation machinery, they may suggest voluntary arbitration, they may permit the parties to decide the issue through a test of economic strength, or they may proceed in some other fashion; but most of them will not take the decision directly out of the hands of the parties, and will not settle the dispute by

143

requiring the contested item to become a subject for bargaining or, conversely, by requiring its exclusion from the negotiations.

The practice in the Netherlands illustrates this general approach:

...the principle of freedom of contract prevails, and the parties are at liberty to give to the agreement such content as they choose. This principle has a dual significance: on the one hand the parties are not compelled to regulate any prescribed topics by their agreement, and on the other hand they are not prevented from regulating anything they like, i.e. any conditions of employment they consider as appropriate for collective regulation, and also any other matter which they regard as suitable.[1]

There are, however, some important exceptions to the general non-intervention of the authorities. Although categorisation is difficult, it seems that the exceptions can be divided into two groups: the first generally reflects the principle that the authorities should allow the parties to define their own issues, but it recognises that departures from that principle may have to be made in certain cases on grounds of an over-riding public interest. The second one goes so far toward the assumption of a more general third-party role by the authorities that it should probably be considered as representing an acceptance of state participation in defining the subject matter of collective bargaining. High on the list of examples of the first group are statutory rules which in some countries prohibit collective bargaining concerning compulsory union membership. Closely associated with this rule is another which prohibits the parties from agreeing to benefit provisions that are limited to union members only. For example, the Constitution of the Federal Republic of Germany, which contains a provision on freedom of association, has been interpreted as not only preventing the parties from agreeing to provisions requiring union membership but also severely limiting their freedom to reserve negotiated benefits for union members.

Along similar lines, legislation in the United States, and more recently in Great Britain, prohibits closed-shop clauses, which means that employers and trade unions may not agree to make prior union membership a condition of employment at the time of hiring. Moreover, federal law in the United States leaves individual states free to impose still greater restrictions on the freedom of the parties to reach agreement on the subject matter of bargaining by prohibiting the union shop, which makes union membership a condition of continued employment.[2] Another example along this general line is the 1927 Act

---

[1] M. G. Levenbach: "The law relating to collective agreements in the Netherlands", in Kahn-Freund, op. cit., p. 106.

[2] Only a minority of states have taken advantage of this possibility. On the other hand it should be made clear that when a union in the United States becomes the recognised bargaining agent for a given group of employees, it must in its bargaining activities represent all of the employees fairly, whether they are organised or not, and it may not discriminate between members and non-members.

on collective agreements in the Netherlands, which declares void any negotiated provision that imposes on an employer an obligation "to engage or not to engage workers of a specific religious persuasion or political opinion or members of a specific trade union".[1] This provision does not *per se* prohibit a union membership requirement; it only precludes the linkage of such a requirement to a particular union—a measure that should be seen in the light of the religious and ideological segmentation of the trade union movement in the Netherlands.

While the practices cited up to this point represent special exceptions to the general proposition that governments prefer to let the parties themselves decide on what subjects they shall bargain, reference must now be made to the existence of a more sweeping kind of public intervention in a small number of countries where the State has chosen to play a significant role in determing the content of agreements. This intervention may take the form of a legislative enactment or administrative action. The legislative approach is exemplified by the French collective bargaining law of 1950.[2] Under that Act, a national agreement, or more accurately one which the parties intend to be eligible for extension to an entire industry or branch, must include an enumerated series of provisions relating to minimum wages, differentials for dangerous or unhealthy work, equal pay for women and young workers, paid holidays, apprenticeship and vocational training rules, and a number of other required items. The law does not specify what the provisions should be; it merely imposes on the parties an obligation to incorporate suitable provisions in their collective agreement. In support of this statutory requirement it has been argued that "agreements of this kind [i.e. extendable agreements] will govern working lives over a vast area of industry".[3]

The United States represents a second instance of substantial involvement by the public authorities in the determination of the subject matter for collective bargaining, although the approach chosen is more administrative than legislative. The relevant law itself, namely the National Labor Relations Act as amended in 1947, imposes on the parties an obligation "to meet at reasonable times and confer in good

---

[1] Levenbach, op. cit., p. 107.

[2] ILO: *Legislative Series,* 1950—Fr. 6 A.

[3] André Brun: "Collective agreements in France", in Kahn-Freund, op. cit., p. 80. Attention should also be called to a rather different form of government intervention in the substance of collective bargaining in France, namely the prohibition of cost-of-living escalator clauses. For reasons dating back to efforts to establish a stable currency in 1958-59, provisions in an agreement whereby a worker's wages, or the wages of a category of workers, are automatically adjusted to changes in the minimum wage or in a general wage or price index are prohibited by ordinances of 30 December 1958 and 4 February 1959 governing sliding scale provisions and by an Act of 2 January 1970; see Jean Rivero and Jean Savatier: *Droit du travail* (Paris, Presses Universitaires de France, 1970), p. 441, and Pélissier, op. cit., p. 733. It should be added, however, that the legal prohibition is not uniformly observed in practice and that in fact some forms of negotiation about cost-of-living adjustment of wages are not uncommon.

faith with respect to wages, hours, and other terms and conditions of employment or the negotiation of an agreement, or any question arising thereunder".[1] As long as the parties agree on what subjects they are to bargain, the question of intervention by the public authorities does not arise; it is only when either side seeks to introduce a question which the other side does not consider a proper or a necessary subject for bargaining that a cause for action by the public authorities could develop. The initiating side, usually the trade union, may file an unfair labour practice charge with the agency administering the law, the National Labor Relations Board, alleging that the other side has failed to bargain in good faith by refusing to discuss a particular question or set of questions. If the complaint is upheld, the Board will order the question in dispute to be treated as a bargainable issue. An order to bargain is not equivalent to an order to agree, but the order to bargain does compel the parties to negotiate in good faith on the new issue, even if ultimately they cannot reconcile their respective positions.

Through this procedure, the subject matter of collective bargaining in the United States has expanded to encompass questions, or aspects of questions, which employers previously considered to be within their sole discretion, including profit sharing, merit-rating systems, bonuses, subcontracting, safety rules, and plant relocation. While on one hand the freedom of the parties to define the scope of their own bargaining unhindered by outside intervention has thus been circumscribed, the prevailing administrative procedure has also ensured the peaceful settlement of a substantial number of questions which otherwise might have been settled only through a test of economic strength. It could also be argued with reasonable plausibility that the need for administrative intervention is greater in a system such as that of the United States, where traditionally a large number of questions have entered into the bargaining relationship at enterprise level, than in systems where the range of issues is more limited because of the prevalence of industry-wide bargaining over minimum terms and the relatively greater importance of labour and social legislation. The point has important implications for industrial relations systems in which plant-level bargaining is becoming more widespread and in which the issues dealt with are becoming more numerous and more detailed.

Application of agreements

In terms of frequency and depth of involvement, the role of the State in the application of collective agreements is a particularly impor-

---

[1] ILO: *Legislative Series*, 1947—U.S.A. 2, sec. 8 *(d)*.

tant one. Though this is not the place for a comparative disquisition on the place of the law in applying and enforcing the terms of collective agreements, the question is sufficiently relevant to the general field of the role of the State in collective bargaining to call for a brief review of representative practices. No attempt will be made to deal with complex questions of legal interpretation or to describe the status of collective agreements under the laws of various countries; instead an attempt will be made to demonstrate the close relationship of public authorities to the application of agreements.

A useful distinction should be drawn at the outset among the purposes which lead to state involvement in the application of agreements. Two main ones may be identified, namely extending the scope of an agreement and enforcing the rights and obligations embodied in it.[1] The latter may be taken here as including the settlement of divergent interpretation of the agreement. Each of these purposes will be dealt with in turn.

Extension

In the ordinary course of events, collective agreements are intended to apply to the parties that negotiated and subscribed to them, the term "parties" here being intended to include the membership of the parties, i.e. the members of organisations of workers and employers. If the parties are fully representative of their constituents, their agreement will cover the entire economic sector for which the negotiations were conducted. However, if representativeness is less than perfect, then some employers (and of course some workers) may not be bound by the terms of the agreement. It follows that their independent position may give them a competitive edge if the benefits incorporated in the agreement create a labour cost differential to the disadvantage of employers and workers bound by the agreement. When this occurs, the disadvantaged parties or their members try to find a remedy. If they cannot find it by widening the circle of their membership and thus the circle of all those bound by their agreement, they may look for protection to the State on the ground that the social value of collective bargaining entitles it to public support. The threat of undercutting becomes particularly acute during periods of economic decline, and it is therefore not particularly surprising that a number of countries first passed legislation permitting the extension of agreements to non-signatories in the depression years of the 1930s.

---

[1] In relatively rare circumstances, government approval may be required for collective agreements whose terms deviate from the provisions of legislation. Section 3 of the German Works Constitution Act of 1972 requires the approval of the Ministry of Labour of the Federal Republic or of a constituent state for collective agreements that alter the statutory system of workers' representation on the works council if the purpose of the alteration is the achievement of a more effective co-operation between the works council and the workers represented on it.

At present, legislation providing for the extension of agreements is in force in several countries, including Austria, Belgium, France, the Federal Republic of Germany, Japan, the Netherlands, Switzerland, the Canadian Province of Quebec and to some extent Australia and Italy. There is no such legislation in the Scandinavian countries, probably owing to the fact that the degree of representativeness on both sides of the bargaining table is very high and that collective agreements cover a correspondingly high proportion of the labour force and of enterprises in the industries concerned. Nevertheless, in certain circumstances the Swedish Collective Agreements Act of 1928 admits of sympathetic strike action for the purpose of achieving the practical extension of an agreement through the exertion of pressure on employers not represented in the negotiations.[1] Extension is also absent from the North American industrial relations systems (with the exception of Quebec) because it is not readily reconcilable with the predominance of enterprise bargaining. This, incidentally, is probably a reason why the statutory provisions on extension in Japan have seldom, if ever, been utilised. It is only through industry-wide bargaining that employers and workers can be brought under a single agreement in proportions sufficiently large to justify the extension of the agreement to the economic and geographical limits of the industry. In Australia arbitration awards under the federal system bind only the parties to a dispute, but an award made under the system of a constituent state may be extended generally throughout the state, thus making it possible for unions "to obtain awards binding on employers who may not even employ any union members".[2]

The specific conditions that must be met before the appropriate government agency, usually the Ministry of Labour, will act on a request for extension vary from country to country, and need not be examined here. It may be noted, however, that in general the parties to the original negotiations are expected to be widely representative of the trade or industry to which the agreement is to be extended (i.e. universalised); there must also be grounds for presuming that the public interest would be served by an extension. The process of extension transforms a private agreement between independent parties into a kind of law for an industry or a branch of it through the intervention of the government but at the request of at least one of the parties. In this connection, the Belgian statute is of special interest because, more than any of the others, it employs the extension procedure for the explicit purpose of giving collective agreements the force of law. At the request of either party or both, as represented on one of the 80 statutory joint committees in which collective agreements are negotiated, the

---

[1] Johnston, op. cit., p. 149.
[2] See Yerbury and Isaac, below, p. 177.

public authorities may within their discretion give their official approval to an agreement.[1] Such approval has the effect of transforming the agreement into "binding rules having the force of mandatory law automatically applicable to all workers and employers in the trade concerned".[2]

This is not the place for a detailed description of the various procedures and requirements concerning the extension of collective agreements. It may be noted, moreover, that in a number of countries where legislative provisions on extension exist, their practical significance is frequently fairly limited.

Enforcement

Collective agreements create rights and obligations for both parties. The employer, for example, assumes an obligation to put into effect the conditions of employment provided for in the agreement. In return, agreements often recognise explicitly his right to manage his enterprise and to direct the workforce. Workers acquire a substantial number of rights through collective agreements, among them the right to be remunerated as agreed upon, to receive various benefits, to be considered for promotion or transfer according to the provisions of the agreement, and to be represented by their trade union (or shop steward, works council, etc.). The precise nature of the rights will vary, of course, in line with national and industry practices. Some agreements, especially in the North American countries, enumerate workers' rights in far more detail than others. Obligations arising from the agreement for the trade union and its members may include an undertaking to use the complaints procedure to resolve differences, and may also include a specific no-strike pledge for the duration of the agreement.

What happens if it is believed by either party, or by its members, that its rights have been infringed or that the other party has failed to live up to its express or implied obligations? By the same token, what happens when the parties differ in their interpretation of the agreement? After all, it is unusual for collective agreements to be so lucidly drafted that they leave no room for divergent interpretations. Are the rights and obligations created by the agreement legally enforceable, or do they depend for faithful performance on the exercise of moral or economic pressure? The choice depends on the view which society and the parties themselves take of the collective agreement, but it is clear that if it is not enforceable at law most of the burden falls on the parties and on devices of their own making, while on the other hand legal

---

[1] For a description of the joint committees and their place in the bargaining machinery of Belgium see pp. 59 and 104-105 above.

[2] André Lagasse: "The law of collective bargaining and collective agreements in Belgium", in Kahn-Freund, op. cit., p. 74.

enforceability becomes a channel—potentially a very important one—for the involvement of the administrative and judicial authorities in collective bargaining.

In Great Britain collective agreements have in the past existed outside the law. Under common law they have not been regarded as being legally equivalent to commercial contracts, and in the absence of a statutory requirement the bulk of collective agreements have not been subject to legal enforcement. This situation has reflected the traditional view of labour-management relations as a matter to be regulated principally by the parties themselves, a view which imposes on the organs of the State the greatest possible self-restraint when considering intervention. An essential reason for the extra-legal character of the agreement must be looked for in the simple proposition "that the parties do not intend them to be contracts" enforceable at law.[1] In its report the Royal Commission on Trade Unions and Employers' Associations recognised a like explanation.

A change in this traditional position has been introduced by the Industrial Relations Act of 1971. While the precise importance of the change remains to be determined, the mere fact of statutory intervention can be regarded as evidence of the increasingly important role of the State in collective bargaining. The Act stipulates that any new collective agreement "shall be conclusively presumed to be intended by the parties to it to be a legally enforceable contract" unless the parties have inserted a provision to the contrary.[2] Since many trade unions have already made known their intention to insist on the preservation of the extra-legal character of their agreements, it remains to be seen whether British practice with regard to enforceability will soon undergo significant changes, but in terms of the intent of the statute itself the position in Great Britain is now much closer to the situation that exists in most other industrialised countries.

A rather different conception has prevailed in the Federal Republic of Germany. Not only is the collective agreement legally binding on the parties that have concluded it, but legal theory has tended to consider unions and employers as something like law-making agents of the State and the agreement as a quasi-legislative act. The participation of trade unions and employers' associations in proceedings before the labour courts also favours the tendency to regard them as agents of the State.[3]

---

[1] Otto Kahn-Freund: "Report on the legal status of collective bargaining and collective agreements in Great Britain", in *Labour relations and the law,* op. cit., p. 26.

[2] ILO: *Legislative Series,* 1971—UK 1, section 34 (1).

[3] Thilo Ramm: "Labor courts and grievance settlement in West Germany", in Benjamin Aaron (ed.): *Labor courts and grievance settlement in Western Europe* (Berkeley, University of California Press, 1971), p. 156.

150

Legal enforceability of agreements is of relatively long standing in most continental European countries: in Switzerland, for example, it dates back to 1911. Since 1947 it has existed in the United States as well. The 1927 Collective Agreements Act of the Netherlands is reasonably representative of the continental European approach in that it permits either party to an agreement to compel faithful performance, if necessary through court order, and also permits suits for damages arising from a breach of an agreement. If agreements have been entered into between employers' associations and trade unions, either the associations or their individual members may seek to recover damages through court decisions. Similar provisions have been incorporated into law in the United States, where collective agreements are enforceable in the federal courts through suits "for violation of contracts between an employer and a labor organization representing employees in an industry affecting commerce...".[1] Although the language seems broad enough to make any contract provision enforceable, most court decisions have dealt primarily with the meaning and application of arbitration clauses. The reason, of course, is that a grievance procedure, with ultimate resort to private arbitration culminating in a binding decision, is almost universally laid down in agreements in the United States and in Canada.

An important aspect of the matter is the "peace obligation", which imposes on the parties a duty to refrain from hostile acts during the life of the agreement. In some countries, for example in Sweden, the law places an explicit obligation on the parties to prevent their members from engaging in unlawful offensive practices or, where such practices have already occurred, to endeavour to put a stop to them. Enforcement of this obligation, where it exists, rests with the ordinary courts or with special labour courts and can thus constitute an additional instance of the participation of public authorities in the collective bargaining process.

Research, information and education

In most of the countries included in this study the public authorities engage in a number of activities with the general purpose of improving collective bargaining through guidance, advice, and other forms of assistance to the parties. Unlike mediation, conciliation, arbitration, fact-finding and similar services that are brought into play in a particular situation to settle a dispute or merely to help the parties to define their respective positions more precisely, the activities to be considered in this section serve a broader and longer-term purpose. They aim, for

---

[1] ILO: *Legislative Series*, 1947—U.S.A. 2, section 301 *(a)*. The commerce in question is inter-state or foreign commerce.

example, at increasing the sources of information available to the parties, at improving negotiating skills, at achieving a heightened understanding of underlying economic forces, at enlightening the constituencies represented in bargaining, and generally at reducing the potential sources of conflict that can be traced to misunderstanding, lack of information, malfunctioning of institutions, failure to use tried and tested methods and other remediable shortcomings.

Of necessity, it is only in the long run that an investment in activities designed to overcome these shortcomings will produce results, which cannot be as immediate and spectacular as the successful mediation of a major dispute in a vital industry. Yet without in the least underestimating the indispensable contribution of competent mediation to the collective bargaining process, it can be said that failure to develop long-run programmes of research and information may be exceedingly expensive. A recent review of the industrial relations system in the United States makes this point as follows:

> In the past, too little imagination has been expended on opportunities for government to influence the conduct of collective bargaining. Discussions of the role of government have oscillated from proposals for drastic regulation to critiques of conventional mediation in particular disputes. Yet there is a vast underdeveloped world between these two forms of governmental involvement in private collective bargaining. An active industrial relations policy would use the government to suggest, to stimulate, to research and to advocate a variety of measures to reduce conflict.[1]

The public authorities in many countries already sponsor or themselves undertake a certain amount of research of direct usefulness to collective bargaining, although the results are not necessarily applicable to a specific bargaining relationship. The information collected and disseminated includes—

information on wages, earnings, and hours of work, usually by industrial, occupational and geographical categories and other subdivisions;

statistics on price movements, especially of consumer price indices, the importance of which is particularly great whenever collective agreements contain provisions for automatic wage adjustments in line with changes in the consumer price index;

data on current changes in employment and unemployment, broken down by area, industrial sector, and other categories;

information on negotiations in progress or recently concluded, analyses of the coverage of agreements and of topical provisions, extension of agreements by ministerial action, industrial disputes, developments in arbitration and conciliation; and

---

[1] Bok and Dunlop, op. cit., p. 247.

summaries of the decisions of courts and administrative tribunals and explanations of new laws or regulations.

Some governments have gone well beyond the preparation and dissemination of this type of factual but highly useful information, and have undertaken or commissioned studies of the industrial relations system as a whole or of separate components of that system. For example, the British Commission on Industrial Relations has been examining labour-management relations in a number of individual industries. The reports emerging from these studies include specific recommendations addressed to the parties, some of which are intended for joint action by labour and management and others for separate implementation.[1] Concomitantly, the research and planning division of the United Kingdom Department of Employment has been conducting its own studies, as exemplified by a recent examination of the prerequisites for effective collective bargaining at plant and company levels.[2] In the United States special industry studies under government auspices have been undertaken for the railways, East Coast longshoring and the atomic energy industry. The Canadian Task Force on Industrial Relations commissioned a large number of industry case studies in conjunction with, and as background for, its review of the system as a whole.[3]

The need for additional research initiated by the public authorities and removed as far as possible from the immediate pressures of an ongoing set of negotiations has been stressed in a number of recent studies and reports. In their survey of the industrial relations system of the United States, Bok and Dunlop repeatedly return to this theme, as in the following passage:

From the 150,000 agreements in the United States, it should be possible to develop a short list of those that produce the greatest concern, both by the frequency of stoppages resulting from a breakdown of negotiations and by the economic impact of the eventual settlements. The maritime, East Coast longshore, construction, newspaper, railroad, airline, and copper industries undoubtedly would be included on the list. Detailed studies of bargaining problems and bargaining structures should be arranged by government officials in each of these industries, preferably with the co-operation of the parties. As a general rule, the studies should be made apart from pending negotiations and disputes.[4]

Very much the same point has been made as regards Canada:

There are probably a number of reasons why independent research and fact finding become of increasing importance in the field of collective bargaining. Two major factors

---

[1] For the summary of an industry study of this kind see "Guidelines to better industrial relations in shipbuilding and shiprepairing", in *Department of Employment Gazette,* Sep. 1971, pp. 807-808.

[2] See United Kingdom, Department of Employment: *The reform of collective bargaining at plant and company level,* Manpower Papers, No. 5 (London, HM Stationery Office, 1971).

[3] For a list of the industries see *Canadian industrial relations,* op. cit., pp. 248-250.

[4] Bok and Dunlop, op. cit., p. 247.

might perhaps be singled out: the fact that the public interest is at stake in an increasing number of employer-employee disputes increases the need for wide-ranging factual information on the basis of which accommodations can be more easily and quickly worked out. The second major factor is the impact that certain labour relations developments (those resulting from technological change for instance) can have on society at large, and in relation to these developments the increasing awareness by governments of their responsibility in cushioning if not eliminating the adverse impact of certain economic and industrial changes.[1]

The Canadian Task Force on Labour Relations has also emphasised the high value which it attaches to a closer relationship between government-conducted or government-sponsored research and the bargaining activities of the private parties, with special reference to individual industries:

In research the Department [of Labour] should concentrate on the policy implications of overall developments in industrial relations and on the maintenance of what might be termed watching briefs in the major industries under federal jurisdiction and those under provincial jurisdiction which are of national significance. The former would better enable the Department to make proposals to keep the legislative and administrative framework up to date. The latter would improve the Department's ability to be of assistance to the parties in their industrial relations. To this end the Department should make the data it gathers and the research it undertakes as relevant and as available to the parties as possible.[2]

Whatever the shortcomings of this research effort, the fact remains that in terms of the allocation of resources, governments tend to place more emphasis on research and its dissemination than on education. This may be because other institutions, notably universities, voluntary organisations and the parties themselves, already try to meet some of the educational requirements. Yet in view of "the serious shortage of competent personnel in virtually every phase of industrial relations" (an observation of the Canadian Task Force which is also valid for other countries) there is a demonstrable case for more active government promotion of education in collective bargaining[3]; the need has recently become particularly acute in the countries where collective bargaining has spread from the industry to the company and plant levels.

One of the most direct and practical kinds of government-provided education for more effective collective bargaining is conciliation and mediation by a government service. Skilled mediators have numerous opportunities of assisting the parties to strengthen their procedures, improve their negotiating skills, seek out reliable information to support their positions and learn to appreciate the problems of the other

---

[1] Félix Quinet: *Collective bargaining in the Canadian context, with references to collective bargaining in the Public Service of Canada* (Ottawa, 1972; mimeographed), pp. 14-15.

[2] *Canadian industrial relations,* op. cit., p. 204.

[3] In Japan the Ministry of Labour has run a labour education programme largely concerned with improving collective bargaining. See ILO: *Government services for the improvement of labour-management relations and settlement of disputes in Asia,* An account of the work of the labour-management relations committee, Fifth Asian Regional Conference, Melbourne, 1962, Labour-Management Relations Series, No. 16, p. 38.

bargaining party. Despite its educational usefulness, however, mediation does suffer from the disadvantage of being normally resorted to only during a dispute or a crisis in labour-management relations. For this reason the Federal Mediation and Conciliation Service in the United States has developed an approach called "preventive mediation". It includes not only the improvement of mediation practices, detailed case-by-case analyses and action to deal with identifiable disruptive factors in particular collective bargaining situations; in addition the service develops educational programmes to help the parties to improve their bargaining performance during periods "when tempers are cool and negotiating deadlines are not pressing".[1]

In a recent report on preventive mediation, the Federal Mediation and Conciliation Service summarised its functioning in the following terms:

There are four basic preventive functions or programs: (1) the joint labour-management committee; (2) consultation; (3) continuing liaison; and (4) training or assistance. Each can be utilised alone or in combination with any of the others. They all have one common goal: providing a plan or technique for encouraging and maintaining communication between the parties to discuss and resolve mutual problems.

The particular form of a preventive effort is usually determined by the mediator based on the need of the individual situation. Often the basis for this determination is made abundantly clear to the mediator during his efforts to assist the parties in reaching a contract agreement at the bargaining table. His close and intimate contact with a bargaining situation gives the mediator a unique opportunity to identify the weak features of a bargaining relationship that could lend themselves to repair through the preventive approach.[2]

The importance of mediation, particularly preventive mediation, as an educational tool in collective bargaining is underlined by the explicit recommendation of the Canadian Task Force to merge the Canadian conciliation service with the consultative services of the federal Department of Labour and the Manpower Department, respectively, because such integration "would lead to a more appropriate balance between dispute settlement and problem solving".[3] It must be recognised, however, that preventive mediation is more relevant to enterprise-level bargaining than to industry-level bargaining, for its success depends heavily on opportunities to deal directly with the parties involved in day-to-day labour-management relations.

Mention needs to be made here also of the advisory services which some governments have established to improve collective bargaining and other aspects of labour-management relations. Among the first to do so was the Government of the United Kingdom, which established a service staffed by professional advisers as early as 1945 in what was at

---

[1] Harold W. Davey: *Contemporary collective bargaining* (Englewood Cliffs, New Jersey, Prentice-Hall, 3rd ed., 1972), p. 202.

[2] United States, Federal Mediation and Conciliation Service: *Twenty-third annual report, Fiscal year 1970* (Washington, Government Printing Office, 1971), p. 42.

[3] *Canadian industrial relations*, op. cit., p. 201.

that time called the Ministry of Labour and National Service.[1] Although the organisational structure has changed over the years, the general notion of having a public agency to provide skilled consulting services has endured.

Wage bargaining and the role of government

The activities of the organs of the State that have been reviewed up to this point demonstrate a widely accepted relationship between public authority and private decision making. With due allowance for national patterns, which sometimes diverge rather widely, it can be said that the generally understood terms of that relationship make the State responsible for laying down the basic rules of collective bargaining as a process, and in so far as necessary for ensuring compliance with those rules, while reserving for the parties the major responsibility for jointly deciding the contents of collective agreements. This general division of responsibility does not preclude a government from playing a role in deciding some major issues of substance, nor does it detract from the great importance of private procedural rule making in supplementing the basic public rules; but until relatively recently it has been agreed in most countries that except in periods of dire national emergency the core of employment relations, namely the determination of wages and related questions, is reserved for collective bargaining between bodies representative of the two sides. That principle, while still widely adhered to, is increasingly being put to the test in some countries in view of the growing involvement of the public authorities in the determination of wage rates.

This is not to say that the State is exercising relentless pressure in the field of wage bargaining. In fact the evidence is quite to the contrary: it shows intermittent rather than continuous participation, which takes place in such a way that periods of relatively unmonitored collective bargaining alternate with periods of more or less close controls. Whatever the extent and character of state influence, it is likely to affect the future shape of collective bargaining in ways that are bound to be significant but the precise effect of which in individual countries cannot yet be clearly determined. The reasons for the increased involvement of the State in wage bargaining are as complex and as controversial as its consequences. They have been the subject of many detailed investigations[2], and this is not the place for yet another. In brief, they are by and

---

[1] For a detailed account of the advisory service between 1945 and 1960 see M. Towy-Evans: "The Personnel Management Advisory Service in Great Britain", in *International Labour Review*, Vol. 81, No. 2, Feb. 1960, pp. 125-139.

[2] See for example, ILO: *Prices, wages and incomes policies in industrialised market economies,* by H. A. Turner and H. Zoeteweij, Studies and Reports, New Series, No. 70 (Geneva, 1966); and Lloyd Ulman and Robert J. Flanagan: *Wage restraint: A study of incomes policies in Western Europe* (Berkeley, University of California Press, 1971).

large the product of policies that have sought to combine the maintenance of full or high employment with reasonable price stability, while striving for a substantial rate of economic growth and the achievement of equilibrium conditions in the balance of payments—objectives considered difficult to reconcile.

At some stage or other over the past few decades, most governments in the group of countries covered in this study have had to cope with severe challenges to their multiple policy objectives, whether because of a rate of inflation deemed to have become intolerable or because of repeated balance-of-payments deficits, or both. An even more complex problem has arisen where, as in the United States, inflation has been accompanied by substantial unemployment. The responses have been very varied, and have included a temporary lessening of emphasis on one or another of the objectives already mentioned, the manipulation of fiscal and monetary tools, the development of special incentives, notably to stimulate productivity, the search for improved techniques for the management of labour markets, and last but not least the development of some sort of wage or incomes policy. In the present context only the last of these will be considered, and only in as far as wage policies have had an effect on collective bargaining methods and practices.

Although categorisation cannot do justice to the variety of complex political moves, three kinds of active government approaches to wage determination under collective bargaining may conveniently be distinguished: they are broad policy statements, the establishment of explicit guidelines, and government assumption of final control over wage changes. Some countries have never moved beyond the first category, others have at different times employed all three; the choice has depended on a host of considerations, but two general observations can be safely made: the political complexion of a government has not been a decisive factor in determining the degree of intervention, and no government has ever eagerly resorted to the imposition of outright controls. The administrative and political problems connected with outright controls are formidable, and this helps to explain why severe controls have only rarely survived for long. Of course, some governments have chosen to have no explicit wage policy at all, at least not for the time being. Examples are to be found in the Federal Republic of Germany and in Japan, where despite substantial inflationary pressure, the opposition of employers and workers to the adoption of an active government wage and price policy has so far prevailed.

Statements by political figures urging limitations on wage movements meet with least objection from the parties but are also the weakest form of intervention. Governments tend to resort to this course near the start of an inflationary cycle, or after the collapse of much more stringent restraints. Their purposes include the creation of public support or pressure and the securing of the voluntary adherence of trade unions and employers and their organisations to a policy of moderating wage and price movements.

The first major case of reliance on this approach after 1945 was the White Paper of 1948 [1] issued by the Government of the United Kingdom, which called attention to the state of the postwar economy, warned of the dangers of inflation, and concluded that there was no room for general wage increases. Unlike some later instances of resort to nothing more than a policy statement, the White Paper commanded the support of trade unions and employers for almost two years, after which it succumbed to the world-wide rise in prices at the outset of the Korean War of 1950-53. Similar efforts were also attempted in other countries, including the Federal Republic of Germany, Italy, Denmark, Canada, the United States, and again in the United Kingdom itself at a later stage in the evolution of its wage policy. The great advantage of this approach, which accounts for its frequent use and wide acceptability, is the avoidance of sharp conflict between the government and the private parties, especially the trade unions, because a policy of exhortation relies on voluntary restraint and entails no direct interference in the bargaining process. That, however, is also its most serious drawback— indeed often a fatal one—for the parties only rarely succeed in bringing the results of their negotiations into line with the appeals of the authorities.

The all too evident shortcomings of exhortation as a way of attaining goals of economic policy have led a number of governments to seek, at various times, a more effective means of gaining influence over the results of collective bargaining concerning wages without, however, going so far as to assert actual control. The establishment of wage guidelines has seemed to certain governments to offer a workable solution to the dilemma of preserving reasonably unfettered collective bargaining and simultaneously holding average wage increases within the bounds of the growth of national productivity. The essence of this policy was succinctly expressed in a report of the Council of Economic Advisers to the President of the United States:

> The general guide for non-inflationary wage behavior is that the rate of increase in wage rates (including fringe benefits) in each industry be equal to the trend rate of overall productivity increase. General acceptance of this guide would maintain stability of labor cost per unit of output for the economy as a whole—though not of course for individual industries.[2]

---

[1] *Statement on personal incomes, cost and prices, presented by the Prime Minister . . . to Parliament . . .*, Cmd. 7321 (London, HM Stationery Office, 1948).

[2] United States: *Economic report of the President, transmitted to the Congress, January 1962, together with the annual report of the Council of Economic Advisers* (Washington, Government Printing Office), p. 189.

The promulgation of guidelines sets up a framework within which the parties are expected to abide in negotiating their agreements. Not all frameworks are equally firm in their delimitation of the bounds of non-inflationary wage settlements, but frequently (though by no means always) they establish a specific target figure expressed as a percentage wage increase in a given year. In the United States the "non-inflationary guidepost" calculated by the Council of Economic Advisers in the early 1960s was 3.2 per cent. In 1962 the Government of the United Kingdom estimated the anticipated increase in national productivity at 2 to 2.5 per cent, and established that range as the appropriate limit for general wage increases at that time; a National Incomes Commission was set up to help interpret and apply the policy to specific cases and industries. More recently, after having sought in the last decade to administer a variety of different types of incomes policies, the Government in 1972 returned to the guidelines approach and sought to contain wage increases within a limit of 7 to 8 per cent a year. Later developments involved more stringent controls. In France, as early as 1960, the Prime Minister urged the National Employers' Council not to grant wage increases exceeding 4 per cent. Several years later the Fifth Economic Development Plan included specific income guidelines expressed as a maximum annual percentage by which the incomes of various groups in the population (farmers, businessmen, workers) could be allowed to rise. In the case of most groups of workers the figure was set at 3.3 per cent. In the Federal Republic of Germany an initial attempt at the development of a wage policy occurred already in January 1960 when, at the request of the Chancellor, the president of the central bank issued a memorandum urging that 4 per cent should be the generally allowable wage increase on the basis of the productivity forecast for 1961.

Although a policy of guidelines is usually expressed through a specific maximum target figure, this need not necessarily be the case. National collective bargaining in Sweden has at various times been preceded or accompanied by the Finance Minister's presentation to the legislature of his fiscal budget, in which he discusses the requirements for economic stability and may (or may not) suggest what level of nominal wage increases would be compatible with the maintenance of economic equilibrium. In the Netherlands, since the collapse of the system of wage controls in 1963, the Government has tried almost every year to obtain the advance consent of the confederations of employers and trade unions to a limit for wage increases in the coming year, without necessarily urging from the very outset that a particular figure should be adopted. The following description of the policy of so-called "concerted action" in the Federal Republic of Germany indicates that it, too, was intended to be a variant of the general category of collective bargaining within the framework of guidelines:

Collective bargaining

In 1966, when there was a temporary economic recession, legislation was enacted requiring the Government to formulate and interpret guidelines for maintaining or restoring economic stability through what was termed "concerted action" by the regional authorities, the trade unions and the employers' associations. This procedure has been repeated at irregular intervals as needed, particularly by means of talks between the Federal Minister of Economic Affairs and the associations concerned. Although the data produced in this way are not binding on the employers' associations or the trade unions, they can prove useful to them in the bargaining process, both in making matters clear to their members and in showing the foreseeable effects of their agreements on the economy and therefore on the whole nation.[1]

That a guidelines policy goes beyond mere advocacy of restraint is evident: by setting up a more or less specific target, it confronts the parties to collective bargaining with a choice between visible and measurable disregard or support of national economic objectives as defined by the Government; it affords trade unions and employers' associations an opportunity to justify the outcome of a given bargain to their constituents in terms of national economic needs rather than in terms of bargaining power; and it also seeks to enlist the forceful support of public opinion by disseminating information about the rationale for the guidelines and by publicly warning against the consequences of bargaining settlements not in line with government policies.

Most governments committed to a guidelines policy strive for the endorsement of the confederations of trade unions and employers, in the reasonable expectation that the moral authority of the confederations will strengthen the effect of the request for restraint on the actual bargainers at industry and enterprise levels. Since the support of the parties is usually obtainable, if at all, only through negotiations on the substance and administration of the guidelines, one of the potential results of a guidelines policy is the emergence of tripartite bargaining at top national levels. For this reason, as has already been observed in a previous chapter, wage policy under the guidelines approach exerts a substantial centralising effect on collective bargaining.

As a rule, a wage policy applied through guidelines is acceptable to unions only if they are assured of equivalent treatment of prices, profits, dividends, interest rates and rents, or at least some of these. Government-set price guidelines or employer commitments to forego price increases may be a condition for union acceptance of wage guidelines. It was in recognition of this relationship that the 1962 report of the United States Council of Economic Advisers, whose statement on wage guidelines was cited earlier, also contained[2] a guide to acceptable price behaviour:

The general guide for non-inflationary price behavior calls for price reduction if the industry's rate of productivity increase exceeds the over-all rate—for this would

---

[1] See Reichel, below, p. 259.
[2] Loc. cit.

mean declining unit labour costs; it calls for an appropriate increase in price if the opposite relationship prevails; and it calls for stable prices if the two rates of productivity increase are equal.

An instance of price guidelines serving to protect wage guidelines has been the British effort in the private sector and in nationalised industries to keep price increases within a 5 per cent annual limit. The Confederation of British Industry has taken the initiative in this effort.

Guidelines policies that have endured over a substantial period of time, such as five years or more, are rare. For most of them, a short life expectancy seems inevitable. The causes of early demise are numerous and not always easy to identify: they may include the inevitable upward pressure on wages in tight labour markets, the efforts of trade unions or employers to improve the relative wage position of members or employees in their particular industries, rapidly rising prices, persistent underestimates of future improvements in national productivity, pressure from trade union members on their leaders to maximise the organisation's bargaining power, and no doubt many others. Even under the most favourable conditions there are difficulties in reconciling over a protracted period of time a policy of wage guidelines with a policy of completely unrestricted collective bargaining. After all, wage guidelines are intended to set limits to collective bargaining even if there is no strict enforcement; therefore after a certain time if the conditions which led to the guidelines policy still exist, the accumulating pressures resulting from restraint tend, in practice, to lead to increasingly widespread disregard of the guidelines.

The problem of maintaining adherence to the guidelines is particularly acute in the case of nationalised industries, for trade unions in private industry will find it difficult to moderate their demands, and employers will have difficulty in resisting them, if nationalised industries grant wage claims in excess of announced limits. This was a key issue in the protracted British coal mines disputes during the winter of 1971-72. The success of the miners in finally obtaining a recommendation for a very substantial wage increase from a specially appointed court of inquiry severely dented the Government's prime objective of reducing over-all pay settlements by the force of examples set in the public sector.

Wage guidelines and the even less compelling policy of exhortation depend ultimately on voluntary compliance. Where such compliance is absent or breaks down after a while, governments may decide to rely primarily on conventional economic instruments, notably monetary policy. However, they may also under certain conditions shift to a policy of actual control over wage changes. Such a step is of great importance. In industrial relations systems marked by a fundamental commitment to collective bargaining, government assumption of review power over wage determination represents an incisive and far-reaching intervention, since the government establishes an administrative or juridical authority over the parties with the right to review, disapprove, and in certain instances modify the results of collective bargaining. The public interest, however defined, tends to be the primary criterion applied in the review process, and the criteria may therefore differ substantially, in kind or in emphasis or both, from those which the parties to collective bargaining customarily employ in their negotiations.

Thus, wage controls that are meant to be effective impinge unavoidably on the freedom of the parties to conclude their own bargain. For that reason, they are as a rule [1] invoked only to cope with unusually severe economic problems; they are expected to be in effect for only a limited time; and their introduction is usually accompanied by assurances that normal collective bargaining will be restored as soon as economic conditions permit. In addition, governments may try to associate the parties with the operation of wage controls either in an advisory capacity or as an integral element of the administrative machinery. An alternative is the establishment of close and continuing consultation with their chief representatives.

One of the most enduring schemes of government-supervised wage determination to which the above-mentioned conditions applied existed in the Netherlands from the end of the Second World War to about 1963. It was assumed from the outset that the success of that scheme, conceived at a time when the urgent needs of economic reconstruction took precedence over other considerations, depended largely on co-operation between the Government, the trade unions and the employers' associations. The Government endeavoured to secure the support of the other parties by linking them to the system in several ways, mainly advisory, policy-making and administrative. In their advisory capacity the trade unions and employers' associations, acting through their chief representatives, helped to prepare the reports and forecasts underlying the Government's social and economic programmes. In their policy-making capacity the representatives of the parties regularly engaged in bipartite collective bargaining for the purpose of working out a national wage agreement within the framework of the Government's economic programme. (Failure to arrive at an agreement meant that the Government would make the final wage decision.) In their administrative capacity they participated in the enforcement of the national wage agreement by scrutinising the collective agreements concluded at industry level to ensure that they conformed to agreed national norms. Although the system eventually had to give way to an accumulation of pressures in the labour market and to other forces which demanded a return to less encumbered collective bargaining, its demonstrated capacity to survive for so long was considered to be due in

---

[1] Australian practice is of course a recognised exception; see below, p. 166.

substantial measure to the existence of numerous channels for co-operation between the public authorities and the private parties.[1]

In 1969 the Government sought to reassert its position of ultimate control over wage policy by enacting a law which granted it the right to institute a general wage freeze in an emergency and also to intervene in individual collective agreements if considerations of the national interest so dictated. The trade unions did not object seriously to the stand-by freeze authority but vigorously opposed that part of the meas-ure which authorised intervention in individual agreements. Two of the trade union confederations decided to underline their displeasure by temporarily withdrawing from all further wage consultation with the Government and employers. Eventually the Government agreed to divest itself of a power which the unions considered to be an inadmis-sible infringement of the autonomy of collective bargaining.

A very recent instance of collective bargaining under wage controls is that of the United States, where a combination of persistent inflation and mounting balance-of-payments deficits led the Government in August 1971 to institute first a 90-day wage and price freeze and subsequently a programme of economic controls aimed at cutting infla-tion to an annual rate of 2 to 3 per cent by the end of 1972. To secure the co-operation of employers and of rather reluctant trade unions in the administration of the wage component of the controls, the Government appointed a tripartite pay board which it invested with broad powers to develop standards for non-inflationary wage increases. The trade union representatives dissented from the over-all 5.5 per cent guideline which the board established as its first major act, mainly because in their opinion the guideline made no allowance for the provisions of long-term agreements already previously negotiated, in which increases in excess of the 5.5 per cent figure were included for the second and third years. Thus from the start the issue of priorities was joined: the trade union representatives maintained that the wage provisions of collective agreements, especially of agreements already negotiated, should pre-vail over standards set by the board so as to preserve the inviolability of the bargaining process; on the other hand a majority of the members of the board held in principle that wage standards that could be over-ridden by collective agreements could hardly be called standards. In certain cases, however, a board majority composed of trade union and employer members approved collectively bargained increases well in excess of the standard for exceptional reasons, notably for the coal miners. Continuing disagreements over the question of standards versus agreements culminated in the case of the West Coast longshore-men, whose wage increase gained through collective bargaining was

---

[1] For a fuller account of the system see Albeda, below, pp. 320-326; and Windmuller, op. cit., pp. 273-279 and Chapter 9.

substantially reduced by a majority of the board's members. This decision led to the resignation of four of the five trade union representatives on the board four months after it had begun to operate.

Although the pay board ultimately disbanded in early 1973 with the institution of "Phase III" of the controls programme, it continued to function for a while as an all-public board with a reduced membership. The experience demonstrated the enormous difficulty of administering wage controls within a system committed so strongly to decision making through collective bargaining as that of the United States. Whether it is possible to administer a national wage standard in the face of determined trade union opposition—and, it might be added, in the face of rising prices—remains an open question, especially in a highly decentralised industrial relations system. The extensive experience of Great Britain in the second half of the 1960s under not entirely dissimilar circumstances would appear to raise doubts in this regard.

It is not possible in the confines of this study to provide an adequate review of the efforts made in Great Britain to move from guidelines to actual wage controls. The course of developments has already been traced in several studies.[1] Suffice it to indicate here only the most salient aspects of the system during its phase of actual controls. The incomes policy of the Labour Government which took office in October 1964 began with a period of voluntary restraint to which the trade unions and employers' associations pledged their full support, in particular by agreeing to keep increases in money incomes in line with increases in real national output and to have the price level kept stable. In 1965 the Government established a National Board for Prices and Incomes to review collective agreements on referral by the Government. Although the Board was not explicitly tripartite in composition, it included at the outset several employers and a member of the General Council of the Trades Union Congress on leave from his trade union post. Despite bipartite support of its policies and despite the Board's efforts, the Government was unable, in the framework of the highly decentralised bargaining system in Great Britain, to keep wage increases within an announced norm of 3 to 3.5 per cent during this initial phase. An attempt by the Trades Union Congress to set up its own internal review procedure to scrutinise the wage claims of affiliated unions went counter to the traditional bargaining autonomy of individual unions and eventually ended in failure.

In view of an increasingly disappointing balance-of-payments outlook the Government instituted a statutory freeze on wages and prices from July 1966 to June 1967, with a few exceptions permitted (for example, on account of inadequate living standards) during the second half of the period. When the Government during the freeze period

---

[1] See for example Hugh Clegg: *How to run an incomes policy* (London, Heinemann, 1971).

forestalled the payment of increases previously agreed upon in collective negotiations, the General Council of the Trades Union Congress withheld its approval but "after the most scrupulous examination of the alternative courses of action genuinely open to them ... reached the conclusion that the interests both of trade unionists and of the nation as a whole ... compelled them to acquiesce in the Government's proposal".[1] During the freeze and the ensuing period of so-called "severe restraint", increases in wages and prices were kept within extremely narrow limits. This span was followed, however, by a period (July 1967 to March 1968) of more flexible standards during which the Board, in recognition of the presence of exceptional factors, approved a substantial number of agreements in excess of the norm which was nominally being held at zero. In April 1968 the norm was replaced by a ceiling of 3.5 per cent, with higher increases permissible when linked to productivity agreements. Actual increases turned out to be well in excess of this limit. From 1969 on, wages increased at an accelerating rate, and in 1970 earnings rose by an average of 15 per cent.

The Conservative Government that came to office in June 1970 decided against maintenance of the controls machinery and disbanded the National Board for Prices and Incomes in March 1971. As reportedly said by Mr. Robert Carr, the Secretary of State for Employment: "Behind the strikes of recent years ... was the fact that there had been a wages policy imposed on top of a system which involved collective bargaining. This was why the Government were opposed to a wages policy and why he believed that industrial relations should continue to improve."[2] The new Government, in its continuing effort to manage inflationary tendencies, shifted its attention to the use of more conventional economic instruments which it sought to reinforce by appeals to public support for wage restraint and by exerting pressure on private industry to keep wage settlements within non-inflationary bounds. It welcomed the already mentioned proposal of the Confederation of British Industry to place a limit on price increases, and indicated that the nationalised industries would be expected to co-operate. The coal strike and the size of the settlement which emerged from it made it doubtful, however, whether this effort at self-restraint in price policy would survive for long.

In another major shift the Government sought to approach the problem of wage policy indirectly by introducing structural and legal innovations through the Industrial Relations Act of 1971, in the hope that these would ultimately produce a more integrated bargaining system. Nevertheless, early 1973 marked the introduction of a more

---

[1] Trades Union Congress: *Annual report, 1966*, p. 326, as cited in Clegg: *The system of industrial relations in Great Britain*, op. cit., pp. 423-424.

[2] *The Times*, 23 Mar. 1972, p. 5.

stringent system of direct controls. Any systematic attempt to draw conclusions of general application from the British experience would require a far more detailed examination than has been attempted here. There does appear to be support for the view that over the long term, controls are very difficult to maintain; that the support of the top organisations of employers and trade unions is helpful or even necessary but by no means a sufficient condition of success; that co-operation further down the line, where the actual bargaining decisions are made, is at least equally important; and that in general a fairly broad national commitment to the maintenance of a wage policy is an essential aspect of a workable scheme, as shown by the success of the wage-price freeze of 1966-67. But even under optimum conditions it is extremely difficult to adjust collective bargaining, especially when it is so highly decentralised, to the constraints of national wage norms.

Not all forms of explicit government involvement in wage determination fit into the categories of exhortation, guidelines, or controls. The Australian system of compulsory conciliation and arbitration stands by itself, and so does the Austrian scheme of tripartite price and wage setting. A brief review of the approaches taken in these two countries will round out the presentation of this important aspect of the role of government. The Australian system has been in existence longer than any national wage policy scheme in Western Europe or North America, but its antecedents are based more on the search for an effective combination of fair remuneration and industrial peace than on the resolution of competing economic policy objectives. As a recent study put it—

> Australian wages policy developed from piecemeal attempts to deal with industrial disputes by compulsory legislation. It remains an adjunct of a disputes settlement procedure, and in wage policy formulation Australian Governments have been reluctant to play the interventionist role adopted by governments in those countries pursuing incomes policies.[1]

Wage arbitration at federal level is in the hands of an independent Commonwealth Conciliation and Arbitration Commission. In practice, many of the tribunals in the constituent states of the federation tend to follow its lead on substantive questions, so that the effect of the Commission's awards is more significant than the legal scope of any particular case before it might seem to indicate. Among its principal tasks is the setting of a basic wage for unskilled workers, plus the establishment of differentials ("margins") for various degrees of skill. Traditionally the key case serving as a vehicle for basic wage determination is that of the metals industry. Arguments before the Commission are presented in public hearings by the appropriate trade unions and employers'

---

[1] J. P. Nieuwenhuysen and N. R. Norman: "Wages policy in Australia: Issues and tests", in *British Journal of Industrial Relations,* Vol. 9, No. 3, Nov. 1971, pp. 353-354.

associations in the industry, as well as by the federal Government. As a rule, the federal Government has not sought to utilise its presentation for the purpose of impressing on the tribunal the need for following a particular wage policy:

In its submissions to the leading wages tribunal, the Commonwealth Conciliation and Arbitration Commission, the federal Government has normally confined itself to advice which is unspecific about the degree of award wages increases it would regard as acceptable. In general, while some cabinet ministers have been prepared spasmodically to adopt a "reasonable" wage policy, federal Governments in the post-war period have carefully avoided immersing themselves in the suasion and cajolery characteristic of, for example, the British experience of incomes policy.[1]

Over the years, there have been several changes in the principal criteria underlying the wage awards. The living wage, the cost of living, industry's capacity to pay, national productivity, the exigencies of given economic policies and the need to maintain industrial peace have at various times played the leading role. On the basis of his review of decisions in the mid-1960s, Professor Walker concluded that "three criteria are at present applied by the tribunal: living standards, industrial peace, and the economic effects of its decisions".[2] The "reasons for decision" which accompanied the 1970 wage award would seem to indicate that the Commission is still guided by this same set of criteria:

We had before us a great deal of debate on inflation, on our role as regards inflation and what effect any general increase in wages would have on inflationary pressures. We regard our role as primarily one of regulating industrial relations though we realise we must consider the economic consequences of what we do and we should not take any step likely to cause adverse economic consequences over-all. In our view, in national wage cases, the Commission should, in the public interest, award the highest rates which, in its opinion, the economy can sustain.[3]

Thus, Australian wage arbitration cannot be regarded as merely another way of administering a national wage policy. Its thrust is considerably broader than wage determination, and its legitimacy is derived not from urgent efforts to achieve wage restraint in an inflationary period but rather from a more basic quest for industrial peace and fair remuneration. Indeed, a recent study of wage policy in Australia concludes on the note "that there may be neither the will nor the ability on Australia's part to undertake an incomes policy on British lines, were the need to arise".[4]

A strikingly different approach distinguishes the Austrian system which, except for slight modifications in the early 1960s, has governed

---

[1] Nieuwenhuysen and Norman, op. cit., p. 354.

[2] Walker, op. cit., p. 107.

[3] Cited by Cyril Grunfeld: "Australian compulsory arbitration: Appearance and reality", in *British Journal of Industrial Relations,* Vol. 9, No. 3, Nov. 1971, p. 342, note 58.

[4] Nieuwenhuysen and Norman, op. cit., p. 366.

decisions on wage and prices in that country since 1957. At its centre stands a tripartite Joint Council on Wages and Prices, composed of top-level representatives of the Government and of the organisations of employers and workers.[1] Administratively, the work of the Joint Council is divided between a subcommittee on wages and a subcommittee on prices, the tripartite structure being retained in both.

A trade union intending to engage in negotiations with employers in its industry over a wage increase or other benefits must first clear its claim with the Trade Union Confederation. Given the highly centralised structure of the Austrian trade union movement, the assessment of the claim will hinge on how well it fits into the general bargaining strategy and social philosophy of the Confederation. Assuming approval, the claim then goes for further scrutiny to the Joint Council's subcommittee on wages, which reviews it in the light of national economic policy and forecasts of wages, prices, productivity, and other economic factors. Of particular importance to the subcommittee's review are likely to be the technical studies and recommendations prepared for it by an Advisory Council on Economic and Social Affairs whose members, deemed to be experts rather than representatives, come only from the economic interest groups and thus do not include the government agencies. If the claim is approved by the subcommittee, the union is then authorised to enter into collective bargaining with the appropriate employers' association.[2] Any agreement emerging from the negotiations still requires final approval from the subcommittee to ensure that the agreement has remained within previously stipulated limits.

As in other Western European countries the wages laid down in collective agreements are considered to be minimum rather than effective rates. The fact that there is room for further increases through plant-level negotiations or through unilateral decision by the employer has helped the system to retain a measure of flexibility; at the same time, however, it creates the possibility of wage drift.

Macro-economic considerations, with particular emphasis on attenuation of inflationary pressures and maintenance of international competitiveness, have been paramount in the deliberations of the Joint Council and its subcommittees. The unions have accepted these considerations as relevant to their own policies, provided that any proposed

---

[1] The employer representatives are delegates of the Federal Chamber of Commerce and Industry and the Federal Chamber of Agriculture. The workers' representatives are designated by the Federal Chamber of Labour, which is also known at the Congress of Chambers of Workers, and the Austrian Trade Union Federation. For a more detailed description of the institutional framework see Anton Proksch: "The Austrian Joint Wage and Price Council", in *International Labour Review,* Vol. 83, No. 3, Mar. 1961, pp. 230-232. See also H. Suppanz and D. Robinson: *Prices and incomes policy: The Austrian experience* (Paris, OECD, 1972).

[2] Approval by the subcommittee has to be unanimous. Failing that, the claim is submitted to the full Joint Council where the unanimity rule also applies.

price changes are accorded the same scrutiny as wage claims, and provided further that the unions participate in the national decision-making process—including the taking of price decisions—on the same footing as employers and the Government. With wages and prices thus closely linked in a structure of national bargaining, the unions have moved a considerable way toward the creation of a system "in which the workers' organisations would have full powers of joint decision in economic matters and through which they could avail themselves of all existing economic instruments to play an important part in determining prices and the general economic development of the country".[1]

Although there appears to be agreement among observers that, as regards wages, the main substantive effect of the review procedure has been to delay and possibly to limit wage increases rather than to deny them altogether, the employers have regarded the opportunities for consultation and negotiation on wages and economic policy at national level as sufficiently advantageous to participate fully in the operation of the system.[2] The willingness of employers to contribute to its smooth functioning may have been enhanced by the relatively low level of industrial conflict.

The Austrian experience, which has so far not attracted as much outside attention as it would seem to warrant[3], demonstrates the feasibility of shared economic decision making between the State and organised interest groups over an extended period. To be sure, the particular economic, social, and political conditions prevailing in Austria, which constitute the essential basis for the joint operation of national economic policy, will not be found in other countries, but the experiment nevertheless deserves close study as a rather uncommon way of reconciling the maintenance of collective bargaining with the exercise of the general responsibility of the Government for the effective functioning of the economy.

---

[1] Proksch, op. cit., p. 244.

[2] Turner and Zoeteweij, op. cit., pp. 102-103.

[3] However, see Barbash, op. cit., pp. 371-387.

II. Recent Trends
in Selected Countries

Recent Trends in Collective Bargaining in Australia

Dianne YERBURY and J. E. ISAAC [1]

Introduction

A<small>N OUTSTANDING FEATURE</small> of Australian industrial relations [2] is the existence of an extensive and complicated network of legally constituted tribunals for the purpose of dealing with industrial disputes.[3] Although generally referred to as the " compulsory arbitration system ", an indication of the ultimate powers of the tribunals, they also use the processes of voluntary conciliation and arbitration. Furthermore, a number of " systems " exist. The tribunals operate under federal and state legislation and vary in name, form, composition, procedure and jurisdiction.

Collective bargaining is not formally precluded by the system. Indeed, one of the objectives of the Commonwealth Act of 1956 which regulates the federal tribunals is " to encourage conciliation with a view to amicable agreement, thereby preventing and settling industrial disputes ". It is inevitable, however, that collective bargaining in an environment of compulsory arbitration tribunals should differ in extent, style and character from collective bargaining operating in other contexts.[4]

---

[1] Lecturer in Economics and Professor of Economics respectively, Monash University, Melbourne.

[2] Among earlier articles to have appeared in the *International Labour Review* on various aspects of this theme are Orwell de R. Foenander: "The achievement and significance of industrial regulation in Australia", Vol. LXXV, No. 2, Feb. 1957, pp. 104-118; idem: "Aspects of Australian trade unionism", Vol. LXXXIII, No. 4, Apr. 1961, pp. 322-348; and Kingsley Laffer: "Problems of Australian compulsory arbitration", Vol. LXXXII, No. 5, May 1958, pp. 417-433.

[3] See J. E. Isaac and G. W. Ford: *Australian labour relations readings*, Second edition (Melbourne, Sun Books, 1971).

[4] The purist may well deny the use of the term collective bargaining to describe the recent developments in Australia because of the constraints of the arbitration system. Instead of pursuing the finer definitional points of what constitutes collective bargaining, we propose to leave the reader to decide whether collective bargaining in some sense prevails in Australia.

173

In Australia, the existence of punitive sanctions against strikes and lockouts, the easy access of parties to compulsory arbitration, the difficulty for any party to opt out of the system completely and the readiness which most tribunals display to determine matters in dispute by compulsory arbitration, must necessarily affect the scope and nature of collective bargaining. More fundamentally, the ethos of Australian society and its institutions perceives industrial relations and the settlement of industrial disputes as being the responsibility of the Government. The entire socio-legal framework has been not only inappropriate for " free " and independent collective bargaining and fraught with formal barriers for those who prefer its operation, but also, in a very real sense, hostile to the values which underlie it. The egalitarian notion referred to as " comparative wage justice " traditionally underlined by arbitration authorities, runs counter to the " bargaining power " concept of collective bargaining.

However, from what follows it will be evident that, despite the constraints on collective bargaining, employers and unions in Australia do settle their differences by direct negotiation and agreement; that strike action in defiance of arbitration awards does take place; and that many disputes which are ostensibly settled by compulsory arbitration are in fact resolved by conciliation or a form of " accommodative " arbitration by which the terms of settlement are either substantially agreed to by the parties or in keeping with their power positions. The changes which have occurred in recent years in the direction of " freer " collective bargaining are due not so much to the parties' philosophical preference for collective bargaining as to the pressure of full employment on the viability of dispute settlement by compulsory arbitration *simpliciter.*

Our article will outline the various types of agreements, the framework within which they are negotiated, their status, and the issues they cover; it will analyse the structure of negotiated agreements in terms of the types of workers covered by negotiations, the levels at which negotiations are carried out and the bodies involved in them; it will also touch on aspects of the administration of agreements; and finally, it will discuss likely future developments in collective bargaining.

The setting

Before embarking on the subject-matter of this article, it may be helpful to set down a few of the basic facts about the workforce, trade unions, employers' associations and industrial tribunals in Australia.

Australia is a highly industrialised country. Out of a workforce of just over 5 million persons, less than 10 per cent are engaged in primary production and about 60 per cent are concentrated in seven metropolitan centres. The level of unemployment in the post-war period has been mostly in the vicinity of 1 to 1.5 per cent of the workforce. For most of the last fifty years, at least half the wage and salary earners have been unionised. The proportion of union members has fallen from a peak of 61 per cent in 1954 to 50 per cent at present. There are over 300 unions and of these over 200 are small with less than 2,000 members, but 70 per cent of the total membership is concentrated in thirty unions. The central inter-union body is the Australian Council of Trade Unions (ACTU) to which some 100 unions are affiliated, including all the larger manual unions. At the state level, inter-union activities are conducted through the state branches of the ACTU known as the Trades and Labour Councils. These inter-union bodies play a leading part in arbitration and collective negotiations. The main white-collar and professional unions, comprising about one-sixth of the total union membership, are affiliated to a separate body, the Australian Council of Salaried and Professional Associations. There are about half-a-dozen important employers' associations concerned with industrial relations. Their industrial relations policy at the national level is co-ordinated by the National Employers' Policy Committee.

The development of Australian industrial tribunals dates back to the end of the nineteenth century, and although over the years many changes have taken place in the manner of their operation, their basic concepts have remained unchanged. Australia is governed as a federal system and industrial legislation is enacted by the Commonwealth (or Federal) Government and each of the six states. Actually, except in relation to its own employees, to employment in territories governed by the Commonwealth and to other special cases, the Commonwealth Government cannot legislate directly on industrial matters but may only set up tribunals for the purpose of settling inter-state industrial disputes by conciliation and arbitration. The states, on the other hand, are free to legislate directly on wages and working conditions, and although they have taken advantage of this power to determine a limited number of matters (hours of work, annual leave, long-service leave, etc.), they have also set up tribunals to deal with most industrial questions. The powers of the federal tribunals reflect the more limited powers of the Commonwealth Government as compared with those of the state governments. These tribunals can act only if an *inter-state industrial dispute* (each word having a special legal connotation) takes place; they must confine their decisions strictly to the terms of the dispute; and their decisions are binding only on the parties in the dispute. In contrast, the state tribunals can act even if no dispute exists and their decisions can be made a " common rule " to cover all those under state jurisdiction. However, in practice, because of the broad interpretation given by the High Court of the relevant sections of the Constitution, the powers of the federal tribunals have turned out to be far less restricted than might have been intended by those who framed the Constitution. The jurisdiction of the federal tribunals now extends to nearly half the total of wage and salary earners. As may be expected, jurisdictional problems are an endemic feature of Australian industrial relations but it can be said that the state tribunals have generally followed the awards and standards of the federal tribunals. Thus, despite the diversity of tribunals a surprising degree of uniformity in awards prevails.

The differences in the form and manner of operation of the various tribunals make it difficult to give a succinct account of their characteristic features, but putting aside complications and fine points, the following brief observations may be made. There are three types of tribunals—the court or curial types, the tripartite board type, and a mixture of these two types.

The federal system (Commonwealth Conciliation and Arbitration Commission) and those of Queensland (Industrial Conciliation and Arbitration Commission) and Western Australia (Industrial Commission) fall into the first category. The Commonwealth Conciliation and Arbitration Commission is composed of legally qualified persons with the status of judges (presidential members) and laymen (commissioners), all of whom have powers of conciliation and compulsory arbitration. Generally speaking, the presidential members deal with matters of national interest while the commissioners are concerned with the more local issues. There are also conciliators who do not have powers of compulsory arbitration. The Queensland and Western Australian tribunals consist entirely of lay members.

The second type of tribunal consists of equal numbers of employers' and employees' representatives and an independent chairman. These tribunals, which operate in Victoria and Tasmania, are known as Wages Boards and are each assigned to a particular trade or group of trades. The wages board system is the earliest form of industrial tribunal in Australia, and although unlike the other types in that its original purpose was to legislate directly on wages and working conditions in order to prevent " sweating " rather than to settle industrial disputes, in practice these functions shade into each other. Boards perform substantially the same functions as the curial type of arbitration tribunals. The differences between them are mainly in their composition and in the greater informality of the board type.

Finally, the states of New South Wales and South Australia combine the characteristics of these two types—at the lower levels a system of the wages board type (known as Conciliation Committees), and at the higher level the curial arrangement (Industrial Commission).

The terms and conditions of employment as prescribed by tribunals in an arbitrated settlement of an industrial dispute are embodied in an " award " or " determination ". An award sets out in considerable detail the minimum obligations of the parties to each other. It is quasi-legislative rather than contractual in concept and its enforcement is quasi-criminal rather than civil in nature.

Until 1956 the main Commonwealth tribunal had arbitral powers to make awards in the course of settling industrial disputes as well as judicial powers to interpret and enforce these awards. In that year the High Court ruled that the federal parliament could not invest in the one body both arbitral and judicial powers. As a result, the Commonwealth Court of Conciliation and Arbitration which had been in existence since 1904 and had carried out both functions was superseded by two separate bodies—the Commonwealth Conciliation and Arbitration Commission concerned with arbitral matters, and the Commonwealth Industrial Court concerned with the judicial functions of interpretation and enforcement as well as the function of administering the laws governing trade unions and employers' associations registered under the Commonwealth Conciliation and Arbitration Act. The Industrial Court consists entirely of judges. The separation of these functions was also instituted in the Queensland system in 1961 and in Western Australia in 1963.

Unions play a vital part in the arbitration system, which would be impossible to operate if it had to deal with individual workers. If for no other reason, this fact ensured the growth and security of trade unions from the very beginnings of arbitration in Australia. The arbitration legislation makes provision for the registration of unions and employers' associations, both of which are thereby accorded full corporate status. From the unions' point of view this provision is extremely important because it entitles them, as registered organisations, to appear as a *party principal* in disputes, as distinct from being merely an agent or representative of workers, a fact which has enabled them to obtain awards binding on employers who may not even employ any union members. Furthermore, in the federal jurisdiction an award only binds the parties to a particular dispute; whereas a state award may be extended generally through the state. It is, therefore, necessary for a federal award to specify the parties which are bound by it—the particular unions and their members on the one side, and the organisation of employers and its members or individual employers on the other. It should be noted that while it is most unusual for an individual worker to appear as a party, it is quite common for individual employers, as distinct from employers' organisations, to appear as such particularly in the case of large employers or where the issues are local. Our discussion below will show that the parties in the case of negotiated agreements are little different from those in arbitrated awards—unions on the one side and employers' organisations or individual employers on the other.

The above remarks provide in outline the setting in which collective bargaining operates in Australia. In our discussion below we shall refer wherever appropriate to those elements in this setting which have affected the character and extent of collective bargaining.

Characteristics of agreements

1. The categories of agreements

There are three main categories of fully negotiated instruments which co-exist with or take the place of arbitrated awards in the Australian arbitration systems—consent awards, statutory agreements and common-law agreements. A consent award is the result of a settlement negotiated by the parties in compliance with the arbitration system and issued afterwards by the arbitrator as if it were an award resulting from his adjudication. Statutory agreements comprise two main types. First, there is the certified agreement, which is often used as an alternative to the consent award in the Commonwealth and which corresponds to it almost exactly except in the manner of its formalisation. Certification is hardly ever used in the state systems where the second type of statutory agreement, the (filed) industrial agreement is found. Such an agreement is negotiated independently of the arbitration systems; after settlement is reached, the parties bring it within the jurisdiction of the system by presenting it for registration [1] and filing. Finally, the common-law agreements are simply private agreements which are not only negotiated entirely independently of the arbitration systems but are never brought within their jurisdiction in any way.

Consent awards, statutory agreements or common-law agreements may either deal comprehensively with the terms and conditions of work in the particular workplace(s) or supplement existing comprehensive instruments by providing " over-award " payments or conditions or by providing for certain issues not covered in the main instrument.

2. The framework of collective negotiations

The nature of these various categories of agreements becomes more apparent when one considers the framework of collective negotiations in the Australian industrial relations system. It is convenient to distinguish between pre-arbitral negotiations, post-arbitral negotiations and negotiations in lieu of resort to arbitration.

Either party may bring a dispute within the scope of the appropriate arbitration system by notifying the tribunal of its existence, or the tribunal may act of its own motion. Only rarely, however, will the tribunal act to settle a dispute by adjudication without first ordering the parties to

---

[1] Whereas a settlement tendered for approval as a consent award or for certification may be rejected by the arbitrator on the ground of the public interest, the Registrars have no power to reject an industrial agreement as long as the technicalities of filing are complied with.

attempt to settle their differences by negotiation and assisting them to do so. Very often, of course, the parties will have already engaged in fruitless or partially successful negotiations before reference to the tribunal. Such pre-arbitral negotiations are nearly always successful in narrowing down the unresolved area of the dispute to some extent, and not infrequently they are fully successful, so that no arbitration at all is necessary. Where the settlement in such cases is fully negotiated, it is " rubber-stamped " by the tribunal as a consent award of a certified agreement.

Once an award has been made, it constitutes legally binding minima but there is nothing to stop parties affected thereby from negotiating over-award wages or some special conditions appropriate to their particular circumstances. Most of these supplementary agreements resulting from post-arbitral negotiations are kept outside the arbitration systems, but considerable numbers of them are brought within the state systems as industrial agreements.

Finally, parties may prefer to establish the rules of their workplace(s) entirely independently of the arbitration systems, without any request for intervention to an arbitrator. (It is only if the tribunal does not exercise its right to intervene or neither party decides to notify the tribunal unilaterally that this is possible.) Where settlement is reached in such a situation, two alternatives face the parties: the agreement may be filed as an industrial agreement in one of the state systems [1], or it may be kept outside the systems as a common-law agreement. In fact, very few of these private comprehensive agreements are kept outside the systems, those negotiated in the Broken Hill mining community, in the Melbourne newspaper printing industry and in parts of the tobacco and brewery industries constituting exceptions to the general rule.

Statistics are not available to show the relative importance of the number of awards, consent awards and certified agreements separately or the number of workers covered by each of them. A substantial increase in the relative importance of industrial agreements is revealed in the New South Wales jurisdiction, between 1960 and 1970. The numbers of industrial agreements and awards increased respectively from 521 and 731 to 966 and 847. The figures for the Commonwealth jurisdiction are less useful because consent awards and awards are lumped together. The numbers of certified agreements and all awards were respectively 58 and 270 in 1960 and 110 and 565 in 1970. In relation to the number of workers covered by the different instruments, the statistics are even less revealing. In 1968, for the whole of Australia, employees fell into the following composite categories:

---

[1] Technically, a settlement cannot be brought within the Commonwealth system unless its making has involved at least some conciliation: this requires that the machinery be complied with as described in the comments on pre-arbitral negotiations.

Commonwealth awards and agreements . 40.1 per cent
State awards and agreements . . . . . 47.3   ”
Unregistered collective agreements . . . 1.4[1]   ”
Not covered by any of the above . . . . 11.3   ”

These figures are much the same as those of earlier years.

3. The status of collective agreements

Like awards, consent awards and statutory agreements are of a quasi-legislative rather than a contractual nature, although they are binding only on the specified parties thereto. Consequently, their enforcement is a public matter and can be sought by a representative of the public as well as by the parties concerned. The proceedings being quasi-criminal, the appropriate sanction is the imposition of a penalty, although " compensatory " orders can also be made. Common-law agreements are probably " gentlemen's agreements ", binding in honour only.

The duration of a consent award or statutory agreement must be specified. It cannot be longer than either three or five years, depending upon the system involved. However, it is provided in all the arbitration systems that an award or agreement continues in operation after the expiry of the set term until a new instrument has been made or the original one has been varied or cancelled.

Provision for the variation and rescission of awards and agreements varies from system to system. In the Commonwealth system, a variation can only be made within the original ambit of the dispute, for which reason the log (or file) of claims is usually framed in unrealistically wide terms. In all cases, variations can be made by the agreement of both parties, although this requires the formal approval of the relevant tribunal to be effective with respect to consent awards and certified agreements. These instruments (and, in some states, industrial agreements as well) can be varied or set aside by the tribunal of its own motion or upon the request of one party: however, a tribunal is very reluctant where one side opposes it to vary a negotiated instrument during its specified term, and will only do so where " good and cogent reasons " exist.

Issues covered in agreements

1. Employee-oriented issues

The range of employee-oriented clauses in comprehensive agreements differs little from that in awards. They consist mainly of the numerous aspects of remuneration, hours of work, the various types of paid leave,

---

[1] This percentage indicates employees covered solely by unregistered agreements of a comprehensive nature. Numerous other unregistered agreements exist as supplements to awards and statutory agreements.

and a limited number of monetary fringe benefits. A noteworthy feature is that they reflect the tendency of Australian negotiations to " settle " nearly all issues by means of a money payment.

The substance of employee-oriented clauses often foreshadows the liberalising of award conditions. This has been the case, for example, with arrangements for four weeks' annual leave, and limited and un-limited accumulation of sick-leave. It is, of course, a common practice for unions to secure favourable conditions with individual companies by agreement, and then, when a sufficient number of such agreements exist, to use them as a lever in obtaining similar provisions in an award, by showing that such conditions are becoming the custom in industry. For this reason, the employers' associations generally have adopted a very firm policy that negotiations for over-award agreements will be restricted solely to above-minima money payments and domestic issues. Such over-award payments have thus been the subject-matter of the vast majority of supplementary agreements in recent years. Until the 1950s they were relatively rare, award minima being usually the rate actually paid. Under the pressure of full employment, many employers found it advantageous to pay an over-award rate in return for stability of costs and guaranteed production. Other employers were forced, by union and market pressures, to follow suit and in recent years over-award pay has become universal practice.[1]

Traditionally, unions have relied on government legislation for welfare provisions (pensions, and sickness and accident benefits). Although a number of agreements and awards contain these provisions by way of fringe benefits, some of the larger unions are only now showing a greater interest in securing these benefits to supplement the legislative provisions. It is important to note too the lack of interest shown by the unions with regard to what might be termed " employee rights " as opposed to material benefits. For example only a few agreements [2] contain substantial provisions concerning the application of the seniority principle to promotion, demotion and retrenchment. Again, managerial discretion in hiring and firing—as long as union preference rights are observed—goes virtually unchallenged in Australia. This lack of interest probably reflects the prevailing view concerning management preroga-tives: a dispute on a matter infringing what management regards as its

---

[1] Often a union agreement with a key employer will force other employers to pay similar over-award rates as attraction and retention money. Many of the actual agreements, moreover, are mere informal understandings rather than formally documented instruments. A survey in 1965 by the Commonwealth Statistician showed that about 10 per cent of earnings were in the form of over-award pay. But this figure understates the position for two reasons. First, it does not include over-award pay in consent awards; and second, the influence of over-award pay in forcing the pace of award increases is not revealed.

[2] These include the airline pilots' agreements where the seniority principle is the basis of rostering, promotions and retrenchment, and the meat industry where supplementary agreements exist to give effect to the seniority principle in retrenchment and re-engagement.

prerogatives can easily be referred to the appropriate arbitration tribunal which will almost invariably order that the matter is one for managerial discretion. Nor have the unions made any strenuous efforts to change this state of affairs, which may be one indication amongst many others of the fact that in the protected environment of a compulsory arbitration system, and given their particular history, Australia's unions are only slowly developing a real " business " orientation with its primary emphasis on job control and the use of industrial strength rather than looking to the State for assistance. None the less, considerable inroads have been made in recent years on total managerial discretion in the case of retrenchment.

The provisions in the few comprehensive agreements which deal with redundancy are mainly limited to the application of the seniority principle, preferential treatment for unionists or, occasionally, long periods of notice. In the late 1960s [1] special supplementary agreements providing for severance pay were concluded in a number of industries, one of the most generous being that negotiated in 1966 with the Gas and Fuel Corporation (a state government agency) to provide for the effects on employment of the introduction of natural gas and the need to retain employees until the Corporation was ready to release them. [2]

2. Union-oriented issues

Unions in Australia have considerable legal protection of their rights, ranging from protection against competing unions by the registration process, arbitral grants of employment preference rights to unionists, legislative guarantees of the rights of union officials to enter and inspect premises and interview members, and so on.

Not surprisingly, perhaps, there has been little emphasis on expanding or developing these rights by negotiation. For example, the check-off principle operates in some areas of public employment, but it does so as a matter of government policy, not as the result of hard union bargaining; disputes over the use of non-union labour and the like are not infrequent, but they tend to be handled on an ad hoc basis and not as bargaining issues in the negotiation of collective agreements. Partly this may be explained by the security of legal protection, but it probably stems also from a lack of awareness on the part of both managements and unions in Australia of the possibilities for using union-oriented issues as bargaining tools.

---

[1] In the late 1950s and even earlier certain special redundancy agreements were made in parts of the mining industry, in the iron and steel industry (over the introduction of electrical furnaces) and in the railways (over dieselisation).

[2] The unions have had some success in using this agreement as a pattern. Mostly, such agreements have been made on an ad hoc basis only where redundancy seems imminent, probably because inadequately staffed unions prefer to concentrate on immediate benefits (particularly when full employment enables their members to be casual about the prospects and consequences of retrenchment).

3. Management-oriented issues

The general " management rights " clause found in American con-tracts—that is to say, a clause reserving as management prerogatives all rights not specifically defined by the terms of the agreement or some other instrument—is almost never seen in Australia. In view of the management rights policy of the arbitration tribunals, managements are unlikely to see the necessity of such a clause. Not infrequently, however, a statutory agreement stipulates that an employer shall have the right to deduct pay-ment for any day the employee cannot be usefully employed because of any strike or through any breakdown in machinery or any stoppage of work by any cause for which the employer cannot reasonably be held responsible. Other specific rights clauses are rare.

While managements in Australia have rarely been forceful about gaining a *quid pro quo* from the unions in return for the concessions they have been compelled or persuaded to make, the disputes or grievance procedure [1] has been receiving much more attention in the last few years. This trend has been accompanied by the increasing significance which the term of the agreement [2] is assuming for management in Australia. Both will be discussed further at a later stage of this article.

Rarely does the *quid pro quo* for management go as far as a pro-ductivity bargain in Australia. In a few areas, particularly in the Broken Hill mining industry and in agricultural implement manufacturing, where management has been engaging in hard and skilful bargaining for some years, the relaxation by the unions of their control over certain work practices has been a definite and often disputatious bargaining issue in a number of predominantly employee-oriented agreements. However, instances of productivity agreements, where the primary purpose of the agreement is to gain a concession from the union with regard to work practices, are very few and far between.

Notable among the few attempts that have been made are the agree-ments in the shipping industry which rationalise manning requirements on the new container ships in return for considerable benefits in terms of wages, hours and other conditions. In the airlines, agreement on a " bidding system " for manning aircraft has provided management with the opportunity of obtaining increased utilisation of aircrew and a more flexible roster in exchange for earnings above a minimum guaranteed

---

[1] In most cases in Australia the disputes procedure is still regarded as a concession by the union, rather than as an administrative device of mutual benefit.

[2] Practically speaking, awards and statutory agreements are of indeterminate life, since they continue in being until varied, rescinded or replaced after the expiry of the specified term. However, in those areas where the rules of the workplace have traditionally been determined by collective negotiations, such as the Broken Hill mining industry and the Melbourne newspaper printing industry, the term of an agreement has always been regarded as an important bargaining issue, and new agreements have been negotiated promptly at the expiration of the term.

salary for those who, subject to seniority, are willing to fly in excess of the hours for which the minimum guaranteed salary is fixed. A Department of the Navy agreement involving the relaxation of demarcation and other practices in shipbuilding, in return for wages approaching those paid in private industry, shows the interest that is beginning to be shown in productivity bargaining in areas of government employment. Sectors of the oil industry are currently attempting job enlargement of semi-skilled work to take advantage of technological changes to plant.

However, these and other instances are fairly isolated and seem likely to remain so for some time. The major barrier to productivity bargaining in Australia would seem to be the lack of awareness of its nature and potential. Moreover, the constraints imposed on ordinary negotiation by the attitudes and characteristics of the parties and the nature and availability of the arbitration system are likely to be even more inhibiting in the case of productivity bargaining, so that greater awareness alone is unlikely to herald many significant experiments. Briefly summarised, these inhibiting factors include management's customary conservatism regarding negotiations, its dependence on employers' associations, the prevailing notion of management rights, the lack of negotiating experience and skills on both sides, the weaknesses of union structure and leadership and union-member relationships, the ready availability of arbitration, and the emphasis on wage uniformity and maintenance of wage relativities which would lead one to expect very strong pressure for a " flow-on " (i.e. an agreement based on a previously arbitrated " master " settlement).

The structure of negotiations in Australia

What categories of employees are covered by collective negotiations in Australia? At what level are the negotiations carried out? What bodies and institutions are involved in the negotiations? The answers to such questions form elements making up the complex and widely varying structure of negotiations in Australia.

1. The coverage of negotiations

In every sector of the Australian economy, at least some elements habitually engage in collective negotiations, and in some cases this represents the preferred practice of entire industries. Space precludes all but a brief consideration, however, of some of the most significant areas. It is convenient to categorise our comments according to the type of employees affected, whether in manual or white-collar (including administrative, technical and professional) employment. A few of the special features of collective negotiations in public employment are also noted.

THE MANUAL SECTOR

The industrial relations system of Broken Hill is usually cited as the purest example of collective bargaining in Australia. Since the mid-1920s and, in particular, the 1930s, negotiations have been carried on in a highly institutionalised manner between the mining companies, represented by their association, the Mining Managers' Association, and the various unions, co-ordinating their approach through their local inter-union organisation, the Barrier Industrial Council. The resulting Mines Agreement is used somewhat as a model in this single industry community, where the Council also negotiates with the various utilities, services and commercial institutions. All the agreements are made—and strictly observed—for a three-year period, with the result that Broken Hill has enjoyed a quite exceptional record of industrial peace and stability. Fears of the limited life of the line of lode in certain mines led to the negotiation in 1969 of a generous supplementary redundancy agreement.

Mount Isa, another mining community, repaired its industrial relations, shattered in 1964-65 by a bitter seven-month stoppage, with the adoption in subsequent years of regular collective agreements bringing excellent results for both sides. More recent mining ventures in remote and underdeveloped areas of the continent have thrown upon management a whole range of issues not normally encompassed in negotiations—housing, provisions, social amenities, schooling, medical and welfare facilities, etc. The isolation of workers and management from official union leadership, employers' associations, industrial tribunals and government departments has forced an independence of action on management and the rank-and-file workers in dealing with these local problems by direct negotiation with each other.

The construction industry has expanded enormously in the last two decades with the development of new natural resources. The demand for skilled labour on such projects and also on construction in the cities tends to exceed the supply, and the unions have made full use of their bargaining strength to put in demands for very high over-award rates, which factors such as the cost of delays, the short-run nature of the construction work and the over-all profitability of the construction projects have encouraged the employers to meet. In Western Australia, in particular, the vigorous and militant unions engage in an effective combination of arbitral techniques and strongly executed negotiations.

The shortage of skilled labour is also the main factor behind the high over-award rates negotiated in the metal trades generally [1]; rare until the 1950s, opposed strenuously by employers until the beginning of the 1960s, the negotiation of over-award rates now constitutes a major part of the work of employers' representatives in this industry.

---

[1] The pressure to maintain traditional differentials has caused over-award amounts to be paid also to semi-skilled and unskilled labour.

In the oil industry, over-award payments dating from the employment market position at the end of the Second World War were first negotiated to supplement arbitrated awards on an individual company basis. The major companies took the lead in the mid-1950s in the formation of a committee for the exchange of information and co-ordination on industry matters generally, which rapidly led to a unified approach to the quantum of over-award rates, followed by the substitution of near industry-wide negotiations on over-awards for the previous company-level agreements. In the late 1950s the practice began of negotiating all the conditions of employment in regular rounds culminating in industry-wide consent awards covering nearly all the major oil companies. There is a distinct possibility that the events of 1970 in this industry, which we mention below, may change this pattern once again, but it is too early to make concrete predictions.

The printing industry has always been one of the most important areas of collective negotiations, the tightly organised and managed unions pursuing these channels in preference to arbitration wherever possible. One of the most successful examples, at least from 1910 until 1968 when the hitherto unbroken record of industrial peace and co-operation began to show signs of strain [1], is the Melbourne newspaper printing industry, where some of the most generous agreements in Australia, outside the construction industry, are regularly negotiated on a fixed-term basis.

There were several pre-Second World War agreements negotiated individually with the various major companies in the pulp and paper manufacturing industry by the appropriate unions. In 1948 the companies co-operated in seeking a partly arbitrated federal award on a near industry-wide basis, and in 1951 they jointly negotiated the first of a long series of agreements, certified in the Commonwealth system, each covering most of the major companies and both production and maintenance employees. In 1968, while the maintenance employees' unions continued to negotiate agreements on their own, the various production employees' unions reached a deadlock over pay rates which was eventually resolved by arbitration. Currently, they take a pragmatic approach, being prepared to use negotiations or arbitration according to which channel looks the more favourable at the particular time.

A surprising development in the direction of collective bargaining has occurred recently in inter-state shipping and stevedoring, two industries with a tradition for poor industrial relations and the dominance of compulsory arbitration as a method of dispute settlement. The substantial reduction in employment opportunities during the 1950s, arising from technological innovations and increased capital intensity in the face of

---

[1] A two-day strike took place when the unions covering skilled tradesmen tried to obtain increases on a par with the substantial benefits awarded to metal tradesmen after a work value inquiry.

severe competition from road and rail transport, created a situation in which the Seamen's Union became receptive to arrangements which would provide greater employment and income security for its members, while the employers, conscious of the need for work continuity to spread overhead costs and to speed up the turnaround of ships to meet competition from road and rail transport, were willing to offer such security. In these circumstances productivity bargaining took place and resulted in the rationalisation of manning requirements in 1964. Although pay and certain conditions of work are determined mainly by the Commonwealth Conciliation and Arbitration Commission, the union has been successful in negotiating separate and improved wage agreements with a number of employers. But the heart of the terms of employment, involving regular and stable employment, was achieved by the 1964 agreement. Since 1964 strikes have declined dramatically in this industry and the turnaround of shipping has improved markedly.

In some ways, the problems of dockworkers in the stevedoring industry resemble those of the seamen. In recent years, container shipping, roll-on roll-off and other developments for reducing labour handling of cargo foreshadowed a serious displacement of labour in what was basically a casual system of employment. The prospects of greater insecurity produced increased industrial unrest and demands for redundancy pay and pensions. In an attempt to meet these problems, the Commonwealth Government set up in 1965 the National Stevedoring Industry Conference comprising representatives of the unions, employers' associations and the Department of Labour under an independent chairman. Negotiations resulted in a consent award on the principle of permanent employment, pension, redundancy pay, retirement and transfer schemes. However, despite early hopes for a reduction in strikes, the last year has seen a return to the high strike loss of the years prior to 1965. In the middle of 1970 a new comprehensive agreement was concluded on wages and conditions of work including a no-strike clause on the issues in the agreement. It should be noted that in addition to the general agreement negotiated under the National Conference, separate and more favourable agreements have been concluded between the union and a number of employers which operate fully containerised or roll-on roll-off terminals using different stevedoring methods and hours of work from the normal stevedoring arrangements.

WHITE-COLLAR EMPLOYMENT

The Clerks' Union, which has members in nearly all industries in both the private and the public sector of employment, has found that the propensity of employers to negotiate has waned and increased in distinct cycles over the last two decades, regardless of the industries or employers concerned. Thus it reports that in the early 1950s the employers evinced a hard-line preference for arbitration, while the years 1955 to 1957 saw a considerable increase in negotiated settlements; from 1958 to 1963 negotiations tended to be fruitless; from that time on, however, the proportion of negotiated settlements increased and there appears to have been a very strong trend in favour of agreements and consent awards in the last three or four years. Certainly a distinct preference for negotiations has been evidenced by many important white-collar unions in the last decade, accompanied by a dramatic reversal of the traditionally passive attitude to direct action and political comment.[1] While this is by no means universal, it has affected such customarily conservative occupational groups as professional engineers and banking staff and has even penetrated the ranks of ballerinas and nurses

One of the most militant occupational groups in this area is that of the airline pilots. Their attempts to handle their industrial relations by collective bargaining constitute a clear example of the difficulties involved in trying to avoid arbitration if one party is determined not to negotiate. Expensive and lengthy resort to arbitration having failed in 1954 to win acceptance of their argument that their salaries should reflect the high ranking which pilots' salaries enjoyed overseas, the pilots tried to win their case by militant negotiations. The airline operators countered with constant insistence on arbitration and successfully sought the imposition of fines to penalise the pilots' strikes. In an attempt to thwart this, the pilots resigned from their federation in 1959 and formed another association not registered within the arbitration system. The High Court ruled in 1961 that although the new association was outside the arbitration system, the individual pilots could be parties to disputes brought within its jurisdiction and could be made subject to the sanctions available in the system. None the less, negotiated agreements held sway for the next few years, while the airline operators pressed for new legislation to tie the new association to the system. Fearing a crippling confrontation with the pilots, the Commonwealth Department of Labour instead masterminded a procedural agreement for the processing of industrial claims.[2] In 1966 and 1967 the procedure was the basis of negotiations which introduced the North American-style bidding contracts into the Australian airlines. However, a twenty-eight-day strike in breach of the agreement which preceded settlement with the overseas airline on this issue led to the introduction of special legislation requiring the association to submit to arbitration by a specially appointed tribunal, even though it was not a registered organisation. The Flight Crew Officers' Industrial

[1] R. M. Martin offers some interesting analysis of this trend and its causes in " Class identification and trade union behaviour: the case of the Australian white-collar unions ", in Isaac and Ford, op. cit.

[2] This seems to be the only important example of such a procedural agreement, other than grievance procedures which are discussed below. Under the agreement, based on procedures in the United States Railway Labour Act, the pilots undertook not to resort to direct action until various stages involving negotiations, mediation, independent inquiry and, finally, a cooling-off period had been observed.

Tribunal, as it is called, has strongly encouraged negotiations and conciliation in preference to arbitration.

Between 1917 and 1955 the terms and conditions of employment of journalists were fixed almost entirely by negotiations. Since this time, negotiations have been successful on many occasions, but on others the union has resorted to arbitration to press its claim, its approach being an entirely pragmatic one. Thus its major or " parent " instrument covering the metropolitan newspapers in all states is either an award or consent award at any particular time, and is supplemented by several minor federal or state statutory agreements which substantially apply the provisions of the major instrument to such groups of employers as the press agencies and the provincial daily newspapers.

Since at least the early 1950s wages and conditions in banking have been settled virtually entirely by negotiations. The major negotiations take place with the group of free enterprise banks, the settlement receiving the *imprimatur* of the Commonwealth Commission as a consent award. This settlement is followed in a number of minor industrial and certified agreements with other banks. Banking also constitutes something of a lead sector in this regard for insurance officers and, on a lower rung in the over-all white-collar pay structure, the various categories of clerks.

The first major industry award for " indoor " clerical staff in the insurance industry was handed down in the early 1920s; from this time, the parties have moved steadily towards more negotiations until now it is customary for consent awards to be made in this area, supplemented by other consent awards for other types of employees, and certified and industrial agreements covering certain individual employers.

The highly integrated combination of arbitration and negotiations through which the professional engineers press their claims illustrates the close interplay between the two channels in this country. Having established satisfactory salary standards in important areas of employment by costly and imaginatively conducted arbitral cases from 1957 to 1962, the engineers' association spent the next six years in widespread and vigorous negotiations in private industry (mainly on an industry or near-industry basis) and in public employment (mainly on a single department or local government level), which were successful in persuading most other employers of professional engineers to sign agreements adopting or bettering these standards. It is interesting to note that conditions of employment other than salaries were negotiated only in the public sector, being left to the individual contract of employment in private industry. Since 1968 the association has largely devoted its attention to the arbitral adjustment of the now eroded salary standards, after which it may be expected that further rounds of negotiations will follow.

A large number of statutory agreements and some consent awards have been made by municipal officers with individual local government authorities and government agencies. The union covering these officers has often stated publicly its preference for collective bargaining, but has none the less been very skilful in processing claims through arbitral processes where it has not been able to achieve satisfactory results by negotiations. Its officers in the State Electricity Commission of Victoria, one of the most militant of the white-collar groups, often act as a lead sector for other municipal officers and white-collar groups. The difficulties they have encountered in using their militant strength in negotiations are, however, typified in the constraints on negotiations in the public sector, to which we now turn.

PUBLIC EMPLOYMENT

Public employment in Australia comprises roughly a quarter of total civilian employment.[1] The division of public employment into those areas subject to the regular arbitral tribunals and those falling within the jurisdiction of special machinery lacks any easily ascertainable basis, and the formal framework of industrial relations in this sector is both varied and complex. In nearly all cases, however, there is scope for pre-arbitral negotiations, and in New South Wales and Western Australia the procedural arrangements affecting the public service emphasise negotiations to the total or near-total exclusion of arbitration. Many settlements in the field of public employment are thus fully negotiated. However, figures such as those showing that agreed settlements affecting the Commonwealth public service outnumber arbitrated settlements by roughly ten to one, can be misleading. Such agreements are frequently no more than " flow-ons " from an arbitrated " master " settlement, where further resort to arbitration would be merely a formality. Again, such are the constraints on meaningful negotiations in public employment, that some agreements represent little more than a resigned accommodation to this fact. Both the constraints and other features of public employment negotiations vary according to the type of employment and the government concerned.

The use of employee bargaining power is severely curbed by substantial or total strike restrictions. None the less, as we have noted, resort by government employees to direct action in recent years has increased significantly mainly, but not only, in industrial-type employment and in the semi-independent bodies. The Government's reaction to such pressures is rarely one of economic rationality. Partly, perhaps, because of the constraint imposed on Government-union negotiations by their continued subjection to public and political scrutiny and partly, in some cases, because of an insulated economic status, the Government has tended to adopt authoritarian and costly postures based on " moral principles " rather than a purely costs-versus-gains approach. These

---

[1] The degree of unionisation in this area tends to be very high, and the public service unions, in particular, are well staffed and financed by Australian standards.

190

reflect, very often, not only an abhorrence of the strike weapon but a rigid adherence to the virtues of arbitration. Nor have the prospects for meaningful negotiations been enhanced by the readiness of politicians to become embroiled in these disputes and to make public statements on their merits. It is in keeping with the equitable values of a system which adopts compulsory arbitration that the Government should see itself as having to be even-handed to different groups of employees in terms of concessions and benefits, regardless of the disparities in their market position; and, on the whole, this approach has the support of the unions concerned provided, of course, that any inconsistencies are corrected by *upward* adjustments. The principle of consistency has extended, in some cases, to the observance of a monolithic wage structure in which the relativities between the widely varying groups and classifications employed by any particular government are rigidly maintained. A further reflection of this perceived need for uniformity is the strong co-ordinating and controlling role played by the bodies responsible for over-all industrial relations policies in government employment, such as the Departments of Labour, often operating under additional constraints imposed by the Treasury Departments.[1]

The policies of the Government on negotiations place it at a considerable disadvantage in the employment market vis-à-vis private enterprise. Not only does the Government typically regard itself as unable to be a lead sector in the negotiation of employment conditions but, in fact, it has failed in a number of areas to match the actual wages established by post-arbitral negotiations in private employment, regarding itself as " unable ", as a matter of principle, to pay over-award rates. However, as a matter of industrial expediency, this attitude has been modified considerably in recent times.

2. The levels of negotiations

As can be seen from the foregoing, no one level of negotiations presents itself as the norm in Australia. Parties often operate, of course, on two or more levels: a formal basic agreement may be reached, for example, on a near industry-wide level, supplemented by informal company and plant agreements made by its signatories, and accompanied by single company agreements made by those employers who prefer to act independently, as is usually the case in the pulp and paper manufacturing industry. Moreover, this aspect of negotiations is extremely variable: while systems such as that of Broken Hill have largely followed the same

---

[1] Such controls prevent " whipsawing " (leapfrogging) tactics being used by the unions but the inevitable consequence is the centralisation of decision-making authority on major industrial issues and even, sometimes, on minutiae. Since negotiations normally take place at the individual department level, this remoteness of authority places substantial obstacles in the path of smooth and responsible negotiations and the satisfactory resolution of individual sources of conflict according to the particular circumstances.

pattern in round after round of bargaining, and norms can already be identified in the negotiating rounds of, say, the Victorian building industry, the majority of negotiating relationships in Australia are too recent in origin or too vulnerable to the constraints on negotiations in this country to have become ritualised. Thus the following comments are only indicative in nature.

National-level economy-wide bargaining on substantive issues is very rare [1], although tripartite consultation takes place on a number of issues—such as economic trends, technological change and, recently, penal provisions and grievance procedures—through a body known as the National Labour Advisory Committee. National-level industry-wide or near industry-wide bargaining has taken place at times, or even regularly in some cases, in such industries as the waterfront, maritime, oil, and pulp and paper manufacturing, though agreements reached at these levels are usually supplemented by company or plant agreements. Also common is regional (usually but not always at the level of the state) multi-employer bargaining, on an industry-wide basis, such as occurs in parts of the printing, mining and building industries, amongst others. Department-level or local government-level bargaining is common in the public employment sector, as is company-level bargaining in all areas of private industry. Plant-level negotiations take place frequently in all industries, particularly with respect to over-award and other supplementary agreements.

3. Involvement in negotiations

Managements acting on a multi-employer basis usually co-ordinate their approach by means of a small industry-based employer group, such as the Mining Managers' Association of Broken Hill, the Melbourne Newspaper Proprietors' Association, or the Airline Operators' Association, in which case they are normally represented in negotiations by their own industrial relations executives; alternatively, they may be represented or assisted by the full-time industrial officers of a broader-based employers' association, such as the Metal Trades Industry Association or the Chamber of Manufactures. The dependence of large numbers of employers in Australia on their employers' associations in industrial relations matters means that managements often seek advice or actual representation even in plant-level negotiations.

Multi-unionism is rife in Australia, at least in the manual sector, although certain big amalgamations of major unions are scheduled for the early 1970s. Even with such amalgamations, bargaining at almost any level involves several unions. These may negotiate separately, reaching

---

[1] The only major instance, relating to a long-service leave code, broke down at the point of ratification when the unions, refusing to regard the code as uniform, wanted to reserve the right to apply more favourable terms under state legislation.

192

individual agreements as did the five major unions in the Melbourne newspaper printing industry until 1968, when they persuaded the reluctant employers to meet the joint unions. More frequently, they engage in composite bargaining by all unions, as in the Victorian building industry, or in functional groups, as seems to be the practice developing in the pulp and paper manufacturing industry with the recent separation of maintenance and production workers.

In Australia the inevitable problems of communications and co-ordination and the balancing of conflicting interests take on an extra dimension with the difficulties sometimes encountered in reconciling a labour movement split by widely opposed political ideologies. Some of the problems are overcome by the practice of acting through informal federations, such as exist in the metal trades and building trades, although unions of an opposing political hue tend to be excluded. Very often, the unions co-ordinate their approach through the ACTU or through the state Trades and Labour Council, an officer of whom may act as the official spokesman. Sometimes the unions use such an organisation because of the convenience; on occasions, as in the Victorian building industry, they do so because they share the employers' belief that more peaceful negotiations and greater observance of the resulting agreement may ensue where the inter-union organisation is involved; at other times, the organisation is automatically involved because of the rules of affiliation which stipulate that any dispute threatening to affect other unions in a stoppage must be referred to the Disputes Committee that is set up in each such organisation to control the power of any one union in far-reaching disputes.[1] A compromise operates in the Broken Hill mining negotiations, where the unions jointly negotiate all matters of common interest but hold separate conferences with the mining managers on matters affecting individual unions.

Finally, third parties, in the form of the conciliators appointed by the arbitral tribunals or members of the tribunals themselves in a conciliatory capacity, may participate in the negotiations; as yet, the use of private mediators in Australian negotiations is extremely limited.

It is important to note that although there are many cases in which individual employers deal at the plant level directly with individual workers by offering extra pay and better conditions in order to retain or attract their services, it is unusual, where a union exists, for an employer to negotiate with groups of workers independently of the appropriate union official or the elected shop steward even if the latter is acting without proper authority from the union branch officials. There are no statistics to show the extent of formal joint consultation committees but

---

[1] The Australian Council of Salaried and Professional Associations, the highest inter-union organisation for white-collar unions, differs from its blue-collar counterpart in having only advisory and consultative functions; it has no power to intervene in the disputes affecting its affiliates and has not as yet been involved in their negotiations.

in many of the larger establishments such committees exist and operate with varying degrees of success. However, these committees are careful to avoid trespassing on recognised union functions directly or indirectly connected with awards. Most of the matters dealt with by the committees relate to welfare amenities, labour efficiency, quality control, safety and the like.[1] The virtual absence of direct employer-employee negotiations on substantive terms of employment reflects the general acceptance of unionism by Australian employers.

Administration of collective agreements

1. Disputes procedures

Before and during the 1950s in Australia there were only isolated instances of disputes procedures other than the provision in statutory agreements for a Board of Reference—a tripartite committee chaired by a representative of the tribunal—to handle questions arising out of the application of the instrument, as a sort of " minor tribunal ".

The indeterminate life of awards and statutory agreements blurs any clear distinction between " rights " and " interests " so that any type of dispute may be referred to arbitration. Moreover, the scope for grievance handling is narrowed in that awards and agreements tend to be very detailed, leaving fewer doubtful issues to be handled by management than would be the case, say, in the United States[2]; again, many contentious issues in that country tend to be regarded as managerial prerogatives in Australia. In the circumstances, grievances are more likely to be confined to such issues as the application of the award to particular situations and the handling of matters which the award does not cover. Given these factors, the dependence of the parties on arbitral tribunals and the legalistic nature of the system, it is not surprising that formal procedures for the handling of grievances by union-management negotiations were very few and far between until the 1960s.

Only limited use was made of the Boards of Reference, and thus grievances which did arise at the plant level were handled, if at all, on an informal basis by management with little union consultation. Nor were (or are) the unions sufficiently well organised, at the plant level, or sufficiently well staffed, to play an effective part in shop-level grievance

---

[1] See L. R. Wall and W. P. Butler: " Management-employee committees—the results of Australian research ", in *Personnel Practice Bulletin* (Melbourne, Commonwealth of Australia, Department of Labour and National Service), Vol. XV, No. 1, Mar. 1959; and W. P. Adkins: " Joint consultation—a case study ", ibid., Vol. XXII, No. 1, Mar. 1966.

[2] F. T. de Vyver: " Settling plant disputes—the Australian experience ", in *Labour Law Journal* (Madras), Oct. 1961.

handling. The result was neglected and badly handled grievances which accounted for a substantial proportion of Australia's high incidence of short protest-type strikes.[1]

The use of the short stoppage was extended in the 1950s to back demands for over-award wages. An American company, the Braun Transworld Construction Company, negotiated with the building trades unions in 1952 to pay over-award wages but insisted in return on a formal disputes procedure being established.[2] This agreement was the forerunner of the Victorian Building Industry Agreement of 1956, in which industry the success of the procedure in grievance handling and the satisfactory nature of the substantive terms of the agreement produced results that were nothing less than spectacular in terms of industrial stability for a number of years. Other companies, mainly but not all in the construction and oil industries, followed suit, experimenting with their own disputes procedures. By the beginning of the 1960s the most reluctant of employers' associations were unable to deny the negotiation of over-award payments, particularly in the metal trades and construction industries, and during the 1960s it became quite common, at least in these areas, to require a disputes procedure in return. The procedures vary considerably as to their nature and the involvement in their various phases of union and management personnel and, sometimes, representatives of the arbitration system. The inclusion or otherwise of a " peace obligation "—either in a blanket form or until the procedure is exhausted —also varies from agreement to agreement.

However, after their initial interest, a number of important employer representatives have announced themselves as being disenchanted with the results, mainly because they are rarely observed. Even the highly encouraging Victorian Building Industry Agreement has been endangered in recent years by the readiness of employees to resort to stoppages before exhausting the disputes procedure.[3] Most often the procedures— in the building industry and elsewhere—are broken by stop-work meetings called on the job by the shop steward, often without the knowledge of the union officers, who nevertheless generally choose to ratify the stoppages at a later stage. In some cases, mainly in the metal trades where strong shop stewards' committees have been formed, the stoppages are unofficial, and have been strongly condemned by the official union leaders. The ACTU executive has repeatedly stressed its conviction that

---

[1] J. W. Kuhn: " Grievance machinery and strikes in Australia ", in *Industrial and Labor Relations Review* (New York), Vol. 8, No. 2, Jan. 1955.

[2] This involved a " cooling-off " period being observed while attempts were made to deal with the dispute by a union-management conference on the spot, culminating in the meeting of a Conciliation Committee consisting of representatives of both sides (including representatives of the Trades and Labour Councils and employers' associations) in an endeavour to settle the dispute without resort to a statutory tribunal.

[3] F. T. de Vyver: " The Melbourne Building Industry Agreement ", in *Journal of Industrial Relations* (Sydney), Vol. 12, No. 2, July 1970.

agreements must be observed and that grievances must be processed through the " proper channels ", and has, in the past, mounted campaigns aimed at weakening and controlling the power of shop stewards' committees.

This is an area where empirical research is badly overdue; at present, one can only surmise as to the reasons underlying the ineffectiveness and lack of acceptance of disputes procedures. It may well be that the procedures are insufficiently dovetailed to the needs of the particular organisation; almost certainly they are inserted into agreements without adequate shop-floor communications, preparation and involvement. The problems of union structure and organisation, particularly those concerning the role of the shop steward, remain unresolved in many unions. There are grounds for suspecting too, that many industrial relations departments are still unable to shoulder the responsibility for resolving disputes. Whatever the reasons, disputes procedures have recently received a solid endorsement from national employers' associations, the ACTU and the Federal Government. Tripartite consultations during 1970 led to recommendations as to the form such procedures might take, based on a series of conferences at different levels, with safeguards built in against undue delay in the processing of grievances on either side. At any stage in the procedure, it was suggested, the parties might seek the assistance of a Conciliator, a member of the Commission or some mutually acceptable person, but should not have recourse to the formal processes of the arbitration system until they had tried to resolve the issue in full accordance with the procedure. The recommendations are no more than guidelines: it remains for individual unions and employers to adopt them, if they choose, and to adjust them, if necessary, to meet their particular needs. The biggest barrier to their success continues to be the lack of attention paid to the contextual problems which, it seems valid to suggest, very largely dictate whether even the best-designed procedures will thrive or falter. The widespread publicity given to the recommendations is an excellent sign, but the mere endorsement of a disputes procedure by individual parties, without sufficient preparation and investigation of their particular difficulties, seems unlikely to guarantee its successful operation.[1]

---

[1] It is important to note that the use of a grievance procedure with a " no-strike " commitment is not generally taken by the unions to exclude strike action for sympathy or political reasons or in support of campaigns called by the ACTU or Trades Hall Councils. Part of the reason for this attitude is the assumption that such stoppages are beyond the scope of an individual plant's dispute procedure and that the workers in a plant cannot be expected to refuse to support such a campaign. This attitude also reflects the absence historically of any strong feeling of obligation on the part of unions to refrain from strike action against " innocent " employers. This feeling may have been promoted by the system of compulsory arbitration which, because it imposes awards on unions, enables their leaders to disown any responsibility for ensuring that stoppages will not occur during the currency of an award. The legitimacy of penal sanctions has, of course, been denied traditionally by unions.

2. The duration and modification of agreements

Not only have the employers been disappointed with the results of dispute procedures, they also have qualms about the unions' approach to the life of agreements. Major disputes occurred on the waterfront and in the railways during 1970, when unions were alleged to have put pressure on managements to vary substantially the over-award payments set down in agreements before the fixed term of the agreements expired. This is another area where the ACTU has guaranteed its support for the observance of agreements; it is also one in which management has to gain confidence in the unions' ability to maintain observance against rank-and-file impatience before collective negotiations will be fully acceptable.[1] The growing practice of staggering increases paid under an agreement over, say, six-monthly or yearly intervals may prove useful in this regard.

The modification of agreements during their term poses considerable problems in Australia, apart from the legal issues indicated earlier. Agreements made on construction sites often specify that they are to operate for the duration of the building project in question; others are usually made for periods ranging from one to three years. During this time, National Wage Cases [2] take place and increases decided upon have general implications for the whole workforce. Reviews also take place with regard to the rates paid under the Metal Trades Award, which has been used as a yardstick for other industries for many years. Agreements which fail to provide for adjustments in line with such increases can often cause disputes. Many agreements now specify that the rates stipulated therein will be varied in accordance with increases awarded on economic grounds for general application in National Wage Cases. Certain others, where parity with tradesmen covered by the Metal Trades Award has been customarily maintained, also provide for automatic variation to maintain this parity in the event of increases being granted under this award (other than those granted solely on the basis of increased work value in the categories of work specified).

Then there is the special problem which affects the negotiation of over-award agreements, namely the relevance of variations made during the term of those agreements to the particular awards which cover them.[3]

---

[1] This point has an important bearing on the proposals put forward by the Australian Council of Employers' Federations on possible reforms to the system (outlined in a later footnote).

[2] An annual review by the Commonwealth Conciliation and Arbitration Commission, based on general economic considerations, of the national basic wage and associated factors. For fuller information see " Wage determination in Australia: basic wage and total wage inquiries, 1964 ", in *International Labour Review*, Vol. 92, No. 2, Aug. 1965, pp. 128-140.

[3] In the negotiation of the Victorian Building Industry Agreement, the question whether such variations in the various instruments covering plumbers, carpenters and labourers and

(Footnote continued overleaf)

This problem caused numerous hours to be lost in the metal trades industry in 1967 and 1968, where in many cases no prior arrangements covering this point had been made. The Commonwealth Conciliation and Arbitration Commission, having awarded substantial increases to certain classifications covered by the Metal Trades Award, suggested that employers might choose to " absorb " some or all of the increases in the substantial over-award payments being paid in that industry. The ensuing industrial action proved to the employers that this was not a feasible proposition, and emphasised the need for some provision to be made in over-award agreements as to the practice to be observed.

The future

The last twenty years have witnessed a significant movement in the direction of collective bargaining in Australia. There are no statistics to show the number of workers affected by this development and our evidence is confined to references to those industries and sections of industries which have entered in recent years into collective agreements and consent awards. Although the proportion will have declined in the last ten years, our judgment would be that at least half of all workers are still covered mainly by awards (excluding consent awards) of tribunals. But the importance of collective agreements and consent awards is not measured sufficiently by the proportion working under them because these agreements and awards tend to set the pace and the pattern of awards prescribed by tribunals.

A combination of factors, some of which are inter-related, have contributed to this development. First, the environment of full employment has profoundly affected the relative industrial power positions of labour and employers. Unions have been quick to realise the capacity of employers in certain industries to concede wages and conditions of work better than those provided in the awards of tribunals. The strategy of unions has been to obtain as much over-award benefits as possible by negotiation and strike pressure and to persuade tribunals to incorporate this higher standard in awards, at the same time resisting successfully any attempt by employers to absorb subsequent award increases in over-award benefits. The over-award elements not only stick but grow larger as, round after round, awards are revised upward. Full employment has thus enabled the unions to use both the market and the tribunals for a succession of inter-acting rounds of benefits. Secondly, the punitive powers of the system have become increasingly ineffective in restraining

---

so on should be absorbed in the over-award payment or paid in addition thereto has been very much a bargaining issue: it is usually agreed that the variations will be absorbed, this factor being taken into account in fixing the amount of the over-award payment and the term of the agreement.

strike action.[1] After repeated statements of its opposition to penal sanctions, the union movement reached the limit of its tolerance in 1969 with a demand for their total repeal and a refusal to pay outstanding fines. To avoid a headlong collision with the risk of widespread rejection of the arbitration system, the Government compromised by amending the Act to meet some of the unions' objections. It is too soon to say how these changes will be applied but in principle they provide the basis for a delay in the availability of sanctions and an opportunity for an extension of the conciliation and arbitration processes.[2] The application of this principle is likely to strengthen the unions' ability to press their claims through negotiations, with the tribunals acting more in the role of conciliators and, if forced to arbitrate, to accommodate the demands of the unions in a way acceptable to them. Thirdly, employers are becoming increasingly aware of the narrow limits within which they can rely on arbitration tribunals to make and enforce awards (which unions frequently believe they can improve upon by resort to strike action). While the unions appear to be able to have the best of both worlds—to rely on the arbitration system where they are weak and to defy the system where they are strong—the employers cannot. This realisation has tended to encourage many employers to believe that collective bargaining may well be the lesser of two evils. They see collective bargaining as at least providing an opportunity for securing a reasonable *quid pro quo* from the unions in the form of a no-strike clause during the life of an agreement or consent award. Fourthly, mention should be made of the influence of an increasing number of American companies in Australia which have successfully applied collective bargaining techniques. And finally, in recent years the formation of industrial relations societies has provided a means for bringing together management, union officers, arbitrators, industrial lawyers and academics for a critical review of industrial relations in general and the arbitration system in particular.[3] It is not an exaggeration to say that these discussions have produced a fundamental change in the standard of perception and sophistication regarding industrial relations problems among these groups.

---

[1] In the ten years to 1967 a yearly average of thirty-nine fines were imposed in the Commonwealth jurisdiction amounting to $18,000. In 1968 alone the unions incurred 454 fines totalling $104,000. Excluding two highly strike-prone but small and atypical industries (stevedoring and coalmining), there has been a steady increase in the number of strikes over the last ten years—508, 867 and 1,488 in 1960, 1965 and 1969 respectively. But even in 1969, the peak of strike activity, only two-fifths of a day per man-year was lost through strikes. The annual average time lost for the preceding ten years was about one-sixth of a day. The relatively small amount of time lost in conjunction with the high frequency of stoppages reflects the short duration of strikes in Australia which, for the last ten years, has averaged one-and-a-half days per worker involved.

[2] See C. P. Mills: " Legislation and decisions affecting industrial relations ", in *Journal of Industrial Relations*, op. cit., Vol. 12, No. 3, Nov. 1970.

[3] See, for example, some of the papers delivered at the 1970 Convention of the Industrial Relations Society of Australia in the *Journal of Industrial Relations*, op. cit., Vol. 12, No. 2, July 1970.

All this should not be taken to imply that in the foreseeable future the arbitration system might be abandoned in favour of a system of " free " collective bargaining. The most that can be expected is an extension of collective bargaining wherever expedient *within* the present system, with suitable changes in the manner of operation of the system. The notion of public responsibility in the settlement of industrial disputes, big and small, is so deeply ingrained in the Australian public mind that it has engendered a wariness of free negotiations and the use of economic coercion. If public opinion polls are a reliable guide, there is strong support still for the retention of compulsory arbitration. Similarly, the official government attitude seems to be one of total support for the retention of arbitration, the " rule of law " in industrial relations, and an anxious disapproval of collective bargaining particularly when strike action succeeds in securing gains for the unions in excess of those indicated by national productivity increases. The hope cherished by some that the restraining hand of the arbitration system, despite its constitutional and procedural weaknesses, might be the means for implementing some sort of incomes policy appears virtually doomed with the extension of collective bargaining.

However, in the long run, much more important than current public opinion and the attitude of the Commonwealth Government [1], are the attitudes of the parties directly involved in industrial relations—the tribunals, the employers and the unions.

There are two aspects in the attitude of the tribunals to be distinguished: their attitude on conciliation as against compulsory arbitration, and their attitude on the basis on which arbitration decisions are made whenever necessary. On the former, in connection with national issues (the national minimum wage, national wage adjustments, standard hours of work, annual leave and long-service leave) we may expect tribunals to continue to determine these issues by arbitration largely because both employers and unions would want them to be so determined. In industry and local disputes, it may be said that, in general, tribunals are showing an increasing preference for conciliation. It is likely that, in the spirit of the new penal provisions, conciliation will be pressed even harder by the tribunals [2] but their success will depend very much

---

[1] The industrial spokesman of the Labour Party, which is the Opposition in the present Commonwealth Parliament, is reported to have said that a Labour Government would recast the arbitration laws to permit a system of fixed-term industrial agreements enforceable on both employees and management as binding contracts. These agreements would be based on the minimum standards of wages, hours, leave, etc., fixed by the arbitration tribunals. However, penalties against strikes concerning these minimum terms would be abolished. The application of this policy would, of course, encourage the tendency towards collective bargaining arrangements. (*The Australian*, 30 Nov. 1970.)

[2] There is considerable support for the proposition that resort to arbitration be limited (except in national cases) to situations where a conciliator certifies that the parties have bargained in good faith and that further negotiations are unlikely to be justified. See A. E. Woodward: " Industrial relations in the '70s ", in *Journal of Industrial Relations*, op. cit., Vol. 12, No. 2, July 1970, p. 120.

on how determined one party or the other is to force the matter to arbitration.[1]

This leads to the second aspect of the tribunals' attitude: the basis of their award when conciliation has failed. Arbitration may be based on a " judicial " or " normative " type of approach in the sense that the tribunal determines the matter on the merits of the argument put before it; or it may be based largely on the power positions of the parties. In the latter, which may be called " accommodative arbitration ", the tribunal may take a " realistic " view of the situation and may be inclined to grant an award which would be acceptable, even if grudgingly so, to the union. The judicial approach may be proper in determining the rights of parties; but arbitration on interest is more akin to legislation and the power position of the parties can only be ignored at the cost of having the decisions of the arbitrators frustrated. What has been said makes it clear that the tribunals' traditional view that the system is a method of " industrial justice " is only viable in today's climate in the case of employers and unions unable or unwilling to defy awards. Australian employers are generally unorganised for lockouts, and even if they were well organised they would probably pass on any " excessive " awards to consumers (and seek government assistance by way of tariffs or subsidies if necessary) in preference to incurring public disapproval by declaring a lockout. In general, employers have an escape route not open to the unions. Thus the relaxation of the penal provisions may be expected to persuade tribunals into accommodative arbitration whenever necessary simply as a matter of industrial expediency. The approach taken by the Commonwealth Conciliation and Arbitration Commission in a recent dispute in the oil industry may well set the pattern for collective bargaining-type solutions in industrial disputes. When negotiations on a new agreement in 1970 failed amidst a strike, the unions took the matter to the Commission which determined the main issues by an award which approximated the terms to which the parties were close to agreeing in their negotiations. The Commission remarked by way of guidance in future cases that " if conciliation fails, any subsequent arbitration would be more realistic if the arbitrators are able to put themselves in the position of the negotiators and to regard the arbitration as a prolongation or extension of the negotiations ".[2] In recent years, even national wage decisions have clearly been made with an eye on the acceptability of the decisions to the trade unions, and economic arguments relating to the

---

[1] For example, a union determined to press for an arbitration award on the assumption (usually correct) that it would not be less favourable than the employer's last offer, makes arbitration inevitable, unless the tribunal is prepared (which it is generally not) to allow a strike to take its course. This was the situation in the recent oil industry dispute which was taken to arbitration after protracted negotiations had failed to persuade the unions to accept the offer of the companies.

[2] Decision in the matter of C No. 1249 of 1970 (mimeographed), p. 5.

inflationary effects of such decisions have taken a secondary position in the considerations of the tribunal.

Another factor affecting the operation of accommodative arbitration is the legal difficulty of distinguishing between interest disputes and rights disputes in Australian awards because of the effectively indeterminate life of such instruments. For accommodative arbitration to operate in the same way as an American contract (with a no-strike provision and a grievance procedure likely to be honoured by the union during the life of the contract) requires either that the law be amended or that the tribunal and the parties firmly accept the award for a stated term only. Furthermore, the unions would have to reject their traditional approach of regarding an award as merely prescribing minima which may be raised during its currency by strike pressure. It is an open question whether many unions would be able to honour such an undertaking.

The attitude of employers, particularly the smaller ones, depends to an important extent on the attitude of the employers' association to which they belong and on which they tend to rely for advice and personnel in dealing with industrial matters. Employers' associations, while opposing the abolition of compulsory arbitration and doubting the unions' ability to handle bargaining and the administration of their agreements, none the less range all the way from those which strongly favour an extension of collective negotiations [1] and advocate changes in the system including a drastically reduced role for tribunals, to those, mainly concerned with the metal trades, where the unions have been most militant, which believe that negotiations outside the compulsory arbitration system are an unfortunate development best described as " industrial anarchy ".

The trade union movement has frequently advocated increased reliance on collective negotiations, particularly after disappointments in major wage cases. With the exception of a few strong and militant unions, this stops short of calls for the abolition of the arbitration system. It is generally submitted by the unions that the arbitration system should remain, at least for the purposes of national issues, to set minimum stan-

---

[1] An important recent paper discussed by the Executive Council of the Australian Council of Employers' Federations, a leading employers' body, deserves special mention. The paper proposed that the Commission should retain the power to arbitrate only in National Wage Cases and on applications for changes in standard hours and paid absences from work. Other matters, it was suggested, could be directed by legislation to be completed by way of direct negotiation between the parties, with the final agreement having to be brought back to the Commission for certification. Arbitration would not be available on such issues unless the parties agreed voluntarily or unless a conciliator issued a certificate that negotiations had failed to produce an agreement. Negotiations between the parties would thus be the formally approved process for resolving issues. Conciliation as it is now practised under the Act would be abandoned, and, to facilitate the negotiation process, a conciliation and mediation service, which would have no power to arbitrate, would be established on a basis independent of the Commission. An agreement would have a fixed life and would be re-opened only where it contained a specific re-opening clause. Enforcement against unions and employers' organisations would be by way of damages.

dards and also to protect the weaker unions (which totally oppose its abolition).[1] However, they argue, unions should have greater freedom to bargain for extra wage and other benefits and they criticise strongly those employers, including governments, which rely on the arbitration system and refuse to bargain in good faith. As has been stressed above, their strategy is that the stronger unions should have the freedom to bargain and to use their economic power to raise the pay and other benefits above the standard prescribed by tribunals in national cases; and then to press the tribunals to apply these higher standards to the awards covering the weaker unions.

Finally, there are certain characteristics of both employers and unions which inevitably inhibit the prospects for collective bargaining. Both sides tend to lack the skills involved in negotiations, being accustomed to the simpler semi-forensic approach of arbitration. The union's approach on over-award payments is often not to negotiate at all, but to demand, with immediate threat of the strike. As often, employers retort by making a firm offer about which they are not prepared to bargain. And when confronted with determined union strike pressure, they frequently refuse to negotiate and run to arbitration immediately or concede the claim. Too frequently, parties who are willing to negotiate assume that all that is involved in negotiations is a round-table discussion; they do little homework on their negotiations and rarely bother to formulate mutually acceptable procedures. Another characteristic of many employers and unions is a reluctance or inability to make decisions and to bear the responsibility for them, a requirement of which they have been relieved by the availability of arbitration, employed both as a crutch and a scapegoat. This is aggravated by the fact that employer representatives often lack the status and authority necessary for effective negotiations and are required to refer to their principals frequently before they can make any concessions. On the unions' side, it is reinforced by the inability of many officials to guarantee observance of an agreement because of their lack of authority over the rank and file, which is partly due to poor communications and the inadequacies of union staffing and structure. The problems of composite union bargaining have already been mentioned.

Most of these characteristics of unions and employers have been nurtured by many years of compulsory arbitration. A determined move by tribunals to refrain from readily making awards on interest matters but to press for conciliation even in the face of stoppages, could well force employers and unions to make the necessary adjustments in their organisation, personnel and attitudes for more effective collective bargain-

---

[1] The arbitration system has spawned and succoured a large number of unions so weak, so poor and so badly led that they are utterly dependent on the system for survival. These unions, whose voices count in the policy decisions of the ACTU, have a vested interest in the system.

ing. There will no doubt be a learning period during which stoppages may become more numerous. What could help the learning process is for the Government at this stage to set up a committee of inquiry to examine thoroughly the state of Australian industrial relations and the institutional and procedural changes which may be necessary for improvements in the system. For the circumstances that surrounded the inception of the system of compulsory arbitration nearly seventy years ago have changed profoundly. What has evolved under the pressure of full employment in the post-war period is an industrial relations system with diverse elements: pure compulsory arbitration working effectively at one end of the spectrum and free collective bargaining at the other; and in between, a peculiar hybrid of quasi-collective bargaining, which could well become the dominant feature of industrial relations in Australia, has succeeded in taking root but is still in the process of defining its features.

Recent Trends in Collective Bargaining in Belgium

Roger BLANPAIN [1]

Introduction

THE PHENOMENON of collective bargaining cannot be fully appreciated without taking into account the cultural and historical environment in which the system has its roots. An understanding of some of the main features of labour relations in Belgium is therefore essential to the study of collective bargaining in that country.

Labour relations in Belgium are still marked by ideological differences. The various trade unions hold conflicting principles on such issues as the role of the State in public life, the place of private enterprise, nationalisation and the programmes and goals of the educational system, and seek to win over public opinion to their way of thinking on these and other questions. Ideological conflicts are so deeply rooted that the trade unions themselves only form part of larger movements. Political parties and cultural organisations that share and defend the same beliefs also belong to these larger movements. [2] Although ideological differences have recently become less acute and a pragmatic approach is now adopted in some matters, the clash of ideologies remains an influential factor in the dynamics of Belgian society and the Belgian system of labour relations. It explains many facts, such as the pluralism of trade unions, that would otherwise be completely misunderstood.

The close links of the major trade unions with the chief political parties and the fact that a large number of present or former trade union leaders are Members of Parliament or even hold government office are also characteristic of Belgian labour relations and help to account for the constant political influences that affect them. The political power of trade unions explains the extensive protective labour legislation, the

---

[1] Professor, University of Leuven (Louvain), Belgium.

[2] See also: Alfred Kamin (ed.): *Western European labor and the American corporation* (Washington, Bureau of National Affairs, 1970); and US Department of Labor: *Labor law and practise in Belgium*, BLS Report No. 372 (Washington, 1970).

absence of legislation regulating trade unions and the existence of almost unrestricted freedom to strike. Labour relations in Belgium are largely dominated by the two major trade union organisations, which are almost omnipresent. At the national inter-occupational or inter-industrial level [1] they participate in the shaping of national economic and social policies through formal consultation, generally at the request of the public authorities. At the industrial level they are represented on the joint committees in which collective agreements are made with binding effect for the industry as a whole. At the level of the enterprise they are represented through union delegations, works councils, and safety and health committees, all of which are described more fully below.

Other features of the Belgian labour relations system are the organised participation of the unions in public life and their collaboration with employers' associations, especially the Federation of Belgian Industries [2], at the national and industrial levels. This working relationship is the result of a long evolution in which the events of the Second World War played an important and special role. During the last months of the war prominent union leaders and representatives of the employers' associations clandestinely signed a " pact of social solidarity " establishing the main principles on which a modern system of labour relations should be built up.

The pact, which was very explicit, was a blue-print covering the main points of social reform to be developed in the post-war period. It concerned: wages, hours of work, social security (pensions; sickness, invalidity and unemployment benefits; family allowances), annual vacations and the establishment of union delegations, joint committees and a national joint council, as well as the settlement of industrial disputes.

The working relationship thus established led in 1960 to " social programming ", in other words the joint programming by employers and trade union organisations of a series of agreements at both the national and the industrial levels under which the social advances envisaged are worked out on a realistic assessment of economic possibilities.

Collective labour relations in Belgium rely almost entirely on practice and on gentlemen's agreements between the social partners. It should be added that Belgian trade unions have no legal personality and that they

---

[1] Embracing the private sector of industry, commerce and agriculture.

[2] The Federation of Belgian Industries (FIB) is a confederation of thirty-six employers' associations. It groups at national level some 35,000 industrial undertakings belonging to ts member federations. The purpose of the FIB is defined in its statutes as follows:

— to bring together the employers' associations representing the different sectors of national industry;

— to defend, in accordance with the public interest, the economic, social and moral interests of national industry as a whole;

— to seek, in conjunction with the public authorities and with the nationally and internationally federated trade union organisations, all solutions conducive to maintaining and furthering social peace and the economic prosperity of the country.

cannot be sued for breach of collective agreements.[1] To strict legalists who look for cast-iron principles and structures, labour relations in Belgium may appear chaotic. But in general the pragmatic approach seems to produce quite satisfactory results.

The structure of collective bargaining

Most representative trade union organisations

The most important trade union organisations are the Confederation of Christian Trade Unions (ACV-CSC) [2] and the Socialist-inclined Belgian General Federation of Labour (ABVV-FGTB).[3] Less important is the Federation of Liberal Unions of Belgium (ACLV-CGSLB).[4] No official statistics of trade union membership are available. The trade unions themselves estimate that out of the total employed population of 2,821,334 in 1967 (1,954,171 male workers and 867,163 female workers), about 1.8 million were organised (Christian trade unions, about 905,000; Socialist trade unions, about 771,000; Liberal trade unions, about 120,000).

Almost 65 per cent of Belgian workers thus belong to trade unions. In the most important sectors of industry, including metalworking, chemicals, cement, petroleum and mines, almost 90 per cent of the blue-collar workers are organised, but white-collar workers tend to be less organised (approximately 40 per cent), and managerial or supervisory personnel hardly at all, although they are legally entitled to join unions and to bargain collectively.

Belgian trade unions are not organised on a craft or occupational basis, and industrial unions predominate. The Socialist and Christian movements have unions specifically for white-collar workers, regardless of the industry they belong to.

Belgian labour relations cannot be understood unless one has grasped what is meant by " most representative trade union organisation ". Only three organisations, the Christian, the Socialist, and the Liberal, are recognised as " most representative " by the Government and the employers' associations.

The most representative organisations enjoy a legal and practical monopoly in representing the interests of the workers at the national,

---

[1] Although section 4 of the Act of 5 December 1968 respecting collective industrial agreements and joint committees provides that damages for breach of an agreement may be claimed from organisations if the agreement contains a clause to this effect. See ILO: *Legislative Series*, 1968—Bel. 1

[2] Algemeen Christelijk Vakverbond—Confédération des syndicats chrétiens.

[3] Algemeen Belgisch Vakverbond—Fédération générale du travail de Belgique.

[4] Algemene Centrale der Liberale Vakbonden—Centrale générale des syndicats libéraux de Belgique.

industrial and enterprise levels. They are the only ones to be represented on the official joint committees, composed of employers' and workers' representatives, in which a great deal of collective bargaining is done. The responsible bodies are: at the national inter-occupational or inter-industrial level, the National Labour Council; at the industrial level, the joint committee; and at the level of the enterprise, the works council and the safety and health committee.[1]

The most representative organisations, for practical purposes the Christian and the Socialist, have to be accepted and dealt with as the duly authorised bargaining spokesmen of the workers. They cannot be excluded at the level of the enterprise by means of, for example, an election among eligible employee voters designating a majority union as sole and exclusive bargaining agent or rejecting union representation altogether.

Institutionalised labour-management relations

1. AT THE LEVEL OF THE ENTERPRISE

At the level of the enterprise or establishment there may be three different representative bodies: these are the union delegation, the works council, and the safety and health committee.

The union delegation. In accordance with one of the points in the pact of social solidarity which, as already mentioned, was signed clandestinely by leaders of workers' organisations and representatives of employers' associations towards the end of the Second World War, a union delegation was to be formed in every enterprise with more than twenty employees. In June 1947 a national inter-industrial collective agreement was concluded between the social partners [2] setting forth the main principles concerning the establishment and the work of union delegations. Each joint committee was asked to adapt these principles to the specific situation of the industrial sector for which it was responsible. More than forty agreements were concluded in different industries and many more at the level of the enterprise or establishment.

The employer is not compelled to recognise a union delegation in his enterprise, but unions will press him to do so if they are strong enough. Union delegates are employees, sometimes elected by their fellow workers though more often appointed by regional trade union officers. Their number varies with the size of the enterprise, and there are generally separate delegations for manual and white-collar workers.

---

[1] In full, *comité de sécurité, d'hygiène et d'embellissement des lieux de travail* (committee for safety, health and the improvement of the appearance of the workplace).

[2] The Federation of Belgian Industries; the Association of Big Distribution Enterprises; the Federation of Insurance Companies; the Belgian General Federation of Labour; the Confederation of Christian Trade Unions; and the Federation of Liberal Unions of Belgium.

The union delegate handles grievances and supervises the application of collective agreements on the spot. If he relies more than in the past on the paid union official, he remains the essential link in the chain of workers' representation and the support of the union guarantees him almost complete security of employment.

The works council. Under the Act of 20 September 1948 for the organisation of the economic life of the country [1] and subsequent government regulations the employer is obliged to establish a works council in every enterprise regularly employing 150 or more persons, including managerial or supervisory personnel. The council is composed of a number of elected workers' representatives and an equal number of representatives of the employer chosen by the latter from among his supervisory personnel. All workers, whether members of a union or not, vote in the elections, with the exception of managerial or supervisory personnel.

The purpose of the works council is to smooth relations between the workers and the employer, who must provide it with regular information on financial and economic matters concerning the enterprise, including the productivity ratings of the various groups of workers. It is entitled to express its opinion on such matters as working conditions, productivity and the principles governing the engagement and dismissal of workers, though the power of decision rests entirely with the employer. It also participates in the drawing up of works rules, the fixing of holiday dates and the administration of welfare activities.

Finally a collective agreement, signed on 4 December 1970 between the employers' organisations and the trade unions, confers new rights upon the works councils; they will henceforth be entitled to be informed and consulted before any decision is taken which will affect employment either quantitatively or qualitatively. The agreement makes it mandatory for employers to draw up and implement contingency employment plans after consultation with the workers' representatives.

The safety and health committee. A safety and health committee must be established by the employer in all enterprises employing more than fifty persons. This committee, whose composition much resembles that of the works council, supervises the application of safety and health legislation and works out other measures for improving safety and health at the workplace. Once again, all power of decision regarding safety and health matters—as well as responsibility—rests with the employer.

* * *

---

[1] *Legislative Series*, 1948—Bel. 8. For sections amended up to 16 January 1967 see ibid., 1967—Bel. 1.

Collective bargaining

To function in a more than nominal way the union delegation, the works council and the safety and health committee require strong union support within the undertaking. In practice there is some overlapping between them, and if it is mainly the union delegation that provides machinery for collective bargaining the other two bodies may do so as well. In several industries, the chemical industry for example, many collective agreements are concluded within the enterprise and the negotiations are then usually carried out between the employer and the union delegation assisted by the paid officials of the unions concerned.

It may be said in conclusion that the system is flexible and permits a great deal of constructive freedom of manœuvre, depending on the state of relations between the two sides, the strength and aggressiveness of the unions and the employer's attitude.

2. BARGAINING STRUCTURES AT THE LEVEL OF THE INDUSTRY: THE JOINT COMMITTEES

Since their establishment on a pragmatic basis in the mining and metal industries soon after the First World War, the joint committees have played an important part in collective bargaining, the settlement of industrial disputes and the application of social legislation and labour standards.[1] They remained relatively few until after the great depression of the 1930s, when a large number were set up.

In the pact of social solidarity signed near the end of the Second World War the employers' and workers' representatives agreed explicitly to re-establish the joint committees at the industrial level, and today there are more than eighty covering almost all sectors of industry and almost all employers and workers.

Legal status was at last conferred on them by the Legislative Order of 9 June 1945 to issue rules for joint committees [2], which confirmed the *de facto* exercise of power by these institutions. The joint committees remained directly built on the employers' and workers' organisations, and the Act of 5 December 1968 mentioned earlier, which repeals the 1945 Legislative Order, does not alter this.

Joint committees are established by Royal Order at the request of or after consultation with the most representative employers' and workers' organisations. They generally cover a sector of industry throughout the whole country, but subcommittees with a more limited coverage may be set up to operate under the supervision of a national committee. A multi-product enterprise may come within the scope of more than one joint committee and separate committees are often set up for manual and white-collar workers.

---

[1] See A. Delpérée: " Joint committees in Belgium ", in *International Labour Review*, Vol. LXXXI, No. 3, Mar. 1960, pp. 185-204.
[2] *Legislative Series*, 1945—Bel. 5.

Members of joint committees are appointed by the King, on the nomination of the Minister of Employment and Labour, who first consults the most representative employers' and workers' organisations. An independent chairman and vice-chairman and two or more secretaries are also appointed.

The following are the chief functions of the joint committees:

(i) to conclude collective labour agreements;
(ii) to provide conciliation for the prevention or settlement of disputes between employers and workers;
(iii) to give advice on problems concerning the activity in question. This advice is offered to the Government, the National Labour Council, the Central Economic Council and other bodies.

The Ministry of Employment and Labour also plays an important part in connection with collective labour agreements. It provides administrative aid by making available officials and premises. It is the depositary for collective agreements and verifies the observance of certain requirements as regards their form. It also takes action if one of the parties asks for an agreement to be made generally binding by the Crown.

3. THE NATIONAL LABOUR COUNCIL

The National Labour Council has had many predecessors, of which it is of some interest to mention two. The Supreme Council of Labour, established in 1892 and composed of representatives of management and labour and of experts in various fields, was a consultative body that played a considerable part till 1918 in the preparation of labour legislation. After a reorganisation in 1935 it had more to do with social and economic policy. It should be remembered that direct negotiations between employers' and workers' organisations were becoming commoner between the two great wars and that their results included the national agreement of 1936 concerning wages, annual holidays, hours of work and trade union freedom. After the Second World War a General Joint Council was set up, its members being leaders of workers' organisations and representatives of employers. Although it was a non-statutory body, the chairman was the Minister of Employment and Labour and it prepared important measures for implementation by law or decree and concluded a number of national inter-industrial collective agreements.

In 1952 the General Joint Council gave way to the public body now known as the National Labour Council. The president of this Council is chosen for his economic and social knowledge and his independence of workers' and employers' organisations. The twenty-two members of the Council are divided equally between the most representative trade union organisations and the most representative organisations of employers in industry, agriculture, commerce and handicrafts. The president and members are appointed by Royal Decree.

The main function of the Council is to give advice to the legislature or the Executive on general social problems concerning employers and workers. It is frequently consulted by the Executive and has acquired great prestige. The Act of 5 December 1968 empowers the parties to the National Labour Council to conclude collective agreements within the Council. It does not affect the advisory functions of that body.

Collective agreements reached in the National Labour Council are of two kinds: those covering the entire country and different branches of activity and those covering a single branch where there is no joint committee or where an established joint committee does not function. It is rare, however, for the Council to concern itself with agreements of the second kind.

Collective agreements have already been concluded in the National Labour Council on the following subjects: the " non-competition clause " [1]; a guaranteed monthly income for manual workers and certain white-collar workers [2] in case of incapacity; the furnishing of additional information to the works council and its consultation by the employer on the general prospects of the undertaking and on questions of employment.[3] New agreements are being prepared on the furnishing of still further economic and financial information to the works council by the employer and on the union delegation. It may be said that the conclusion of important collective agreements is tending to make the National Labour Council a kind of social parliament enacting general rules that apply to the whole private sector of the economy.

Collective bargaining and the law

Over the years a number of legislative measures, by confirming existing practices, have had a major impact on collective bargaining.

First of all, as far as the workers are concerned, only the most representative trade union organisations have the right to conclude legally enforceable collective agreements. The criteria of representativity are of the same nature as those already applicable to the works council, the safety and health committee, the joint committee and the National Labour Council. The Act of 5 December 1968 provides the following criteria of representativity for workers' central organisations: (1) they must have an inter-occupational character; (2) they must be established at the national level; (3) they must be represented on the Central Economic Council and

---

[1] 12 February 1970. This clause imposes on the worker some restrictions concerning his employment by another employer in the same field of activity after his labour contract has been terminated.

[2] 9 June 1970.

[3] 4 December 1970.

the National Labour Council; (4) they must have at least 50,000 members. In accordance with these criteria, the most representative workers' central organisations are, as we have seen, the Confederation of Christian Trade Unions, the Belgian General Federation of Labour and the Federation of Liberal Unions of Belgium. Workers' occupational organisations affiliated to, or forming part of, these central organisations are also considered representative.

Both individual employers and employers' associations can be parties to a collective agreement. The criteria of representativity mentioned above for workers' organisations normally apply to employers' organisations as well, with the obvious exception of that requiring at least 50,000 members. However, an employers' organisation in any branch of activity that does not meet these criteria may be declared to be representative by the Crown, and in fact some representative employers' organisations are not affiliated to an inter-occupational organisation. Moreover, certain middle-class organisations are considered to be representative in accordance with the Act of 6 March 1964 (" to provide for the institutional structure of the middle classes ").[1] It should be remembered that only the most representative organisations have a seat on the National Labour Council and the joint committees in which national agreements are concluded.

National bargaining is also favoured by the existence of the centralised bargaining structures of the joint committees and the National Labour Council, as well as by the binding effect that may be given to agreements concluded in these bodies, according them precedence over regional and local agreements.

Until the promulgation of the 1968 Act Belgian law regulated only the binding effect of the individual normative rules of a collective agreement. The agreement affects all employers and workers operating within the territorial and industrial scope of the agreement, except where an employer agrees with a worker to include different terms in the individual contract of employment.

The normative part of the agreement, including both the collective and the individual rules, had a more binding effect through the intervention of the Government by Royal Decree. But only agreements concluded within the framework of the joint committees may be extended. Once the Royal Decree is published, every clause in the works rules or in the individual labour contract that is contrary to a stipulation of a collective agreement rendered binding is deemed to be null and void. Such an agreement

---

[1] At present the following organisations are represented on the Central Economic Council and the National Labour Council (in addition to the three trade union centres): the Federation of Belgian Industries; the Federation of Belgian Non-Industrial Undertakings; two agricultural organisations (the Belgische Boerenbond and the Fédération nationale des unions professionnelles agricoles); the middle-class organisations; and the Flemish Economic Association.

is then imperatively binding upon all employers and workers operating within the industrial, territorial, and personal scope of the joint committee.

The 1968 Act regulates collective agreements more fully. It also establishes more firmly the precedence of national agreements over regional and local agreements.[1]

Ten years of " social programming " [2]

During the past ten years collective bargaining in Belgium has been carried on in accordance with the principle known as " social programming ". The term was first used in 1960, and although its meaning was never clearly defined, it has been generally applied to collective agreements concluded since then. " Social programming " reflects the need for a special relationship between the social partners based on dialogue and concertation, instead of on conflict. The main idea is that by means of concertation taking account of objective criteria the workers' share in the growth of the national wealth will be " programmed " over a certain fixed period. Collective agreements resulting from this social concertation are called " social programming " agreements.

There is no doubt that social programming has favoured the centralisation of collective bargaining; nation-wide inter-industry agreements

---

[1] This follows clearly from a reading of section 51 of the 1968 Act, which establishes a hierarchical order of legal sources:

" The sources of the obligations arising out of the employment relation between employers and workers shall be as follows, in descending order of precedence:

(1) the law in its peremptory provisions;

(2) collective industrial agreements declared to be generally binding in the following order:
   (a) agreements concluded in the National Labour Council;
   (b) agreements concluded in a joint committee;
   (c) agreements concluded in a joint subcommittee;

(3) collective industrial agreements which have not been declared to be generally binding, where the employer is a signatory thereto or is affiliated to an organisation signatory to such agreement, in the following order:
   (a) agreements concluded in the National Labour Council;
   (b) agreements concluded in a joint committee;
   (c) agreements concluded in a joint subcommittee;
   (d) agreements concluded outside a joint body;

(4) an individual agreement in writing;

(5) a collective industrial agreement concluded in a joint body but not declared generally binding, where the employer, although not a signatory thereto or not affiliated to an organisation signatory thereto, is within the jurisdiction of the joint body in which the agreement was concluded;

(6) work rules;

(7) the suppletory provisions of the law;

(8) a verbal individual agreement;

(9) custom."

[2] See also R. Blanpain: " La négociation collective et l'autonomie des partenaires sociaux dans les Etats membres de la CEE ", in *Revue du travail* (Brussels, Ministère de l'emploi et du travail), June 1970, pp. 773-795.

have strongly affected the over-all climate of labour relations, while most industrial sectors are covered by national agreements. This central-isation has led to agreements that are of longer duration, for a fixed period, and of a more comprehensive and technical nature. In addition the character and tone of bargaining have undoubtedly been influenced, especially in the areas of union security and the safeguarding of social peace. Social programming at the national level does not automatically exclude bargaining within the enterprise, however, and bargaining con-tinues to take place at different levels.

Principles and implementation

The first social programming agreement was concluded at the national inter-industrial level on 11 May 1960. Trade unions and employ-ers' associations laid down three fundamental principles:

(1) A concerted policy of economic expansion must enable workers to share in a regularly improving standard of living.

(2) This must be realised through collective agreements, concluded at the national inter-industrial level, programming the share workers are to have in the growth of the national wealth over a fixed period. National agreements by industrial sector and agreements at the plant level may programme supplementary advantages. Programming takes into account government social security benefits financed through employers' contri-butions.

(3) Social programming is possible only if industrial peace is observed during the life of the collective agreement.

Originally social programming dealt with family allowances and annual holidays. Further agreements have extended its scope to cover the third week of annual holidays with double pay, manpower policy, hours of work, paid public holidays, pensions, the works council, time off for union delegates, a guaranteed income for blue-collar workers and the revision of collective agreements, among other matters.

Late in 1970 the Confederation of Christian Trade Unions for the first time organised a written referendum to find out what members want the Confederation to bargain about in national inter-industrial social programming.[1] More than 25,000 answers were obtained.

After negotiations lasting more than four months, a new two-year agreement covering the years 1971 and 1972 was finally concluded on 6 April 1971, providing, among other matters, for pensions, ten paid public holidays, trade union education, hours of work and travelling expenses.

---

[1] Among union claims put forward at the national inter-industrial level are: statutory pensions amounting to 75 per cent of wages; free transport; payment of wages for time lost during trade union education; four weeks of holidays with pay.

Since 1960 negotiation at the national level has also been brought under social programming. Many industrial sectors are covered by national agreements. In 1960 programming at the national level started in the steel and metalworking industries and social programming agreements were reached in the metalworking industry for various periods between August 1960 and December 1963. In 1964 no national agreement was concluded, for bargaining took place mainly at the plant level. But two-year national agreements were made for 1965-66, 1967-68 and 1969-70.

The national agreements in the steel and metalworking industries cover wages and benefits and hours of work, among other things. Except for the year 1964, essential bargaining since 1960 has been conducted at the national level. National agreements are supported by the majority of trade union leaders and generally favoured by the employers' federations, partly because negotiations at the national level greatly reduce the personal animosity in discussion and conflicts.[1]

There has been hardly any research in Belgium on the actual procedure of collective bargaining. The following account of collective bargaining procedure is the result of personal inquiries that are not at all exhaustive or definitive. Again the metalworking industry provides a good example.

Trade union claims in both the Socialist and the Christian trade unions for metalworkers are first formulated by regional councils of union delegates. The various claims assembled at the regional level are then transmitted to the national committee of union delegates and trade union officers [2], which formulates the definitive claims. Recently the Christian trade union organised a written referendum, asking its members to draw up a priority list of claims, and more than 34,000 members replied.[3]

Trade union officers of the two trade unions meet to work out a common programme, which is transmitted to the employers' association, Fabrimetal, and senior representatives of unions and management meet to work out a time-table for negotiating and concluding a collective agreement.

Bargaining on the employers' side is carried out by a committee composed of staff members of Fabrimetal. They are advised by a larger committee on which the different employer members are represented. The latter may reject a draft agreement reached by the negotiating committee.

---

[1] G. Spitaels: " Changes in union organisation and collective bargaining in Belgium ", in B. C. Roberts (ed.): *Industrial relations: contemporary issues* (London, Macmillan, 1968), p. 196.

[2] Composed of two-thirds union delegates and one-third trade union officers in the Socialist trade union and of union delegates alone in the Christian trade union. In both unions only the trade union delegates vote.

[3] About 25 per cent of the members concerned.

The actual negotiations take place in a number of mixed committees composed of workers' and employers' representatives. These committees submit a written report to a plenary meeting, composed of all the negotiators in the different mixed committees. This meeting is presided over by the president of the national joint committee of the metalworking industry. Union delegates do not attend the mixed committees or the plenary meeting. The actual bargaining is done by full-time trade union officers. The union delegates' committees, however, are kept informed by interim reports on the negotiations in the mixed committees and they can formulate desiderata or counter-proposals for the benefit of the negotiators. The president of the joint committee acts as mediator in order to settle disputes between unions and managements.

Once a draft agreement has been drawn up, the national committees of union delegates have to state whether they accept or reject it, after an informal consultation with other union delegates and members through the trade union press, meetings and the like. When a draft agreement has been accepted it must be formally concluded in the national joint committee.

Programming and bargaining at the level of the enterprise

Although programming at the national level may have resulted in a general reduction of bargaining activity at the plant level, collective agreements are still concluded in many establishments. National agreements fix minimum terms of employment which can be improved on. In some industries, for example the chemical industry, the real bargaining is done at the enterprise level, and bargaining at the national level is insignificant or non-existent.

Local bargaining at the plant level is carried out by the regional trade union officers, assisted by the union delegation. It should be remembered that in Belgium the works council also has its say in the establishment of works rules, the fixing of the dates of annual holidays and the administration of the welfare activities of the enterprise.

In many cases the national agreement only constitutes the first round of bargaining. There are two main reasons for this: firstly, as just noted, collective agreements provide only for minima, which can be improved on by further bargaining at lower levels; secondly, the relations between employers' associations and their members and between national confederations of trade unions and the unions allow almost complete freedom to negotiate at the plant level within the framework set by the more general agreements. In practice the minimum terms established by national agreements remain applicable only to marginal employers.

In some national agreements, however, that of the metal industries for example, the national trade unions have agreed that general claims such as higher wages or shorter hours of work for all employees in an enterprise or certain categories of them will not be made at the level of the enterprise.[1] This means that the national agreement is in principle definitive. But many companies that have been paying better wages or that want to attract labour may pay above the national scale. In fact, the employers' associations and national trade unions are not always able to control what happens at the grass roots.

Claims, sometimes approved by the rank and file, are mostly formulated by the union delegates in agreement with the paid union official. At the plant level too it is usual for a joint package of claims to be presented to the employer by both trade unions. Negotiations are conducted by the paid union officials, who are generally accompanied by a number of union delegates. There is an increasing tendency for the results of the negotiations to be submitted to the rank and file for approval, and not infrequently bargainers are sent back to the negotiating table.

Lately, especially during 1970, labour relations have been marked by a growing number of unofficial strikes at plant level.[2] From January to October 1970, about 170 strikes were recorded. A first analysis of sixty of them shows that thirty-three started as unofficial strikes, though these were quickly recognised by the trade unions. Most of them broke the industrial peace provisions laid down in national collective agreements.

Different reasons are put forward to explain this rise in the number of unofficial strikes: the fact that most national programming agreements on wage packets were concluded for a period of two years at the end of 1968, when economic forecasts underestimated economic growth and profits for the two years to come; the growing lack of contact between negotiators and rank and file; the complexity of trade union objectives; and the influence of outside groups such as students.[3]

The changing character of bargaining

Social programming has certainly influenced the character of collective bargaining, which was formerly a traditional trade union activity carried on in an atmosphere of struggle and strong opposition from the employers. Union demands were supported primarily by strikes or threats of strikes and trade union activity was for the most part concentrated at plant level. The chief aim of trade unions was to extend through national agreements the benefits that had been obtained in a few enterprises.

Negotiations are now less emotional and more technical, relying more heavily on statistical data and information and more frequent

---

[1] This of course does not exclude individual wage adjustments on grounds of age, seniority or personal merit, changes in a wage structure resulting from a change in the organisation of work or the reconsideration of special cases.

[2] In the first half of 1970 there were sixty-one industrial disputes involving 52,466 workers and the loss of 871,379 working days, compared with eighty-eight disputes for the whole of 1969 involving 24,691 workers and the loss of 161,999 working days.

[3] External groups were active in thirteen of the sixty strikes analysed.

218

contacts between the two sides in a climate of co-existence. Trade unions act as a common front. This means that they meet beforehand in order to fix common goals and claims and bargain on common proposals with the employers' associations.

Social programming has also resulted in collective agreements being signed for a fixed and in practice longer term than the customary indefinite agreements. The agreements in the metalworking, petroleum, textile and building industries run for two years.

Another significant element is the more comprehensive nature of the collective agreements, the tendency to group all items in a single agreement. Most of the conditions of employment negotiated in national collective bargaining in, for example, the metalworking, textiles, petroleum and building trades are contained in one document. The collective agreement for the metalworking industry for 1969 and 1970 covers wages, cost of living, holidays, hours of work, income security, union security and general terms. Separate agreements, which are concluded for an indefinite period, with the possibility of termination, cover: young workers, absence with pay (civic and other obligations), the closing down of enterprises and the employment of handicapped and retired workers.[1]

Bargaining for social peace and union security

One of the fundamental principles of social programming, as indicated above, is that it calls for the observance of industrial peace while the agreement is in force. Consequently, most agreements contain a " no-strike clause ", through which trade unions guarantee " social peace " during the life of the agreement. This peace obligation is generally accompanied by a clause providing benefits for union members only and gearing the payment of benefits to the faithful observance of the collective agreement and the maintenance of social peace during the life of the agreement.[2]

Unions have successfully argued that a situation in which those who do not pay union dues also benefit from trade union achievements secured thanks to the dues and contributions of members is no longer

---

[1] It should be borne in mind that many questions concerning individual labour relations as well as social security are the subject of detailed legislation. Acts dealing with individual labour contracts for manual and white-collar workers regulate the different forms of contract, damages for breach of contract, redundancy, the period of notice in the event of dismissal, illness, working conditions, public and annual holidays with pay, and the like. There are also very detailed social security regulations dealing with unemployment, sickness and health insurance, pensions, occupational diseases and family allowances. With so much social and labour legislation there is, of course, less room for collective bargaining: so while the statutory standards could generally be improved on, the range of collective bargaining topics in Belgium is not so wide as in systems with fewer legal provisions.

[2] It should be remembered that Belgian trade union organisations cannot be sued for damages if they fail to observe the obligations of a collective agreement (see the Introduction to this article).

acceptable, and that it is only fair that the employer should reimburse union dues in the form of a special benefit paid only to the union or its members.

The first important agreement reserving benefits for union members only was signed in the cement industry in 1954 as part of an effort by labour and management to establish a long-term budget of labour costs. It was only in the 1960s, however, that the practice was introduced on a large scale. It covered only 45,000 workers in 1961 but now extends to more than a million, although the demand by the unions was at first vigorously resisted by most employers. Special bonuses are now usual in the most important industrial sectors, including textiles, garments, coal mining, cement, petroleum, chemicals, tobacco, laundry and dry cleaning, gas and electricity, steel and metalworking, and food.

The benefit takes various forms, such as a productivity bonus, supplementary unemployment and pension benefits as well as a flat-rate payment. There is also great variety in the ways the money involved is administered and distributed to the members.[1] The amount of the benefit or dues reimbursed varies from 250 Belgian francs ($5) a year to 2,000 ($40) and may sometimes exceed the annual union dues.

Typical of this development, through which social programming, the financial stability of the trade unions and social peace have been combined in a fairly satisfactory way, are the various agreements concluded in the metalworking industry which, in return for social programming, offer the employers social peace during the life of the agreements. The agreements contain an explicit clause to the effect that so long as they are in force no claim of a general or collective nature shall be made either at the level of the enterprise or at the local, regional or national level and that no strike can be called and no lockout imposed before the elaborate procedure of conciliation agreed on has been exhausted. This means that trade unions accept the enormous task of safeguarding social peace during the period of the agreement. They thus undertake to prevent unofficial strikes and to get the workers back to work within a period of three days should one occur. If workers continue to strike, trade unions may not give their members strike pay. In return for safeguarding social peace, trade unions receive from the employer (via the employers' association, which collects the money), a financial subsidy of 0.6 per cent of gross wages.[2] If the trade unions support striking employees, the subsidy is diminished by $2.50 daily for each worker on strike. The reduction becomes $5 daily per striker if the strike continues for more than twenty days. An exception is made when a strike breaks out because an employer does not himself observe the collective agreement. An independent board

---

[1] It may be distributed through special funds administered jointly by the employers and unions or paid direct by the employers or the unions.

[2] In the latest collective agreement of 11 January 1971 it was decided to devote 0.5 per cent to benefits reserved for trade union members and 0.1 per cent to union security.

composed of impartial civil servants, chosen by the social partners themselves, will decide—in case of disagreement between labour and management—whether a collective agreement has been violated by the employer
or not. Similar provisions exist in steel, petroleum, textiles, and other
industrial sectors.

It should be pointed out that the building trade unions reject the
idea of benefits for union members only. However, the administrative
formalities and red tape in the Belgian construction industry are so
complicated that membership of unions is virtually a necessity for workers, as is the formation of associations for employers. The existence of
special financial allowances, paid through a special social fund provided
for by collective agreement, in case of lay-off on account of bad weather
is of itself sufficient to convince building workers of the merits of belonging to a union.

Bargaining for different categories of employees

Social programming has not, however, affected the existence of
separate bargaining for manual and white-collar workers. This is due
mainly to the clear-cut and far-reaching distinction between the two
groups; almost all important structures within the labour relations system
take this distinction into account.

There are different union delegations for manual and white-collar
workers, different joint committees[1], different chambers of the labour
courts and—most important of all—different trade unions. White-collar
workers are not organised by industry, and, as already stated, each
national trade union centre has its own inter-industrial white-collar union.

Senior personnel are not involved in collective bargaining. This is not
due to the absence of bargaining machinery, since the joint committees for
white-collar workers represent all white-collar employees. But an examination of collective agreements concluded in joint committees shows clearly
that the salaries and conditions of employment of supervisory personnel
above the level of foreman are generally omitted. The main reason is that
senior personnel do not join a representative trade union.[2]

Bargaining in certain state-controlled industries

Labour relations and employment conditions in the public sector are
marked by two features of the utmost importance: the cabinet system and
the centralised fixing of wages and conditions of work. Under the cabinet

---

[1] Some joint committees that are competent for both manual and white-collar workers
negotiate separate agreements.

[2] R. Blanpain: " Le rapprochement des statuts de l'ouvrier et de l'employé. Etude
juridique comparative ", in *Revue du travail*, op. cit., Sep.-Oct. 1968, pp. 1257-1322.

system the Executive, which negotiates, will find the legislature almost automatically willing to implement the decisions or agreements reached through the necessary budgetary measures and other legislative action. The centralised system of fixing wages and conditions of work means that the national Government is the main locus of decision-making and the trade unions concentrate their efforts at that level.

Although collective bargaining in the public sector is relatively new [1], there is a long tradition of bargaining in state-controlled industries such as the railways, the airlines, the trams and the buses, whose activities are closely linked with, or are comparable to, those of private industry and commerce. Important differences with the public service in general can be noted, especially in labour relations. In the railways, collective bargaining was legally established in 1926, and Sabena (the national airline), the trams and the buses have the bargaining structure prevailing in the private sector. In Sabena, the trams and the buses, the union delegations are active and works councils and joint committees have been established.

The most striking example is undoubtedly the railways. The Act of 23 July 1926 creating the National Corporation of Belgian Railways provides in section 13 for the establishment of a national joint committee, composed of ten representatives of the management and ten representatives of the most representative trade union organisations. This committee, whose decisions require a majority of two-thirds, examines all questions regarding individual labour contracts, industrial accidents, accidents on the way to and from work, occupational diseases, safety, health, and all other questions regarding the interests of the personnel. It also gives advice on all questions of a general nature that may be of indirect importance to the personnel and jointly administers the social activities established for the benefit of the personnel.

Section 13 of the 1926 Act provides further for the establishment of regional joint committees to examine suggestions by the employees concerning safety and health as well as productivity. If no satisfaction can be obtained, the suggestions are referred to the board of governors, which can decide on the matters at issue. The regional committees also give advice concerning the regulation of work.

---

[1] Social programming in the public sector came into full swing at the beginning of the 1960s. The national collective agreements, covering a period of nearly two years, are a typical example of centralised bargaining. They cover all public employees and are negotiated by the two big trade union organisations and the Government. In fact, the Government bargains with one partner, the unions forming a common front for this purpose. The agreements are formally signed by the Prime Minister and other members of the cabinet as well as by the representatives of the trade unions. The latest agreement (for 1970-71) was signed on 29 July 1969 and preceded the preparation of the budget. This type of collective bargaining, which covers a whole range of wages and conditions of work, is not generally governed by laws or regulations. The social programming agreements are not enforceable as such. They only engage the political responsibility of the Government to take the necessary legislative, executive and other steps to implement them.

Conclusions: an appraisal of social programming and the need for adjustment

Ten years of social programming, characterised by national fixed-term agreements of a more comprehensive nature, providing for social peace and union security, have undoubtedly proved to be advantageous on the whole to the workers concerned. Firstly, a number of items, such as cost-of-living clauses, hours of work and certain income-guarantee clauses can be dealt with reasonably only at the national level and within a general context. Secondly, programming has also ensured a continuous increase in wages during years of reduced prosperity. Thirdly, programming and agreements offer the possibility to less developed regions or sectors of industry of obtaining a more equitable share of the wage increases than could be obtained by ordinary bargaining at the regional or sectoral level. In other words it has provided opportunities for solidarity between stronger and weaker groups of workers.

According to some commentators, however, social programming leads to a growing gap between the workers and their unions; it almost completely eliminates trade union activity at the grass-roots level, with the consequence that the technicalities of the action carried out at the top are not always understood by the workers, and this in turn explains a number of unofficial strikes. Others feel that clauses (especially those concerning wages) fixed at the national level for a considerable period will be too rigid and not adapted to changing circumstances. Moreover, social programming at the national level implies the fixing of wages and conditions of work on the basis of the possibilities of the average or even the marginal enterprise. Hence, there is a fear that it will not be possible to adjust wages upwards where there are special circumstances, such as the introduction of various changes or improvements, that would justify such a rise.

It is generally felt that agreements should be reviewed when changes occur in the economic and social conditions that existed at the moment of their conclusion. The social partners agreed at the latest economic and social conference on 16 March 1970 that collective agreements could contain revision clauses for this purpose. In some sectors the duration of wage agreements has been reduced. In the metalworking industry the latest agreement (January 1971) contains a wage package covering one year, while the other points dealt with (hours of work, union security, etc.) fall within the traditional two-year pattern. The same is true of the petroleum industry. Trade unions also propose that bargaining on some matters should be possible at the level of the enterprise; this bargaining often occurs, in any case, even if the contrary is stipulated in the national agreement. Finally, there is a search for more creative ways of communication to bridge possible gaps between union leaders and members, such as the referendums organised by some trade unions.

Recent Collective Bargaining Trends in France

Yves DELAMOTTE [1]

COLLECTIVE BARGAINING has never bulked as large in France as it has in other countries, where it tends to be regarded as the trade unions' chief function, the most effective protection for the wage earners' interests and the best way of settling industrial disputes. Nor has it any past or tradition behind it since, leaving out of account brief bursts of activity (1919-20 and the Popular Front in 1936), it did not really take root until the passing of the Act of 11 February 1950 (still in force), which established its legal framework.[2]

A large number of collective agreements have been negotiated within this framework. They have secured new rights for wage earners and have undoubtedly been a force for social progress. As the purpose of this article is to explore the types of relationship underlying collective bargaining (between the employers and the trade unions and between both sides and the State), there is no need to make a detailed analysis of the terms of these agreements, except where it is necessary to illustrate the working of a relationship. In recent years, new trends have made themselves felt, especially since 1968, but their novelty can only be appreciated if some distinctive features of industrial relations during the previous period are borne in mind.

I. Some distinctive features of industrial relations in France

Some characteristics of French industrial relations, as revealed by practices and behaviour during the fifteen years or so following the passing of the 1950 Act, are briefly touched on below.

Bargaining: the setting and the participants

Under the 1950 Act collective agreements are normally concluded for a particular industry (or " occupation " to use the French termino-

---

[1] Director of the Institut des sciences sociales du travail, Paris (Sceaux).

[2] Industrial relations and collective bargaining in France have been the subject of several articles in the *International Labour Review*. See, *inter alia*, Paul Durand: " The evolution of industrial relations law in France since the Liberation ", Vol. LXXIV, No. 6, Dec. 1956, pp. 515-540; Jean de Givry: " Impressions of a mission to some French undertakings ", Vol. LXXV, No. 5, May 1957, pp. 412-436; " Works agreements of the 'Renault type' ", Vol. LXXXI, No. 3, Mar. 1960, pp. 205-232.

logy). As the Act gives no indication of what is meant by an " industry " or " occupation ", any separate economic or technical entity is entitled to negotiate its own agreement. For example, side by side with the national collective agreements for natural textiles and chemicals, there are others —nation-wide also—covering the manufacture of buttons and umbrellas.

In some industries the national agreement is supplemented by regional or local arrangements, for which provision was also made by the 1950 Act, e.g. natural textiles. In the metalworking industries, for reasons connected with the strategy pursued by the employers' organisation, the Union of Metal and Mining Industries (UIMM), the bargaining unit is invariably regional or local.

Multi-industry agreements, which are neither mentioned nor forbidden by the Act, were also negotiated during this period in order to establish national insurance schemes for old age (National Union of Wage Earners' Retirement Institutions (UNIRS), 1957) or unemployment (National Union for Employment in Industry and Commerce (UNEDIC), 1958), supplementing social security or public unemployment benefits. These schemes are run by joint committees and the technical justification for this type of agreement, which is not common and is in any case of a special character, is the need to have the largest possible membership.

Plant agreements, on the other hand, are explicitly allowed by the 1950 Act; they may also be concluded for a whole firm. Their function is to adapt the relevant industry-wide agreement to the special circumstances of a particular factory (or company) and they may therefore be much more favourable from the wage earners' standpoint. This was clearly demonstrated in 1955, when an agreement concluded by Renault (a nationalised concern, but subject to the 1950 Act) set off a wave of plant agreements on higher wages, holidays with pay, various forms of compensation and benefit, etc. These agreements were viewed by the employers' associations with some alarm.

In industry-wide bargaining the employers are generally represented by a single organisation, affiliated as a rule to the National Council of French Employers (CNPF).

The workers are represented by a number of organisations, each of which stands for a particular brand of trade unionism and is usually affiliated to a confederation which is recognised by the Government as being a representative body, viz. the General Confederation of Labour (CGT), the General Confederation of Labour-Force ouvrière (CGT-FO), the French Democratic Confederation of Labour (CFDT), the French Confederation of Christian Workers (CFTC), and the General Confederation of Executive Staffs (CGC).[1]

---

[1] The CGT was founded at the end of the last century and is the oldest of the trade union confederations. Its philosophy is based on the Marxist doctrine of the class war and some of its leaders are Communist party members. The CGT-FO came into being in 1947,

In the same occupation any employee can choose between several trade unions in accordance with his personal preferences and leanings, so that in the same workshop one operative may be a member of the CGT union for the industry, while another may belong to the CFDT union, etc. The law preserves the freedom of any worker to join or leave a trade union, by prohibiting such practices as the closed shop or the deduction of union dues by the employer, and French trade unionists do not represent the clear-cut, organised, stable group suggested by the English word " membership ".

The fiction is maintained that the trade union organisations taking part in the negotiations between them represent all the workers concerned, even though it may be obvious that some in fact have relatively few members. During the negotiations each organisation can hold out for any points to which it attaches special importance. Tactical ingenuity may take other forms as well, since refusal on the part of one or even two trade union federations to sign an agreement in no way affects its validity (at most it may affect its chances of being extended by the Minister of Labour [1]).

Under the 1950 Act an agreement applies to all firms affiliated to the employers' organisations signing it and to all workers employed in those firms, whether they are trade unionists or not. In other words, a trade union organisation which has taken part in the negotiations is at liberty to refuse to sign the agreement, even though it has been accepted by the other organisations, and to denounce its shortcomings instead. This has no practical consequences for the wage earners, since they all benefit by it if they happen to be working in a firm affiliated to the signatory employers' organisation.

Intermittent bargaining

In some countries where collective bargaining is the keystone of industrial relations, agreements are generally concluded for a specified period, e.g. two or three years. Trade union acceptance of a contract covering such a long period is usually secured by sliding-scale clauses or provision for progressive wage increases.

---

when the anti-Communists split off from the CGT. Although its philosophy is basically socialist, it pursues a policy of collective bargaining. The CFDT is the former French Confederation of Christian Workers, which in 1964 severed all denominational links and adopted a markedly anti-capitalist line. The CFTC consists of trade unionists who have retained the Christian connection. The CGC comprises executives, foremen, commercial travellers, salesmen, technicians, draughtsmen and senior clerical workers.

Gérard Adam calculates that the CGT has 1,500,000 members, the CFDT 600,000, the CGT-FO 500,000, the CGC 200,000 and the CFTC 100,000; the degree of unionisation would seem to be somewhere between 20 and 25 per cent. See G. Adam, F. Bon, J. Capdevielle, R. Mouriaux: *L'ouvrier français en 1970* (Paris, A. Colin, 1970), p. 16.

[1] The Minister of Labour may, by order, extend a collective agreement to all establishments in the geographical area and occupation covered by the agreement, thereby making it applicable to firms that do not belong to the signatory employers' organisations.

In France the usual practice has been to conclude national and regional agreements for one year in the first instance. However, since it would be a pity to allow such complex settlements (which the employers' and workers' organisations have sometimes taken years to hammer out) to last such a short time, there has generally been a tacit understanding to extend the agreements when they expire. Legal support for this practice came with the ruling of the 1950 Act that, unless otherwise stated, a fixed-term agreement would remain in operation after expiry in the same way as an agreement for an indefinite period. In other words, if the parties cannot agree on the changes to be made, the initial agreement remains in force.

Subsequently, of course, it can be denounced by the trade union organisations or a demand for renegotiation submitted. But denunciation does not usually stop it from being observed by the employers formerly subject to it. As for a demand for renegotiation, if it is made as and when prescribed by the collective agreement, the other party is certainly under some sort of obligation to negotiate; but there is no certainty that the negotiations will be successful and if they fail, the entire collective agreement, although disputed on individual points, will continue in force.

Thus, whatever the uncertainties and results of subsequent negotiations, the agreement itself goes on. It underpins the negotiations, which occur at irregular intervals and may prove abortive. Any account of collective bargaining in a given industry would show how sporadic bargaining sessions are and how often they fail. During these years, therefore, collective bargaining in France has been an erratic phenomenon; this is in sharp contrast to the situation in other countries where it is concentrated into short spells of intensive negotiations which are known in advance and recur at regular intervals. It is obvious, on the other hand, that there is a connection between the intermittent character of bargaining and the permanence of agreements—the knowledge that agreements will continue makes the failure of negotiations less serious.

Bargaining and action

When it is known with certainty that an agreement will expire at a given time, that new negotiations will be required for a better settlement and that every scrap of support will be needed to support the new claims, it is only natural that, for the trade union, the bargaining period is also the time when strike action may be most necessary. It forgoes the right to strike during the life of the agreement, knowing that thereafter it will be able to mobilise all the workers within the bargaining units. There is an obvious link between the fixed duration of the agreement, the renunciation of strike action for a given time and the union's relationship with the workers, whose sole representative it is.

These conditions clearly do not exist in France, as is clear from the above remarks on the practice of intermittent bargaining and the existence of a number of separate trade union organisations. The French unions in any case value the surprise element of direct action and have always been opposed to any statutory regulation of the right to strike. Collective agreements usually confine themselves to stating that in the event of dispute, the parties will meet to exchange views. But this conciliation procedure may not take place until the strike has broken out.

In other words, clauses of this type are quite different from the " labour peace " undertakings given by unions, whereby they forgo the right to strike during the life of the agreement over any of the questions covered by it. According to leading commentators on the 1950 Act [1], such an undertaking would be limited in scope because there would be nothing to stop the members of the signatory organisations from withdrawing their labour to secure a change in the agreement; it would merely prevent a union from taking active steps to instigate the strike, which would have to break out spontaneously.

But even though the only obligation on the union is to stand aside, this amounts to washing its hands of members' demands and refusing to back up their actions. For a trade union such an attitude is risky, especially when the workers have a choice between several unions. For some confederations especially, it would mean forgoing a feature of their strategy to which they attach cardinal importance, viz. the ability, while collective bargaining is going on for the industry as a whole, to take action in the factories in support of their members' claims, especially for higher wages.

This aspect of union strategy is due to the limited impact of industry-wide bargaining (which only lays down minimum pay scales) on the wages actually paid by large firms. Action at the plant level, which may take the form of general stoppages, rolling strikes, etc., brings pressure to bear on the nearest decision-making centres, namely the individual employers, who, under industry-wide agreements, are left a good deal of discretion in settling actual wage rates. These concessions at plant level can then be used to strengthen the union's case in the industry-wide bargaining.

Such, greatly over-simplified, are a few of the features that might have struck a foreign observer of French industrial relations during the fifteen years following the passing of the 1950 Act. As can be seen, the system was not restrictive; it safeguarded a number of freedoms and gave trade union organisations in particular a wide choice of tactical options.

The tense used in the previous paragraph might suggest that these practices are now a thing of the past. In fact, however, they are permitted by current legislation and, within the French system of industrial relations, continue to form a hard core where sociology and law overlap. Nevertheless, as will be seen, some of these practices have been challenged in recent years.

---

[1] See, in particular, Michel Despax: *Conventions collectives* (Volume VII of the *Traité de droit du travail* published under the direction of G. H. Camerlynck) (Paris, Dalloz, 1966), pp. 271-276.

II. Before May 1968: signs of change

In the years following the passing of the 1950 Act, a network of nation-wide collective agreements covering a large part of the economy was somewhat laboriously built up. By 1960 there were 189 national collective agreements in force. In the metalworking industry the collective agreement for the Paris area was negotiated in July 1954 and, by the end of 1955, seventy-four agreements had been negotiated covering more than 80 per cent of the labour force.[1]

The intermittent character of collective bargaining did not prevent gradual additions or improvements from being made to most of the key agreements on a variety of questions, e.g. holidays with pay, payment for public holidays, supplements to social security benefit in the event of sickness or maternity and redundancy compensation. The authorities played a far from negligible part in these developments, labour inspectors, for example, often acting as chairmen of the committees in which collective agreements were worked out and thereby playing the role of conciliators.

A second period opened in 1960 and culminated in the stabilisation plan introduced by the Government in 1964; during these years bargaining slackened and in some industries even came to a halt. The employers' organisations attributed this to the pressures brought to bear on them by the Government, either directly (as early as 1960 the Prime Minister at the time urged the National Employers' Council not to grant wage increases exceeding 4 per cent) or indirectly. Whatever the reason, trade union demands to reopen negotiations had no effect, which proved that the employers' organisations could refuse to bargain, both in law and in fact. One of the results of this slackening was the growing gap between minimum wage rates (laid down in the schedules attached to collective agreements) and actual rates.

During a third period, beginning around 1965, collective bargaining was resumed to some extent. The workers made a number of social gains in some of the major agreements, e.g. payment of wages by the employer within certain limits for days lost through sickness, especially in the Paris metalworking industries and the chemical industry. More regular negotiations over wage scales were resumed with the aim of progressively closing the gap between negotiated and actual wage rates. However, in the case of the agreement for the Paris metalworking industries, the wage schedules were not signed by the CGT and the CFDT. It was during this third period that certain new trends emerged. Since they foreshadowed subsequent developments, they deserve some mention: first, collective bargaining was extended to employment questions and it was discovered

---

[1] Olivier Drague: *Le statut de l'ouvrier métallurgiste* (Paris, Librairies techniques, 1966) p. 90.

that they lent themselves to novel forms of treatment; second, government encouragement to negotiate became more explicit and pressing; third, the trade union organisations sought to widen the scope of negotiations and to bargain with the National Employers' Council over a number of questions on a multi-industry basis.

Employment questions and the social agreement for the Lorraine iron and steel industry (1967)

Because of the seriousness of the employment problems created by industrial conversions, mergers and modernisation, a National Employment Fund was set up in 1963 under the Ministry of Labour to provide various forms of assistance to workers affected by industrial change.

Collective agreements at first did not go very far in dealing with this question, and confined themselves in the main to providing for redundancy compensation—often, however, for salaried staff only. The first agreement of any significance was concluded for the sugar industry in September 1966, but it can now be seen, looking back, that it was the " social agreement " for the Lorraine iron and steel industry, signed in July 1967, that has served as a model for the settlement of employment questions by collective bargaining. This warrants some description of its contents and also an attempt to define the type of relationship it created among the firms it covered and between these firms and the State.

The preamble lays down the principle that, generally speaking, the employment problems facing the iron and steel industry in Eastern France should largely be solved through natural wastage, which amounts to a request to the iron and steel firms to improve their employment forecasting. Since it is acknowledged that all employment problems cannot be solved in this way, the agreement makes provision for other steps to be taken by managements, e.g. early retirement of workers over the age of 60, transfers within the same plant, transfers between firms by mutual agreement and with the consent of the workers concerned and, if the worst comes to the worst, termination of the employment relationship with a job being found elsewhere. The order in which these measures should be taken is not laid down in as many words, but is plainly suggested by the order in which they are listed in the agreement. Special importance is attached to keeping the works councils informed, and dismissals involving more than 100 wage earners must be notified to them six months beforehand (three months if due to economic reasons and not to reorganisation).

As regards the operation of these measures, the agreement does not merely define the obligations of each firm towards its employees—it also defines its obligations towards the employees of other firms. If, for example, a firm after discharging its workers over 60 years of age then has to dismiss a number of workers under that age limit, it is agreed that, should there be any difficulty in finding alternative employment for them, neighbouring steel works or—if necessary—the other plants covered by the agreement, will dismiss their workers over 60 years of age in order to create the necessary vacancies. In the event of such an agreed transfer between two firms, a worker normally keeps his grade and seniority and if not, he receives appropriate compensation. Of course, as Jean-Daniel Reynaud points out [1], each firm is at liberty to carry out the agreement in its own way. Even so, these rules are designed to create a link between the firms covered by the agreement and to make each firm accept a concept of the employment market as wide as the bargaining unit itself. A joint committee was set up under the agreement to keep a check on employment trends in the Lorraine iron and steel industry. In short, the social agreement is a constructive experiment in collective bargaining for a particular industry at the regional level. This is perhaps not unconnected with the fact that the bargaining unit consists of a handful of large firms, which constitute a fairly homogeneous group.

The dovetailing of the measures provided for in the social agreement into the schemes operated by the State constitutes another new feature. Although the Government gave initial encouragement, it did not interfere in the negotiations once they had begun. Nevertheless, the clauses of the agreement show that the Government was never far from the negotiators' minds, since they naturally made the most of all the forms of aid available, not only from international bodies such as the European Coal and Steel Community, but also from such national agencies as the National Employment Fund (for redundancy compensation, special early retirement allowances, etc.) and agreement was reached as to the way these facilities should be used. In other words, the Government not only gave its encouragement or acted as a conciliator, but was involved as a source of finance. Without actively taking part in the negotiations, it was not entirely absent either. The negotiators could not do without it and at a given point in the bargaining, they had to make sure that the proposed spending of publicly controlled funds was in fact approved by the Government. Thus the negotiations were direct in that there were no third parties, but the Government nevertheless stood in the background.

Government encouragement to negotiate and the trade union demand for multi-industry bargaining

The two other novel features of the years preceding 1968 are closely linked and cannot be examined separately.

Government encouragement to negotiate became direct and explicit after ordinances were issued in July 1967 with the aim of promoting an active employment policy, with ample funds to back it up. On 3 August

---

[1] Jean-Daniel Reynaud: " La convention sociale de la sidérurgie lorraine ", in *Droit social* (Paris) No. 4, Apr. 1969, pp. 219-227.

1967 the Prime Minister sent a letter to the leaders of the employers' confederations and the national representative trade union confederations. Referring to the recent ordinances, he expressed the Government's hope that the general principles laid down therein would be supplemented by collective agreements containing additional safeguards, and he urged the employers' and workers' organisations to carry out a joint examination of five questions, viz. the appointment of joint employment committees (like those already in existence in iron and steel and in the metal-working industry in certain areas); higher benefits for the unemployed; adequate notice of redundancies; the procedure to be followed in the event of mergers or concentrations; and compensation for partial unemployment.

Although the invitation was sent to the confederations, it did not necessarily mean that the negotiations should be held on a multi-industry or national basis. The National Employers' Council, which gave a cool reception to what it regarded as interference in contractual relationships, refused to negotiate except on the traditional industry-wide basis. For their part, the trade union organisations, especially the CGT and the CFDT, felt that in view of the disappointing results of industry-wide bargaining, the encounter should take place at the top, i.e. the level from which mass movements invoking working class unity could be set in motion. Disagreement on this point lasted until May 1968.[1] The reader will recall how a wave of unrest which began among French students in that month quickly spread to industry and by 20 May, between 8 and 10 million workers were on strike.

When, at the end of the month, the leaders of the trade union confederations held a meeting with the representatives of the National Employers' Council and the Association of Small and Medium Enterprises at the Ministry of Social Affairs (in the rue de Grenelle) in the presence of the Prime Minister, Mr. Pompidou, and the Minister of Social Affairs, they felt that at long last they had secured the inter-industry bargaining they had been demanding. Indeed the Grenelle " statement " (statement and not agreement because it was not signed by the trade union organisations) provided *inter alia* that the National Employers' Council and the trade union federations would meet to discuss various aspects of employment and vocational training.

III. Collective bargaining after " Grenelle " (May 1968 to November 1970)

Even leaving out of account the spate of agreements which marked the return to normal after the events of May 1968, the dominant impres-

---

[1] Although a multi-industry agreement on compensation for partial unemployment was signed in January 1968.

sion of the period from then until November 1970 is one of a remarkable expansion in collective bargaining:

(1) It was extended to cover new subjects such as hours of work, salaried status and profit-sharing [1], and dealt with various aspects of employment and vocational training on a much wider scale than the social agreement for the Lorraine iron and steel industry. Each question was the subject of special negotiations, resulting in a series of specific, quite distinct agreements. The subject of an agreement came to the fore and was used to describe it, e.g. employment, training and salaried status agreements.

(2) It also took place at levels other than that traditionally used for collective bargaining, i.e. the industry. The employment agreement (February 1969) and the vocational training agreement (July 1970) are nation-wide instruments negotiated by the National Employers' Council and the five nationally representative trade union organisations. They cover between 8 and 9 million wage earners. The question of salaried status also led to meetings at the top (e.g. the joint declaration of April 1970 and the recommendation on maternity benefits issued in July 1970). Simultaneously, profit-sharing agreements at the level of the undertaking became far more common and it seems likely that plant-level agreements were negotiated more frequently. Everything suggests therefore that the mere fact of tackling a question separately and on its own made it possible to break out of the traditional framework (industry-wide bargaining) and to decide the question of coverage on its merits.

(3) It was introduced in sectors where it was virtually unknown (civil service and nationalised enterprises set up by statute and therefore—unlike Renault—excluded from the 1950 Act).

Some of these developments were directly due to government initiative (e.g. the ordinance on profit-sharing dated July 1967 and Mr. Pompidou's letter of 3 August 1967) or to trade union demands dating back to before 1968 (e.g. for multi-industry bargaining). The events of May and June 1968 and the " Grenelle " meetings broke the deadlock and started things moving. Jean-Daniel Reynaud has indeed noted the paradox of this " half-successful revolution which caused general consternation, yet had no effect on the questions at issue, or, in certain cases, on negotia-

---

[1] Salaried status as defined by the Government and implemented in the agreements, is designed to give wage earners the same social benefits as monthly-paid employees. As regards profit-sharing, the ordinance of 17 August 1967 making it compulsory to give wage earners a share in the benefits of industrial expansion, provides for special participation funds to be established on their behalf calculated as a proportion of the net profit for tax purposes. These funds can be administered in a number of ways, e.g. through the distribution of shares, deferred saving, etc., the method employed in each case being normally agreed upon between the management and workers' representatives. The ordinance applies to all establishments with over 100 wage earners.

tions that had already begun ".[1] However, these observations do not apply to some of the latest developments—the agreements on salaried status and those for the nationalised industries.

Of course, efforts had already been made to reduce the difference in status between office staff and manual workers in a number of firms and even in certain industries, but the question of salaried status rarely figured among trade union claims before 1968. It is likely that the process would have been slower if the Government, acting on Mr. Pompidou's statement, had not helped to crystallise the interest of both sides of industry in this objective as a result of which they were more willing to respond to the Government's invitation to negotiate. By September 1970 agreements had been signed in metalworking, building and civil engineering, chemicals and coal mining, covering a total of between 4 and 5 million workers. Even though the agreements for the nationalised industries ultimately dated back to trade union proposals made in 1963, they nevertheless marked a conscious departure from the former procedure, known as the " Toutée procedure ", of which more will be said below.

In other words, after " Grenelle " there was a good deal more collective bargaining in France. The social crisis of May 1968 and trade union insistence both had a good deal to do with it, but there was also a change in the employers' attitude, encouraged by the emergence of new men and a government policy of introducing collective bargaining into the nationalised industries (and even the civil service), which in turn fostered it in the private sector as well.

If our purpose were to draw up a social balance sheet, it would mean examining the contents of all these agreements. But if the aim is rather to detect the forces at work in the collective bargaining process, two new developments attract attention, since they are at variance with previous practice. These are the growth of nation-wide and multi-industry bargaining, and the introduction of bargaining in the main nationalised industries. On the other hand, these recent trends should not be allowed to overshadow developments at the industry level, where collective bargaining has traditionally taken place, and in the private sector.

IV. Multi-industry agreements and redistribution of roles between the Government and the " social partners " (1969-70)

The multi-industry bargaining provided for in the Grenelle statement led to two nation-wide agreements, the first covering job security (February 1969) and the second, vocational training (July 1970).

There is no need to dwell on the job security agreement here since it adopts the same approach as the social agreement for the Lorraine

---

[1] Jean-Daniel Reynaud: *Les événements de mai et juin 1968 et le système français de relations professionelles* (mimeographed), p. 7.

iron and steel industry and therefore requires no special comment.[1] Like that agreement it provides for joint employment committees to be set up, defines the procedure to be followed and the period of warning to be given to works councils when redundancies occur, and lays down degressive scales of temporary compensation for workers who are downgraded.

It marks an improvement over the Lorraine agreement in that it defines in greater detail the procedure to be followed in order to soften the impact of company mergers and reorganisations on the labour force; in addition it emphasises the need to include forecasts of employment consequences in the planning of operations of this kind. It does not go as far as the Lorraine agreement as regards the warning period or the rates of degressive compensation, thereby reflecting the limitations of a multi-industry agreement. Similarly, the arrangements to co-ordinate the efforts of the companies covered by the regional agreement are inevitably missing from the multi-industry agreement.

Like the Lorraine agreement, this scheme provides for very extensive use of the available state compensation and training facilities. Significantly, the negotiators suspended their talks at one stage to hold a meeting with the Minister of Social Affairs, at which they asked for clarifications about the working of the Vocational Training Benefits Act of 30 December 1968, which had just been passed, and the conditions in which the National Employment Fund would intervene. As a result of the Minister's statement, the negotiations, which at one time seemed to be deadlocked, were resumed and when the agreement was finally signed, the statement was included in an appendix. This showed plainly enough that the bargaining process also had the effect of clarifying the Government's own intentions and commitments.

But this connection was already obvious in the case of the Lorraine agreement and therefore had nothing to do with the fact that bargaining was on a national and multi-industry basis. On the other hand, the relationship between the " social partners " and the Government in the conclusion of the vocational training agreement suggests a new form of bargaining at that level.

The national multi-industry agreement on training and further training (July 1970)

Title I of the agreement, which comprises a preamble and two parts, deals with the *initial training* of young workers. Where general and theoretical training are concerned, the agreement is designed to facilitate admission to existing courses (attendance, now required by law up to the age of 17, will henceforth continue until completion of the 18th year;

---

[1] The reader wishing to find out more about this agreement and the way it was negotiated should refer to an article published in *Droit social* (Paris), Sep.-Oct. 1969.

training will take up 320 hours a year as against 200; and the trainees will be able to attend during working hours without loss of pay, whereas previously most of the courses were held on Saturdays). As regards vocational training itself, which lasts for anything from one to three years and leads to a recognised qualification, the agreement lays down the principle that whenever the training is provided by employers or employers' associations (and not in state training colleges) it is preferable to set up joint centres " operated by a group or association of employers ". Whether the centres are run by individual employers or joint bodies, workers' representatives will sit on their boards of management, the responsibilities of which are defined. The agreement leaves it to industry-wide collective agreements to prescribe scales of pay for apprentices, while setting minimum standards which must be observed.

Title II contains clauses dealing with *further training*. It draws a distinction between wage earners affected by redundancy and those still in employment.

A worker who is declared redundant can, if he wishes to take a course of training, apply for leave of absence during the period following receipt of warning (given in accordance with the employment agreement of 10 February 1969) and during his actual period of notice.[1] His wage is paid in full until the period of notice expires. If his course of training is longer than this, he becomes entitled to an allowance at the same rate as his former earnings, payable by the joint unemployment insurance agency (the National Union for Employment in Industry and Commerce, or UNEDIC). The training period may not exceed one year.

For workers still in employment, the principle is laid down that each is *entitled* to apply for leave of absence to take a full- or part-time course of training.

The leave of absence allowed is equal to the length of the period of training, subject to a maximum of one year in the case of a full-time course. The agreement lays down the conditions that must be fulfilled by applicants (at least two years' service with the employer and more than five years to go before the normal age of retirement), the proportion of workers who can be absent at any given time on courses of this kind (2 per cent), how a scale of priority is to be established among applicants and the minimum interval between two courses of training taken by the same individual. Finally, the agreement regulates the payment of trainees, which depends on whether the course is run by the firm (in which case the wage is paid in full) or is freely chosen by the employee. In the latter case, it is only when the course is held by a body approved by the joint

---

[1] The warning period required under the employment agreement varies with the cause and extent of the redundancy. For example, if the redundancy is due to a closure and affects more than 300 individuals, three months' warning must be given. Under an ordinance issued in 1967, a further two months' notice must be given to any worker with two years' service or more.

employment committee covering the employee's firm that an allowance is payable, viz. full pay for four weeks, with such reductions thereafter as the joint employment committee may decide.

This analysis, though brief, shows how the negotiators (some of whom had represented their confederations during the earlier bargaining over job security) set out to make use of official schemes for the provision and encouragement of vocational training. The approach is the same as that described earlier in connection with the Lorraine agreement and the national agreement on job security. Just as these two agreements would not have been possible without the passing of the 1963 Act setting up the National Employment Fund, so the 1970 agreement is the outcome of the Vocational Training Act of 3 December 1966 and the Vocational Training Allowance Act of 31 December 1968. Most of the training courses covered by the agreement will be given in centres that have concluded a convention with the Government under the 1966 Act and receive financial aid as a result. Allowances payable to trainees under the agreement take account of the forms of official aid available under the 1968 Act.

Even more novel is the fact that the agreement lays down the conditions in which workers still in employment can obtain leave of absence to take a course of training, i.e. the agreement not only takes advantage of the facilities provided by law, but actually regulates the operation of the Act of 3 December 1966, which introduced the principle of entitlement to leave but stated that detailed regulations would be issued in a subsequent decree. This was in fact never published and the agreement serves in its stead. What could be more natural [1] than that arrangements making allowance simultaneously for employees' wishes and the operating demands of industry should be worked out jointly by representatives of wage earners and managements? Indeed, the initiative was encouraged by the Government.

But the text of the agreement makes it clear that the new role of the employers' and workers' organisations is a dynamic one and that their interest in giving effect to the law extends also to its content. The first clause expresses the hope of the signatories that the legislation on vocational training courses for young workers will be amended, and suggests specific changes. On the subject of finance for vocational training, the parties declare themselves to be " fully aware that, taken in conjunction, the arrangements embodied in this agreement raise the general problem of finance, which cannot be solved by the parties alone but will involve consultation with the public authorities ". In other words, they are advocating that the whole system of financing vocational training should be recast.

---

[1] It will be noted that in a related field, the Act of 23 July 1957 allowing workers to take unpaid leave to take trade union training courses was in fact followed up by an order of the Minister of Labour prescribing the maximum number that could be released according to the size of the firm.

These suggestions arose naturally out of the construction placed by the architects of this major agreement on the nature of their role, namely to question the present system of vocational training, which does not meet the needs of either industry or individuals, and to outline a comprehensive policy. Such an ambitious undertaking could not be carried out if the public authorities themselves were spared from criticism and if no suggestions could be made about their sphere of responsibility. But it seems likely that the suggestions were in fact welcomed by the Government and in no way surprised it. After all, the legislation in need of reform dates back to 1919, and the Government's own attempt to overhaul the system of financing vocational training had run into difficulties. The negotiators themselves helped to break the deadlock, and collective bargaining was found to be a means of achieving a consensus that had eluded the Government's own proposals.

Salaried status: joint recommendation on the reform of maternity insurance

The negotiations on the introduction of salaried status call for the same comments. They are being held on the traditional industry-wide basis, but this does not exclude national and multi-industry meetings.

The first of these gave rise to a joint statement (20 April 1970) in which it was agreed that " details of the introduction of salaried status will be settled at the industry level ". It was also agreed to hold another meeting in an effort to find an answer to the problem of maternity leave. The point is that in industries employing a high proportion of women, it would be an expensive proposition to grant full pay during maternity leave to all female staff as is already done in the case of office staff. This problem had to be tackled first if salaried status was to be extended as rapidly in these industries as in the others.

The meetings held for this purpose led to the signature of an agreed protocol (2 July 1970), which was unusual in that it was not operative, since it merely spelt out the changes that should be made in the maternity insurance scheme, namely a maternity allowance for manual workers at the rate of 90 per cent of the assessable wage instead of 50 per cent and the levying for this purpose of a maximum over-all contribution at the rate of 0.20 per cent of assessable wages. Of course, this implied that the employers agreed to accept the proposed increase in contributions. In December 1970 the Government announced, to nobody's surprise, that it had accepted the proposed amendment and would make appropriate changes in the law; this was done in a decree issued in January 1971.

A new type of relationship between the " social partners " and the State has thus resulted from these inter-industry agreements. The traditional roles are redistributed in the sense that the State recognises that employers' and workers' organisations, being directly affected by certain legislation, are well fitted to decide how it should operate and that when changes are desirable they can be introduced more readily if they are actively sought by the parties concerned than if they are imposed from above.

What has been established under the name of " concerted action " (*concertation*, in French) amounts, in fact, to a form of participation in the State's political authority. This need be no cause for surprise when it is remembered that the organisations taking part represent from 8 to 9 million wage earners, as well as the managements employing them, and are therefore more representative than any trade union or political party on its own. The agreement, which was facilitated by the fact that part of the cost would be borne by the Government, is a striking acknowledgement of their representative character and greatly strengthens their hand in dealing with the public authorities.

V. " Progress agreements " and the return to normal in industrial relations (1969-70)

Whereas the reallocation of roles just mentioned seems mainly to have been an unforeseen by-product of the enlarged scale of collective bargaining, " progress agreements " are the outcome of a conscious political determination to promote collective bargaining in the nationalised industries and to define the rules governing relations between the signatories.

Collective bargaining was not completely unknown in the public sector. In 1965 a procedure (known as the " Toutée " procedure from the name of the member of the Conseil d'État who had advocated it in a report requested by the Government) was introduced in four of the largest industries—electricity and gas, railways, coal mining, and the Paris transport authority.

The " Toutée " procedure involved three stages. At the end of each year the total wage bill for the year was assessed; next, the Government decided on the amount by which this wage bill could be increased during the coming year; finally, the ways in which this increment was to be distributed (by an increase in the basic wage, bonuses of various kinds, or additional payments to certain grades) were selected. The trade union organisations took part in the assessment, were consulted before the Government made its decision, and negotiated with the managements over the distribution. But after some time, they came to the conclusion that consultation had no practical effect and that they were bargaining with managements whose hands were tied since the final decisions were taken elsewhere by the appropriate government departments. As a result, their interest in the procedure dwindled and, with the Grenelle statement, vanished altogether. Nevertheless, the need to make the assessment did help the participants to clarify a hitherto very confused issue, to agree on certain concepts (such as the definition of the total wage bill) and to work out a method of analysing data for the purpose of the wage policy. In these respects, there had been an unqualified gain.

The Government of Mr. Chaban-Delmas, who was appointed Prime Minister in June 1969, decided to make a clean break with this procedure and to grant greater autonomy to the nationalised industries. For example, it gave up its claim to decide the permissible increase in the wage bill for each of these industries every year. In submitting his programme to the National Assembly in September 1969, Mr. Chaban-Delmas declared:

> New wage-fixing procedures will be worked out for the nationalised industries in conjunction with the trade union organisations and will be introduced in 1970. They will be designed to give the workers in the public sector a share in the benefits of national expansion and in the progress of their own industries. In this way, progress agreements covering periods of several years will be negotiated for each industry, covering among other things improvements in working conditions and ways and means of ensuring that service to the public remains efficient and reliable.

On the latter point, the Prime Minister announced the Government's decision to regulate the right to strike in the nationalised industries. The relevant legislation at the time consisted mainly of an Act dated 31 July 1963, under which five clear days' notice must be given of any strike. This Act, which applied only to public services, had in any case been ignored in May 1968.

The social agreement for the electricity and gas industries

The first major agreement reflecting this shift in government policy was concluded for the electricity and gas industries (120,000 wage earners) on 10 December 1969. This " social agreement " is divided into two complementary parts: wage trends and wage fixing, and the regulation of industrial relations.

As regards wages, the rate of increase r between year $n-1$ and year n in the total wage bill is calculated by the formula:

$$r = 1 + 0.5\,P_n + 0.15(V_n - 2.5\,X_n)$$

The first two terms of the formula $(1 + 0.5\,P_n)$ define the employees' share in the expansion of national output, P_n being the percentage rate of increase in the gross domestic production [1] in terms of value between year $n-1$ and year n. The third term corresponds to more specific criteria

---

[1] French national accounts are based on gross domestic production (*production intérieure brute*), which has no counterpart in the United Nations system of national accounting. Gross domestic production is the sum of the value added in each branch of productive activity in France plus import duties and levies (minus subsidies).

and relates the wage bill directly to the performance of the industry and inversely to the size of the labour force. V_n is the percentage rate of increase in the volume of sales of electricity and gas, and X_n is the percentage rate of increase in the total number of wage index points for the labour force as a whole.

For the year 1969 the formula would have resulted in an increase over 1968 as follows:

$$r_{1969} = 1+\frac{15.9}{2}+0.15\,(10.2-2.5\times1.4) = 8.95+1.02 = 9.97\text{ per cent.}$$

Thus, the share of the increase due to specific factors seems bound to be fairly small. The reference to the value of the gross domestic production means that if the latter rises mainly because of the growth in output, wages can also be increased even if the rise in prices is small, i.e. in such a case, the formula is more favourable to the labour force than the sliding scale. If, on the other hand, the rise in the value of gross domestic production is due mainly to price increases, the system is less favourable than the sliding scale whenever the rise exceeds 2 per cent. Should this happen, the unions would probably be compelled to denounce the agreement, which therefore is not open to the charge—levelled against the sliding scale—of fuelling inflation. As an example of the way the system works, the increase in the value of gross domestic production between 1969 and 1970 was estimated at the beginning of 1970 to be 9 per cent, which, allowing for the specific factors, should under the formula entail an increase in the total wage bill of 6.3 per cent. During the year the estimates of the value of gross domestic production were adjusted upwards and the permissible increase in the wage bill therefore went up to 7.9 per cent in November 1970. Over the same period, i.e. from January 1970 to September 1970, the price index went up by 4.3 per cent.

The agreement lays down when and how a joint committee is to calculate the increase in the total wage bill and then share it out. This distribution must first and foremost be made in such a way as to maintain the purchasing power of all employees. Next, " it must result in higher purchasing power for all, with more index points being allocated to the lowest-paid grades ". In other words, the agreement does more than simply define a formula and a procedure; it lays down what amounts to a wages policy. Under this policy, the basic wage—index figure 100—was increased by rather more than the rise in prices in 1970 (which enabled all employees to do a little more than maintain their purchasing power), while the remainder was distributed in such a way that for the lowest grades the rate of increase in purchasing power was twice as great as for the highest grades. For the former, the over-all increase in purchasing power in 1970 was 8.3 per cent, whereas for the latter it was 6.7 per cent. All in all, these arrangements clearly show that the management has regained the ability to bargain and agree with the trade union organisations in formulating a wages policy.

The second part of the agreement consists of clauses dealing with relations between management and unions. The agreement is for a specified period, being concluded for two years with effect from 1 January 1970. " As long as it has not been denounced, it implies that there is no dispute with respect to its contents." This means that disputes can occur on points other than wages while the agreement is in force, but that disputes over wages are ruled out unless the agreement is denounced. One clause stipulates that the signatory unions (but not the management) are entitled to terminate the agreement on three months' notice, but that this period must be used " to settle without a dispute [1], and in conjunction with the general management, the issue which led to the termination ". Thus, despite the limited duration of the agreement, there is nothing to stop it being ended at any time, provided the period of notice is observed; nor, as G. Lyon-Caen points out [2], does it mean that there will not be a dispute (occurring perhaps over a point covered by the agreement) if on the expiry of this period of notice the issue has not been settled. It follows, as this author emphasises, that there is no real restriction on the right to strike, but simply a requirement to give notice and follow a conciliation procedure before taking action. This is not, however, the first time in a nationalised industry that the unions have agreed to observe a specified procedure and hold discussions before striking. The point will be reverted to later on, since it was partly because it considered that the proposed system would curtail its freedom to strike at the most suitable moment that the CGT refused to sign the agreement.

Subsequent agreements: guaranteed increases in purchasing power

During 1970 agreements were also negotiated in the other nationalised industries and undertakings—in the railways (23 February), the coal mines (2 March), and the Paris transport authority (13 October).

Unlike the agreement for the electricity and gas industries, these only covered the year 1970 and did not include " labour peace " clauses.[3] Nor did they contain any formula for expanding the total wage bill from one year to the next. Instead, they provided for a guaranteed increase in purchasing power over the year. For example, the agreements for the railways and coal mines provided for a phased increase in wages of 6 per

---

[1] This is without a strike.

[2] G. Lyon-Caen: " La convention sociale d'EGF et le système français des relations professionnelles ", in *Droit social* (Paris), No. 4, Apr. 1970, pp. 162-173.

[3] Although an agreement on the consequences of railway modernisation signed on 11 July 1968 contains the following clause: " the signatory parties undertake to endeavour to settle between themselves any fundamental difficulties that may arise out of the interpretation of any of the clauses of this agreement and to submit any unsettled issues to a conciliation. . . .''

cent, which, allowing for the anticipated rise in the price index of 4 per cent, gave an improvement of 2 per cent in purchasing power. Should the price index go up by more than 4 per cent between December 1969 and December 1970, it was stipulated that wages would be increased on 1 January 1971 by the difference between the actual rise in the index and 4 per cent. This " escape clause " guaranteed in other words that purchasing power would improve by 2 per cent whatever happened. Discussions on the renewal of these agreements in 1971 began in the early part of the year. In the case of the railways they resulted in a new settlement once more guaranteeing an increase of 2 per cent in purchasing power and providing for a further reduction in working hours.

This guaranteed increase in purchasing power is a characteristic feature of " progress agreements " in 1971, since an annex to the wage agreement for the electricity and gas industries signed on 9 February 1971 also provides for a minimum growth in purchasing power of 2.5 per cent in 1971. In other words the 1969 formula will only be used if it results in an increase of more than 2.5 per cent. On the other hand, the clause requiring a period of notice before the agreement can be terminated, which was one of the distinctive features of the original version, has been superseded by a less restrictive provision worded as follows: " The signatory managements and federations agree to meet to discuss any disagreement or dispute arising out of the operation of this instrument and undertake to make every effort to settle the disagreement or dispute by negotiation in order to avoid termination by the signatory trade union federations ".

But while the " labour peace " clauses are omitted or toned down, the fact remains that these wage agreements seem bound to lead to a new type of relationship between management and trade unions. For one thing, they involve frequent meetings to keep track of certain developments such as the level of prices, wages and the parameters of the electricity and gas agreement, and decide on the action to be taken; for example in October 1969, when it was plain that the rise in prices had been greater than anticipated, the railway management and unions agreed to speed up the original timetable for raising wages, thereby making use of the " escape clause ". The electricity and gas agreement allows the unions to choose between certain policies (shorter hours of work or a larger increase in basic wages, bigger rises for the lowest-paid workers or flat-rate increases all round) and even, as Jacques Delors points out [1], to concern themselves with the way the industry is run. These changes in the unions' status and powers, coupled with regular contacts and the prospect of clearly defined short-term gains, may do at least as much as the dubiously effective social peace clauses to place industrial relations on a sounder footing.

---

[1] Jacques Delors: " La nouvelle société: I ", in *Preuves*, second quarter 1970, p. 102.

VI. Collective bargaining in privately owned industries and firms

Multi-industry, nation-wide bargaining and the wage agreements negotiated in the leading nationalised industries are the most novel and striking developments of recent years and the clearest departure from earlier methods. It is harder to put a finger on the changes that have taken place in traditional bargaining by industry and in plant-level bargaining.

(1) As regards the former, a distinction should be drawn between negotiations over such new issues as hours of work and salaried status, and those that merely continue earlier procedures (e.g. concerning minimum wages).

Collective bargaining has coped admirably with its new objectives. According to the Ministry of Labour, between the end of May 1968 and 30 October 1969, seventy-one agreements on the reduction of working hours were concluded for entire industries, whereas before May 1968 the Ministry only had record of three agreements of this type. Most lay down a timetable for reductions in the working week and the way in which the resulting loss of earnings is to be offset. As regards salaried status, eighteen national or regional agreements were recorded by the Ministry of Labour between 20 April 1970 (the date of the joint statement by the National Employers' Council and the trade union confederations) and the end of the year. It was estimated that by this latter date, nearly 5 million wage earners were covered by the new arrangements.[1] In the case of hours of work as in that of salaried status, the impulse came from the top. At the rue de Grenelle meeting, the employers and trade union confederations reached agreement on the principle of negotiations over shorter working hours. The first nudge towards salaried status was given by the Government, but the joint statement of 20 April 1970 showed that the National Employers' Council and trade union confederations had come round to the Government's view. It is also possible that the proposal to give wage earners staff status, by relieving the negotiators of the need to think up anything new and providing them with a clear-cut objective, helped the negotiations to progress much faster.

It is harder to detect the changes that have taken place in bargaining on such traditional subjects as wages. Of course, the tempo has been speeded up, especially when an agreement allows negotiations to be reopened as soon as the cost of living rises beyond a certain point (according to an estimate from a trade union source, nearly 5 million wage earners are now covered by sliding-scale clauses); but this bargain-

---

[1] For details of the position in November 1970 see Monique Bellas: " La mensualisation: un bon départ ", in *Projet*, Nov. 1970, pp. 1128-1131.

ing only deals with minimum wages, which in most cases are still well below actual rates. The last collective agreement for the Paris metal-working industries (16 February 1971) was not signed by the CGT and the CFDT, which had demanded an increase of 30 per cent in wage rates instead of the 13 per cent actually granted. In the chemical industries the last national meeting (11 February 1971) did not lead to any agreement. In other words the old procedure is still in force, and this suggests that while new patterns have certainly been explored in recent years, the fundamental conditions governing the relationship between employers and trade unions have not been greatly affected.

(2) At the plant level, it is clear that agreements on a wide range of subjects are still being concluded in a small number of firms; these agreements are known and published and in some cases are found to contain innovations. For example an agreement signed by Berliet (a heavy-vehicle manufacturer with 17,000 workers) at the beginning of 1970 is reminiscent of the progress agreements signed in the nationalised industries. In drawing up a social balance sheet it might be worth including the most significant clauses of these agreements, but the fact is that they only cover a fairly small number of wage earners.

While collective bargaining at the plant level has become much commoner since 1968, it has certainly not resulted in more comprehensive agreements, but rather in more agreements on specific points. When they deal with profit-sharing, such agreements are due to a statutory obligation and so it is hardly surprising that there should be a large number of them. Indeed, the total filed under the 1967 Ordinance amounted to 5,800 by 1 December 1970, most of them having been negotiated with works councils. (Whereas plant agreements are normally concluded by manage-ments with the representative trade unions, the 1967 Ordinance allowed profit-sharing agreements to be negotiated with these councils.) In other cases, plant agreements merely repeat industry-wide settlements on the subject while adapting them to local conditions. Between June 1968 and October 1969 the Ministry of Labour was notified of 101 plant or company agreements dealing with the reduction of the working week. There have also been many agreements on the introduction of salaried status.

There is one subject on which industry-wide agreements do not always lead to plant-level bargaining. François Sellier, in his account of collective bargaining in the French metalworking industry [1], notes that for the employers' organisations the agreement on hours of work (con-cluded nationally, whereas normally bargaining in the industry is con-ducted on a regional basis) was to be applied as it stood. By and large, when agreements are of a pioneering character (such as the nation-wide

---

[1] F. Sellier: " L'évolution des négociations collectives dans la sidérurgie et la métallurgie en France (1950-1969) ", in *Droit social*, Sep.-Oct. 1970.

agreement on employment, the industry-wide agreements based on it and the nation-wide agreement on vocational training) plant agreements improving on their standards are usually few and far between.

It may be that the impulse from the top has given managements the impression that there is no need for them to go any further, thereby strengthening a fairly long-standing tradition among French employers of leaving bargaining to their trade associations. On the union side, it is also possible that the immediate aim is often to secure general observation of the employment agreements (nation-wide or industry-wide) and vocational training agreements (nation-wide) before trying to add new clauses to suit conditions in particular enterprises. Perhaps, therefore, the sweeping changes introduced at the national level—and which could only be introduced at that level, as L. A. Moller has shown in the case of salaried status [1]—mean that the initiative in industrial relations must now come from above and that the time is past when major innovations foreshadowing future developments were first introduced at the plant level.

This does not mean that employers and trade unions do not agree in recognising that plant-level bargaining should play a larger part in future. The events of May 1968 revealed the importance of the factory as the place where the problems that matter to the workers are actually encountered, e.g. wages, conditions of employment, place in the industrial hierarchy, etc. At the same time that the social responsibilities of managements were thrown into relief, an Act was passed in December 1968 at long last giving official recognition to factory trade union branches. The changes in men's minds as well as in the law are such that there can no longer be any question of refusing to bargain at this level, and it is significant that a reform of the 1950 Act now in hand is designed among other things to foster the conclusion of plant agreements. But while the National Employers' Council is now far readier than formerly to accept plant-level bargaining, it still insists that it must fit into an orderly framework and that its primary function is to adapt agreements concluded for the industry as a whole. For example, in complying with industry-wide agreements on salaried status, some firms have had trouble combining their terms with existing practices, and special agreements have often been negotiated on this point. The trade unions, on the other hand, regard plant-level bargaining as an opportunity of taking industry-wide agreements one step further. So, while both approaches seem to accept the idea of bargaining " further down the line ", in fact it is not interpreted in the same way on both sides. The trade unions can still, of course, take direct action in the factories, and it may also be taken spontaneously by the workers themselves. The unions do not disown

---

[1] L. A. Moller: " La mensualisation: bilan des accords professionels signés à la fin de 1970 ", article due to be published in *Droit social* in March 1971 (my thanks are due to the author for communicating his manuscript).

247

them when this happens, but try to take over, knowing that this is the level at which demands are most closely related to needs and that direct action in the factories must supplement and so to speak counter-balance the negotiations at the top. These, by a paradoxical twist, thereby help to keep the old style of collective relations alive in the factories.

VII. The extent of the change

These remarks suggest that while major changes have occurred in recent years, they have largely taken the form of additions and innovations rather than the complete reshaping of industrial relations. In privately owned industry and firms—where the two sides confront one another more directly, the negotiating machinery is less elaborate and government influence is less pervasive—it is far from certain that the old pattern is being questioned at all. More generally, this realisation of what has not changed prompts a backward look at the effects of the most visible changes—multi-industry agreements and " progress agreements "—especially on ideologies and strategies.

The policy of " progress agreements " has forced the trade unions to reconsider more carefully the criteria that make an agreement acceptable and the social and political significance of the collective bargaining process.

Over the electricity and gas agreement in 1969, the CGT reiterated its previous standpoint. It does not rule out the signature of agreements with employers—the class enemies—but such agreements are no more than short-term compromises reflecting the balance of power at a particular time. They can be accepted as long as they entail an adequate improvement in workers' pay and conditions; at the same time, they must leave the unions free to deploy their full strength at any time and impose no restriction on the right to strike. On the ground that the electricity and gas agreement did not involve sufficient gains and also because of its opposition to the " social peace " clause, the CGT refused to sign after holding a poll of the entire labour force. It argued from the results of this poll that the majority of the electricity and gas workers were not in favour of the agreement signed by the CFDT and Force ouvrière federations, thereby casting doubt on the latter's representative character. The reason why the CGT did not sign progress agreements without " social peace " clauses concluded in other nationalised industries in 1970 was that in its view they did not grant sufficient concessions. It also seems probable that it was unwilling to give the impression by signing these agreements that it endorsed the Government's new social policy, of which they formed an essential part. It is difficult otherwise to explain why it should have signed with a private firm, Berliet, an agreement which is quite similar in many respects to the progress agreements in the nationalised industries and even includes a " social peace " clause.

248

Thus, while the CGT's attitude is consistent and clear-cut, each agreement is assessed with an eye to its social and political implications as well as its content. This is noted by René Mouriaux when he states that " the CGT fears that the present Government may use these agreements as a device to spread the ideology of class collaboration " and he adds: " The CGT's tactics cannot be reduced to a single formula and it is perhaps necessary to take into account not only the content of the agreements but also the direction in which they point ".[1] The fact remains, however, that in 1971 the CGT, taking the view that the agreements for the railways and electricity and gas industries marked an advance on their predecessors, finally decided to sign them.

Understandably, in this context of a government policy of encouraging progress agreements and refusal by the CGT to sign, the CFDT felt bound to justify to the labour force in general and to its own members in particular, its decision to sign most of the agreements and to define its own approach to collective bargaining. It did so at a time when it was going over to a policy of sharper opposition to capitalist society (at the Congress of March 1970). In other words, the present policy of the CFDT towards collective bargaining is not so much a response to circumstances as a new line altogether. Henceforth, the CFDT regards bargaining within the capitalist system as a reflection of the relative strength of the two sides at a given moment (conclusions published by its executive on 9 January 1970). When agreements relate to particular points, they must be for very short periods only and it must be possible to reopen the issues as soon as the balance of power has shifted in the workers' favour. Agreements must be judged solely from the standpoint of the workers' advantage and the growth of trade union power. It follows that they must be in no way allowed to restrict the unions' ability to oppose.

The determination not to be drawn, not to be tied down, is very clearly stated, therefore. It is also apparent through the formal language of the agreements themselves (although the union prefers the term " statement " to " agreement " and even more to " contract "). Moreover, if an agreement is merely a truce, the union must emphasise what remains to be done and ensure that its signature does not make the workers lose interest. This means that the agreement must be presented as part of a wider struggle; for example the signature of the vocational training agreement is described as a " fighting measure ".[2] Lastly, the fact of signing must not be falsely interpreted as signifying integration into capitalist society (" negotiation is not integration " [3]) or as an endorsement of government policy.

---

[1] René Mouriaux: " La CGT depuis 1968 ", in *Projet*, Nov. 1970, p. 1089.

[2] *Syndicalisme hebdomadaire*, 9 July 1970, p. 4.

[3] Laurent Lucas: " La négociation n'est pas l'intégration ", ibid., 24 Dec. 1969, p. 1.

Even so, the idea of agreements covering a specified period and involving definite commitments is not rejected by all the trade union organisations. For example, the CGT-FO Metalworkers' Federation decided at its last congress in January 1970 that short-term commitments could be entered into by its member unions and that any points settled in such agreements could only be reopened in accordance with the prescribed procedure (i.e. for denunciation, notice and consultation as in the 1969 social agreement for the electricity and gas industries).[1] This, however, is a minority view. On the whole, the extension of " progress agreements " has not been accompanied by any new readiness on the part of the majority of unions to commit themselves—quite the reverse. This coolness is perhaps not simply a question of ideology. It is also due in all likelihood to greater awareness of attitudes among the rank and file resulting from the growing practice of holding consultations with the member unions before signing an agreement.

The growth of nation-wide or multi-industry bargaining has its drawbacks for both sides. In the trade union movement it is realised that questions like vocational training do not generate much passion and that it is hard to work up mass support for the kind of demands put forward at the bargaining table. Furthermore, since the negotiations affect all the industry federations, it is essential to keep in contact with them throughout the discussions; but since there is only room in the trade union delegation for the representatives of the main industries, there must also be regular consultations with those left out.

A similar problem faced the National Employers' Council over its links with the employers' federations, and in order to clarify the question it decided to amend its rules. Under the old rules it had no clear right to engage in inter-industry bargaining, since this was considered to be a matter for its member federations, which were entitled to argue that the Council could only represent them with their specific authorisation and if this were not given, they were not bound by the agreement. In the new rules which came into force at the start of 1970, the principle is laid down that " wages are a matter for individual employers and their trade associations ". At the same time, however—and this is the new feature—an exception is allowed: " in other fields, the French National Employers' Council may in exceptional cases and with the approval of its Permanent Assembly be empowered to negotiate and sign general agreements for all . . . occupations ". On the other hand, each federation is explicitly entitled to opt out of such an agreement before it is signed. A number of them took advantage of this right in the case of the vocational training agreement signed in July 1970. This procedure may reduce the coverage of an agreement, but it also increases the likelihood that it will be

---

[1] " Le contrat collectif à durée déterminée ", in *F.O. Hebdo*, 28 Jan. 1970.

something more than a catalogue of minimum standards based on what the least go-ahead industries can afford.

Because the Council now accepts nation-wide multi-industry bargaining to the extent of having thought it necessary to amend its rules, it should not be concluded that bargaining of this type will become more widespread in the future. Trade union demands to discuss various new topics at this level (union rights, hours of work, the lowering of the retirement age, etc.) were recently turned down by the Council, which still regards multi-industry bargaining as an exceptional measure, although this does not by any means rule out exchanges of views or joint statements at the top to lay down principles for the guidance of collective bargaining further down. The changes that have taken place do not therefore involve any general questioning of ideologies and strategies. The employers and trade unions are still unable to agree which subjects should be dealt with in multi-industry bargaining, the levels at which various questions should be discussed, the function of plant-level bargaining and so forth.

In the past few years the employers' and workers' organisations have managed to find new purposes and new functions for collective bargaining, together with novel ways of tackling the problems they faced. Government encouragement, as part of the policy of " concerted action " has sometimes been a great help. Nevertheless, the legal status of collective bargaining is still subject to an Act passed twenty years ago and ideologies and behaviour only change slowly. The striking creativeness of industrial relations is therefore due to the discovery and exploitation of opportunities inherent in the existing French system rather than to any departure from it. Such changes as have taken place are those that are possible within the system. This explains their limitations, without in any way diminishing their value.

Recent Trends in Collective Bargaining in the Federal Republic of Germany

Hans REICHEL [1]

The scope and effects of bargaining autonomy

IN ORDER TO UNDERSTAND the evolution of collective bargaining in the Federal Republic of Germany it may be useful first to consider the most important of the legal and constitutional provisions in this area. Collective bargaining between employers' and workers' associations occupies a particularly important place in the social and economic life of the country because the wide degree of autonomy in negotiation allows these associations a relatively free hand. Generally speaking, the only limits are set by the need to observe the interests of the public and the State and by certain inalienable rights of the individual citizen enshrined in the Federal Constitution. Article 9, paragraph 3, of the Federal Constitution, and the Collective Agreements Act, 1949 [2], endow employers' and workers' associations with far-reaching powers and latitude of action, corresponding fully to the requirements of the Freedom of Association and Protection of the Right to Organise Convention, 1948 (No. 87), and the Right to Organise and Collective Bargaining Convention, 1949 (No. 98), of the ILO, both ratified by the Federal Republic of Germany, the Collective Agreements Recommendation, 1951 (No. 91), of the ILO and the European Social Charter. Under the Collective Agreements Act the validity of a collective agreement is not conditional upon government approval. Although collective agreements must be communicated to the Federal Minister of Labour, neither this formality nor that of the registering of agreements is a condition for their effective operation. Similarly, the freedom of action of the contracting parties is not restricted

---

[1] Ministerial Counsellor, Chief of the Collective Labour Law Section, Federal Ministry of Labour and Social Affairs.

[2] For the consolidated text, as amended up to 1969, see ILO: *Legislative Series*, 1969—Ger.F.R. 4.

253

by the establishment of minimum conditions of employment, since the relevant Act of 1952 [1] expressly recognises the precedence of collective agreements.

Since German statute law has nothing to say regarding the actual process of collective bargaining or the settlement of disputes arising in that connection, any rules in this respect have largely been worked out in the past twenty years by court decisions, mainly by the Federal Labour Court and the Federal Constitutional Court. Rulings of this kind are accordingly very important for relations between employers' and workers' associations.

The course of collective bargaining in recent years has raised new problems of substance and law with which the associations, the Government, legal experts and the courts are confronted. New and tougher forms of bargaining tactics and labour disputes have been seen to develop. Many established practices have been upset and need to be reconsidered. Positions that seemed to have been set for years have been called into question. There is increasing uncertainty in the relations between the social partners as well as in the relations between the associations on either side and their respective members. It is still impossible to say how or when this situation will be resolved.

The following observations are intended to give a brief but by no means complete outline of significant aspects and practices in the field of collective bargaining and industrial disputes in the Federal Republic.

The influence of the occupational associations

Collective bargaining and the conclusion of collective agreements in the Federal Republic are characterised by the fact that the trade unions are mainly organised at industry level. Each of the sixteen trade unions that together make up the German Confederation of Trade Unions (DGB) aims at covering a particular branch of activity (e.g. the chemical industry or commerce) and everyone employed in that branch, irrespective of the actual type of work performed. This means, for example, that the Metalworkers' Union includes not only metalworkers, both wage earners and salaried employees, but also masons, joiners and commercial and technical staff employed in this industry. The exception to this rule is the German Union of Salaried Employees (DAG) [2], whose membership is open to all salaried employees, whatever branch of the economy they are employed in. Consequently, the employer deals only with one union in respect of matters affecting wage earners, and with the same union plus the DAG in regard to salaried employees. Apart from strengthening these unions' bargaining power, this arrangement normally facilitates the course

---

[1] *Legislative Series*, 1952—Ger.F.R. 1.

[2] The DAG, however, is not affiliated to the German Confederation of Trade Unions.

of negotiations as well. In this respect there has been little change in recent years.[1]

Principal among the central organisations of the employers' and workers' associations are the Confederation of German Employers' Associations (BDA) and the German Confederation of Trade Unions (DGB). Neither of these normally acts as a contracting party in collective bargaining, and neither has ever yet included in its statutes any provision with binding effect on the bargaining activities of its individual affiliates. Naturally, however, it is common for consultation to take place between the central organisations and their affiliates as well as among individual member associations. One reason for this has been the desire to create and maintain a uniform general position in the negotiation of agreements involving comparable territorial, occupational and individual circumstances. For the same reason the DGB and the BDA have special departments concerned with collective bargaining matters from which their affiliates can obtain information and advice. The possibility for a central organisation to bring indirect influence to bear on its member associations exists in the provision contained in the statutes of the DGB empowering it to issue guidelines on direct action that are binding on its affiliates, and it has done so.

The central organisations have rendered substantial services to their affiliated associations through newspaper, radio and television publicity campaigns, some of them with very wide coverage. In addition they have organised polls and surveys through their economic and public information institutes. In some instances they have been able to strengthen the economic position of a member association—for instance, in the case of an affiliated trade union involved in an industrial dispute, by contributing to the strike fund, or, in the case of an affiliated firm, by arranging for risk-sharing among the undertakings affected or by supporting the strike-hit employer through the transfer, or alternatively the non-transfer, of orders, deliveries and so on.

Another way in which the central organisations have been able to play a more or less direct role is through occasional top-level meetings at which the representatives of both sides have come together to exchange views on matters of topical concern.

In some branches of activity there has been a preference for collective agreements covering specified areas rather than the whole of the country. But even where this has been the case the executive committee of the respective industrial trade union has retained certain powers of guidance over the local constituents in regard to the negotiation, signature or termination of regional agreements and the initiation and conduct of labour disputes.

---

[1] Cf. E. G. Erdmann, Jr.: " Organisation and work of employers' associations in the Federal Republic of Germany ", in *International Labour Review*, Vol. LXXVIII, No. 6, Dec. 1958, pp. 533-551, and in particular pp. 536-540; and F. Lepinski: " The German trade union movement ", ibid., Vol. LXXIX, No. 1, Jan. 1959, pp. 57-78, and in particular pp. 66-67.

Deciding which trade union should be recognised as bargaining partner for a particular industry or undertaking has become a matter of increasing practical importance. This is due principally to the fact that technical and economic progress has caused firms to pursue new purposes or to engage either wholly or partly in operations that may make it difficult to determine to which branch they predominantly belong. This has been of special importance for the trade unions because most of them are, as indicated above, organised on industry lines.

Since the DAG covers all salaried employees in every branch of private enterprise and the public service, it is entitled to sit at the bargaining table alongside the other unions concerned, and in particular those affiliated to the DGB. It is common, particularly in the public service, for both of these central organisations to be signatories to a collective agreement, although separate agreements also exist.

In 1970 the Federal Labour Court issued a decision that has had a considerable impact on collective bargaining, whereby it ruled that each union's statutes would determine the question of competence for negotiation.

The question whether specific collective agreements should be sought for the whole of the country, or only for limited areas, such as particular Länder, smaller regions or individual firms was obviously a matter of top-level policy decision in the national organisation concerned. Agreements having a broader territorial and occupational coverage have normally fixed the limits for supplementary agreements of more restricted scope, but the local or Länder associations have had a reasonable say in the negotiations leading up to the signature of a more comprehensive agreement. In addition to laying down general provisions governing such matters as the conclusion and termination of the contract of employment, regular hours of work, or holidays with pay, it has become accepted practice for country- or industry-wide agreements to standardise occupational classifications, wage categories and other factors so that the regional agreements can then establish the appropriate earning schedules. This has produced a firm basis of action for the parties to supplementary agreements at regional or enterprise level.

As part of a move towards enterprise-level agreements, the trade unions have been endeavouring for some time to negotiate separate arrangements for firms already covered by a regional agreement. This is something quite different from the attempts by works councils, as distinct from trade unions, to by-pass collective agreements and settle certain matters direct with the employer; further reference will be made to this subject later on. As regards enterprise-level agreements, the trade unions have particularly in mind some large and powerful firms that pay rates well above those laid down in collective agreements, because regional collective agreements have generally tended to make things easier for the less powerful firms. The unions' primary concern has been to guarantee continued high wage levels for the employees of the more powerful firms, but this policy is liable to jeopardise the smaller firm and the livelihood of those employed there. Even within the respective associations, attitudes towards separate agreements for individual undertakings tend to diverge. The principal misgiving expressed in this connection is that this tendency may undermine the position of employers and their associations as spokesmen for the whole industry, as well as the strength of the individual firm in its dealings with a union having a broader area of reference; this is seen as a threat to the theoretical parity of position and power which are normally regarded as a vital condition for autonomy in collective bargaining. Enterprise-level and local considerations might affect the interests of the community at large, which are balanced between the various regions and industries.

There are also legal problems, involving such aspects as the lawfulness and enforceability of clauses in regional agreements that authorise supplementary arrangements at the level of the undertaking. In the first part of 1970 a significant endeavour launched in this direction by a major union with specific reference to the rubber industry was thwarted primarily through the combined resistance of the firms concerned and their employers' association. In joining the association these firms had renounced their right to engage in negotiations or conclude collective agreements without the association's consent. In so doing they were guided by compelling tactical considerations as well as by feelings of solidarity with the other affiliated firms, but at the same time they were not prepared to empower the association to conclude separate agreements for the firms. In the event, the trade union did not force the matter to a dispute. Following further talks between the two sides it was agreed that the industry-level agreement for the whole of the country should be reinstated but that wage rates should in future be fixed not by a single national agreement but by regional agreements.

Collective agreements which, on the employers' side, cover individual undertakings are something quite different. These are not infrequent and, as of 31 March 1970, out of the roughly 20,000 collective agreements in force about one-third were at enterprise level, only a small number of these being of any importance for the rest of the economy. Most of these enterprise-level agreements concern employers who are outside the competent association and are therefore not bound by its negotiated agreements. Here again the principle of the industrial peace obligation inherent in any collective agreement is applicable to both sides. The most celebrated instance in this connection concerned a dispute which occurred in 1963 between the Federal German subsidiary of the Ford Motor Company, which did not belong to the employers' association, and the Metalworkers' Union. The union called a lawful strike against Ford because it refused to enter into an enterprise-level agreement proposed by the union. The collective agreement covering other firms in the industry in the same area was still in force, and the parties to it were bound by its industrial peace clause. Fords then joined the employers' association, which meant that it was automatically covered by the agreement in question and was thereby protected by the industrial peace clause obliging the union to call off the strike.

Some observations are called for at this point regarding the application of collective agreements to employers or workers who are not automatically covered because they do not belong to one of the contracting associations. Any employer is free to apply the collective agreement appropriate to the industry and the locality to all of his employees, and this is often done. It is particularly common in times of labour shortage because workers cannot be recruited or retained if the wage rates remain below the contractual levels. The parties to a collective agreement cannot prevent its provisions from being applied to outsiders. Conversely, it is often in their interest to force non-affiliated employers to apply the provisions of an agreement, with the purpose of depriving such employers of the competitive advantage of paying lower wages, or alternatively of securing contractual advantages for members of the trade union concerned who would otherwise have no legal entitlement to them. Special statutory powers exist whereby the Government may in specified circumstances declare an agreement to be generally binding and thus extend its applicability also to outsiders. For this procedure to be put into force an appropriate request must be made by at least one of the parties to an agreement, and a committee composed of representatives of the respective central organisations must also give its approval. In recent years such requests have generally been made only in a small number of industries, and except in the case of the building industry they have related almost entirely to small territorial areas. But this procedure is becoming more widespread: there were 42 such requests in 1967, 59 in 1968, 120 in 1969, and 159 in 1970.

A particularly interesting agreement was concluded some time ago with a major undertaking which has branches in a number of different areas in the Federal Republic. It was agreed that the higher rates for the central factory should be paid in the other works as well, even if the collective agreement normally applicable where they were located provided for lower rates. This arrangement may have set the tone for a new policy approach which could result in a further reduction in regional differences in conditions of employment, especially in regard to wages and salaries.

Participation by outside bodies or persons in collective bargaining

Since the end of the Second World War the Government has not seen any reason to restrict the bargaining autonomy so jealously guarded by the employers' and workers' associations, and in particular to exert direct influence or impose binding instructions. The Government has in fact repeatedly proclaimed its intention of further strengthening bargaining autonomy. While this relieves the two sides of any danger of forcible state intervention, it also places on them a heavy burden of public responsibility.

Neither side objects to the fact that the Government sees itself as entitled and obliged in its function of protecting public interests to give the organisations and authorities concerned its views on the present economic situation and probable developments, provided this is not felt to be a form of pressure.

The same applies to the annual reports on the over-all economic situation that have been submitted by government order since 1963 by a neutral expert council. The Government publishes these reports and transmits them to Parliament together with its own comments. The council's terms of reference are to report on any undesirable trends and to recommend ways of avoiding or overcoming them; its mandate obviously covers wage policy as well, but its reports are not supposed to make any recommendations respecting specific economic or social action.

In 1970 the Federal Minister of Labour and Social Affairs initiated a system of social policy talks at which problems are discussed with representatives of the trade unions, the employers' associations and social insurance institutes as well as economists. Here again there is no question of any direct influence being brought to bear on the two sides in regard to the provisions of collective agreements.

In 1966, when there was a temporary economic recession, legislation was enacted requiring the Government to formulate and interpret guidelines for maintaining or restoring economic stability through what was termed " concerted action " by the regional authorities, the trade unions and the employers' associations. This procedure has been repeated at irregular intervals as needed, particularly by means of talks between the Federal Minister of Economic Affairs and the associations concerned. Although the data produced in this way are not binding on the employers' associations or the trade unions, they can prove useful to them in the bargaining process, both in making matters clear to their members and in showing the foreseeable effects of their agreements on the economy and therefore on the whole nation. The Minister has described the process in the following terms: " The purpose of this ' concerted action ' is not to negotiate specific prices and wages; it is to promote understanding, and especially the realisation that there is a limit between the reasonable interests of individual groups and economic necessities. " At the meeting of 12 October 1970 the participants " agreed with the Minister that the talks within the framework of the ' concerted action ' procedure were designed to bring about collaboration among all concerned in order to combine stability with growth, by means of an exchange of information and opinions between the Government, the Federal Bank, employers, trade unions and the council of experts regarding the general economic situation ".

So far the Government's role has been merely to address appeals to the two sides within the framework of the " concerted action " procedure, in Parliament and through public information media. The Government has expressed the hope that collective agreements will avoid endangering the economy, particularly through rising costs due to higher wage bills.

Not everywhere did the Government encounter the response it had anticipated [1], and when it found that its requests were not sufficiently heeded in wage negotiations, it issued urgent and strong appeals to the respective associations. It was not until the 21st Concerted Action Meeting on 4 June 1971 that the two central organisations came to a loose general arrangement laying the foundations for co-ordinated action to promote economic stability. The central organisations plan to set up a standing committee to examine profit and cost trends so that the same basic figures will be available as the point of departure in negotiations. They want to describe and clarify the economic situation and its anticipated evolution to their member associations, which have to conduct the actual negotiations. In recognition of their own responsibilities they want to bring it home to their members that the criterion for action should not be dictated by price and income expectations in a boom period but rather by the necessities of a phase of general economic consolidation. It remains to be seen to what extent the various associations will follow these admonitions in their bargaining procedure. Neither on the employers' side nor on the trade union side are the central organisations empowered to dictate policy to their member associations.

In the public service the Government is anxious to maintain some degree of uniformity, especially in regard to wage and salary groups and the relevant rates of remuneration. In this way it hopes to prevent trouble in any branch of the various administrations and public undertakings. Negotiations involving federal competence are conducted by the Minister of the Interior, with the participation of two bargaining bodies representing respectively all the Länder and all the municipalities in their capacity as employers. The railway and postal authorities each deal separately with their own trade unions but they consult the federal authorities. Public corporations generally join in the negotiations and subscribe to their results.

The actual workers whose conditions of work are under discussion have no right of direct participation in these meetings. They are represented by their organisations, to which they grant full powers in this respect through the act of joining the union and accepting its statutes;

---

[1] Although the Government had indicated that average wage increases of 7 to 8 per cent at the most would be tolerable, the wage levels negotiated in industry in June 1971 were on the average 16 per cent higher than in June 1970.

this means that they have really agreed to accept whatever results are forthcoming. But this has not prevented workers from availing themselves of the principles of internal democracy in order to state their personal views to the association and perhaps influence the line of conduct followed. The workers have often shown their own union and the employer exactly what they feel by voting for or against a move to begin or to end a strike.

In 1969 a number of wild-cat strikes, warning strikes and other forms of action in the metalworking industry clearly demonstrated to the employers and to the union concerned what the workers expected, but the effect was also felt in other industries as well as by the public at large. This behaviour went on in meetings after the collective agreement had been signed, and there were some quite vehement statements by union members and lower-level union officials.

It is only the members of the associations directly concerned who are entitled to participate in bargaining discussions. Workers who are covered by the negotiations but who are not union members, or who belong to a different union, have no say, officially at least. But they have quite often been able to play a part by joining a strike called by one of the competent organisations. If the proportion of the particular union's members in the workforce is fairly small, the decision of other workers either to join or to stay out of a strike can be of vital importance.

Reference should be made here to the efforts of some trade unions to secure advantages for their own members that are not granted to non-organised workers. Their desire is perfectly natural, although the unions affirm in other connections that they speak for all workers. In regard to the collective settlement of conditions of work, however, the unions consider it their primary responsibility to defend the material interests of their members, who expect appropriate representation in return for paying their dues. There have been several attempts to introduce a distinction in collective agreements as between workers belonging to the contracting union and those belonging to another organisation or to none at all. In a basic ruling given in 1967 the Federal Labour Court held any such distinction to be incompatible with the Federal Constitution.

In metalworking, agreements have been concluded to ensure a certain amount of freedom of action in the undertaking for union shop stewards and youth representatives and to protect them against reprisals on account of such action, where such protection is not already afforded by law.

The workers' interests in matters outside the scope of the undertaking are represented only by the trade unions. This is also true as regards negotiations and the conclusion of agreements in respect of a single undertaking. In the fixing of general conditions of work, including wage rates, collective agreements take precedence over plant-level agreements, so that there is no formal direct participation of other representatives or spokesmen of the workers in the collective bargaining procedure. This applies in particular to works councils as elected by the employees under the Works Constitution Act, 1952 [1], and their individual members as such.

The Act limits the extent to which the works council, as distinct from the trade union, can negotiate with the individual employer regarding conditions of work and the conclusion of agreements between the two of them, but in practice the limits laid down have been exceeded. It is usual for these so-called plant-level agreements to cover such matters as normal hours of starting and finishing work, breaks, the time and place of payment of wages (remittances to workers' accounts in savings banks are becoming increasingly common), the establishment of the holiday schedule (which now frequently involves a collective shut-down of the whole works or of individual units), vocational training in the light of new statutory requirements, the administration of welfare facilities at plant or enterprise level, and internal regulations including workers' conduct. The last of these items covers such delicate subjects as clocking-in, checks to prevent filching, no-smoking rules, and fines for offenders.

Other matters that have been paid particular attention include the fixing of time and piece rates, the establishment of principles of remuneration, the introduction of new methods of remuneration, and to an increasing extent the evaluation of jobs newly created or radically altered as a result of rationalisation.

Wages and other conditions are not usually dealt with in enterprise-level agreements but rather in a collective agreement, this principle being followed in the interests of the respective associations; and it is rare for a collective agreement specifically to authorise supplementary enterprise-level arrangements on these matters. This clearly shows the desire to leave the collective settlement of conditions of work to the bargaining parties. Nevertheless, because such questions are not always covered by collective agreements, there has recently been an increase in the number of arrangements between individual employers and works councils designed to soften the hardships liable to affect older workers or long-service employees as a result of rationalisation, automation, production changes or mergers. There have been instances of comprehensive social plans providing for certain wage guarantees in the event of transfer to lower-paid jobs, retraining grants, or lump-sum compensation in the event of unavoidable redundancy.

Union shop stewards in undertakings (who may also be members of the works council or of the staff council in the public service) are not empowered by virtue of their status to participate in their respective unions' collective bargaining activities. Some who also belong to their union's negotiating committee for individual firms' collective agreements

---

[1] *Legislative Series*, 1952—Ger.F.R. 6.

have, however, had a considerable say, even after the conclusion of negotiations. Nor is there any reason why they should not offer their union useful hints about the feelings of the workers on the basis of their own experience and their close contacts with the firm's employees. On this basis they can advise on any changes they think should be introduced in the collective agreement; they can also say whether the workers, including those who are not union members or who belong to another union, would be willing to take action to support the union's claims or to vote in favour of the bargaining results obtained by the union. Employers are showing increasing willingness to recognise the status of these union shop stewards in the undertaking. Some collective agreements, especially in the metalworking industry, provide for the recognition and protection of such trade union representatives at plant level. It has sometimes proved difficult to establish a demarcation line between a worker's activity as a member of the works council or staff council, in which he is bound to observe strict neutrality even in regard to trade union matters, and his functions as the union shop steward, and there have even been occasional clashes in this connection.

Negotiating tactics

Collective bargaining tactics have become more sophisticated and tougher in the past twenty years, with a distinct hardening of positions in recent times. This has sometimes caused increasing difficulty for the individual association, especially when it has to take the interests of members in different categories into consideration, while bearing in mind the position of other associations and allowing for the fact that nowadays, as a result of the increasingly close links between the different branches of the economy, collective agreements have repercussions far beyond the particular industry concerned. The associations on either side have not always found it easy to arouse or maintain sympathy among the workers themselves and the officers in close contact with them, or among member firms, for the tactical and general economic considerations underlying the actions of their executive bodies. In the recent past the unions have not been able to take it for granted that the workers would be satisfied with what has been negotiated with the employers or achieved through conciliation, or that a vote on the negotiating committee's proposals would be favourable. Negotiating tactics have also been affected in some cases by more or less spontaneous action that cannot always be averted. On the employers' side this has taken the form of a refusal by individual firms to toe the line, either by accepting trade union demands that were still in dispute or by paying wages for working time lost through strikes. On the workers' side it has taken the form of wild-cat or warning strikes. The employers have not taken any action against the unions or the workers involved, but where such events have occurred during a period of application of the contractual industrial peace obligation resulting from a collective agreement in force, they have reminded the unions of their obligation to dissuade the workers from taking such action.

In the normal course of negotiations the two sides generally agree finally on a set of provisions which the leaders of the bargaining teams then submit for approval to the competent committees of their respective organisations. If approval is forthcoming the procedure is formally concluded by having the text of the agreement set down in writing and signed by the authorised representatives, as required by law. The text is then deposited for entry in the register of collective agreements kept by the Federal Ministry of Labour and Social Affairs. This means that the individual members of the trade union or the employers' association concerned are not asked to endorse it, the leaders of the bargaining teams or the executives being fully empowered to act on their behalf. But if a negotiating committee decides that it cannot give its consent because it is not certain of finding majority support among the association's members, it submits the proposals to the membership for a vote, normally adding its own opinion, recommending either the acceptance or the rejection of the draft agreement or the proposed conciliation award. Then the proposals are considered to be approved by the workers' side unless at least 75 per cent of the members entitled to vote call for their rejection and in some cases for direct action as well. Voting is by secret ballot. A contracting union is not bound to follow a declaration of opinion in this respect by workers coming within the scope of such an agreement but not belonging to the union. It can happen that the vote by union members reaches the minimum prescribed under union rules but represents only the minority view in the workforce, as when the proportion of union members in the firm or the industry is relatively small.

Instances have become more frequent of trade unions having given notice of the cancellation of a collective agreement but not having said straight away what provisions they wanted instead, and particularly what wage and other claims they intended to submit. It was not until later, and sometimes when negotiations were already under way, that they advanced specific proposals, once they had tried to get the employers to say how far they were prepared to go.

In the metalworking and chemical industries, which are the pacesetters for the other branches of the economy in the field of collective agreements, there has recently been a tendency to get away from country-wide agreements in favour of agreements concluded at the Land level. This was not just a matter of district union officers wanting to assert their authority vis-à-vis their membership and the other side. It was also a question of bargaining tactics consisting of seeking out and dealing with a weaker opponent first. Another justification advanced was that contractual wage rates and thus actual earnings had not moved at the same

264

pace in different Länder, with substantial variations in some cases. The Metalworkers' Union also found that the circumstances were no longer such as to justify a uniform approach to the payment of additional allowances such as annual bonuses, Christmas bonuses or holiday bonuses. Nevertheless, the main claim by this union in the autumn of 1970 was the same in all of the Länder, namely a straight 15 per cent rise in wage rates. It has also been found that regional negotiations and settlements may confront the organisations concerned with difficulties of a kind that they do not encounter where there is national coverage.

In the meantime both sides have recognised the importance of securing public support for their bargaining tactics. They have made increasing use of interviews in the press, radio and television, and have recently taken to buying considerable space in major newspapers, often eliciting counter-attacks from the other side. The results of these propaganda campaigns have enabled them to adapt their future line of action in this running conflict according to the reactions of workers and employers, the general public, the newspapers, radio commentators, the Government, and economic authorities and institutes.

Up to now collective agreements have tended to be established for a fairly long period, especially master agreements dealing with general conditions such as hours of work, holidays or periods of notice. Two years or more remains a very common period of validity. Agreements governing joint arrangements such as supplementary old-age provident schemes are invariably contracted for a considerable period of time because otherwise they would be incapable of attaining their ends. So long as there was little danger that the rates laid down in wage or salary agreements would be rapidly outstripped by the development of the national economy or the industry or undertaking concerned, it was by no means unusual for the period of validity to be fixed at two years and almost always adhered to in practice. More recently, however, since the situation has started to evolve at an accelerating pace, leading to a more rapid growth of productivity, a rising cost of living and a tightening of the supply of manpower, some unions have pressed for shorter-term agreements. Their motives have been not only to catch up with wage rates in some undertakings going beyond the collectively agreed rates but also to prevent any discontent among members for whom the adjustment of earnings to higher prices or improved productivity has not been taking place quickly enough under long-term agreements.

The resulting uncertainty has caused concern on both sides. The employers have feared that their longer-range pricing systems would be undermined. The unions have not wanted to be caught off their guard by a repetition of the sort of wild-cat strike that occurred in the autumn of 1969.

At the same time the unions have not seen fit to ask that collective agreements should be of indefinite duration so that they would be subject to immediate termination at any time and the obligation to respect industrial peace would no longer apply in practice at all. Any such development would also release employers from their obligations or make them less willing to enter into such agreements. In fact the whole system of collective bargaining would be threatened.

Other ways of overcoming these difficulties have therefore been discussed, and some measures have already been cautiously put into effect. The idea has been to introduce regulations permitting an immediate change in contractual wage rates or early amendment or renewal of a collective agreement by mutual consent. Although sliding scales linking wages to changes in the cost-of-living index have not yet been introduced into collective agreements, the parties to an agreement have occasionally contracted to get together for an exchange of views or for actual negotiations before the expiry of the current agreement if a particular index, generally for the cost of living but sometimes for productivity, changes to the extent specified by the parties. In some instances provision is made for early termination or expiry of the collective agreement in these circumstances.

One particular case is so unusual and significant as to call for separate mention. In April 1971 secret talks were held to establish a new collective agreement for the financially languishing and publicly subsidised Ruhr coal-mining industry, in contrast to the clamorous publicity that usually surrounds such negotiations on both sides and despite the fact that the existing agreement still had a fair time to go. A settlement was reached remarkably quickly, providing for substantial wage increases. Thanks to the unusual legal structure of the industry and of its principal undertaking, the trade union concerned plays a decisive role on the employers' side as well, a feature which does not fit in easily with the existing national system of bargaining autonomy and the nature of collective agreements. The employers' willingness to consent to an indisputably heavy extra financial burden was partly due to their expectation—based both on the law and on past experience—that they would not have to foot the bill themselves, because the State, meaning the community at large, would provide further subsidies. Shortly after the conclusion of these negotiations it was admitted that the undertaking had, within a period of two years, suffered losses amounting to DM 700 million which their creditors had to write off; a few weeks afterwards the undertaking had to ask the federal and Land authorities to stand surety for more than DM 900 million in order to obtain further credit.

The settlement reached may be held to mark the farthest extent of what can be accommodated in a genuine collective bargaining system as hitherto conceived in the Federal Republic of Germany, especially in view of the obligation incumbent upon both sides to use their supreme and jealously guarded right of bargaining autonomy strictly within the limits of their duty to respect the interests of the whole community.

Mediation and conciliation in collective disputes

There is no statutory provision in the Federal Republic for mediation prior to direct action affecting all or particular industries.[1] There have never been any cases of compulsory government arbitration, and this is not provided for in law either. Accordingly there is no means whereby the Government or one of its representatives, in the case of a collective dispute, can impose a binding decision, particularly one laying down conditions of employment, on all concerned against their will. Nor is there any legal basis for the Government to prohibit direct action or to defer it for a specified or unspecified number of days.

Voluntary mediation and conciliation have played an important role in the Federal Republic. The procedure may be freely chosen or it may be laid down in the relevant collective agreements. The employers' and workers' central organisations were soon at pains to promote voluntary conciliation machinery in order to avert serious disputes, and especially direct action, wherever they could. In so doing they were anxious to maintain the contractual arrangements and to avoid provoking the Government into imposing compulsory conciliation or arbitration or some other form of intervention if things came to a head.

On 7 September 1954 the BDA and the DGB agreed on a model conciliation procedure, which their respective affiliates were recommended to include in their collective conciliation agreements, with or without amendment.[2] Conciliation agreements of this kind abound, but only a handful are of any significance for the establishment of employment conditions in general or for the national economy. Among these are the conciliation agreements for the metalworking industry [3], the building industry, printing and allied trades, the chemical industry, and seaports and maritime transport. Such agreements are remarkable by their absence in the iron industry, coal mining, textiles, and the public service.

In recent years formal procedures have not always proved satisfactory in achieving the peaceful settlement of disputes. Sometimes one of the sides has rejected the conciliation board's findings, but in certain of these instances, and in other wage disputes with direct implications for the public, prominent independent personalities, mainly politicians, have managed to arrive at a settlement by unconventional means and so avert a clash. It has often been the federal or Land minister of labour or of economic affairs who has undertaken this task, naturally with the political consequences of any breakdown particularly in mind. In some cases the

---

[1] See H. C. Nipperdey: " The development of labour law in the Federal Republic of Germany since 1945 ", in *International Labour Review*, Vol. LXX, No. 1, July 1954, pp. 26-43, and No. 2, Aug. 1954, pp. 148-167.

[2] See *Industry and Labour* (Geneva, ILO), Vol. XIII, No. 3, 1 Feb. 1955, pp. 121-122.

[3] See *International Labour Review*, Vol. XC, No. 4, Oct. 1964, pp. 380-381.

associations involved in a dispute have requested this form of assistance, while in others the minister has himself intervened in view of the political or economic importance of the issue.

Direct action

Since there is no statutory law regulating the right of employers' and workers' organisations to engage in direct action, the onus has been laid on the judiciary and the Federal Labour Court in particular to derive this right from the Federal Constitution, especially from the right of association, and they have thereby had a decisive influence in determining the way in which such action should be conducted. The number of working days lost through strikes in the Federal Republic of Germany in the past ten years has, in fact, been relatively small.[1]

Collective agreements for the public service and for public institutions and utilities (hospitals, gas-works, water supply, etc.) can be concluded along the same lines as for private undertakings, so that the right to strike exists in principle there too, provided there is no danger of serious harm to the public. But major disputes have never yet occurred in this sector, although not so long ago there was a phase of working to rule in the postal services, and something of the same sort in the air traffic control service, the effects being to some extent comparable to those of a strike.

With the above exception, just about every group of employees has participated at some time in a strike movement, and they are normally entitled to take part in a lawful strike. This holds good equally for wage earners and salaried employees, whatever their grade, and even for university people, but can hardly be held to apply to top managers and certainly not to board members in undertakings governed by company law. Although borderline cases could well be difficult to decide no serious cases of dispute have yet been notified.

In order to rally their members' combative spirit in the event of a strike or a lock-out, both sides take more positive action than just threatening them with personal disadvantages under the association's statutes if they ignore a strike call or similar appeal. When members are on strike or locked out, their unions pay them strike money; over the years the rates of assistance have risen closer to net earning levels and in exceptional cases have drawn almost level. In certain circumstances the DGB's strike rules provide for financial assistance for unions heavily hit by strike payments. The employers have in turn begun to promote the idea of solidarity among their affiliated associations and member firms, and guidelines have been issued in this respect in a number of industries. The intention is that the firms concerned should in their mutual interest

---

[1] *Year book of labour statistics, 1970* (Geneva, ILO), p. 790.

help strike-hit undertakings to keep their losses down to a minimum and should refrain from aggravating the situation by taking over their orders. Members are asked not to steal away customers, transfer their own orders to other firms or employ workers from strike-hit firms. Employers' organisations now have support funds as well.

The right of public servants to strike has so far been denied by the Government, and this attitude has also been very largely upheld by public opinion, although recently certain views were expressed suggesting a possible change. There have been some impressive protest demonstrations by tax officials, teachers, policemen and regular soldiers. Apprentices also have taken part in strikes involving their undertakings and have been affected by lockouts. It is after all difficult to provide proper training in an establishment where there is a complete stoppage of work and the instructors are also absent.

Under the strike guidelines issued by the DGB, a strike involving the collective settlement of employment conditions (not a political strike) may be called by an affiliated union if a secret ballot shows at least 75 per cent of the members eligible to vote to be in favour of it. Identical or similar provisions were included in the statutes of most of the affiliated unions. More recently the statutes of some unions have been amended so as to authorise a strike without a prior vote in special circumstances.

Every union's statutes stipulate that the members then have to follow their executives' instructions. There is no union that recognises the right of non-members affected by a strike call to be heard.

Very recently there have been quite a few brief warning strikes without a preliminary vote among the members concerned.

According to a ruling by the Federal Labour Court a wild-cat strike is a collective stoppage of work by a group of employees where such stoppage has not been authorised in advance and initiated by a competent trade union, or subsequently approved and sponsored by it, or which is pursued against the wishes of that union.

Recently, collective bargaining has no longer been conducted by the two sides merely in the knowledge that they could always fall back on the traditional weapons of strike or lockout in the event of a breakdown. In some industries there has also been a greater or lesser element of pressure coming from the danger of an unofficial strike or of certain employers breaking rank. The pattern of negotiations, which had hardly ever strayed from the normal and predictable course, was disrupted in the autumn of 1969 by a series of wild-cat strikes in the metalworking industry, where the existence of current collective agreements involving an obligation to abstain from direct action did not deter workers in some undertakings from advancing claims without union endorsement or even against their union's wishes. Although these local or plant-level clashes were rapidly settled, partly because the employers concerned met the claims without delay and paid for lost time, it was clear that the calm and steady course of negotiations had been interrupted by a new sort of unrest. These events also led writers on the subject to question the propriety of continuing to outlaw unofficial strikes.

In 1955 the Federal Labour Court confirmed that, alongside the lawful right of trade unions to call a strike, there also existed the right of employers and their organisations to impose a lockout as a legitimate form of direct action. In this way employers were given the possibility of terminating the employment relationship of striking employees without notice as a means of self-defence if the trade union, as normally happens in practice, had called the strike without observing the proper period of notice for termination of the employment relationship. It was understood that, once the dispute had been settled, and if no express provision had been made concerning reinstatement this should lie within the employer's fair discretion. This has in fact been the regular procedure, except that the trade unions have usually insisted that new collective agreements should guarantee the reinstatement of those concerned, thereby affording them general protection against any adverse effects.

One case that was of no consequence in itself (a lockout against croupiers on strike at a casino) nevertheless caused the Federal Labour Court to reconsider this question, which is of vital importance for the continuation of the employment relationship and the workers' willingness to strike. The Court's fundamental decision of 21 April 1971 was in some ways a reversal of its earlier position, because it ruled that lockouts should in principle, just like strikes, not terminate employment relationships but simply suspend their effects. But in order to ensure a fair balance of bargaining power, a lockout terminating the employment relationship may be allowed if there are aggravating circumstances, which may have to be confirmed by judicial inquiry. The normal procedure is for the court to recognise the right of the workers concerned to immediate reinstatement, with the possibility of judicial supervision of the employer's compliance. But in special cases the employer may be allowed to refuse reinstatement, particularly if a post no longer exists or has been given to someone else.

In recent years lockouts have only been imposed as a rejoinder to strikes already under way, and no cases have been notified of employers taking the first step.

The position of workers' representatives in the event of direct action

Members of works councils are certainly in the most difficult position if it comes to direct action. As workers they will generally be in favour of a strike designed to improve their own economic situation and will want to join it themselves. But as members of the works council they are bound to observe strict neutrality. The law requires the employer and the works council to refrain from any action liable to jeopardise the operation of the undertaking or industrial peace; it specifically forbids them to engage in any direct action one against the other. But there is nothing to stop members of the works council from participating in a strike in their capacity as employees. Shop stewards in an undertaking will naturally be inclined to back a strike called by the union to which they belong, and union rules require them to give their support even if they do not personally approve of the strike or some lawful action proposed by the strike committee.

Workers serving on their undertaking's supervisory board [1] must not misuse this function in the event of direct action because they have the same obligations as the representatives of the shareholders in this respect. As employees, on the other hand, they can join a strike.

Interim injunctions

In some cases courts have responded to a plea from one of the parties by issuing an interim injunction forbidding certain forms of action. The infringements against which this protection was sought were connected not with the actual determination of the members' employment conditions but with such matters as violation of a statutory or contractual obligation to maintain industrial peace, failure to follow the agreed conciliation procedure, and so on. Where courts have provisionally banned direct action in such circumstances they have exerted a decisive influence on the relations between the two sides.

---

[1] See Professor Wilhelm Herschel: " Employee representation in the Federal Republic of Germany ", in *International Labour Review*, Vol. LXIV, Nos. 2-3, Aug.-Sep. 1951, pp. 207-215.

Recent Trends in
Collective Bargaining
in Italy

Gino GIUGNI [1]

The background to the new trade union strategy

WHEN TAKING STOCK of the situation in these pages in 1965 [2], I noted that in the whole history of the Italian trade union movement there had never before been a decade in which industrial relations had undergone such sweeping changes. After a lapse of only six years, however, the point can be made again even more strongly. Beyond doubt, the years between 1968 and 1971 mark a turning point in the history of the Italian trade union movement, and this in all probability will affect the political life of the country as a whole. But, as I pointed out in 1965, the far-reaching changes then taking place in the industrial relations system were a product of the economic and social evolution of the country, which in the space of a few years had become an industrial power in its own right, whereas developments since 1968 must be looked at in a very different light.

The fact is that the new trends and patterns in collective bargaining have been profoundly affected by the wave of unrest that has swept across Europe in the past three years, leading to a complete reappraisal of the whole purpose of social movements in general and—in some countries—of the trade unions in particular. This climate of cultural and intellectual unrest certainly accounts to a great extent for the change in trade union strategy. Another reason, however, especially in the case of the thriving metalworking industry, is that from 1960 onwards a set of younger, more militant and critically minded leaders emerged.

---

[1] Professor of Labour Law, University of Bari, and Legal Adviser to the Minister of Labour.

[2] Gino Giugni: " Recent developments in collective bargaining in Italy ", in *International Labour Review*, Vol. 91, No. 4, Apr. 1965, pp. 273-291.

The second point to be borne in mind is that although Italy's post-war economy grew remarkably rapidly and quickly recovered from the 1963-65 recession, it has been subject to very little public control. The attempt at economic planning in the mid-1960s proved disappointing. And it is in the mood of impatience and restlessness mentioned above that the country has found itself faced with a whole series of acute problems created by this self-same process of industrialisation and economic development, e.g. the influx into the rapidly expanding cities and the formation of a large new class of unskilled factory workers, nearly all immigrants from other parts of the country, usually the south. Other problems are the housing shortage, the gross inadequacy of urban and suburban transport, the lack of welfare, hospital and educational facilities, especially in the new centres of industry, etc. Thus social policy, instead of being regarded as secondary to economic development policy, is now seen to be its fundamental prerequisite.

The change in the trade union movement

This new situation is not easy to describe concisely for an international public.[1] Indeed, it can hardly be compared with the kind of situation encountered in other highly industrialised States. The general trend of the Italian trade union movement in the 1960s seemed to be, and in fact was, towards consolidating a system of industrial relations that was already to some extent institutionalised. In other words there was considerable scope for trade union action and collective disputes, but within a framework (established by collective agreement) of clearly defined bargaining rights and levels, together with the possibility of recourse to procedural rules applicable in the event of direct action. The whole of this system of bargaining, which in the absence of special legislation [2] operated autonomously, has passed through a crisis in the past few years entailing a painful reassessment of the entire situation.

Another major development in the Italian trade union movement is the fact that the three principal confederations, namely the CGIL (mainly comprising communist and socialist workers), the CISL (largely made up of Catholic workers) and the UIL (chiefly socialist, social-democratic and republican workers, with the first group slightly in the majority), during the past five years have been moving towards trade union unity. If achieved, this will be an event of unprecedented importance. It has been encouraged and indeed made possible by the joint trade union

---

[1] See in this connection F. Sellier: "Les transformations de la négociation collective et de l'organisation syndicale en Italie", in *Sociologie du travail*, No. 2, 1971, pp. 141-158, and, in particular as regards the political and trade union framework, A. Pizzorno: "Les syndicats et l'action politique", ibid., pp. 115-140.

[2] Regarding the failure to pass trade union legislation implementing article 39 of the Constitution, see my previous account.

action that has begun to develop in the past few years, especially during the so-called " hot autumn ", i.e. the last quarter of 1969. In the metal-working industry, which has always been the pace-setter, the practice of holding joint meetings of workers and joint sessions of union committees, etc., has resulted in common union policies and gradually helped to forge a common will. Progress towards trade union unity in Italy has thus gone a long way and must be borne in mind if recent collective bargaining trends are to be understood. For example, the metal-workers, at a conference held in July 1971, resolved to achieve unity during the next year. The confederations to which their unions belong endorsed this programme, but for the time being they are having to reckon with increasingly important minorities who are opposed to these moves. In August the UIL " excommunicated " its metal-mechanical workers' federation which is in danger of undergoing a split, while the CISL and its metal-mechanical workers' federation are in a state of open conflict.

Another very significant development is the fact that, during the extensive industrial strife of the past few years, the unions have found themselves providing guidance and leadership to other, sometimes reluctant, groups. It was in 1968 that the first big disputes, especially the strike against the Pirelli Company in Milan, broke out under pressure from small, unofficial groups which played a prominent part throughout the upheavals of this period. However, it is fair to say that the trade union organisations were on the whole successful in maintaining their position of leadership. They achieved this, and neutralised the " spontaneous " pressures from below, by breaking completely with their practices of the past and adopting a policy of constant communication with the rank and file and the totality of the workers. This in turn has led to considerable democratisation of the decision-making process, and as a result the unions, instead of representing only their own members, are tending to become the spokesmen of the working class as a whole.

The consequences of this state of affairs can be assessed only over the long term. What is already clear, however, is that in a very short space of time certain trade union organisations (especially those affiliated to the CISL) have had to abandon their policy of representing only their own members and bargaining solely on their behalf (even to the extent of trying to deny negotiated benefits to non-members). Today the movement appears to have emerged as the spokesman of great numbers of workers who are not themselves union members (the degree of unionisation has risen sharply, but over the country as a whole still averages less than 50 per cent [1]) yet are deeply involved in the unions' struggle.

---

[1] In the metalworking industry, however, this figure is much higher—presumably of the order of 70 per cent—and there has been an increase of 250,000 members in the past two years.

It was in this broader representative capacity that, immediately after the disputes over the renegotiation of collective agreements in 1969, the unions dealt direct with the Government about what became known as the " reform strategy ". They had come to realise that, whatever concessions might be extracted from the employers, the workers' fundamental needs could not be met unless certain vital reforms were undertaken, e.g. in respect of health services, housing, transport, taxation, and—less urgently—education. The unions, in short, were no longer mere bargaining agents restricted to the field of employment conditions but bodies able to hold their own with the Government in discussing the latter's own political programmes. Even the Government's plans for the south, the most backward part of the country, were discussed exhaustively on a bipartite basis; the unions insisted that this problem was the key to the solution of all the others, arguing rightly that the existence of a backward area within the country affected the economic development of the remainder. The Government was technically correct in describing its dealings with the unions as " consultations ", but in actual fact they were nothing short of negotiating sessions which went on for several days and nights.[1]

Evolution of the bargaining system

Let us now take a brief look at the pattern of industrial relations before 1963 and the way in which the new system established in that year has evolved. For fuller details reference should be made to my previous article; suffice it to say here that from the end of the Second World War until the early 1960s, the Italian system of collective bargaining was characterised by exclusive reliance on collective agreements concluded at the national level, whether in the form of general agreements for the whole of industry or special agreements for particular industries. This system was virtually universal. It began to show signs of inadequacy towards the end of the 1950s, however, when plant-level agreements became more common (even though usually negotiated with non-union bodies such as the works councils), while simultaneously there was a widening of the gap between the conditions of employment in large firms and those in small firms. Reverting to the diagnosis made

---

[1] On the constitutional implications of these talks with the Government—which completely bypassed the National Economic and Labour Council, a representative body which has been in a state of crisis from the beginning—see G. Giugni: " Stato sindacale, pansindacalismo, supplenza sindacale ", in *Politica del Diritto*, No. 1, 1970. They were, in fact, a form of " political bargaining " of the kind dealt with by Selig Perlman in *A theory of the labor movement* (New York, Macmillan, 1928), p. 173. Political bargaining in Italy is non-partisan and is not to be equated with lobbying; it is genuine negotiation with the Government, which recognises the workers' representatives, even though not officially, as spokesmen of public opinion on a par with the political parties. Naturally, this action by the Government has given rise to criticism and controversy. See for example G. Negri: " Governo e sindacati ", in *L'Europa*, 1970.

in a recent but already classic article by two British authors [1], it can be said that the distinguishing feature of the collective bargaining system in these years was a high degree of anomie.[2] Nation-wide collective bargaining was in fact a façade which concealed widening discrepancies between individual firms.

This phenomenon grew even more marked after 1960, when plant-level bargaining with the unions or (more rarely) works councils over internal conditions of work gradually became more widespread.[3]

The growth of trade union pressures from below, especially in the metalworking industry, led to a new development in 1962. In July of that year, the state-controlled concerns managed by the IRI and ENI [4] signed a " protocol of intentions " for the metalworking industry in which they accepted that the nation-wide agreement could be supplemented by plant-level agreements dealing with such specific points as piece rates, new systems of job classification and output bonuses. This was tantamount to recognition of plant-level bargaining, though not without reservations, since the bargaining agent for the workers was not the union in the plant concerned but the trade union organisation for the province. There was, in short, no recognition in these agreements of plant unions themselves; this is something that was to change radically in the years that followed.

This method was called " articulated bargaining " and in due course became widespread in publicly and privately owned industry alike, to the extent of being codified in " protocols " preceding the agreements. The division of responsibilities was not always closely respected on either side, but the experiment was a major step towards acceptance of supplementary plant agreements within the industrial relations system. However, the working of this articulated system was hampered by a number of factors such as the economic recession that began in 1963, which made bargaining very difficult on the type of subjects covered by plant-level agreements, e.g. output bonuses. These bonuses were established in virtually all plants but, very often, instead of being linked to productivity,

---

[1] Alan Fox and Allan Flanders: " The reform of collective bargaining: from Donovan to Durkheim ", in *British Journal of Industrial Relations* (London), Vol.VII, No. 2, July 1969, pp. 151-180.

[2] Defined by the authors as " a state of normlessness resulting from a breakdown in social regulation ".

[3] Works councils are elected bodies representing all the workers employed in a plant, usually elected from trade union lists. For the past ten to fifteen years the councils have been cold-shouldered by the unions, which look upon them as dangerous competitors too ready to accept paternalism from the employers and suffering from a general lack of toughness. In practice, however, the councils are now fading out of the picture (see below for a discussion of new forms of representation).

[4] The two main public holding companies, the former of which controls all or most of the telephone network, radio and television, iron and steel, shipping and air transport, together with a number of large engineering firms (such as Alfa Romeo), while the ENI operates in the petroleum, chemical and textiles industries.

were in reality nothing more than fixed wage supplements. The first experimental period came to an end with the recession itself; in the circumstances it would have been unreasonable to expect the practice of plant-level bargaining to spread very fast.

The 1966 metalworkers' agreement—a cautious compromise

The metalworkers' collective agreement expired in 1966. As was noted in the previous article, it had increasingly tended to become the pace-setter, and the negotiations over its renewal took place in a strained atmosphere, both sides finding themselves in a rather ambiguous position. For one thing, the effects of the recession were still being felt while, on the trade union side, as the political differences between the confederations became increasingly blurred, they tended to crop up further down the line in relations between the confederations and their industry-wide federations. It was this latent conflict between the metalworkers' federations, which were increasingly inclined to go their own way, and the national confederations that formed the background to the hard bargaining over the 1966 agreement. The economic recession affected the whole of industry, so that trade union attempts to renew the many collective agreements due to expire made no progress. Under government pressure, the deadlock in bargaining was finally broken through talks at the level of the confederations, and in this way the confederations regained the initiative, but their attempts to strengthen their position as the final arbiters in the collective bargaining process were thwarted by the failure of a proposal for a " model " or " protocol " agreement aimed at covering the whole of industry.

This idea of the " model " agreement, which was much favoured in CISL circles, would have involved defining the powers of the parties at each level and the bargaining procedure at each stage. This would have strengthened the system of articulated bargaining, which was by now widespread throughout industry, and at the same time would have reinforced the position of the confederations themselves. Under the arrangement the unions would have been recognised as entitled to bargain with plant managements. But no detailed proposals in this sense were ever put forward and, while the model agreement was discussed for some time, none of the confederations had any precise suggestions to make. The crux of the matter lay not so much in what points should be covered by the agreement as in the whole idea of giving overriding responsibility to the confederations. This idea nevertheless influenced the setting up of the Government's planning machinery, which inevitably gave rise to proposals for Swedish-type centralised control of wages in close collaboration with the planning authorities. Events since 1967, however, have completely swept aside this scheme for a " model " agreement, which had only come to the fore as a topic for discussion around 1966.

Despite the lack of progress in collective agreements as a result of the recession, negotiations were resumed between the employers' and workers' confederations on a number of important points affecting the whole of industry, but the results were not very striking. Between 1965 and 1966, three agreements which had been in force since 1947 (dealing with individual dismissals; redundancies; and works councils) were renewed with a number of marked improvements. As regards works councils, the new agreement for the whole of industry concluded in 1966 stated explicitly that they were not empowered to conclude agreements at plant level, but did not specify any other bargaining agent.

The principles governing individual dismissals agreed on between the employers' and workers' confederations were embodied in Act No. 604 dated 15 July 1966 [1], which was already under consideration when the agreement was concluded and was one of the items of legislation later consolidated to form the so-called " Workers' Charter ". On the whole, therefore, when allowance is made for the pressures created by the passing of legislation on dismissals and the fairly minor importance of the changes in the status of works councils, collective bargaining at the top during this period (1966-67) can be summed up as a phase of administrative tidying-up and, above all, of filling in gaps created by the absence of industry-level bargaining.

The resumption of industry-level bargaining

In 1966 bargaining at the industry level once more got under way, the pace-setter being the metalworkers' agreement. This was first renewed by the state-controlled concerns after long drawn out negotiations and then by private industry (this had by now become standard practice). It did not involve any major innovations and, looking back, can be regarded as a setback for the unions. The real reason for this setback was the lack of bargaining power, mainly due to the recession from which the Italian economy was still recovering.

But apart from the distinctly meagre wage concessions (a 5 per cent increase over three years), the agreement did contain a number of interesting points. For example, although plant-level unions were still not recognised, the provincial union organisations were empowered to appoint workers to special committees set up to negotiate such matters as job classification and piece rates. In practice, this gave the unions plant-level representation, even if by a roundabout route. Minor relaxations were also made in the rules governing the conduct of trade union

---

[1] ILO: *Legislative Series*, 1966—It. 1.

business in the factories, e.g. the granting of time off and permission to post notices. The most significant gain in the state-controlled concerns—even though in practice it was scarcely observed—was the requirement that managements should make premises available close to the factories for trade union business to be carried on. The agreement also regulated the deduction of union dues from wages, thereby doing much to stabilise the incomes of the Italian unions, which now can no longer be regarded as " poor ". The employers, for their part, received undertakings regarding strikes in continuous-process industries and other trades where stoppages of work without warning might endanger life and limb or damage equipment.

The example of this agreement was as usual followed in other industries, which took as their model the agreement signed by the private firms; this was slightly less advanced than the one concluded by the state-controlled undertakings. During this period ending in 1968 the most significant innovations occurred in the chemical, petro-chemical, petroleum and textiles industries.

The crisis in articulated bargaining

With the end of the recession, which had considerably restricted the opportunities for articulated bargaining, it might have been expected that from 1966 onwards the system would grow in effectiveness and gradually develop through a progressive expansion of the coverage of plant-level bargaining. Back in 1962 this had been permitted only in extremely cautious terms; indeed, word-chopping was taken so far that sometimes even the word " bargaining " was avoided—on grounds which paradoxically led on occasion to extensive bargaining! In short, a policy of progress in industrial relations covering the period up to the end of 1968—a policy which was clearly stated in a publication of the state companies [1]—could be discerned in the actual enlargement of the scope of articulated bargaining and the strengthening of the procedural standards designed to regulate the conduct of disputes or to cushion their effects. The inevitability of industrial conflict was regarded in advanced management circles not any more as an evil but simply as a fact of life and even as a healthy sign, provided only that a few rules of procedure were observed.

Some at least of the agreements concluded at this time bear the stamp of this approach. For example, the agreements for the petroleum industry enlarged the list of points on which plant bargaining was allowed, and there was also a tendency—if not formally, at least in practice—towards direct negotiation between individual employers (sometimes

---

[1] Associazione sindacale Intersind: *Dieci anni di attività contratuale (1958-1967)* (Rome, 1968).

assisted by their employers' associations) and trade union representatives who were in the firm but who might, for the principle of the thing, be delegated by the provincial organisations. Economic gains under these agreements continued at much the same rate up to 1969, despite the fact that the recession was by then over.

In 1969, however, there was a decisive change. The year opened with heavy and partly uncontrolled pressure from the trade unions in the form of wildcat strikes. Sometimes these consisted of alternating (" rolling ") strikes and sometimes of repeated brief stoppages without notice by groups of workers who seemed to be acting for no particular reason. One important new development occurring in this unsettled phase and affecting the negotiation of the plant agreements that followed it was that, instead of the normal forms of representation consisting of works councils and factory trade union branches (which in any case were now only being formed with the utmost difficulty), a new type of worker representation sprang up in the shape of the so-called " delegates ". These spokesmen, who are now playing a key part in the revival of the trade union movement and are discussed in greater detail later, are elected direct by their fellow workers in workshops or departments or sections. Sometimes these elections are conducted in association with the trade unions (which may put up candidates), and at other times completely independently, although the bargaining itself is usually carried out jointly with the unions.

In short, at the beginning of 1969 the traditional representative structure fell apart, while the principle of the division of responsibilities involved in articulated bargaining crumbled with the spread of agitation in the factories, which often led to the conclusion of far more comprehensive agreements. In virtually all cases the trade unions joined forces with the delegates' movement during the bargaining stage proper and took over strategic control. Simultaneously, however, it became common practice for workshop meetings to decide on the instructions to be given to their delegates or to the trade unions. It is impossible to give a clear-cut account of the situation because the whole pattern was, and still is, extremely blurred and complex.

It is not the purpose of this article to explore the reasons for this revival of working-class militancy, although some of the internal factors at work were mentioned in the first section. It is, however, worth mentioning two external factors which undoubtedly had some effect: the events of May 1968 in France, and the efforts of the student movement, which urged on the most extreme workers' groups and, although in practice playing only a marginal part in the struggle, managed to inject into it some of the themes of the radical student organisations, e.g. the struggle " against the system ", workers' control, and rejection of the idea of delegating authority on the ground that all decisions should be taken directly by meetings of all the workers.

281

The hot autumn of 1969

Whether through hope, or fear of a general explosion as a result of industrial strife, public opinion was kept on tenterhooks throughout the whole of this period. In point of fact the " Italian May " was a long time coming and the " events " were more spaced out, but their impact was all the greater for that. In the spring of 1969 strikes of all kinds broke out in a number of large firms in the north. Most of them were short, unofficial rolling strikes, and in a large number of cases resulted in the conclusion of plant agreements. But once the trade unions had reasserted their authority, the movement was successfully harnessed to a clearly defined strategy designed to bring maximum pressure to bear when the most important national agreements were due to expire, i.e. in the autumn of 1969. It should be noted that the unions had already regained the initiative between 1968 and 1969 and following an agreement between the leading confederations which, after a bitter struggle, led to the introduction of a single national wage structure (and therefore the abolition of regional differentials).

The unions won several notable successes about this time, showing that they had by no means abandoned their position of leadership on the social front. Another significant achievement was the adoption, after a series of strikes for reform of the pension scheme, of much more advanced legislation in the spring of 1969.

Events unfolded punctually in accordance with the strategy mentioned above. The campaign for the renewal of the collective agreements was planned well in advance, especially in the metalworking industry, where 1.5 million workers were affected. Between 2,000 and 3,000 well-attended meetings were held which hammered out lists of key demands on which only very limited room for manœuvre was allowed. The meetings in no way served just to endorse programmes decided at the top. For instance, the FIOM (the CGIL metalworkers' federation), which was in favour of percentage wage increases, had to abandon its stand because of egalitarian pressure at the meetings for flat-rate increases all round. Unlike the practice in previous years, the lists of items for inclusion in the new agreements were not simply an assorted catalogue of demands which would later be whittled down to a few key points, but from the start represented a careful selection concentrating on certain well-defined objectives, which under the new strategy were to be fought for until they were all achieved.

Although the front-line troops during this hot autumn were the metalworkers, close behind were the unions in other major industries whose agreements were also about to expire. Agitation invariably began several months beforehand. The first agreements to be concluded were for the building industry, chemicals and cement; in the case of chemicals the " protocol " agreement on articulated bargaining was terminated, and in the cement industry representation at plant level was explicitly recognised. But the question which gripped virtually the whole country and formed the main topic of the nation's political life for two or three months was the negotiation of the metalworkers' agreement.

In all, some 4 million industrial workers were involved in the strikes of this hot autumn—not to mention another 1.5 million in agriculture. A total of 520 million working hours were lost, 400 million of them in industry. Picketing was energetic and there were quite a few incidents with the police, management personnel and blacklegs, as well as a few cases of sabotage. The extremist groups often engaged in provocation, which the trade unions tried to counteract or contain, in the main successfully. They relied heavily on mass demonstrations, culminating in an imposing but peaceful march through Rome by 150,000 metalworkers in November 1969.

The country went through a period of acute tension and indeed fear, but it is only fair to say that the mass demonstrations such as the one in Rome were kept well under control. In fact they did a great deal to defuse the situation, since they proved that the movement was under proper leadership and that the unions' ultimate purpose was a settlement and not the overthrow of the system.

The Workers' Charter

Side by side with these negotiations, legislative action was being taken in the form of a Bill promulgating the so-called " Workers' Charter ".[1] This is a somewhat vague term dating back as far as 1952, when the CGIL proposed that there should be a " charter of workers' rights " regulating the exercise of their civil and political rights at their place of work, as guaranteed by the Constitution.

The Workers' Charter announced by the Government in June 1969 represented a somewhat unusual approach. On the one hand it set out to implement the constitutional principles guaranteeing the workers' freedom and right to fair treatment (recognition of political freedom at the place of work, prohibition of unreasonable disciplinary practices and prohibition of equally unreasonable checks on absenteeism, etc.). On the other hand it was imbued with the notion much favoured in socialist circles and advocated by the then socialist Minister of Labour, Giacomo Brodolini, that obstacles to trade union action at the factory level should be removed by law. This notion, which undoubtedly owed much to the precedent of the French Act of 1968 and also the Wagner

---

[1] Passed into law as Act No. 300 dated 20 May 1970 (ILO: *Legislative Series*, 1970—It. 2).

Act of 1935 in the United States, held that representative trade unions should be granted recognition at the workplace. By " recognition " was meant not so much the right to be treated as representative or to bargain with the employer as the right to special facilities for the conduct of trade union business, although this in turn might be construed as a precondition for some form of intervention or bargaining. The Act is silent on this point. Neither the Bill nor the Act as finally passed dealt with the bargaining powers of the trade unions at the plant level. The unions themselves were vigorously opposed to any definition on the ground that it would be restrictive in effect.

The Workers' Charter was thus mainly designed to modernise methods of personnel management by introducing an element of respect for the law and democracy, and to strengthen the trade unions at the workplace at a time when their position appeared to be undermined from two sides—as a result of pressure from employers who were still hostile to the recognition of trade unions within the factories, and pressure from spontaneous groupings and small-scale movements which questioned the whole function of a trade union. In short, the Charter sought first and foremost to put the unions on a firm footing at the factory level.

Owing to its introduction of an exceptionally rapid procedure for dealing with disputed cases, the Workers' Charter has had a considerable impact and has given rise to a large volume of case law, nearly all of it favourable to the unions. But leaving aside the practical effect the Charter has had since its entry into force in May 1970, if we go back to the period under review, i.e. the hot autumn of 1969 when the Charter was still before Parliament, its value lay mainly in the influence it had as a statement of legislative policy which would ultimately be binding on the parties. The unions welcomed the proposal to recognise their activities in the factories, while the employers found it difficult to maintain their position when faced with the Government's declared intention of proceeding along these lines by law. There was thus a direct relationship between the framing of the Workers' Charter and the unions' actions—a relationship that worked both ways. The Bill's provisions were embodied in the unions' demands, and these in turn, since they preceded the passing of the Bill into law, provided material for modifications to the Government's original version, which emerged from the debates in Parliament in a considerably amended form. The Workers' Charter therefore has also been a fundamental factor in bringing about the major changes in the Italian system of industrial relations.[1]

---

[1] The Charter consists of forty-one articles and is partly inspired by the international labour Conventions on freedom of association (Nos. 87 and 98). For details of the legal and constitutional background to the trade union movement in Italy, see my previous article in the *Review*.

The metalworkers' agreement of 1969

The bitter dispute over the renewal of the national metalworkers' agreement began in September 1969 and ended on 21 December 1969 with the signing of the new agreement by the private employers' delegation. The settlement for the state-controlled concerns had taken place two weeks earlier.

Before briefly summarising the contents of the agreement, which need not be analysed in detail here, it is worth recalling certain distinctive features of this vitally important round of negotiations. First, the bargaining began before the existing agreement expired, and indeed the new agreement was concluded before this date as well, so that there was no gap between the two. It should be added in passing that in almost all previous cases there had been a time-lag between the expiry of one agreement and the conclusion of another—sometimes of as much as a year or more. A second noteworthy feature is that the negotiations went on at the same time as the strikes, whereas it had been the established practice in Italy for the employers to refuse to bargain and for the Government to refrain from mediating while a strike was in progress. The third point deserving emphasis is the way the campaign was conducted, for not only did large numbers of workers take part in the stoppages but they also helped to take the actual strike decisions as well. What happened in practice was that the trade unions announced the number of hours for which workers were to strike each week and left it to the various workers' meetings to call the strikes as and when they thought fit.

Reference was made earlier to the fact that there was some disorder and violence—much less, however, than one might have expected in such a hard conflict. In the months immediately following, a whole series of prosecutions—denounced by the unions as a " wave of repression "—were instituted as a result of incidents which occurred during the campaign, mainly during the picketing, mass demonstrations and manning of road-blocks. In the end, however, Parliament intervened with an amnesty.

The democratic conduct of the campaign culminated in the ratification of the settlement reached by the trade unions. The negotiations had naturally been carried on by small groups of representatives, but the settlement was submitted to the workers' meetings, which voted on it; the pattern varied, but on the whole there was a large majority in favour of ratification. This, too, was an innovation in Italian practice, where bargaining at the national level had always been conducted entirely at the top with only very limited participation by local representatives.

A point worth emphasising is the heavy participation by young workers, and the motivating force constituted by the unskilled operatives, many of them immigrants from other parts of the country doing the simplest jobs and also the most restive under discipline, whether exercised by employers or unions. The white-collar workers, especially the technicians, likewise played a prominent part.

The final and by no means the least important point to be made about this dispute concerns the mediation exercised by the Minister of Labour. This gave rise to bitter criticism.[1] The intervention by the Minister, Mr. Donat-Cattin (a left-wing Christian Democrat), in early November met with an unenthusiastic response, not to say hostility, on the part of the workers' organisations, But the Government felt that action had become essential because the negotiations between the parties themselves had been a disastrous failure. In actual fact, once mediation had been offered, the negotiations could not be transferred back from the Ministry, and from being a mediator the Minister was bound to become a virtual arbitrator. Indeed, the announcement of any settlement was almost always made by the Minister in official communications to the parties, with the result that the employers' organisations complained that agreements were imposed and not genuinely negotiated. It is true that the Minister's settlements " imposed " on the employers were extremely close to the unions' position. For the unions it was a notable success, since the concessions granted fell little short (a mere 20 per cent) of their demands. But a willingness to direct the final solutions towards achieving a marked increase in wages, a shorter working week, and a reduction in the gap between white- and blue-collar workers was announced at the very beginning of the mediation process as being the official policy of the Minister.

As regards the contents of the agreement—it would really be more accurate to speak of agreements, since there was one for state-controlled industry and another for private industry—one need only single out the main points in order to illustrate the changes in the bargaining pattern. Both agreements introduced, with a number of unimportant variations, a whole series of changes in pay and conditions. The increase in pay amounted to 65 liras an hour for operatives and 15,500 liras a month for salaried staff. This flat-rate increase reflected the egalitarian trend and the tendency for skill differentials to narrow; as was mentioned earlier, this was one of the demands that emerged from the stormy workers' meetings held during the bargaining. Other clauses provided for the gradual reduction of the working week to forty hours by the end of 1972; equal treatment for hourly paid workers and salaried staff in the event of sickness and injury; the drastic limitation of overtime; and a whole series of minor points (such as the overhaul of the pay structure to take account of the shorter working week, which was a very expensive concession). The points on which the unions' demands were rejected, or to all intents and purposes shelved, mainly concerned

---

[1] See G. Giugni: " L'autunno 'caldo' sindacale ", in *Il Mulino*, No. 207, 1970, and now also under the title " L'automne chaud syndical ", in *Sociologie du travail*, No. 2, 1971 pp. 159-177.

the provision of a career structure for salaried staff. The additional cost to industry of the agreement was estimated at about 16 per cent during the first year and a total of 28 per cent over the three years. It is undoubtedly one of the most expensive agreements to have been concluded in the past twenty years. The Minister of Labour, however, argued that it was necessary to expand domestic demand and to promote employment by cutting working hours and curbing overtime.

The second group of demands made by the unions, which also led to a good deal of hard bargaining, concerned the points subsequently regulated by the Act of 20 May 1970 (the Workers' Charter). The negotiations over the clause dealing with the right to hold meetings on working premises were particularly tough. One of the concessions to emerge from the negotiations was the right of workers to attend meetings during working hours without loss of pay, up to a maximum of ten hours a year. This innovation did not form part of the Government's original Bill, but was subsequently endorsed by Parliament and is now a statutory requirement. On the subject of time off with pay for workers engaged on union business, the two agreements differ in that the one for private industry followed the terms of the Bill, while that for state-owned industry makes more generous provision. The part dealing with disciplinary sanctions also contains a number of important innovations although, by and large, it does not come up to the standards that were laid down in the Government's Bill. The agreement will remain in force until the end of 1972.

The new bargaining pattern

On the morning of 21 December 1969 the hot autumn came to an end and a new chapter opened in the history of Italian industrial relations. The metalworkers' agreement marked an unprecedented success for the trade unions. It introduced major changes in a number of non-economic spheres, but even so, at the express desire of both sides, did not contain a definition of what at one time appeared to be the prime bone of contention, viz. the exact extent of plant-level bargaining.

It is fair to describe the bargaining pattern in Italy today as passing through a transitional stage in which the opposing positions are for the time being irreconcilable. The private employers' delegation had laid down as a prior condition to the opening of negotiations for the metalworkers that there must be a discussion on the exact scope of plant-level bargaining and a restatement of the principle that once a subject has been settled by negotiation it cannot be reopened elsewhere until the agreement has expired. The unions had rejected any prior definition of powers and the " protocol " on articulated bargaining was neither terminated nor confirmed.

The difference of opinion was fundamental and insoluble, and only a stopgap compromise could be found. On the insistence of the Minister of Labour, the employers' confederation had withdrawn its condition, but the Minister himself acknowledged the need to tackle this problem at some later date after the new national agreement had been in force for some time. By the end of the first half of 1971, however, the talks envisaged by the Minister had still not been held and do not seem likely either. The result of negotiations on this point, therefore, was that the parties agreed to differ. The trade union organisations reserved the right to reopen issues in plant-level bargaining which had already been settled in the national agreement and denied that the latter in any way constituted a final settlement or even a truce. The employers' delegation based its case on the fact that the " protocols " of 1962-63 had not been specifically abrogated and must therefore be considered to be still in force. In practice, as was to be expected, plant-level bargaining expanded considerably in the months that followed, though it partially dealt with issues that were not covered by the 1969 national agreement.

The extent to which the agreement has bound the unions to a temporary truce has also been questioned. The actual behaviour of the parties suggests that the new agreement " was signed merely to put an end to the current dispute and in no way guarantees employers against possible future disputes ".[1] Thus, from the point of view of the collective bargaining pattern as well, the hot autumn has brought about a major change—to the point where a jurist might be prompted to ask whether a collective agreement can actually be considered to constitute a contract imposing legal obligations on both parties. While this is plainly going too far, it is based on the assumption, considered to be obvious though unprovable, that any contract implies a legally enforceable truce (rather than in this particular case a reasonable *political* likelihood that the national dispute will only be resumed when the agreement expires). If there were not such an implied no-strike clause, this would mean that the duration of the agreement would be binding only on the employers. A third hypothesis can also be put forward, namely that there is an obligation to observe a truce but only on the points which were actually renegotiated in the national agreement.

The subject offers plenty of scope for argument and it is sufficient for our purpose to sum up the main issues involved. What is certain is that plant-level bargaining is on its way in and that, if only to a limited extent, it also covers matters which are the same as or similar to those settled in the national agreements.

Developments in 1970 and the first half of 1971

In 1970 and the early part of 1971 a number of major agreements at the national level covering some 2.5 million workers came up for

[1] G. Giugni: " L'autunno 'caldo' sindacale", op. cit.

renewal. Broadly speaking, the changes introduced were much the same as in the case of the agreement for the metalworkers. The main industries involved were textiles, glass, ready-made clothing, rubber and plastics. The increases granted—once again the same for everybody—ranged from 60 to 85 liras an hour. In some industries the principle of the monthly wage was accepted and other innovations were a reduction in the number of grades for operatives, the lowest being eliminated, while the experiment in job evaluation is being wound up. One agreement (in the rubber industry) conceded longer vacations, a point that had not been dealt with in the metalworkers' agreement. Almost all these settlements granted much more extensive bargaining powers to the unions at plant level.

The agreement for the rubber industry explicitly recognised trade union bargaining rights at the plant level, especially over such matters as working conditions and the determination of maximum permissible levels of toxicity. Similar clauses appeared in the agreement for the glass industry, which also terminated the " protocol " on articulated bargaining. Lastly, major gains were also secured in the agreement for agriculture.[1]

Thus the years 1970 and 1971 witnessed not only the conclusion of a number of nation-wide agreements but also a remarkable upsurge in collective bargaining at the plant level. It is estimated that as many as 4,400 plant agreements of various kinds covering more than 1.5 million workers are now in force. In some cases they implement national agreements, the most significant examples being those concluded with Fiat in 1970 over the reduction of working hours, in which the trade unions adopted a policy of linking their own demands to the more general problems of national development. As a result, they agreed to spread the reduction in working hours over a longer period in return for an undertaking by Fiat to take active steps to create plants and jobs in the south.

In other respects the unions are not so consistent because, while they demand direct action to reduce congestion in the northern cities, the fact remains that shorter working hours and less overtime may actually mean a rise in the number of workers attracted there. So far, the rise has been very small, but the main reason for this is the stagnation of the national economy.

The plant-level agreements vary considerably in content. They are of course most numerous in the metalworking industry. The majority deal with direct and indirect wage increases (allowances, annual bonuses, etc.) as well as incentive payments. A smaller proportion are concerned with grading systems and hours of work, especially the arrangements for introducing the shorter working week. Relatively few reflect the new approach which has become apparent among the trade unions and which is discussed immediately below.

---

[1] For further details of the trade union campaign in agriculture see Bruno Veneziani: " L'autunno caldo dei braccianti ", in *Economia & Lavoro* (Padua), No. 4, 1970, pp. 379-411.

As we saw earlier, the unions in negotiating with the Government on a series of wide-ranging national problems concentrated on the need for institutional changes in the social services in the widest sense of the term. This policy has undoubtedly had satisfactory results, but it is equally sure that the participation of the workers in these negotiations has been less active than in the collective agreement negotiations of 1969. On the other hand, the informal agreements reached with the Government have not met with the full support of Parliament, where resistance to their implementation through legislation has become marked.

At shop level the pattern of claims has undergone a remarkable change. Hitherto, industrial organisation has been the prerogative of management and the unions' task has been to bargain over the consequences of any changes in industrial conditions, especially as regards wages. Nowadays, however, they question the whole organisation of work within industry. The symbol of this campaign is the assembly line, which is singled out as the source of the workers' alienation and degradation. In this drive for a new type of organisation, particular importance is attached to such matters as the working environment, the pace of work and job classification. The demand is for an upgrading of jobs and a guaranteed career, combined with the abolition of incentive payments. The complete elimination of the lower grades, the introduction of job enlargement or job enrichment and the end of the practice of breaking down the work into simple operations have become common claims. The limitation of output, instead of allowing the pace of work to be set by the management, has also become far from infrequent. Nevertheless, in practical terms agreements dealing with these questions are still fairly few in number. A dispute broke out at the Fiat works in April this year largely over these points and led to some hard bargaining. This proved the most important test so far of the new union policy. The settlement, reached in June through the mediation of the Minister of Labour, substantially acknowledged the new union policy, but it was accepted that the changes in working conditions must be introduced gradually.

The emergence of demands of this type links up with the growth of the workers' delegate movement mentioned earlier. According to the (incomplete) information supplied by the metalworkers' unions, there are more than 22,000 workers' delegates in the industry belonging to 1,400 factory committees [1]; taking industry as a whole, the delegates

---

[1] Information supplied by the second joint metalworkers' conference held in March 1971. An inter-industry survey showed the degree of unionisation among the delegates to be higher than in the metalworking industry alone. It is also worth noting that the average age of the workers' delegates is between 30 and 35, so that it is possible to speak of the emergence of a whole new class of workers' leaders. Only 30 per cent belong to a political party. See R. Aglieta, G. Bianchi and P. Merli-Brandini: *I delegati operai* (Rome, 1971); extracts published under the title " Les délégués ouvriers: nouvelles formes de représentation ouvrière ", in *Sociologie du travail*, No. 2, 1971, pp. 178-190.

are strongest in textiles and clothing and the rubber industry. Their representative character can be gauged from the fact that there is usually one delegate for every thirty or forty workers.

The growth of the delegates' movement has also had an influence upon collective bargaining: while it was possible during the early post-war period to deny that plant-level agreements existed, now there is a close network of agreements right down to formal and informal arrangements between departmental managers and workers' delegates.[1] These delegates in turn are controlled by the departmental workers' meetings and are liable to be relieved of their posts at any time. Thus, although this description is something of an oversimplification, it can be said that the bargaining process has now become extremely decentralised, democratic and representative.

It is precisely through this extension of participation in the bargaining process that new issues are being raised, such as working conditions, piece rates and other types of incentives and grading systems. This can lead alternatively to great progress or simply to a reversion to highly restrictive work rules and practices. To a certain extent the introduction of some practices of this kind has been spontaneous and widespread (such as absenteeism), although it should be borne in mind that in the past Italian workers' output has been very high. To some extent also, this slackening is in accordance with the experience of other highly industrialised countries.

Conclusions

Thus the Italian bargaining system has undergone a drastic change since the hot autumn of 1969.

It is easier to say what has disappeared from the old system than to describe what has taken its place. For example, the whole question of workers' representation raises a series of problems on which the unions themselves are not in agreement. Sometimes the workers' delegates are union members and sometimes they are not. They may be elected from lists put forward by the unions or alternatively they may be selected without reference to their union membership. They should normally combine to form "factory committees", appointing their own executive bodies. These committees in turn, according to a proposal of the metalworkers, should form the basis for a new comprehensive metalworkers' union (rather fewer than 50 per cent of the delegates are union members at present). But while the proposal enjoys wide sup-

---

[1] This can be compared with the often informal "fractional bargaining" described by Neil W. Chamberlain in "Determinants of collective bargaining structures", in Arnold R. Weber (ed.): *The structure of collective bargaining* (New York, The Free Press of Glencoe, 1961), pp. 3-19. See also the analysis of "fragmentation" in Allan Flanders: *Collective bargaining: prescription for change* (London, Faber and Faber, 1967), p. 24.

port in the metalworking industry, this is not the case in other industries, where the tendency has been for the unions to take over the workers' delegate movement and to impose their own candidates for election or simply to appoint them direct.

Thus it can be seen that the situation is wide open and any number of outcomes are possible. The ultimate solution will depend on the speed at which the process of trade union unification goes forward, for it must be obvious that a representative structure such as the one just described will vary considerably in its effectiveness, depending on whether the unions manage to maintain their progress towards unity or whether the deep wounds inflicted prior to the period 1960-65 are reopened.

As regards the pattern of bargaining, the live issue of the moment is the definition of the bargaining powers to be exercised at each level. In purely descriptive terms the present situation is characterised by bargaining conducted at a number of levels (national, plant and sometimes company) without any co-ordination and therefore leaving the unions free to lodge claims at one level after they have been settled at another.

Another change has been in the significance attached to collective agreements, with the parties no longer agreeing to observe a period of truce and bargaining liable to be reopened at any time during the period of validity of the agreement. This means of course that in practice agreements are binding on employers but not on trade unions.

A system of this kind may seem extremely unstable and precarious and it undoubtedly is. " Permanent conflict ", which is the motto of the more militant unions [1], nevertheless requires a medium-term strategy and entails occasional lulls in the hostilities even if they do not take the form of an agreed truce.

A choice has to be made between an explicit, formal definition of bargaining powers and deadlines, and an approach based on informal political practice adapted to the circumstances. The present trend is undoubtedly towards the latter, in which case it is easy to foresee that, especially since the recent battle over the definition of the national minimum wage, bargaining at the top between employers' and workers' confederations covering the whole of industry is bound to lose its erstwhile importance.

As regards the subject-matter of collective agreements, it may be recalled that bodies like the works councils are also fading away and certain subjects such as dismissals are now regulated by law. On the other hand, agreements between the employers' and workers' confede-

---

[1] Naturally—and not only in Italy—forecasts about the trend in this field often prove wide of the mark; see for example Arthur M. Ross: " Changing patterns of industrial conflict ", in David B. Johnson (ed.): *Proceedings of the Twelfth Annual Meeting of the Industrial Relations Research Association, Washington, DC, December 28-29, 1959* (Madison, Wisconsin, IRRA, 1960), in which he speaks of the " withering away of the strike ".

rations might regain importance where social matters are concerned (for example such matters as manpower policy and vocational training), on the lines of the recent experiment in France.

The national collective agreement for branches of industry, on the contrary, will continue to occupy a key position for a number of reasons. Despite the considerable gains secured by action on the shop floor, it has been shown that the unions' strength and bargaining power are greatest when the negotiations are nation-wide. This was the experience of the " hot autumn ", when participation in the strikes reached its peak. In any case it is unlikely that as long as the unions engage in politics (as, for instance, on the occasion, referred to above, of their negotiations with the Government over various reforms), even if independently of the parties, instead of confining themselves to bread-and-butter issues, they will forgo an instrument with such obvious opportunities for political pressures and leverage—provided they can preserve their feelings of class solidarity. Furthermore, national collective agreements affect the conditions of workers in small firms, which is important since industrial concentration in Italy still has a long way to go.

Plant-level bargaining, now becoming increasingly widespread, has a twofold function: to blaze a trail for national agreements, especially in the big firms; and to improve and supplement these national agreements, especially in the smaller firms. Since it is improbable that nation-wide bargaining will disappear, it can reasonably be anticipated that the most advanced settlements will tend to be made in the largest firms, which will therefore enjoy a good deal of latitude. These settlements in turn will serve as pilot agreements for national bargaining purposes.

With all these changes in the forms of representation and assuming trade union unification as probable, bargaining will tend to be decentralised to the maximum extent until it merges into what is normally understood by the administration of a collective agreement (depending on the degree of flexibility of the standards to be observed).[1] At this level responsibility will fall mainly on the workers' delegates in the workshops or departments, who will end by combining the enforcement of plant or national agreements with the setting of new work standards. As regards this latter point, it is obvious that the current union demands to negotiate over industrial organisation and working arrangements are merely the thin end of the wedge. This situation is a challenge to the unions' (and also to the employers') inventiveness and initiative, as well as to their ability to co-ordinate and consolidate their demands in the interests of a common strategy. The imposition of work rules may help to humanise industrial employment and may even therefore be worth a falling-off in efficiency

---

[1] Allan Flanders: " Collective bargaining: a theoretical analysis ", in *British Journal of Industrial Relations*, London, Vol. VI, No. 1, Mar. 1968, pp. 1-26.

which should in any case be balanced by the increased pace of technological progress; if this does not happen, there will be a corresponding slackening in the rate of increase of the national income. On the other hand, the practice must not be allowed to result in privileged positions for certain groups to the detriment of others.

The present bargaining pattern can thus be described as an unco-ordinated, multi-tiered system ranging from what are virtually political negotiations with the Government at the top to informal bargaining by workers' delegates at the bottom. In the latter case, the bargaining merges into collective agreement enforcement and involves joint settlement of working practices. In turn, this development involves a major encroach-ment on the prerogatives of management and marks the end of the idea of the national agreement as a medium-term stabilising factor in industrial relations. In the other case—that of the unions' political activities or " bargaining " with the Government—the process clearly runs counter to the theory that industrial conflict should be treated in isolation [1] and opens up prospects for the unions of relationships with the political parties different from the traditional ones of subjugation together with a feed-back to the parties themselves and their leadership. These, however, are only general tendencies and some time must elapse before they can be verified and brought into sharper focus.

---

[1] Ralf Dahrendorf: *Class and class conflict in industrial society* (London, Routledge. 1959).

Recent Trends in Collective Bargaining in Japan

Tadashi MITSUFUJI [1]
and Kiyohiko HAGISAWA [2]

COLLECTIVE BARGAINING IN JAPAN is mainly conducted at the level of the undertaking, i.e. between the employer and an " enterprise union ", while the national or industrial trade union organisation to which the latter is affiliated seeks to influence the course of the negotiations as best it can. There is no reason to suppose that this general pattern will not continue, at least for the foreseeable future. Nevertheless, the balance of power between the various forces involved in the collective bargaining process has recently been shifting and the system as a whole has tended to become more flexible to take account of this.

To enable the reader to appreciate the latest trends taking place in this field, we propose to start by giving a general account of the structure, content and particular problems of collective bargaining in Japan.

Collective bargaining at the level of the undertaking

Enterprise unions

An enterprise union, as generally conceived in Japan, has two main features. First of all, it groups all workers—white-collar and blue-collar, professional and technical—who are employed in an undertaking operated by a single management (not an individual plant or workshop). Of course there are exceptions to this general rule. There are cases where workers in the same undertaking form or split into several unions organised on job or craft lines, or where several unions coexist within one undertaking as a

[1] Professor, Seijo University, Tokyo.
[2] Professor, Seikei University, Tokyo.

result of two or more companies having merged. In large concerns unions may be organised within each establishment (when they are known as locals) and form a federation (" headquarters " union) for the undertaking as a whole. Furthermore, workers in two or more medium or small-scale undertakings in the same locality sometimes organise themselves into a union on the basis of their craft or industry, or form a general union cutting across craft and industry. Cases also exist where workers in the same industry organise themselves into an industrial union on broader lines.

The second principal feature of an enterprise union is that as a rule it is open only to the permanent or regular employees of the undertaking. Temporary workers, who have inferior status and do not enjoy the same terms and conditions of work, are often barred from membership and are excluded from the application of the collective agreement. Even where a permanent workers' union takes up the problems of temporary workers, it is generally reluctant to assist them in forming a union of their own, so that, apart from the few cases where temporary workers have succeeded in organising a union by themselves, they usually have nobody to represent their interests within the undertaking.

Collective bargaining at this level naturally concentrates on matters within the direct purview of the undertaking and its operation. Indeed, problems are rarely dealt with in the context of a job, an industry or the economy as a whole. For instance, wages are determined, as a rule, on the basis of a worker's age, educational background, years of service and occupational status within the undertaking. While the size of a general wage increase may be roughly in line with the target established in the so-called spring wage offensive (see below), the actual figure will depend on the economic situation of the undertaking. On the other hand, as will be seen, the range of subject-matters dealt with at the bargaining table is wide, extending to practically every aspect of conditions of work and employment.

While collective bargaining is generally conducted between the management and the enterprise union, there are exceptional cases where it is entrusted to employers' and workers' organisations at the industrial level. Moreover, in large undertakings bargaining may take place both at the local level between the representatives of management and the officers of the locals, and between the management and the headquarters union officers at the centre. At the latter level the parties generally conclude a basic or framework agreement, while at the local level they work out the details of the agreement and deal with problems specific to the workshops concerned. Cases also exist where everything is decided through bargaining at the headquarters level without any scope being allowed for local bargaining.

The situation becomes more complicated where several unions coexist within the same undertaking. As noted earlier, a plurality of unions can arise as a result of *(a)* a split over union policy; *(b)* a merger of companies whose unions maintain their separate existence; and *(c)* the organisation of different craft unions within a single undertaking. There is no problem in the last case, but in the first two the situation becomes complex in that each rival union purports to cater for all the firm's employees. Each union has the right to bargain collectively, so several sets of negotiations take place simultaneously and separate agreements are concluded between the management and the unions concerned. Confused though this system may be, the general practice has been for the parties to conclude agreements with roughly the same contents because both labour and management are anxious to provide for uniformity in the establishment of conditions of work throughout the undertaking. Recently, however, the deepening confrontation between the central (i.e. national and industrial) organisations has begun to have repercussions on the activities of their affiliated unions at the base. Thus instances have begun to arise where rival unions in the same undertaking conclude agreements with differing provisions, especially as they relate to criteria for productivity-based wage increases. Even in the above three exceptional cases, however, it can be seen that collective bargaining remains confined to the individual undertaking.

The real problem arises where bargaining involves negotiation with a union whose members include employees of other undertakings, e.g. a general union or an industrial organisation to which the enterprise union is affiliated. Japanese employers and workers strongly believe that conditions of work should be determined uniformly within the context of the undertaking and share the view that outsiders should not intervene in the collective bargaining process. As far as the employers are concerned, there is the fear that intervention by a representative of a central organisation would be harmful to the preservation of friendly relations in the undertaking, disrupt negotiations by the injection of policy directives from the central organisation and possibly lead to the divulgence of confidential business information. As for the workers, they still have a clear recollection of the confusion and hardship caused by the excessive politicking of the central organisations' leaders immediately after the Second World War. They have a firm conviction that collective bargaining should mean " *our* negotiations to determine *our* working conditions within *our* company ".

The content of bargaining and collective agreements

Wages and bonuses naturally form one of the main subjects for collective bargaining. With the progress of rationalisation, however, such questions as the distribution of the benefits of increased productivity, the reduction of working hours, longer holidays and leave with pay are increasingly being dealt with at the bargaining table. Management policy (especially with regard to rationalisation), production plans, etc., are also discussed, although problems of this type are normally referred to joint consultation bodies (see next section).

Personnel questions (transfer and reassignment of employees, disciplinary sanctions, dismissal, retrenchment, etc.) constitute another important item for collective bargaining. Disputes often arise over the question whether personnel matters are a fit subject for negotiation, as many employers consider them as falling within the scope of managerial prerogatives. Generally, however, they are considered as being negotiable. In the post-war years there were many cases of mass dismissal which were necessitated by the shift from a war-time to a peace economy and which were smoothly effected according to criteria that had been agreed on between management and labour. More recently, with the structural changes and rationalisation taking place in industry, questions of transfer and collective dismissal have begun to take on renewed importance as a central issue of collective bargaining and of what has become known as the " struggle against rationalisation ". Of late, as the manpower shortage grows more acute, retirement allowances and the age of compulsory retirement have also become important bargaining issues, while worsening environmental pollution has lent added urgency to questions of occupational health and safety.

Collective agreements cover a good deal of ground. Usually they consist of *(a)* general provisions defining the scope of application of the agreement (including union security provisions); *(b)* provisions dealing with the status of the union within the undertaking and covering such matters as union activities during working hours or the use of company facilities for trade union purposes; *(c)* provisions relating to conditions of work, such as wages, hours of work, holidays and leave; *(d)* provisions covering personnel matters, such as disciplinary sanctions and procedures; *(e)* provisions governing labour disputes, industrial peace clauses, etc.; *(f)* provisions relating to grievance machinery, joint consultative machinery and other joint bodies or committees; and *(g)* provisions concerning the period of validity of the agreement and procedures for its renewal.[1] It is usual for the actual amounts of wages, bonuses and allowances to be fixed separately and to figure not in the collective agreement itself but in a separate supplementary " wage agreement " or " agreement on temporary allowances ". In the same way, the recent tendency has been for basic collective agreements to remain unmodified while separate agreements are concluded to incorporate such changes as prove necessary. One other recent trend that may be mentioned here is that, as opposed to their former lenient attitude, the employers have

---

[1] Also important for the determination of working conditions are of course the works rules unilaterally established by the employer; these constitute part of the employment contract, but it is statutorily laid down that in case of conflict with the collective agreement the latter shall be given precedence.

298

become more stringent in their application of provisions governing union activities during working hours and the use of company facilities.

Under the law the period of validity of a collective agreement may not exceed three years but in practice agreements are normally renewed every year; this is especially the case with regard to wage agreements. While collective agreements are sometimes disregarded by workers or employers, the basic agreement seldom contains any matter lending itself to enforcement by coercive measures. This explains why few applications have been made for court injunctions in connection with collective agreements. Claims for damages resulting from their violation have likewise been rare. It is far more common for an employer to take disciplinary measures against workers who act in defiance of an industrial peace or dispute clause. Such action by the employer may be challenged either before the appropriate Labour Relations Commission [1] or, on appeal, before a court of law. Where it is the employer who violates the collective agreement, the workers sometimes riposte by strike action.

As regards the extension of application of collective agreements, two possibilities are provided for by law but neither is much used in practice. The first concerns regional extension. When a majority of workers engaged in similar work in a certain locality are covered by one collective agreement, the Minister of Labour or the prefectural governor may, at the request of either or both of the parties to the agreement and on the recommendation of the Labour Relations Commission, decide to extend its application to all remaining workers of the same kind employed in the same locality and to their employers. A similar procedure is used for the determination of regional minimum wages. Given the fact that most collective agreements are concluded at the level of the undertaking, however, and that there is therefore a multiplicity of agreements in any one region, instances of such extension are rare. The second type is the general extension of application within the undertaking. Where more than three-quarters of the permanent workers employed in a plant or establishment are covered by the same collective agreement, the agreement can be made applicable to the remaining permanent workers in the same plant or establishment. However, since this cannot be done where the remaining workers are organised into another union and have concluded a separate collective agreement, instances of general extension are also extremely rare.

A good many collective agreements include provision for grievance machinery, though in practice it is seldom used. There are a number of reasons for this. To begin with, collective agreements and other rules governing the workplace are not detailed enough to make it obvious whether there has been a breach of the rules or not. Secondly, Japanese workers as individuals are not used to, and feel inhibited about, present-

---

[1] See below, in the section " Collective bargaining and the Government ".

ing grievances to their employer. Finally, grievances in the private sector in Japan are not normally taken to arbitration. Unresolved grievances are normally referred to joint consultation machinery or collective bargaining, so workers naturally feel inclined to submit their grievances to the union in the first place.

Joint consultation machinery

One of the more significant recent trends in collective bargaining is the development of joint consultation machinery within the undertaking. According to a survey by the Ministry of Labour in 1969, joint consultation is quite common in Japan. Of the 1,203 unions covered by the survey, 51 per cent participated in joint consultation bodies. The proportion tends to increase slowly each year.

Joint councils are normally established by collective agreement at the level of the undertaking, factory or workshop and are composed of an equal number of management and union representatives. They discuss such matters as management policy, the production plan, the introduction of new technology, social welfare and occupational health and safety. At the same time they may often deal with matters relating to general conditions of work, such as wages or working hours, which should normally be discussed at the bargaining table. Given the fact that collective bargaining is conducted at the enterprise level, it may be wondered whether joint consultation under Japanese conditions is not competitive with and detrimental to the collective bargaining system. This supposition is not entirely groundless, but may not be the whole truth either.

As regards its relationship to collective bargaining, joint consultative machinery is of three main types. The first type deals almost exclusively with matters relating to conditions of work and does in fact form a substitute for collective bargaining. The second functions independently of collective bargaining in the sense that the subjects to be discussed are apportioned between two different sorts of machinery: management, production and social welfare topics are discussed by the joint council on a consultative basis with a view to securing a mutual understanding of the problems involved, whereas matters relating to conditions of work are handled by the collective bargaining negotiators with a view to the conclusion of a collective agreement. The third type is where subjects relating to management, production and social welfare are discussed side by side with those regarding conditions of work. When an identity of views can be reached on the latter, a collective agreement is drawn up and concluded. When it cannot, the matters in dispute are referred to collective bargaining. Other subjects are discussed only on a consultative basis.

Clearly the first type does compete with collective bargaining procedures, particularly in medium and small-scale undertakings where unionisation is less developed. In fact there was a time when it not only weakened the collective bargaining system but also led to the weakening of the unions themselves. Yet in other cases it has served as a stepping-stone to collective bargaining.

The second and third types of joint consultation machinery are prevalent in large undertakings. The second presents no particular problem as far as collective bargaining is concerned. The third type takes advantage of the fact that in Japan the parties to collective bargaining and joint consultation are identical in order to deal with a broad range of problems of mutual concern in a comprehensive and systematic manner. It aims to negotiate conditions of work in an amicable atmosphere relieved of the tensions so often encountered in collective bargaining, but without trying in any way to subvert or weaken the function of collective bargaining. Indeed it serves above all as a preliminary step to collective bargaining. According to the Ministry of Labour survey, it is this third type of joint consultation machinery that has been adopted most widely in Japan. As industrial relations mature, the role of joint consultation vis-à-vis collective bargaining can become an independent, supplementary one; the majority of joint consultation systems now functioning in Japan may be said to have already reached this stage.[1]

Advantages and disadvantages of collective bargaining at the level of the undertaking

It is often argued that collective bargaining at the level of the undertaking suffers from the following defects: *(a)* its narrow base results in a somewhat blinkered view of wider interests and thus makes harmonisation of conditions of work on the basis of the industry, craft or occupation harder rather than easier; *(b)* a union whose members' interests are so closely bound up with the employer's is unlikely to act militantly and, in extreme cases, may even turn into a " company union "; *(c)* the restriction of union activity to individual undertakings makes it difficult to mount a large-scale attack on the employers, private or public, at the industrial or national level.

Disadvantages such as these certainly exist. However, the blinkered outlook of enterprise-level collective bargaining has now begun to be compensated by the growth of the workers' and employers' central organisations and the greater guidance they are now in a position to give. It cannot be denied that by exchanging and supplying information, " they are strengthening the links between industries and between undertakings in matters of wages and other conditions of work. . . . If this trend continues, the scope of wage determination will come to extend beyond

---

[1] See " Workers' participation in management in Japan (No. 7) " (prepared by Tadashi Mitsufuji and Toshio Ishikawa), in *Bulletin* (Geneva, International Institute for Labour Studies), No. 7, June 1970.

the framework of the individual undertaking."[1] Moreover, the sharing of a common fate with the undertaking may not necessarily weaken the bargaining power of the union. It is the workers' conscious identification with their undertaking that has given vitality to labour-management relations and contributed powerfully to the post-war economic recovery of Japan. Where the danger lies is rather when, owing to the egoism of labour and management in a particular undertaking, collective bargaining fails to take into account the broader interests of the working class, the public and the economy as a whole, and is treated as a purely private matter. And the difficulty experienced in mounting a large-scale and effective campaign at the industrial or national level owes more to the lack of influence exerted by the trade union federations than to the structure of collective bargaining itself.

Conversely, collective bargaining at the level of the undertaking is considered to have the following merits. First, it enables the parties to relate conditions of work and employment closely to the actual operation of the undertaking and to examine and deal with them in a pragmatic and realistic manner. The question of wage fixing, for example, can be fully discussed in the light of the undertaking's performance and profitability. The whole process makes for flexibility and avoids the duplication of effort involved in re-negotiating at the enterprise level conditions of work that have already been determined at the industrial level. One side-effect of associating workers more directly with the collective bargaining process is that unofficial or wild-cat strikes are virtually unknown in Japan.

Secondly, all the problems arising at the workplace can be taken up in a comprehensive manner within the context of the industrial relations system in the enterprise. Even such matters as management policy, the production plan and productivity schemes, which are not normally subject to collective bargaining, can be discussed in detail. Depending on the nature of the problems, they can be appropriately dealt with through the three complementary channels of collective bargaining, joint consultation machinery and personnel management.

Thirdly, there is the fact that collective bargaining at the level of the undertaking can cope relatively well with the changes induced by technical innovation, which has brought about greater differentials in wages and working conditions between enterprises. Finally and more generally, the power relationship between labour and management tends to centre on the undertaking. This stems from the propensity of the Japanese to organise themselves vertically according to their traditional social relationships. Thus it may be said that collective bargaining at the enterprise level is well suited both to Japanese business conditions and to Japanese social concepts.

---

[1] Ministry of Labour: *Rôdô Hakusho* [White Paper on labour] for 1970 (Tokyo).

The role of workers' and employers' central organisations

Workers' organisations

Enterprise unions have combined among themselves to set up national, regional or industrial organisations or federations, with a view to co-ordination and the consolidation of their organisational strength. The fact that trade unions have from the outset been organised at the level of the undertaking, however, has necessarily limited the role played by these federations in collective bargaining, with the result that they have concentrated their activities essentially in the political and politico-economic fields in close association with the political parties.

There are four major national trade union centres in Japan: the General Council of Trade Unions (Sôhyô) (with a membership of about 4.3 million); the Japanese Confederation of Labour (Dômei) (membership about 2 million); the Federation of Independent Unions (Chûritsurôren) (membership about 1.4 million); and the National Federation of Industrial Organisations (Shinsanbetsu) (membership about 74,000). Policy with regard to collective bargaining varies considerably from one centre to another.

The main feature of Sôhyô's policy is its " spring wage offensive ", which has been launched repeatedly every year since 1955 and appears to have become firmly institutionalised. In early spring a target figure for wage demands is decided and a schedule of warning strikes is worked out, timed to rise to a peak which will induce the employers to concede to the unions' demands a couple of months later. The schedule often takes account of political considerations, e.g. electoral issues or campaigns against the Mutual Security Treaty, as well as of economic considerations. By contrast, it is not the policy of Dômei to set a target figure for wage increases or to concentrate strike action in a particular period. Dômei makes specific wage demands, in consultation with its members, when collective agreements come up for renewal, resorting to strike action where necessary. Another feature of Sôhyô's policy is its adherence to a rigid strategy of collective bargaining backed up by strikes. Dômei's approach to collective bargaining is more flexible in that it supplements militant collective bargaining with the use of joint consultation machinery. Unions affiliated with Chûritsurôren frequently keep in step with Sôhyô's spring wage offensive but their bargaining tactics are generally less rigid. The fact that Chûritsurôren does not profess any specific collective bargaining policy of its own attests to its being a very loose liaison council. Finally, it is important to note the strong desire of all national centres to conduct collective bargaining at the industrial level or at least between individual managements and the industrial trade union federations concerned.

303

The role played by the central organisations in the collective bargaining process may best be illustrated by taking the example of the spring wage offensive noted above. At its annual extraordinary convention in February or early March Sôhyô decides the amount of the wage increase to be claimed by all its affiliates, and at the same time draws up a schedule whereby they should call strikes during the period from mid-April to mid-May. Each member industrial federation then advises each of its enterprise union members as to the precise amount of the wage increase to be claimed. The amount claimed by each enterprise union is not necessarily the same, nor is it quite the same as the target set by Sôhyô. The amount fixed depends on the economic position of the undertaking and the bargaining power of the union concerned. Nor are all demands submitted at the same time. Each union chooses its own date so as to synchronise its peak bargaining effort with the schedule of strikes drawn up by Sôhyô. It is only up to this point in the spring wage offensive that Sôhyô and the industrial federations exercise their leadership, after which their role is reduced to watching over the bargaining of their affiliates and the implementation of the strike schedule. This does not mean that they remain idle. They provide information on the over-all progress of the bargaining campaign and where necessary advise on tactics and timing, but it is rare for their officers or organisers to take part directly in the negotiations at the level of the undertaking. For one thing they do not have enough organisers, and for another neither the employer nor the enterprise union welcomes such participation. Nevertheless, when one of their affiliates goes on strike, they do often dispatch an organiser to give guidance and assistance.

Given the limited role of the central organisations in the determination of wages, it may be asked why Sôhyô should set a target figure for wage increases and what makes its affiliates conform faithfully to the strike schedule. An answer to this may be found in the rather special nature and function of strike action in Japan. Strike ballots are usually taken before bargaining has even begun. Even if the ballot is positive, it does not mean that a strike will be called immediately: the actual timing of a strike is decided by the union officers in the light of progress made in collective bargaining. A strike is called not when bargaining has broken down but when a breakdown appears imminent. Thus a strike ballot is held not so much for the purpose of consulting union members on the necessity for strike action as to impress upon the employer their determination to have their demands met. Consequently, if a strike proposal is voted down, the actual negotiations tend to lapse. Strike action is used not to break the deadlock in collective bargaining but to elicit a new counter-offer from the employer. In other words, no clear functional demarcation may be drawn between collective bargaining and strike action: they are both regarded as parts of the same process. By setting a target figure for wage increases Sôhyô aims to rally the fighting spirit of its affiliates and to demonstrate to the employers the nation-wide nature of the campaign. And by observing the strike schedule unions seek to bring home to the employers their sense of discipline and their determination to secure their demands. Sôhyô's target figure is also significant in that it provides a guideline for other unions regardless of their affiliation, and even for unorganised workers.

Despite this, the role played by the national and industrial trade union centres remains a very restricted one. How is this to be explained? Partly, of course, by the fact that the focus of trade union activity and strength has always lain within the undertaking. But lack of funds is another reason. The central organisations are financed by contributions from their affiliates, but their combined share amounts to less than 15 per cent of union dues, which is not even sufficient to enable them to provide adequately the guidance needed by their member unions, let alone build up a strike fund. In practical terms, this means that the national and industrial trade union federations are limited, besides their political activities, to the following tasks and functions: holding an annual conference at which policy matters are decided; drawing up a programme of action to secure higher wages and bonuses; dispatching officials to give on-the-spot guidance to affiliates on strike and canvassing for contributions to assist them; and helping affiliates to obtain loans for their strike funds from the Labour Bank.

To illustrate the obstacles to collective bargaining by industrial trade union federations, mention may be made of the experience of the Federation of Metal Miners' Unions (Zenkô) and the Federation of Synthetic Chemical Workers' Unions (Gôkarôren). Towards the end of the 1950s both these centres proposed holding negotiations with the managements of the undertakings where they had affiliates, but in both cases management refused. The two cases were brought before the Central Labour Relations Commission (CLRC) as constituting an unfair labour practice, whereupon the CLRC ordered a number of undertakings to engage in collective bargaining with Zenkô, whereas it considered the refusal of other undertakings to be justified. As for the Gôkarôren case, the CLRC ordered management to agree to representatives of Gôkarôren taking part in the negotiations but did not approve of bargaining between management and Gôkarôren alone. In the Commission's view both Zenkô and Gôkarôren lacked the organisational strength and authority to negotiate directly on behalf of their affiliates.

Nevertheless, a number of industrial federations do engage in collective bargaining, jointly with negotiators from the affiliated unions. This is the case in coal mining, textiles and privately owned railways, for example. But only the Seamen's Union (Zen-Nikkai) is capable of independent bargaining at the level of the industry. It negotiates directly with the shipowners, who are divided into four groups according to the size and nature of their operations. In fact Zen-Nikkai is not a federation but an industrial union in the Western sense—the only one in Japan.

Employers' organisations

On the other side of the fence the Japan Federation of Employers' Associations (Nikkeiren) is composed of nine regional employers' associations, including the prefectural associations, and forty-seven industrial organisations. Its main tasks are liaison between the member organisations, the harmonisation of management policy, the carrying out of studies and research on labour questions, and the preparation of recommendations to the Government. While a federation by its structure, Nikkeiren is more of a liaison centre where collective bargaining is concerned. The same may be said of its regional and industrial affiliates. Their influence over collective bargaining at the level of the undertaking is thus limited, much more so than in the case of the unions. This is one further factor hampering the establishment of industry-wide bargaining.

Nikkeiren's approach to collective bargaining may be illustrated by its reaction to Sôhyô's spring wage offensive. As soon as Sôhyô has announced its target figure for wage increases, Nikkeiren denounces it as excessive and recommends its member organisations to stand firm against such demands. It also collects and disseminates information on labour disputes and offers a limited amount of guidance, but the terms on which disputes are settled are left entirely to the discretion of the member undertakings. For instance, in the spring wage offensive of 1971 Sôhyô set a target wage increase of 15,000 yen, which Nikkeiren countered by emphasising that wage increases should not exceed the rate of productivity increases. Despite Nikkeiren's recommendation, however, some employers settled for increases of more than 10,000 yen, and a survey by the Ministry of Labour showed that the average rate was 9,522 yen (16.6 per cent), far more than Nikkeiren had anticipated.

Collective bargaining in the public sector

It is in the public sector that many of the more intractable problems concerning collective bargaining are found.[1] The public sector's economic importance, its large and powerful unions and its direct impact on the public interest combine to give collective bargaining in this sector a place of special significance in the spring wage offensive and in wage determination generally.

Collective bargaining in the public corporations (i.e. the National Railways Corporation, the Japan Monopoly Corporation[2] and the Nippon Telegraph and Telephone Corporation) and national enterprises (postal services, forestry, etc.) is usually conducted at three levels— national, regional and local. As far as the National Railways Corporation

---

[1] The term " public sector " covers public corporations, national enterprises and local public enterprises but does not include the national and local civil services.

[2] This corporation operates the salt, tobacco and camphor monopolies.

is concerned, there is also joint consultation machinery established in each workshop. Collective bargaining at the national level deals with basic questions of principle, whereas negotiations at the regional or local level deal with the detailed regulation of the agreements concluded at the national level or with problems specific to the region or locality concerned. Collective agreements are concluded between the representatives of the employing authorities and union officers at each level at which bargaining is conducted. Joint Grievance Adjustment Boards are likewise set up at all three levels.

Needless to say, the main subjects of collective bargaining in the public sector relate to general conditions of work, such as wages and working hours, transfer, dismissal and disciplinary sanctions. Lately, however, problems of employment and changes in conditions of work arising from the rationalisation of public undertakings have begun to come to the fore. In addition, because little use is made of the grievance and joint consultation machinery, problems which should normally be dealt with by these bodies are now frequently referred to collective bargaining.

In spite of its importance, collective bargaining in the public sector is inefficient and the rate of voluntary settlement of disputes is low. Most of the issues negotiated at the national and regional levels are referred either to the National Enterprise and Public Corporation Labour Relations Commission (NEPCLRC) or its regional Mediation Commissions for mediation, or to compulsory arbitration for settlement. Strikes and other forms of direct action (although prohibited by law) are often resorted to before a solution is found.

The weakness of collective bargaining in the public sector is due to a number of factors. First of all, there is the constraint imposed by the Treasury's tight control over the money supply. This obviously restricts the autonomy of the public corporations very severely: in fact the only way to persuade the financial authorities to loosen the purse strings is to refer a claim to the NEPCLRC for mediation or arbitration. (It is true that submitting a claim to the Commission can also be a useful face-saving device.) Moreover, in spite of their size and complexity, there is very little delegation of power in public undertakings, which explains why negotiated settlements at the regional and local levels are few and far between.

Secondly, there is the negative attitude of the public authorities towards collective bargaining. This may well be a reaction to the political activities of the unions, which are often imbued with a class struggle ideology and are directed against the Government. It may stem also from the traditional reluctance of bureaucrats to commit themselves, an attitude that can generate unnecessary antagonism between the parties concerned. It may be recalled that prior to the ratification by Japan of the Freedom of Association and Protection of the Right to Organise Convention, 1948

(No. 87), there was a legal provision to the effect that no person could hold office in a public undertaking union unless he was an employee of the undertaking. This gave rise to cases in which the public authorities concerned dismissed union officers on disciplinary grounds and then refused to engage in collective bargaining because the unions maintained these former employees in office. Today, the public undertakings frequently rely on a legal provision to the effect that " no matters relating to the management and operation of public undertakings shall be subject to collective bargaining ". While this presents no problem in itself, the public authorities tend on the strength of this provision to refuse to bargain even on such matters as conditions of work and employment, which they prefer to regulate unilaterally.

The third factor contributing to the weakness of collective bargaining in the public sector is that since strikes are officially prohibited here the unions are unable to place much reliance on direct action in order to force the public authorities to the bargaining table.

Finally, one of the most important problems in the public sector today is how to deal with the staff reductions necessitated by rationalisation (for with the exception of the Monopoly Corporation all the public corporations and national enterprises suffer from a low rate of productivity). It seems an obvious prerequisite for the solution of a problem of this sort that the workers' side should have a democratic say in the decision-making process, yet no such machinery exists in any of the public corporations or enterprises. Moreover, inasmuch as the public authorities claim that the question of rationalisation is also a matter pertaining to the management and operation of the undertaking, they refuse to discuss it even in a joint council, not to speak of collective bargaining sessions. Consequently, problems associated with redundancy, such as transfers, dismissals and changes in conditions of work, have to be settled case by case through the NEPCLRC.

It will have been gathered from the above that industrial relations in the public sector are in a poor way. Lack of communication between the parties has resulted in mutual distrust, with collective bargaining being looked upon more as a lull in the hostilities than as an opportunity to lay the foundations of industrial peace. It is not surprising in these circumstances that reliance on a third party (the NEPCLRC) has now become virtually complete. This has the advantage of reminding the two principal parties of the importance of the public interest, which is often neglected in the heat of collective bargaining, but it suffers from the drawback that it undermines their will to seek voluntary settlements and may cause unnecessary friction between management and labour.

There are none the less one or two brighter spots in this somewhat gloomy picture. Shortly after it ratified Convention No. 87 in 1965, the Japanese Government set up an Advisory Council on the Public Service Personnel System which began to carry out an over-all review of industrial relations in the public sector, taking into consideration the findings and recommendations of the Dreyer Commission.[1] It is true that the Council's deliberations have not yet yielded anything of substance. On the other hand, for several years now arbitration awards have been implemented fully and promptly, which was not always the case before. Joint consultation machinery established at the workshop level in the National Railways Corporation is functioning quite effectively. However, no progress has yet been made in the vital respect of supplementing collective bargaining through the development of workers' participation in management for the solution of problems arising from rationalisation.

Collective bargaining and the Government

Collective bargaining in Japan is essentially based on the voluntary principle. Since the recognition of freedom of association and the right to collective bargaining in Japan's new Constitution of 1946, government policy has been to assist the development of voluntary collective bargaining. This policy has found expression in a number of ways. One is the provision of machinery to deal with unfair labour practices through the Trade Union Law, another the establishment of a system for the peaceful adjustment of disputes under the Labour Relations Adjustment Law. A third is the granting of legal effect to collective agreements by the judiciary and the extension of the application of collective agreements by administrative action. A fourth is provision for minimum wages and conditions of work under the Minimum Wages Law and the Labour Standards Law. A fifth is the establishment of special administrative agencies or commissions to deal with these matters.

With regard to the handling of unfair labour practices and adjustment of labour disputes, cases in the private sector and local public enterprises are dealt with by the Central and Prefectural Labour Relations Commissions; those involving seamen by the Central and Prefectural Seamen's Labour Relations Commissions; and those in public corporations and national enterprises by the NEPCLRC. As for the implementation or revision of the Labour Standards Law, there are the Central and Prefectural Labour Standards Deliberation Councils, whereas for the fixing of minimum wage rates Minimum Wages Councils have been set up at the national and prefectural levels. The extension of collective agreements is also the concern of both the Labour Relations Commissions and the Minumum Wages Councils. All these special administrative agencies are tripartite, composed of representatives of labour, management and the public interest.

---

[1] Report of the Fact-Finding and Conciliation Commission on Freedom of Association concerning Persons Employed in the Public Sector in Japan, in *Official Bulletin* (Geneva, ILO), Vol. XLIX, No. 1, Special Supplement, Jan. 1966.

No doubt it is this tripartite structure that explains the confidence placed by the unions in the impartiality of these bodies. Certainly considerable and frequent use is made of them, especially the Labour Relations Commissions and the NEPCLRC. And in fact, through their disputes adjustment work, it has been possible for these agencies to make their voice heard as regards the substance of negotiations instead of being simply confined, as in the past, to the administrative and procedural aspects of collective bargaining or the enforcement of agreements. In this way they reduce the danger that the parties will act arbitrarily or selfishly in defiance of the public interest.

While prices and wages are both rising rapidly, the spiral is not yet so serious that it cannot be dealt with by economic and fiscal policies. So for the present, at any rate, the likelihood of government intervention in collective bargaining through the introduction of an incomes policy seems remote.[1]

Conclusions and latest trends

In Japan the need for collective bargaining is not questioned. The key role played by the unions and by collective bargaining in the country's post-war recovery and its subsequent economic development is generally recognised. There is also a general consensus that collective bargaining must be the nucleus of any dynamic modern system of industrial relations. As regards the level at which bargaining takes place, there seems little likelihood that the days of the present enterprise-based system are numbered—indeed there are signs that it may gain still further strength in the future.

At the same time, a subtle change has come over the power relationship between the various forces influencing the course of collective bargaining, such as the undertakings and their unions, the workers' and employers' central organisations, the Government, the political parties and public opinion. Its cause may be found in the new economic and social needs created by rapid economic growth, the liberalisation of capital and foreign trade; and the emergence of a mass high consumption society, as well as the need to reconcile the requirements of rapid economic development with those of social justice. The system of collective bargaining itself must also evolve in order to meet these challenging needs.

The change may be seen in the fact that workers' demands in Japan are increasingly focusing on the active promotion of their interests rather than on passive defence and protests. On the one hand, as noted earlier, there has been a shift of emphasis with regard to the content of

---

[1] See Taishirô Shirai: "Prices and wages in Japan: towards an anti-inflationary policy?", in *International Labour Review*, Vol. 103, No. 3, Mar. 1971, pp. 227-246.

collective bargaining. Concern with the distribution of material benefits obviously remains primordial, but the workers' side is steadily extending its interest, through questions of higher productivity and better management, to broader problems of co-operation and respect for workers' dignity. On the other hand, the workers' preoccupations go beyond the problems that can be treated within the undertaking and extend to such questions as prices, housing, taxation, structural change in industry, social security and environmental pollution. Unions are being urged to take up these problems energetically. Increasing emphasis is being placed on the need for private undertakings to display a sense of social responsibility, to pay more attention to safety and stability than to profitability alone, while there is a greater recognition that in a pluralistic society the government's role must be that of a peacemaker as well as a rulemaker. As the problems that arise in labour-management relations become more complex and sophisticated, so it is natural that the various systems set up to resolve them should be adjusted and diversified accordingly; this is in fact what is happening in Japan.

The first phenomenon to which attention may be drawn is the spread and development of joint consultation and advisory machinery. Experience has shown that reliance on collective bargaining alone, even at the level of the undertaking, is not sufficient, tactically speaking, to ensure labour-management co-operation on a basis of mutual understanding. The function of collective bargaining is inherently limited, but the structure of enterprise unionism facilitates the adoption of flexible tactics. This explains the growth of joint consultation—often taking the form of " preliminary bargaining "—as a means of participating in management. The establishment of joint consultation machinery is making headway even among unions affiliated to Sôhyô which, because of their strongly anti-capitalist stand, have up to now opposed any form of joint consultation on the ground that it weakens the unions. This trend is spreading to labour-management relations outside the undertaking. The diversification and increasing sophistication of workers' demands, coupled with the realisation that collective bargaining and political action in a constant atmosphere of class warfare are insufficient to achieve their ends, have compelled the unions to redouble their demands for participation in the formulation and implementation of economic and social policies at the industrial and national levels. (This development is not unrelated to the recent trade union unity moves to which reference is made below.) A number of bipartite conferences have accordingly been organised for different industries, starting with synthetic fibres and textiles and continuing, especially since 1968, with electricity generating and supply, electrical appliances, automobiles, shipbuilding, metal mining, and so on. Most of the unions participating in these conferences at present are affiliated to Dômei and Chûritsurôren but even among the Sôhyô affiliates, e.g. those in metal mining, iron and steel and synthetic fibres, there is now a stronger move towards such participation. At the national level it has been the Government's policy for some time to set up committees composed of labour, management and government representatives and people with special knowledge and experience to advise it on labour and social policy. This practice has recently been extended to the field of economic policy. The Price Stabilisation Board, the Economic Deliberation Council and the Industry and Labour Consultative Board are typical examples of the new consultative machinery established, but because of acute tensions between the Government and the unions they are not functioning very effectively.

The second major trend is towards new relationships among the parties involved in or influencing collective bargaining. While there is no outstanding change in relations between labour and management, nor in the Government's policy of non-intervention in collective bargaining, two notable changes are taking place on the side of the unions. The first has to do with the power relationship between the enterprise union and its locals on the one hand, and the enterprise union and the industrial and national organisations on the other; the second has to do with the relations between the central organisations themselves on the one hand, and between them and the political parties on the other.

In Japan, as we have seen, bargaining has traditionally been conducted at the level of the undertaking. However, with the emergence of huge oligopolistic companies, there has been a growing tendency for collective bargaining to be conducted at the level of each local plant. This has resulted, because of concern that there should be as few differences as possible between the conditions of workers employed by the same firm, in considerable importance being attached to collective bargaining carried out at company level by a federation of unions organised within each plant. This same demand for an end to discriminatory conditions of work is also being voiced at the industrial level, which is one of the factors accounting for the noticeably stronger influence that the national and industrial organisations have been exercising over bargaining at the level of the undertaking in recent years. Other factors include the greater maturity, the growing flexibility and the realistic leadership of the central organisations, as well as the impact on wage determination of the spring wage offensive in a context of rapid economic growth and shortage of manpower.

In the view of some observers, however, the national and industrial trade union federations are unlikely to consolidate this position unless they can overcome their present organisational weaknesses and sever their ties with the political parties, which have lasted since the pre-war days and have now grown cumbersome. Herein lies the significance of the second change mentioned above. This is the movement for the " unification of the labour front " which was launched in the autumn of 1969 by some of the powerful industrial federations—mainly in the private sector—affiliated with Sôhyô, Dômei and Chûritsurôren. The idea is to reorganise and strengthen the national and industrial trade union centres on a broader base transcending the existing organisational and political framework with its inevitable clashes of policy. The movement is most active in key industries such as iron and steel, automobiles, machine tools, electronics, oil, petro-chemicals and synthetic fibres, textiles and metal mining, and it is interesting to note that it is precisely these industries whose growth and increasing complexity in recent years have most affected the general policy and practice of collective bargaining at both the industrial and enterprise levels. Opposition to the movement is strong. However, if the unification comes about, it will bring a new orientation to the power relationship not only between the unions and the political parties but also between the upper and lower echelons of the trade union movement itself. And, not least important, it will significantly affect the relations between the Government and the unions with regard to the formulation of industrial and social policies.

Recent Trends in Collective Bargaining in the Netherlands

W. ALBEDA [1]

THE INDUSTRIAL RELATIONS SYSTEM in the Netherlands should be viewed in the light of some basic characteristics of the country. The Netherlands is small with a relatively large population, the greater part of which lives in the western provinces where the big cities (Amsterdam, Rotterdam and Utrecht) form a triangle that for practical purposes may be considered as one metropolitan area.

Industrialisation started rather late. Traditionally agriculture was strong and the development of the services (transport and commerce) was closely related to the one invaluable national resource—the splendid situation of the Netherlands in the delta of the Rhine and the Meuse; this factor and the large colonial empire overseas were of key importance for the national economy. With some notable exceptions (Unilever, Shell, Philips) manufacturing took place in small, family-owned firms with a paternalistic system of labour relations.

The trade union movement, as a result, got off to a slow start. From the beginning, moreover, the movement was split into three independent organisations: the social democratic Netherlands Federation of Trade Unions (NVV), which now has 558,000 members; the Netherlands Catholic Federation of Trade Unions (NKV), with 398,000 members; and the Netherlands Federation of Protestant Christian Trade Unions (CNV), with 238,000 members. Up to the Second World War the three federations were unable to achieve close co-operation with one another. There were often strong differences of opinion between the NKV and the CNV on the one hand, and the NVV on the other, as to what was desirable policy. The two denominational unions were more reluctant to strike and less hesitant about collaborating with the Government than the socialist NVV, which was regarded with suspicion by the authorities.

---

[1] Professor, Netherlands School of Economics, Rotterdam.

The same tendency to base their organisations on religious belief developed among the employers. The farmers, the small entrepreneurs and the manufacturers are organised in three associations which, while traditionally co-operating closely with one another, are independent of each other. Since the war the employers' denominational organisations have tended to integrate and the distinction between Catholics and Protestants for purposes of industrial association is disappearing. Such a trend is less noticeable, however, in the trade union movement. Here the three organisations are slow to come together, although the Catholic federation seems to show less hesitation about further integration with the NVV than with the CNV. In the last few months, a proposal to unite the three federations in a single confederation has been under serious consideration; a common Institute of Social-Economic Research has already been established.

The collective agreement in the Netherlands

In the Netherlands the collective agreement was accepted as a legal instrument at a fairly early stage. As far back as 1907 it was recognised in labour law and in 1927 an Act respecting collective agreements was promulgated which is still in force, although it was partly amended by the Extraordinary Decree of October 1945 respecting labour relations, which formed the basis for the Government's wage policy.

Since 1937 the Minister of Social Affairs has had the possibility of extending to non-organised workers and employers the terms of collective agreements with the exception of certain provisions—for example those limiting freedom of association—and it has become normal practice for this to be done. The collective agreement in the Netherlands ordinarily is valid for one year and contains a provision to the effect that several months before its expiration the parties concerned will consider revising, extending or cancelling it. The Extraordinary Decree of 1945 prescribes that for as long as no new agreement is reached the old agreement shall be extended on a month-to-month basis. Some agreements are of longer duration than one year. Thus in the metal industry and in the firms of Philips and Hoogovens (steel manufacturers) the practice is to conclude agreements of two or three years' duration. Such long-term agreements of course either prescribe in general terms that wages can be increased during the period of their validity or provide for wage increases of a given percentage on specific dates.

Within the private sector most firms are covered by collective agreements. The exceptions are some of the smaller retail undertakings. Workers in the public sector (public utilities, public transport), which is rather small, are considered legally as civil servants and the level of their remuneration is regulated by law. In some cases private institutions (for example private schools) which are highly subsidised are obliged by the subsidiser to adhere to the rates of remuneration set by the ministry concerned. In the public sector the Dutch railway system, however, has since the end of the Second World War been covered by a collective agreement. Like all civil servants in the Netherlands, railway workers do not have the right to strike. The present agreement, which is of three years' duration, follows the remuneration policy laid down by the Ministry of Internal Affairs for civil servants. However, the whole system of wage groups and grades differs from that in the rest of the public service. Railway workers do not participate in the civil service pension fund.

The position of the Dutch airline, KLM, is a little different from that of the railways. KLM, which is a mixed company, has a standard collective agreement with no special features. Wages and salaries of KLM employees are not tied to those in the government sector.

Plant-level agreements and industry-wide agreements

Most workers are covered by industry-wide collective agreements, this being in line with what has been from the outset the express policy of the trade unions—namely to increase the size of the bargaining unit. This policy may be explained by the relative weakness of a divided trade union movement in a labour market characterised by unemployment throughout the period between the First and Second World Wars, and bearing in mind the fact that in a situation of unemployment it is important to exclude competition between firms so as to avoid the depressing influence of the weakest employer. Admitted, this hardly explains why during the post-war period, with full employment and fairly close co-operation between the unions, the number of company collective agreements continued to decrease (from 1,159 in 1940 to 406 in 1968). However, a policy does not always end when the background changes and, moreover, a centralised wage policy is conducive to agreements covering a greater number of firms. Broader agreements offer greater possibilities for the use of " scientific " incentive systems, job classification systems and so on.

The employers' attitude towards plant-level bargaining has not always been clear; but one gets the impression that employers' organisations have taken a more positive attitude towards industry-wide agreements since the Second World War, possibly as a result of the change in the power relationship on the labour market in the last twenty-five years. Nevertheless, the number of agreements covering entire industries decreased between 1940 and 1968 from 1,544 to 274.

A substantial proportion of all workers are now covered by a small number of agreements (250,000 building workers are covered by one agreement, 360,000 metal workers by two agreements, for instance). It is interesting to note that there are no important differences in the contents of company-wide agreements and industry-wide agreements. Company agreements are found in the very large companies, where they may contain some provisions concerning the social policy of the firm [1], as well as in smaller companies in the chemicals, foodstuffs, wood-working and transport industries, where mostly their provisions do not differ from those of industry-wide agreements and where the only reason for their existence seems to be that in these sectors the variety of undertakings is much greater than in others. The trend towards larger bargaining units may have been counteracted in the last few years by the emergence of more big firms, which naturally prefer to have company agreements.

Collective agreements are concluded between the trade unions on the one side and the employers or employers' organisations on the other. There are no legal rules concerning the procedures which the parties have to follow in order to obtain their respective members' approval of an agreement, the implication being that the trade unions themselves determine which internal bodies have to give their approval before the text can be finalised. The only legal stipulation is that a copy of the collective agreement must be provided to all workers who are covered by its provisions. The unions in manufacturing industries have a highly decentralised structure, within which each industrial sector has its own governing body, representative of the local unions, that can take decisions concerning a new collective agreement. Other unions—for example the building unions—have a more centralised structure and their sector committees have only advisory powers. There is, however, a tendency for groups of five or six unions to amalgamate into federations and this tendency is accompanied by decentralisation within the individual unions concerned.

Bargaining procedures

From an early stage the Dutch trade unions and employers' organisations felt the need for formal bargaining machinery. As long ago as 1933 the Government took the initiative in this respect by providing through the Industrial Councils Act for the establishment of industrial councils *(bedrijfsraden)*. These councils, which may have a permanent secretary and some staff, offer a meeting ground for the leaders of both sides, where collective bargaining with a view to the conclusion of new agreements takes place, problems arising from the functioning of existing agreements are discussed and decisions required under collective agreements (as regards, for instance, the fixing of holidays, the introduction of incentive systems, etc.) are taken. The councils may also in some cases authorise exceptions respecting the application of the provisions of agree-

---

[1] For example the Hoogovens agreement, which contains a preamble stating the company's policy with regard to trade unions.

ments. Councils for the building and printing industries play an important role as a kind of governing body for the industry.

Formal structures at the industry level, like the councils, are of course needed because of the multiplicity of bargaining organisations (three or more trade unions on the one side and at least two employers' organisations on the other). The idea of setting them up was inspired also by the hope that they could pave the way for lasting industrial peace, based on close co-operation between employers and workers in fields of common interest, and by the concept that continuous bargaining concerning the attainment of common goals (integrative bargaining) would facilitate bargaining on controversial goals (distributive bargaining).[1]

In 1950 Parliament adopted the Organisation of Industry Act to replace the Industrial Councils Act of 1933. The main objectives of the new Act were to create a permanent form of co-operation between employers and employees, to ensure the promotion by trade and industry of their own interests and (and this was the new feature) to give the bodies established under the Act statutory powers enabling them to lay down rules and develop activities by which all undertakings in a specific sector of trade and industry could benefit and to which all of them could make a financial contribution.

The industrial boards set up under the Act can as a result of their statutory powers do things which organisations under private law would be unable to do, or would do less efficiently. In the present context it is interesting to note that they can transform a collective agreement into a statutory regulation, the difference between the two being based essentially on the way in which they come into being. A regulation is the result of a decision of the board and a strike protesting against such a decision would be impossible. Some forty industrial boards created under the new Act are now in existence, most of them in the smaller industrial sectors consisting of many undertakings. The industrial board for agriculture is one of the most important. It has taken over many functions which in other countries are executed by the government. In a large number of manufacturing industries, however, the establishment of industrial boards has met with strong resistance on the part of the employers, who fear that they could make decisions not only in the social but also in the economic field, and in this sector such bargaining bodies as exist have a private status, based upon contract and not upon the Organisation of Industry Act, and hence do not have the statutory power to lay down rules for the sector. Of course a collective agreement may provide for the setting up of other, more specialised joint bodies (a vocational training institute or a pension fund, for example). In many cases collective agreements also provide for industrial tribunals.

---

[1] R. E. Walton and R. B. McKersie: *A behavioral theory of labor negotiations* (New York, McGraw-Hill, 1965), pp. 1-10.

Grievance procedures

In the Netherlands a collective agreement is enforceable under the law, so that a worker may place his complaints before the normal courts. However, this is a complicated and cumbersome procedure and other means of action are therefore provided for in most collective agreements.

Both industry-level and plant-level agreements generally lay down a grievance procedure prescribing that, if an amicable settlement—in the first instance between the worker and his immediate supervisor or at a subsequent stage between union and management representatives—cannot be reached, the case shall be placed before an arbitration board. Such a board consists, in the case of Shell for example, of three members appointed respectively by the unions concerned, by the firm and by the two together. The metal workers' agreement establishes a similar, more elaborate procedure.

In practice, however, these procedures are hardly ever used. Normally workers bring their individual complaints to their local union, which tries to find a solution through informal contact with the personnel department. If the worker is not a member of a union, the complaint is usually handled directly by the personnel department at the request of the worker himself. National union officials deal essentially with broader complaints involving basic questions respecting the administering of collective agreements. This package of complaints is put on the table when a new agreement is being negotiated. Another procedure followed where an industrial board or council exists is for basic matters to be brought forward at regular meetings and general rules to be laid down after some discussion.

The centralised wage control system

The Dutch system of collective bargaining as it exists at present cannot be understood without a brief look at developments after the Second World War. In the post-war years the Government centralised the process of wage fixing. The reorientation of the economy, it was felt in 1945, required an economic climate that would foster the growth of modern industry. One of the basic prerequisites was seen to be a wage level that would be low enough to permit new industry to compete with older and more experienced firms abroad and at the same time would induce a high rate of saving by keeping consumption at a relatively modest level.

Under the centralised wage control system the Government, through its Minister of Social Affairs, had the right to prescribe the wage level for all industries. It used this right to impose a highly uniform wage structure by linking wage rates to a standardised method of job evaluation and to the level of productivity, first in the economy as a whole and then in the industry concerned.

The system was not as arbitrary as it might appear. The Minister of Social Affairs delegated his authority to the Board of Government Mediators [1], which used its powers only after consultation with the Foundation of Labour as the representative organisation of the employers and employees. It was felt that the wage policy involved a high degree of government interference which needed to be counterbalanced by the creation of a " partner " that would be able to meet the Government on an equal footing. The Foundation of Labour is a private bipartite body set up by the three trade union federations and the employers' federations, in which the workers' and employers' representatives have equal voting rights. In the course of time a complicated but not illogical procedure was developed by means of which the process of evaluating economic possibilities and examining basic economic data was carefully separated from the bargaining process. The former process was handed over to the Social and Economic Council, established under the Organisation of Industry Act to advise the Government on all social and economic matters, and composed of fifteen employers' representatives, fifteen trade union representatives and fifteen experts nominated by the Government.

The Council, assisted by the Central Planning Bureau, and following discussion of the matter with the Foundation of Labour (a discussion based on common documentation and which was in fact part of the collective bargaining process), made a recommendation to the Board of Government Mediators concerning the possible wage increase in the coming year. Where the recommendation was unanimous the Board required industry to apply the proposed increase. Otherwise the matter was referred for decision to the Minister, who was confronted with a delicate task, knowing that his ruling would be examined with the closest attention by Parliament.

The wage increase accepted at the national level had to be incorporated in the collective agreements of the various industries, though in many cases of course better rates could be obtained through bargaining. Inventive trade union leaders could always find arguments why some job or some industry had a right to a greater increase than the centrally agreed average. Moreover, by using piece-rate or incentive systems the wages ceiling could be pierced. The Board found that it had to lay down very detailed rules for the application of systems of job evaluation, incentives, merit rating, profit sharing and so on in order to prevent their being used as a cover for " black wages ". Moreover, the wages mentioned in the collective agreements were not only minimum but also

---

[1] Set up in 1945 to mediate in labour disputes. Its members, though appointed by the Minister of Social Affairs, were independent and, except for the Chairman, served on a part-time basis. The Board was abolished in 1970 when the new Wages Act was adopted.

maximum wages. It is probably no exaggeration to say that the Dutch system of wage control was more comprehensive than any other in the free enterprise economies.

The collapse of the system

The 1960s saw the collapse of this system as a consequence of economic pressure from abroad and of the stress that the whole arrangement put on employees, trade unions and undertakings. In a way it is easier to understand why the system broke down than why it worked so well during the whole period from 1945 until 1963. A system of wage control is effective only in as far as the workers (of whom in Holland not more than one-third were members of one of the three trade union federations) and the employers accept it. When labour is in short supply—and this was nearly always the case in at least part of the country—it is evident to the workers that they can obtain wage increases if they wish to. For the employers there is always the temptation to use wage increases to get a better share of the labour force. Although in some industries (for example the building industry) " black wages " were a normal phenomenon in the 1950s, in general wage control was accepted and there was no considerable wage drift.

The explanation is not simple. Perhaps it could be said that Dutch workers were used to paternalistic employers and trade unions, and to following the leader. Before the Second World War (and also after the war, although to a lesser degree) organisation at the social, cultural and political levels in the Netherlands was based on a system of ideological blocs. Everybody became a member of the organisation of his " colour " and the leaders at the top worked closely together. Moreover, the workers remembered all too well the unemployment of the 1930s. The leaders of the trade union federations accepted wage control because they were convinced not only that the Netherlands could not industrialise with a high wage level but also that the Government should direct the economy and that there should be strong control of prices and incomes. For them wage control was a first step towards a more centrally controlled economy and not an emergency measure. Another argument which played a role was that wage control promised industrial peace. Last but not least it should not be forgotten that from 1945 to 1959 the country was ruled by governments which could, by their composition and policy, convince the trade unions of their good intentions.

Especially during the first few years, when the economic situation left only limited scope for big wage increases, the system worked quite well. Sharing poverty proved to be easier than sharing wealth. From 1945 to 1950, when the Dutch economy was running at a deficit, compensated by Marshall aid, it was clear to everyone that wages should be kept at a very modest level. After 1951 successive productivity gains made it possible to debate the criteria for wage increases. Private consumption was curtailed when this was necessary during the short recessions of 1951 and 1957 by a decline in real wages.

As long as conditions in the pre-war period remained fresh in people's memories, wage rounds (all wages went up at the same time) came regularly and the trade union federations supported the system whole-heartedly, the workers in general believing in it. Rival unions either accepted the wage policy, as the independent (white-collar) unions did, or they failed to organise enough workers to break the system.

Slowly, however, the climate changed, as the Government loosened its grip on the economy. Wage control, being essentially part of the broader system of a controlled economy, became an isolated instrument of economic policy. It gave the workers the impression that they were the only group subject to a rather strict curb on their income. The Christian unions were the first to ask for freer wages, followed by the employers' federations, who wanted greater scope for horizontal wage differentials. It became increasingly clear that trade union leaders who continued to support the Government's wage policy were running the risk of alienating the membership. They were criticised from without, and later on also from within, for their lack of aggressiveness and revolutionary zeal.

The confidence of the membership in wage policy was further shaken when a new system of wage control was introduced by the Government in 1959. This system was based on an attempt to link wages to productivity by industry and was highly unpopular. How to explain to mine-workers that they would have to accept a smaller wage increase than metalworkers because productivity was going down in the mines and up in the metal industry, when at the same time mineworkers were in shorter supply than metalworkers? How to explain to everyone that the fifteen-year-old slogan " equal pay for equal work " should be changed to " equal pay for equal productivity "? As more and more firms paid " black wages " the discrepancy between the centrally agreed rates and the actual rates in the labour market became too evident to be disregarded by workers (both organised and non-organised) and employers alike. When some of the larger firms in the Amsterdam metal industry stated openly in August 1963 that they would no longer accept the guidelines set by the Foundation of Labour, widespread social unrest developed.

It was clear to everybody that not only the Government and the employers but also the trade union federations had been too careful. The employers should be capable of judging for themselves what they could afford. It was a bad time for the trade union leaders and some workers gave up their trade union membership. The unions did not hesitate long, however, and decided that the only way to maintain their influence was to get ahead of events. The three metalworkers' unions asked for an 8 per cent increase in wages. The three trade union federations followed suit and asked for a " substantial increase ". When the employers and the

Government accepted these demands (they could not risk the total collapse of the system) the result was a " wage explosion ". The most important outcome, however, was the introduction of a minimum wage for unskilled workers.

During 1964 wages increased by 16 per cent. What was most astonishing, however, was that as the result of an unprecedented productivity increase of 9 per cent the national economy adjusted itself to the big wage increase. Instead of the prophesied unemployment, unexpected high real earnings were the result of this aggressive wage policy.

It is understandable that confidence in the Government's and the Foundation's ability to assess possible wage increases was still further weakened when the wage explosion was such a success. Had the unions been too cautious throughout the post-war years? Was the relatively low standard of living in the Netherlands a result perhaps of the meekness of the trade unions? Would a more aggressive wage policy not have led to greater efficiency and increased mechanisation and investment? The powers of the Board were transferred to the Foundation in 1963 so that the burden of implementing the policy was placed on the employers' and workers' organisations. The idea behind this change (effected within the existing legal framework) was that perhaps a wage policy administered by the social partners themselves would encounter less opposition than the Government's policy.

But how could the trade union members of the Foundation be expected to hold back the wage increases which the unions had gained within their industries with the approval of the employers concerned? Moreover, the labour shortages throughout the country were not being reduced by the repeated big wage increases within certain industries. The trade unions became less and less prepared to come to central agreements on wage increases within the Foundation. Although the procedures were maintained theoretically—the legal framework in fact did not change until 1970—in practice the Government relinquished its powers in respect of wages and step by step the network of regulations implementing the wage policy was dismantled. While all collective agreements were required to be submitted to the Foundation, they were in fact always accepted.

In the years following the wage explosion of 1963 it became increasingly clear that it was no longer possible to formulate a wage policy that could get the support of the three partners involved—the Government, the employers and the trade unions. The Government tried (and still tries) every year to obtain an understanding on the limits for the wage increases in the coming year. It became evident, however, that even when it succeeded in obtaining such an understanding (as in 1964 and 1965) the three partners were unable to implement the agreement reached. The situation in the labour market did not permit the Foundation or the Board to use their powers to curb the rise in wage levels, and recourse to the old government-dominated wage policy was equally impossible.

Apart from a temporary interruption due to the mild recession in 1967-68, the labour market situation continued to push wages up faster than the increase in productivity. At the beginning of 1969 the introduction of the new value-added tax led to a record price increase in the first three months of that year. This situation seemed to create the atmosphere for new concerted action on the part of the Government, the employers and the trade unions.

In the middle of 1969 the three trade union federations accepted an invitation by the Government to attend a round-table meeting, during which it was decided to accept a ceiling on wage increases in 1970. This agreement, concluded in June 1969, gave hope that at least a minimum amount of wage control could be practised in the coming years.

The latter part of 1969, however, brought about a set-back. The Government (in the person of Minister Roolvink, himself a former trade union secretary) decided to strengthen its position with regard to wage policy by introducing a new Wages Act. This Act enables the Government not only to require a general wage freeze in a national emergency situation but also to interfere with individual agreements in the national interest. A clear symptom of the changing attitude of the trade union movement was the strong opposition of the NVV and the NKV to this last possibility. Both federations stated that they would refuse to participate in central consultations within the Foundation and the Social and Economic Council on wage matters if the Act was accepted with these provisions. For the first time since 1945 no real consultation of the social partners at the national level preceded the adoption of the Act by the Second Chamber of Parliament in November 1969, and the Government is left with a Wages Act which it cannot easily use, as can be seen from the social unrest in 1970.

At the same time various developments have proved that in the Dutch economy central negotiations cannot easily be discarded. A strike in a shipbuilding yard in the Rotterdam area in September 1970 resulted in a decision that all the workers concerned would receive a one-time payment of Fl. 400 as an advance on an increase to be provided for subsequently in the relevant collective agreement. Although there was a particular reason for the decision in question, demands for a similar payment were rapidly made at other firms within the area and elsewhere. The Foundation reacted promptly by deciding that the amount of Fl. 400 should be fixed as the limit for any such payments granted elsewhere. The trade unions regarded the Foundation's decision as the go-ahead signal for making the demand a general one and so a new wage round took place, resulting in the first general, uniform wage increase since 1959.

Agreement was simultaneously reached between the employers and trade union leaders within the Social and Economic Council to propose that the Government should revoke (or " put on ice ") the provision in the new Wages Act opening the way for the Government to interfere with individual agreements. This proposal was accepted by the Government (the provision was temporarily set aside) and so the way was paved for the resumption of tripartite central consultations. These consultations came to nothing, however, and the Government thereupon decreed a " wage freeze " under which wages were allowed to increase by 3 per cent on 1 January and a further 1 per cent on 1 April. In July fresh bargaining will be possible. This decision was taken, and accepted by Parliament, notwithstanding a one-hour protest strike by the three federations. It led to a further deterioration of relations between the trade unions and the Government.

The industrial relations system in a time of transition

Even before 1940 the Dutch industrial relations system was characterised by a high degree of centralisation and a strong tendency towards institutionalisation.

By increasing the cost of a strike, centralisation of the bargaining process may lead to a reduction in the number of strikes. Especially during the era of the centralised wage policy it could be argued that every strike was directed against the Government and could easily develop into a general strike. Therefore the trade union federations resorted to this weapon only in exceptional circumstances. An interesting case was the strike in the building industry in 1960. When the employers would not accept the conditions that the Government had attached to a wage increase, the building unions launched a strike against them. They forced them to accept the conditions set by the Government (no price increase) and to raise wages as proposed by the Foundation of Labour. Before the collapse of the wage policy, industrial peace was almost complete. Only in some difficult pockets of the labour market (the building industry in the big cities, the docks, etc.) wild-cat strikes now and then reminded the Dutch population that such action was a possibility in the Netherlands.

Strikes are still an exception rather than the rule. They are not legally recognised and are forbidden in the case of government employees and railway workers. After the war many people thought that the strike was an outmoded weapon in industrial relations, not only at the national but also at the plant level. However, a change of climate seems to be on the way.[1] The conviction that industrial conflict is not necessary in the Netherlands because the bargaining machinery works smoothly and justly under the benign supervision of the Government is being shaken more and more. The younger generation does not seem to have the same patience as its elders. Moreover, the slow but steady coming into being of the European Common Market, bringing with it the example of the

---

[1] The number of days lost through labour disputes increased from 19,000 in 1968 and 20,000 in 1969 to 262,000 in 1970 (though this is admittedly still a rather low figure by international standards).

more aggressive policies of the Netherlands' neighbours, may cause the break-up of the peaceful Dutch labour situation. This consideration makes it all the more necessary that the legislation on the right to strike (which is really non-existent) should finally be put in order. A new Act is now in preparation.

Developments at the undertaking level

Since the 1930s there has existed in the Netherlands a well-developed system of national regulations governing industrial relations both at the national level and at the level of different industries. At the level of the individual firm and of the shop floor the trade unions have in general been inactive (even shop agreements do not normally provide for trade union activities within the firm). With some notable exceptions (the railways, the PTT) the only contacts between trade union officials and particular firms have concerned individual grievances regarding the application of the collective agreement. In general there are no institutions comparable to the shop-steward in Great Britain or similar structures elsewhere, by means of which a direct influence on work and working conditions can be exerted.

In many firms (especially in the metal industry) the trade unions appoint their spokesman *(vertrouwensman)* who represents the union on the shop floor. He does not bargain like the shop-steward, but acts as the representative of the union. He informs the workers of their rights and he is the person responsible for ensuring that the trade union is informed of grievances and developments in general in the firm. He is in a rather difficult position because he receives complaints and passes them on, but normally he himself does not take an active part in resolving grievances.

The weak position of the trade unions at the shop floor level is understandable in view of the relatively late industrialisation of the Netherlands and the rather slow development of the trade union movement, which only achieved numerical strength after the recession had taken away its power on the labour market. Moreover, the division of the movement into three separate federations has made representation within (on the average rather small) firms difficult. The first twenty years after the Second World War saw a development of outstanding importance— permanent unemployment was replaced by full employment. The agricultural labour force was decimated and modern industry sprang up, marked by more manufacturing and bigger firms. Continued growth replaced stagnation. Of course the effects of such changes could not be confined to the technological and economic fields. Traditional views on authority and subordination were undermined, and on top of this, as far as management was concerned, came the fact that employers could no longer resort as freely, in their personnel policy, to the formerly effective threat of dismissal.

327

In the new situation the trade union movement gained influence in national life, but the fact remained that its influence was smallest where the workers could best observe it—on the shop floor level. When gradually the national wage policy turned out to be a failure, the trade unions started to doubt whether they were on the right road. These doubts became certainties when sociological research revealed that workers within the firm did not feel any influence of the trade unions, and that they did not expect anything from the trade union movement at their own level.

The 1960s were for the whole of the trade union movement a period of " agonising reappraisal ". A re-evaluation of the structure of the movement, of its tactics and even of its ideology and inspiration could not be avoided.

The re-evaluation and re-orientation have not yet been concluded. It is certain, however, that they will lead to a change in the attitude of the unions as regards individual firms. The union spokesmen had no real influence. The developments in personnel management were the result of the labour shortage rather than of trade union pressure. Moreover, the Act of 1950 to provide for works councils has not strengthened the position of the trade unions within firms. In the first place the trade unions play only a limited role with regard to the composition of the works council. They have the right to present lists of candidates but groups of non-organised workers may do likewise. Although normally the percentage of organised workers in the council is higher than in the firm as a whole, many councils have important minorities or even have majorities of non-organised workers in their membership. A survey undertaken by the NVV revealed that most members of works councils do not view themselves as trade unionists but as members of the personnel. It is interesting to note that those who view themselves first as trade unionists look upon the council as a bargaining instrument. The others see the council as an instrument of joint control.

What, in reality, is the function of the works council? The Act describes it as an organ of the firm which advises the employer (who is ex officio chairman of the council) on social matters. The employer is required to keep it informed about matters relating to the economic functioning of the firm. The members have to respect the " independent position of the employer ". Of course the borderline between advising an employer and bargaining can be very thin. The trade unions do not like to see the councils taking over their job, but obviously a discussion on such matters as the introduction of an incentive wage system, the regulation of shift work, the hiring of foreign workers, the fixing of holidays, the need for overtime, etc., will more often than not develop into a sort of bargaining. In this sense it is clear that the works councils fulfil functions which could be performed by the trade unions or trade union representatives.

During September and October 1970, when a state of social unrest existed in most undertakings in the Netherlands concerning the question of the one-time Fl. 400 payment mentioned earlier, the trade unions left it in most cases to the works councils to put the demand for this payment before the employer. This, however, is an exceptional example of a case in which the trade unions left bargaining to the works councils.

It may be of interest to point out that new legislation (based on proposals of the Social and Economic Council) is in preparation which will strengthen the position of the works councils. Under this legislation the council would be able to meet without the presence of the employer (officially this has been impossible up to now); members could request the attendance of experts; and they would have the right to veto the nomination of a member of the board of directors of the undertaking. The council would also have the right of inquiry, meaning that, in case of suspicion of mismanagement, they would have the right to order an official inquiry by a special court.

If this legislation is adopted, it will clearly give the works councils greater possibilities of influencing management policy in all fields. But the trade unions will not have new possibilities of influencing the composition of the councils or their functioning.

It is not surprising, therefore, that within the trade union movement more and more voices are heard seeking a new union presence on the shop floor. The metalworkers' union affiliated to the NVV was the first to propose a fresh approach[1] in the form of so-called plant work *(bedrijven-werk)*. In all plants employing trade unionists, a plant representative would be selected, with the following functions: he would act as chairman of all trade union meetings within the plant, inform the trade union of developments within the plant, receive complaints regarding work and working conditions and inform the members of the works council or the trade union of such complaints. He would also act as chairman of the trade union committee within the plant. The underlying idea is that the more or less passive attitude of the former trade union representative would be replaced by the active role of the new-style agent. The representative could fulfil his new role as a result of more active assistance and guidance on the part of the trade unions. Experienced trade union officials are being trained to advise plant representatives on how to fulfil their role and to direct their attention more to those areas which are not normally dealt with by the trade unions (work content and organisation for instance).

This new approach first met with resistance on the part not only of the employers but also of some members of the works councils. The employers opposed it because they felt that it stemmed from an attitude

---

[1] For a more detailed description see John P. Windmuller: *Labor relations in the Netherlands* (Ithaca, New York, Cornell University Press, 1969).

whereby the trade unions more than ever viewed their role as being to check on management policy. As of now the new policy has been introduced successfully in about 150 firms, which constitute of course only a small minority.

It is evident that the presence of an active trade union plant committee could pose a problem for the works council and in a few cases the works council opposed the new system. However, as is often the case, the initial resistance to something new is disappearing. The real problem is whether the trade unions have the necessary knowledge concerning management problems and can transfer this knowledge to their agents so as to put them in a position to present management with alternatives to its policy—a policy which in the eyes of the trade unions is " one-sidedly guided by economic interests ".

It is by no means impossible that the new trade union presence in the firm may encourage the unions to start official bargaining at that level, for it may open their eyes to the special needs of individual firms.

Development of the collective agreement

The post-war period saw a marked acceleration in the development of collective agreements. Not only did they begin to cover an increasing number of workers, but also the scope of their provisions was expanded. The inclusion of provisions relating to systems of job classification and merit rating was, of course, influenced by the system of wage control. In addition the agreements began to regulate the length of annual holidays with pay as well as hours of work, and to provide for vocational training, the introduction of arbitration systems, etc.

As in most countries, the collective agreements in the different industries have a strong influence on one another. An improvement in one industry tends to spread to others. Therefore it is possible to observe general trends in collective bargaining. Notwithstanding the propaganda made for differentiation in wages in different industries, the high degree of uniformity in wages which was a result of the centralised wage policy persisted throughout the 1960s.

The slow growth of the unions and their difficult financial position as a result of prolonged inflation may explain the action taken by them to obtain extra benefits for their members. This action started in 1960 when the Catholic factory workers' trade union proposed the inclusion in an agreement covering two electric light factories of a provision prescribing a slightly higher wage for organised workers. This provision was rejected by the Board of Government Mediators on the grounds that it had not received the unanimous support of the Foundation of Labour. In 1961 a similar proposal to give special benefits to organised workers in the Ankersmit's Chemical Works in Borgharen was again rejected by the Board and on this occasion it sent a detailed note to the Foundation of

330

Labour explaining its general position in this matter, because it was expecting more such proposals. The subsequent discussions within the Foundation took a considerable time because the trade union federations themselves needed time for reflection on this highly controversial matter.

In April 1964 a proposal was made for the inclusion in a collective agreement for the printing industry of a provision requiring unorganised employees to pay a slightly higher contribution towards their old-age pension than organised employees (in the Dutch printing industry blue-collar workers have a union shop agreement; white-collar workers, however, are free to organise or not). In this case the Foundation decided to accept the provision without prejudice to other cases. The following year a discussion on this important issue was initiated both within the trade union movement and the Foundation but was constantly interrupted by the need for decisions to be taken on proposed agreements in individual firms, which was a clear indication that the trade unions at the branch and firm level were no longer willing to delay action until the Foundation had decided on a common stand. In fact a common stand was never achieved.

In 1966 the demands of the trade unions in different industries led to disputes. These demands were essentially directed towards ensuring that (i) organised workers should obtain certain privileges (freedom to attend union meetings during working hours, the right to pay lower social insurance contributions, the right to be reimbursed for part of their trade union dues), and (ii) some union activities should be subsidised by the employers (trade union education, trade union recreation centres, trade union social welfare funds, etc.).

After two more disputes (one in the ready-made clothing industry in Groningen and one in the ceramics industry in Maastricht) the three trade unions for the manufacturing industry and the General Employers' Federation (AWV), whose members and affiliated associations are engaged in miscellaneous industries, concluded an agreement. This agreement, after guaranteeing the independence of the trade unions, provides that the three unions will open a common account into which the members of the AWV will pay Fl. 15 per member per year. The unions will use this money only for such purposes as are acceptable to the employers. It may not be used for the reimbursement of individual dues but it may lead to an extension of the benefits trade unionists derive from their membership.

In 1969, when a similar agreement was not accepted by the employers in the so-called small metal industries, the metalworkers' union threatened to take action against all the firms concerned. Successful strikes in a few firms were sufficient to convince the other employers.

During the last ten years two tendencies have emerged in most industries: there are common collective agreements for blue-collar and white-collar workers, and piece-rate and other incentive wage systems are being discarded. As in many other nations, white-collar workers in the Netherlands traditionally had a different status and position in the firm from blue-collar workers. In the private sector white-collar workers had their own unions (generally affiliates of the three federations), which concluded separate collective agreements with the employers but of which only a small proportion of the workers concerned were members. Thus many white-collar workers, especially those in supervisory posts, were never covered by a collective agreement.

The white-collar workers' agreements differed from those of the blue-collar workers in several respects: they provided for shorter working hours; they established broader wage groups (leaving more scope for individual bargaining); they provided for monthly (instead of weekly) wages and for their amount to increase with the age of the worker over a longer period than in the case of a blue-collar worker. White-collar workers at a comparable level to most blue-collar workers had longer holidays, better pension rights, etc.

Several factors combined to undermine the privileged position of the white-collar worker. First there were developments in the labour market, with the number of blue-collar workers decreasing as a percentage of the total labour force. Then the differences within the blue-collar group increased, so that in some cases their qualifications were not lower, and sometimes were even higher, than those of white-collar workers. At the same time the differences in status between the two began to disappear. Moreover, since 1945 the three trade union federations have accepted the principle of industrial unionism, whereby blue-collar and white-collar workers should join the same union.

Obviously the integration of white-collar workers into the industrial unions, along with the lessening of the traditional differences between the two groups, opened the way to including both within the scope of a single collective agreement. The agreements of a few large companies set an example in this respect. Thus the Hoogovens steel company in Ijmuiden now has such an agreement and bargaining within Unilever seems to be heading in the same direction.

The tendency to do away with piece-rate systems is closely related to the trend towards integration of the provisions applying to blue-collar and white-collar workers. On the one hand technological advances in many industries have led to the development of types of work that afford no possibility of measuring the amount performed. On the other hand workers are objecting more and more to wage systems that make their income too variable. In an increasing number of cases blue-collar workers, like salaried employees, are paid by the month, get seniority pay, receive wages for a thirteenth month and are given a share in the profits. The Government's wage policy stimulated the development of profit-sharing plans: as the profits of an undertaking could not be translated into higher wages, profit sharing was an attractive alternative. Moreover, the distribution of profits to the workers, theoretically at least, does not lead to higher costs and higher prices. Many firms now have profit-sharing plans, but distribution of profits does not really take place in all cases. Profit sharing is often a disguised form of wage increase. The trade unions, as well as the Foundation of Labour, have accepted the principle that profit-sharing plans should be based on an agreement between the firm (or an employers' federation) and the trade unions.

In 1964 the three trade union federations published a report prepared by a joint study group on the participation of workers in the growing capital formation in Dutch industry. A plan was put forward to make workers the owners of any capital deriving from non-distributed profits. A combination of profit sharing and property ownership for workers was worked out. By participating in social investment societies workers would be able to share in the accumulation of capital in the Dutch economy. To make the plan general, a system of investment wages was recommended for civil servants and other workers in non-profit-making institutions. The plan proposed by the working group was widely criticised on account of its complexity and the dangers for the future of private enterprise alleged to be inherent in it. Up to now there have not been any notable examples of its practical application.

Because of the strong inflation in the entire post-war period, and especially since 1964 after the failure of the wage policy, provision for sliding wage scales has been made in collective agreements. Traditionally the agreements had contained so-called re-opener provisions prescribing that, although the text was valid for one or two years, in exceptional circumstances (a government decree to increase wages, an unexpected price increase, etc.) the parties could break the agreement and re-open bargaining on wages.

In April 1968 the Philips company entered into an agreement (covering 66,000 workers) providing for automatic wage increases of up to 2.5 per cent on 1 January 1970 and 1.5 per cent on 1 January 1971 to compensate for price increases. The collective agreement for the metal industry which entered into force on 1 January 1970 provides for automatic wage increases of 3 per cent every six months or a maximum of 6 per cent a year. The collective agreements in some other branches set no maximum for compensatory wage increases, though normally they fix a threshold for the level of price increases after which wage increases will be granted.

There could be substantial repercussions if an important precedent set by the trade unions in the printing industry should be followed by other unions. As a result of the rapid concentration taking place within that industry in the Netherlands, many workers were concerned that they might suddenly find themselves without a job. Accordingly, in 1967 the printing unions proposed that the employers should carry the costs involved in the temporary unemployment, retraining or resettlement of dismissed workers. This principle was included in the collective agreement for the printing industry concluded in that year. Every worker in the printing industry is, in the case of lay-off as a result of integration or re-organisation, entitled to an amount equal to one week's wages for every year of the first ten years that he worked for his last employer, to one and a quarter times his weekly wages for every year of the second ten years so worked and to one and a half times his weekly wages for every year of all subsequent years, the maximum amount he can receive not exceeding one year's wages. For workers of 60 years of age or more who have worked in the same undertaking for twenty years or more, this severance pay is replaced by a guarantee on the part of the employer to continue to pay the worker up to the time of his 65th birthday the normal wages that he would have received if he had continued to work (including statutory benefits, etc.). The same ruling applies to women workers of 55 years of age or more. In a recently published report the NVV made proposals that regulations of this kind should be applied in all industries. In an economy which is increasingly characterised by rapid technological change such proposals have strong chances of being accepted in more branches of industry.

The winds of change in Dutch labour relations

Unquestionably the climate in Dutch labour relations, as in the whole of Dutch society, is changing. The time when trade union members were complaining that it was difficult to see where trade union policy ended and government policy began is past. The Government can no longer count on the moderation and support of the trade unions. The years when the trade union movement co-operated with the Government to limit consumption (1951 and 1957) seem very long ago.

Even so there is evidence that the trade unions through their more aggressive attitude have still not regained the confidence of all the workers. The picture is not quite clear. As already mentioned, in some cases works council members opposed the attempts by the metalworkers' unions to introduce their new, more aggressive approach within under-takings. During the 1960s the three trade union federations saw only a limited increase in their membership. Their growth has not kept pace with that of the national labour force. The proportion of workers orga-nised in the three federations has fallen (from 27 to 26 per cent of the total labour force) over the last ten years. The independent unions have fared a little better, but together they do not have more than 300,000 mem-bers and the increase in their membership is largely due to the fact that they are stronger in the government sector, where there has been the most rapid growth in the labour force (the number of government employees who are members of the three federations is also constantly increasing).

On the other hand there are signs of social unrest, which, where it manifests itself, is directed as much against the trade unions as against the employers. A disturbing example is the sequence of events which developed from the action taken in the strawboard factories in the north of the country, in Groningen. Because of the chronic underemployment in the region and the weak position of the industry concerned (with about 2,500 workers), wages lagged behind those in the more prosperous parts of the country. During 1969 a skilled agitator organised a strike, against the wishes of the union leaders, in which most of the workers—union members and non-members alike—participated. The strike was very successful and the official unions could do little more than sign the resulting collective agreement providing for better wage rates. Similar action then followed in the rest of the region, and in other parts of the country there were also spontaneous strikes (for instance in protest against the partial closing of a firm) which placed the trade unions before the uneasy choice of following the lead of the " action committee " or denouncing the strikers, many of whom were members in good standing. The year 1970 saw a further wave of social unrest.

Conclusions

The present industrial relations system of the Netherlands is clearly passing through a period of transition. On the one hand the era of the wage policy jointly implemented by the Government and the Foundation of Labour seems to be definitely over. On the other hand most of the parties concerned have reservations about the total decentralisation of the system of bargaining. Everyone is seeking a new way of solving the difficult predicament of free trade unions in a full employment economy. A centralised and government-controlled wage policy threatens the independence of the trade union movement and perhaps even the existence of free trade unions based on the voluntary membership of the workers. Wages which are freely fixed may give a strong impetus to the ever-present threat of inflation.

Perhaps the whole concept of an anti-inflation wage policy is too narrow. It places wage earners in a position different from that of all other income groups. Would a general incomes policy be the solution? Since May 1970 the Social and Economic Council has been studying the possibilities of an integrated incomes policy.

At the same time voices warning that control of the process of income distribution merely concerns symptoms are becoming more insistent. They argue that the management of a full-employment economy through monetary policy and the elimination of monopolistic tendencies in many markets would constitute a more fundamental attack on the problem of inflation.

The question of centralisation or decentralisation of bargaining, however, is broader than that of inflation control. Centralisation of the bargaining process provides possibilities for the elaboration of a more rational wage structure. In a way the trade union movement is confronted with an uneasy choice. Should the unions opt for the centralisation of the wage fixing process in order to achieve their ideal of a more rational or more equal wage structure? Or should they focus their attention on the needs and wishes of the smaller groups of workers at the shop floor level? For the first fifteen years after the war Dutch trade unions adopted the first course. It is not yet clear whether they are prepared to switch to the other alternative in the years to come.

Obviously this question cannot and should not be decided on the basis of arguments concerning the rationality or effectiveness or equity of the wage structure only. As long as importance is attached to workers having a say in the fixing of wages, either through the unions of their choice or through their direct participation, a certain degree of decentralisation of the wage fixing process is inevitable.

The ideal solution, of course, would be a combination of centralised bargaining in respect of wages and decentralised action at the shop floor level in respect of secondary benefits, day-to-day conditions of work and work content. Whether this solution can be approached in some way remains to be seen. Windmuller[1] gives three conditions as being necessary for the smoothest possible transition to a lower level of bargaining: the Government should have confidence in the ability and the willingness of the contracting parties to accept their macro-economic responsibilities; the employers and their organisations should be prepared to carry the heavier burden of bargaining at the industry and the undertaking level; individual unions should strengthen their bargaining capability. It must be borne in mind that for more than twenty years the bargaining process was centralised in the hands of the Foundation of Labour and the Government, which meant in a way that both employers and trade unions were relieved of this responsibility. They have to regain the strength and capability needed for real bargaining at their own level. Certain developments are taking place which could facilitate this process: in the first place, as a result of the rapidly spreading practice of mergers, the average size of the Dutch firm is increasing; in the second place, within the three trade union federations there is a marked tendency towards reorganising the membership in many fewer but larger unions. Both developments could very well pave the way for the fulfilment of the conditions mentioned by Windmuller.

---

[1] John P. Windmuller, op. cit.

Recent Trends in
Collective Bargaining
in Sweden

Gunnar HÖGBERG [1]

IN SWEDEN the rates of pay and other conditions of employment of the majority of wage and salary earners are settled by collective agreement. This is so both for manual and for white-collar workers, in the private and public sectors alike.

In the private sector, which is predominant, the Swedish collective bargaining system is built on a long-standing tradition of strong employer and employee organisations and a well-established pattern of industrial relations. The employee side is characterised by an exceptionally high degree of unionisation. To take an example, around 95 per cent of the manual workers and 70 per cent of the white-collar workers employed in manufacturing industry belong to trade unions.

In the public sector, the present system of collective bargaining derives in major respects from the events of the past six years or so. It was not until 1966 that the parties in the state and municipal areas of the labour market may be said to have come to enjoy the same negotiating freedom and the same legal rights as their counterparts in the private sector. As a result, substantial organisational changes have had to be made in recent years, especially by the State in its capacity of employer, and there has not yet been time for the system of collective bargaining in the public sector, at least as far as the negotiating machinery is concerned, to become stabilised to the same extent as in the private sector. It may be considered symptomatic of the position in the public sector in recent years that it has not been possible to complete wage negotiations without touching off awkward conflicts in the form of strikes and lockouts. This has led to demands from various quarters that the Government should legislate limits to the relatively new-won

---

[1] Director, Swedish Employers' Confederation.

freedom to bargain in the public sector. However, no such legislation has yet been enacted. Instead, the parties in the state domain (central government and its agencies) have started negotiations with a view to the conclusion of a " new " basic agreement. The object of these negotiations is to preserve the bargaining rights of civil servants and at the same time to formulate a procedure which promotes union-type negotiations and prevents open conflicts—for example strikes and lockouts—that are liable to have adverse effects on society or individuals.

The Swedish collective bargaining system and the way it is shaping must be judged with reference to various institutional factors that have marked the development of Swedish society generally. These factors are economic, social, political and cultural, not to mention many others that are harder to define. It would take us too far afield to try to describe or analyse the development of the collective bargaining system against such a background. Nor is that really necessary, since the present article seeks only to give a picture of recent trends. It should be quite sufficient to indicate, as a general background to these trends, what the Swedish labour market looks like at present, mainly in terms of how the different parties to collective agreements are organised.

Some characteristic features of the Swedish labour market

The system of collective bargaining and the emerging tendencies within that system are intimately bound up with the structure of the labour market and with its organisational relationships. In both these respects the Swedish picture exhibits peculiar features which distinguish it from that of many other industrialised countries.

Composition of the labour force

The Swedish labour force consists of about 4 million people. Of these, about 3 million are employed in the private sector. Public employment numbers about 400,000 persons working for the State and 600,000 in the service of the municipal authorities. Out of the total of 4 million or so in the country's labour force, about 3 million are manual workers (wage earners) and 1 million are white-collar workers (salary earners). This twofold breakdown is arrived at on the basis of two assumptions: first, that all employees are organised; and second, that their organisational affiliation is determined by the traditional classification of jobs into white-collar and blue-collar ones. If one looks instead at the working conditions now applying to the different types of employees, the ratio of manual to white-collar workers appears in a somewhat different light. The traditional disparities between the working conditions of these two categories have been gradually ironed out. The number of workers who have white-collar terms written into their contracts of employment has increased in both absolute and relative terms. This development has been most pronounced in the public sector where, as from 1 January 1972, all manual workers employed in the state and municipal administrations were given white-collar status. This step, which has affected about 55,000 employees, will probably build up pressure for the eradication of all the disparities in working conditions as between manual and white-collar workers across the whole labour market.

The employee organisations

The Swedish Confederation of Trade Unions (LO) organises manual workers and is the largest employee organisation. It has a total membership of 1.7 million distributed among 27 unions. Most of the LO's members are employed in the private sector. The largest white-collar workers' organisation is the Swedish Central Organisation of Salaried Employees (TCO), with around 650,000 members. Of these, slightly less than half are in public employment (the State and the municipalities). Like that of the LO, the membership of the TCO is distributed among different unions. The largest white-collar unions in the private sector are the Swedish Union of Clerical and Technical Employees in Industry (SIF) and the Swedish Union of Foremen and Supervisors (SALF). These two organisations, together with the Swedish Association of Graduate Engineers (CF), which belongs to the Swedish Confederation of Professional Associations (SACO), are parties to an agreement on composite bargaining, which means that they present a common front in central negotiations. Together, these three unions represent about 300,000 white-collar workers in the private sector.

The employer organisations

The leading representative of management is the Swedish Employers' Confederation (SAF), which speaks for about 25,000 firms in the private sector. All told, nearly 1.3 million employees—820,000 manual and 440,000 white-collar—work for SAF-affiliated firms. The firms belong to the SAF through membership of one of the 41 employer associations of which it is formally composed; each employer association caters for a specific industry or line of business. In the public sector there are separate organisations of employers at the national and local levels. The leading body in this group is the National Collective Bargaining Office (SAV) which was constituted in 1965. The SAV attends to management-oriented issues and represents the State in its capacity of employer in negotiations affecting government offices. State-owned firms are covered by a separate body, the Negotiating Organisation of National Enterprises (SFO), formed in the autumn of 1970. In the municipal sphere, the

STRUCTURE OF THE LABOUR MARKET

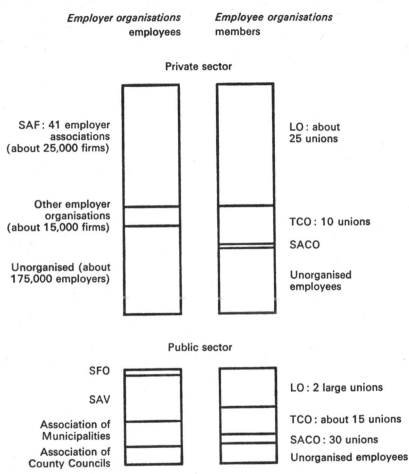

Employer organisations
employees

Employee organisations
members

Private sector

SAF: 41 employer
associations
(about 25,000 firms)

LO: about
25 unions

Other employer
organisations
(about 15,000 firms)

TCO: 10 unions

SACO

Unorganised (about
175,000 employers)

Unorganised
employees

Public sector

SFO

SAV

Association of
Municipalities

Association of
County Councils

LO: 2 large unions

TCO: about 15 unions

SACO: 30 unions

Unorganised employees

employer side is represented by the Association of Swedish Municipalities and the Association of Swedish County Councils.

The essential organisational features of the Swedish labour market may be summarised as in the figure above. The most important, valid for both the employer and the employee sides, is the presence of a small number of organisations, each large enough to bring crucial influence to bear on the development of bargaining issues across the whole labour market. This institutional factor has contributed powerfully to the evolution of Swedish collective bargaining into a system that may be described as " economy-wide bargaining ".

Current trends

As regards trends in the organisational relationships, it may be noted that the various central organisations are undergoing a process of structural change. This development has been most pronounced in the LO. In the past ten years amalgamations of LO trade unions have reduced their number from over 40 to 27. Parallel therewith, several trade unions have been reorganised by merging union locals and plant unions into " big departments " covering larger geographic regions. This development reflects a trend towards organisational centralisation that will probably continue, even though it has come under fire from the trade unions' own members. Only recently, some 1,000 stevedores belonging to the Swedish Transport Workers' Union, an LO affiliate, voiced their protest by seceding to form their own organisation separate from the LO.

Another tendency under this head is for the public sector to carve out an ever larger employer role not only in absolute terms but also relative to the private sector. During the past ten-year period the number of government employees and persons employed by local authorities increased by close to 70 per cent, while the labour force in the private sector remained more or less constant. Moreover, the number of organised white-collar workers is tending to increase faster than the number of organised manual workers: in the past 20 years the LO has grown by 30 per cent from 1.3 to 1.7 million, while the ranks of the TCO have more than doubled, from 300,000 to 650,000.

It is impossible to foresee how the organisational relationships will develop with reference to the traditional classification of employees into manual and white-collar workers. As pointed out earlier, the disparities between the working conditions of the two groups have tended to even out, from which it follows that the blue-collar versus white-collar dichotomy has become less and less relevant. On the other hand, the fact that both the blue-collar and the white-collar organisations are very powerful guarantees that the traditional classification will persist for the foreseeable future and leave its imprint on the bargaining system. A tentative forecast for the near term is that the difference in strength between the two groups of organisations will narrow progressively and that each will compete ever more keenly with the other. The longer-term trend may conceivably be towards the constitution of one organisation for those we now call " workers " and " lower-grade salaried employees " and another for " higher-grade salaried employees ". Incidentally, it may be relevant here to observe that even now there are circumstances in which the LO and the white-collar unions in the private sector—that is, the SIF, the SALF and the CF—find it is in their mutual interest to present a common front to the SAF on certain matters. A current example of this kind of situation is to be found in the negotiations that were started recently on the question of granting educational leave. Of late, too, the LO has joined forces with the SIF/SALF/CF group to negotiate on the co-determination issue.

Developments in the bargaining system

As noted earlier, the development of the Swedish collective bargaining system, which in several respects is unique, is intimately bound up with the organisational relationships and the structural changes in the labour market. Under the system of economy-wide bargaining that has evolved, the negotiations and agreements in the SAF-LO domain—i.e. that part of the economy for whose labour relations these two confederations and their member organisations are responsible—have so far set the pattern for contractual relationships across the whole labour market.

The trend towards central negotiations in the SAF-LO domain

Before the Second World War and during the immediate post-war period up to around 1950, collective bargaining in the SAF-LO domain was to all intents and purposes strictly a matter for the different employer associations and trade unions. The negotiations at this level were conducted without any appreciable interference from the central employers' and workers' organisations. Wage rounds took their course without any systematic attempts being made to co-ordinate the substance or duration of the collective agreements concluded for the various industries.

The next few years saw a gradual and hesitant evolution in which recourse was occasionally had to central negotiations but always as an " emergency " measure. Since 1956 the negotiations in the SAF-LO domain have taken quite a different turn, and collective bargaining between the employer associations and trade unions has been regularly preceded by central agreements between the employers' and workers' confederations which set limits to the cost increases resulting from new contracts. Formally, these central agreements between the SAF and the LO have amounted to recommendations for the guidance of the employer associations and trade unions. In practice, however, the recommendations have had binding effect. That is because once the parties at industry level have decided to apply a central agreement reached between the SAF and the LO, they are bound by a " peace obligation " that is guaranteed by each central organisation.

The tendency to co-ordinate or centralise collective bargaining in the SAF-LO domain should be seen against the background of the lessons learned from the earlier decentralised system, under which the employer associations and trade unions bargained with one another without any real direction from above. These experiences showed, especially during the late 1940s and early 1950s, that the bargaining tended to be obstructed

342

by each union having to keep an anxious eye on the others to see what became of their particular negotiations. As a result, every agreement reached more or less set a precedent for subsequent negotiations. As a rule, the collective agreements that were concluded at the end of a wage round contained more favourable terms for the workers and incurred higher costs for the employers than those which were signed at the beginning of the same wage round. This gave a strong push to inflation. With the trade unions constantly jockeying for position in the queue (the later the better), moreover, the wage rounds tended to become unduly protracted.

By international standards, the technique of central bargaining applied in the SAF-LO domain is unique. Some of the reasons why the parties have deliberately chosen this method reflect common interests. Thus both sides believe that improved co-ordination of negotiations can reduce the risk of conflict. For the rest it can be said that the employers favoured the central approach because they thought it would give them greater bargaining strength vis-à-vis the opposite party. One of the chief inducements for the LO was the hope that central negotiations would provide a better means of implementing its policy of " wage solidarity ". With centrally unified negotiations no blue-collar group in the SAF-LO domain would end up the worse for having settled ahead of the others. One drawback of which the parties were aware, the employers in particular, was that central negotiations would mean formulating contractual solutions in relatively general outline, which in turn could limit the scope for reaching agreements tailored to specific industries.

Bargaining at the industry and company level

In any analysis of recent trends in collective bargaining in Sweden it is natural to concentrate on the process of centralisation, since this has been the most characteristic feature of developments over the past 15 years or so. At the same time, however, it is important to emphasise that collective bargaining in Sweden is still basically a decentralised affair which in practice leaves a good deal of room for the negotiation of agreements both at the level of the industry and in individual firms.

The trend towards centralisation of collective bargaining has meant that the wages and conditions of employment laid down in collective agreements have increasingly been fixed in accordance with the guidelines the confederations have agreed to recommend to their respective affiliated organisations (employer associations and trade unions). However, these organisations are still the real partners in the collective agreements at industry level, and the practical application of the various terms of an agreement depends on the state of a company's relations with the local trade unions. If disagreement should arise between the employer and his employees concerning the interpretation of a point in the collective agreement, the procedure requires that the dispute shall first be the subject of negotiations between the parties within the company. If agreement cannot be reached in these negotiations, the dispute is referred to the organisations at the industry level and, if agreement is still impossible, the only remaining course is to have the dispute settled by the Labour Court or by means of arbitration, providing the parties are agreed upon that method. This procedure, which has been established by law in Sweden since 1928, has in no way been affected by the centralisation of collective bargaining.

It should also be emphasised that country-wide collective bargaining has been concerned with questions which the parties have considered to be of such a nature as to require the most uniform possible regulation throughout the labour market. Questions not of this type have been negotiated on a local basis. As examples of the major questions which have recently been solved specifically on the local plane, mention may be made of the local union representative's status in the company, employer co-operation in the collection of trade union dues, and the wages and salaries payable to employees re-assigned to other jobs within the company.

There are no indications that the bargaining system will become so centralised that there will not continue to be considerable scope for negotiation at industry level of matters that are of particular concern to the industry in question.

Experience of central bargaining

As mentioned earlier, the wage rounds in the SAF-LO domain have formed the subject of central negotiations on a regular basis ever since the mid-1950s. Up to now a total of ten wage rounds have been conducted under the central bargaining system. The experience has been favourable for the most part. Compared with the state of affairs during the immediate post-war period, when the extent of co-ordinated bargaining in the SAF-LO domain was very small, the contractual and other relations between the parties have become stabilised. The central bargaining system has clearly met a need by preserving industrial peace. As against that, it has not left much room for adapting contract structures and cost commitments to the varying capabilities of different industries. Even though this effect was foreseeable, it is now perceived to be more and more of a drawback. On both the employer and the employee sides, the need for greater flexibility on contractual issues has encouraged ideas about enlarging the scope for substantive negotiations between the parties at industry and local plant level. But such ideas have run up against a dilemma: how can negotiators below the central level be given greater elbow-room without undermining the central agreement's function of preserving the peace? Another negative experience of the central bargaining process is that it has scarcely produced the intended result where the LO's policy of wage solidarity is concerned. Nor has it short-ened the wage rounds to the extent that had been hoped for at first. Disappointment with these results has been especially pronounced in the two latest wage rounds, 1968-69 and 1970-71.

Mounting criticism of central negotiations

Following the most recent wage rounds in the SAF-LO domain, the central bargaining system has come in for mounting criticism. As indicated earlier, one reason is the inordinate length of time the whole process takes. On both the last two occasions the central agreements could not be concluded until several months (in the case of the 1970-71 wage round, as much as six months) after the old collective agreements had legally expired. Another cause of the growing criticism is that the central agreements, owing to their ever greater preoccupation with de-tails, have become more and more technically complicated and hence harder and harder to implement. From the general cost aspect, more-over, the central agreements have regularly burst through the macro-economic ceiling and contributed to cost-push inflation, and this even though the parties have each time professed to agree that negotiated pay increases must not exceed what the national economy can bear.

Although criticism of the central bargaining system in the SAF-LO domain has intensified during the past year, it has not so far been constructive in the sense of having led to any proposal for a realistic alternative. Moreover, closer analysis of the criticism reveals that it is not levelled at the central bargaining system as such. The negative ex-periences ascribed to centralised bargaining on the basis of the most recent wage rounds stem mostly from other circumstances. One such circumstance has been the LO's ambition to co-ordinate the SAF-LO talks with negotiations in other areas of the labour market. It has not been possible to translate this ambition into practical action without playing upon the potential for conflict contained in the negotiating procedure, and in that way invoking mediation by the State. There is con-siderable evidence to suggest that the LO's demands for co-ordination of collective bargaining throughout the economy basically explain why the last two wage rounds have been so prolonged. The latest wage round is the clearest example of this.

The course and outcome of the latest wage round, 1970-71

The latest wage round on the Swedish labour market embraced not only the SAF-LO domain but also the whole public sector. It got under way in May 1970, when the SAF and the LO began to discuss the feasibility of ironing out certain remaining disparities between the social benefits granted under agreements covering privately employed manual workers and white-collar workers. The stand taken by the LO from the outset was that no new wage contract could take effect as from 1971 unless provision was simultaneously made to put manual and white-collar workers on an equal footing as regards pensions and sickness benefit. Examination of this problem was entrusted in the first place to a joint expert group, who by February 1971 had already reached an agreed proposal covering both types of benefit.

Negotiations between the SAF and the LO

The main negotiations between the SAF and the LO began on 18 November 1970. Apart from wages these negotiations took up a wide range of other issues, among them income maintenance in cases of temporary or permanent transfer of workers within the company; certain conditions of employment of part-time workers; rules governing check-offs; and rational methods of wage payment. This agenda was cumbersome enough to complicate the negotiations, but an even greater obstacle was that the LO felt it could not specify its wage claims in view of uncertainty as to the outcome of concurrent negotiations in the public sector. As a result the first round of talks lasted until 19 February 1971, when the parties were obliged to observe that their opinions diverged so greatly as to render an agreement impossible. A joint request was therefore made to the Government for the appointment of a mediating commission. At the same time both the SAF and the LO declared their intention of maintaining direct contacts with one another—parallel to those established through the mediating commission—with a view to concluding the negotiations on pensions and sickness benefit.

After a few more weeks, on 15 April to be precise, the mediating commission issued the draft of a proposed three-year contract. It was estimated that the draft agreement would incur aggregate cost increases of about 24 per cent over the whole contract period. The commission's proposal was rejected by both the SAF and the LO, but the commission continued its work. In the meantime, the negotiating situation became critical. Repeated contacts took place not only between the SAF and the LO directly but also between the parties at industry level. On 13 May, after another month, the commission reported that this third stage of the negotiations had not succeeded either. The distance separating the parties was too great for there to be any point in putting forward a final draft contract, so the commission declared that the negotiations had broken down.

The next step was for the LO unions to give notice terminating all collective agreements which had been provisionally extended during the negotiations. So as from 25 May workers throughout the SAF-LO domain were no longer covered by a contract. In that situation the mediating commission resumed its efforts, but the negotiations broke down again on 4 June. The LO issued an order banning all overtime work, taking effect on 15 June, after which it escalated the campaign by serving notice of selective strikes by about 80,000 manual workers to begin on 23 June. The SAF held its fire but declared that it would provide dispute pay to member firms hit by the LO's action. After yet another attempt by the mediating commission to bring the parties to terms, a central agreement finally emerged in the early hours of 22 June.

Negotiations in the public sector

Parallel with the negotiations in the SAF-LO domain, intensive negotiations were being carried on in the public sector. These had already reached a critical stage by the beginning of 1971. In protest at the lack of progress made during January and February, 9,000 government employees went on strike, and the employer side issued a lockout order against 35,000 employees, mostly teachers. At the end of February the National Collective Bargaining Office (SAV) served notice of intention to lock out 3,000 officers in the armed forces, a step that naturally received a great deal of publicity, and not only in Sweden. More than anything else it was this last move by the State in its capacity of employer that prevailed upon the Government to intervene by speedily enacting an emergency law, under which agreements in the state and municipal areas were extended to 25 April and direct action, whether planned or already in force, had to be suspended. After further negotiations before the mediating commission, a three-year agreement for the municipal area was reached on 17 May. It was not until 17 June, i.e. after yet another month, that an agreement was signed for the state area.

This account of the course taken by the latest wage round would not be complete without drawing attention to the influence exerted on the negotiations in the SAF-LO domain by the concurrent negotiations in the public sector. A circumstance not mentioned above but which was of crucial importance in this respect is that the SAV, representing the State as employer, proposed special increases in the wages of the lower paid before the negotiations had even got under way in earnest. This far-reaching proposal came to set a precedent for the municipal area and later for the SAF-LO domain as well, a fact that has been criticised by both the SAF and the LO. The SAV's high opening bid at the very outset of the negotiations, in particular its proposed deal on behalf of the lower paid, engendered great expectations among all employee parties that the forthcoming agreements would introduce big improvements in wages and other conditions. This had a paralysing effect on the willingness of employee spokesmen to negotiate in the private sector. The LO did not want, or felt unable, to specify its wage claims in detail before it was in a position to size up the implications of pay settlements reached on behalf of government employees.

Interaction of negotiations in the private and public sectors

Thus a cardinal problem brought up by the latest wage round is the public sector's influence on the level of remuneration. As noted earlier, the public sector has enlarged its employer role in consequence of its rapid expansion. Inherent in this development is the prospect that rates of pay and other conditions of employment in the public sector will have an increasing impact on those in the rest of the labour market. However, the question is whether the public sector's expansion must necessarily make tomorrow's wage rounds more and more dependent on wage policy initiatives by the State. Up to now the outcome of collective bargaining in the private sector has usually shaped the pattern of collective bargaining elsewhere. As to the scope for wage increases and other increases in labour costs, that has traditionally been calculated mainly on the basis of the capacity to pay of the sector of private enterprise exposed to international competition. In that respect the latest wage round signifies a new allocation of roles between the private and public sectors. It constitutes the first example of collective bargaining in the public sector having decisively swayed the course and outcome of negotiations in the private sector of the economy. A question that must be left open is whether the 1970-71 wage round is an isolated case or whether it is a first indication that the initiative in matters of wage policy will continue to shift from the private to the public sector. Most qualified observers seem to agree that in this respect the latest wage round constitutes a warning that must be heeded.

The long-term outlook for the collective bargaining system

The most recent wage round, as we have just seen, revealed the desirability of co-ordinating negotiations covering the public employment domain on the one hand with those covering workers in the SAF-LO domain, i.e. manual workers in the private sector, on the other. In earlier wage rounds the co-ordination requirement mostly pertained to the negotiations for the blue-collar and white-collar areas within the private sector.

The problem of co-ordinating negotiations for manual workers with those for white-collar workers in the private sector

Up to now the LO's demands for complete co-ordination of collective bargaining in the private sector have got nowhere, except to induce the white-collar organisations to assert their considerable independence by rejecting any form of co-ordination with the blue-collar sphere, at least where remuneration is concerned. A clear manifestation of this is the five-year agreement, running from 1970 to the end of 1974, which was reached between the SAF and the SIF/SALF/CF group in December

1969. Another remarkable aspect of this agreement is that it is the first real long-term contract on the Swedish labour market.

By virtue of the five-year agreement, the white-collar camp has seen to it that no wage round will have to be undertaken in parallel with the LO for a fairly long time to come. Since the agreement runs up to the end of 1974 and the latest SAF-LO agreement expires at the end of 1973, the white-collar and manual wage rounds cannot coincide until 1974 at the earliest, and then only provided that the SAF-LO negotiations due to begin in the autumn of 1973 result in a one-year agreement. Should 1974-75 turn out to be a wage round concerning both manual and white-collar workers in private enterprise, it is likely that the need for co-ordinating negotiations on behalf of these two employee groups will be felt in the same way as it was in the case of the SAF-LO domain and the public sector in the latest wage round. An interesting problem that beckons on the horizon, therefore, is whether such co-ordination will be feasible in the private sector, or whether competition between the blue-collar trade unions and the increasingly strong white-collar organisations will intensify to the point of precipitating direct state intervention in wage determination. Employers and employees have so far been agreed that they must retain their freedom to bargain at all costs. So it does sound strange to hear, in the public debate on the co-ordination problem, trade union officials argue that it may be necessary to circumscribe this freedom. Underlying such views, no doubt, is the realistic recognition that without some such limitation the co-ordination of collective bargaining, whether it is confined to the negotiations of manual and white-collar workers in the private sector or extends to those of all employee groups in both the private and public sectors, may well prove impossible.

The employers propose a new bargaining procedure

As long ago as 1967 the SAF proposed a new bargaining procedure, based essentially on the same principle of co-ordinating negotiations for the blue-collar and white-collar areas that the LO has come to advocate more recently. The fundamental idea in this proposal was for the parties to join forces in objectively estimating an " over-all margin " for the increased labour costs employers would have to bear. In calculating the margin account was to be taken of any increased social costs imposed on the employers by legislation, plus the anticipated wage drift, i.e. the amount by which, depending on local market conditions, actual wages exceed negotiated wages. The remainder of the margin would then be distributed between the blue-collar and white-collar categories. Lastly, after agreement on this distribution had been reached centrally between the SAF and the LO as well as between the SAF and the white-collar organisations, negotiations at industry and plant level would take place in the same way as before. The SAF's proposal provided that the wage round in the private sector could be divided for this purpose into stages, each of which would have to be concluded by a specified date. The idea was to have the parties jointly determine an over-all framework, to preserve the possibility of negotiations between different groups, and to set a more or less definite deadline for the negotiations.

The SAF's proposal did not arouse any enthusiasm to speak of on the employee side. Even so, the SAF, the LO and the TCO did appoint a joint expert group to explore the feasibility of building an objectively based model illustrating the role of wage determination in the national economy, which could serve as a data base for an agreed estimate of the macro-economic margin for cost increases. By the autumn of 1968 the experts had already presented their findings on wage determination in relation to the economy as a whole in a report that received a great deal of attention. This report came to bear crucially upon the genesis of the five-year agreement between the SAF and the SIF/SALF/CF group. Inasmuch as the report discussed the secular factors involved in assessing the movement of wages in the Swedish economy, it may help to focus more attention on longer-range considerations of economic growth, profitability and investment needs than has been the case in the past. Moreover, agreement in principle on the role of wage determination in the national economy such as the parties have achieved at expert level in their work on the report should help to maintain and reinforce the tendency towards economy-wide bargaining that has asserted itself in both the blue-collar and white-collar spheres during the post-war period.

Trends in the content and form of central agreements

There has been a tendency of late for central negotiations to culminate in longer and longer contract texts and increasingly intricate wordings, which in turn gives rise to difficult problems of application both at industry and at local plant levels. The causes of this development must be sought, first, in the fact that an increasing number of issues other than remuneration have been introduced into the negotiations; and second, in the ambition of the central employee parties to play a greater role in bargaining. In these respects, too, the latest wage round in the SAF-LO domain sheds some revealing light on the most recent trends.

The 1970-71 round of SAF-LO negotiations was concerned not only with wages but also, as was partially indicated above, with pensions and sickness benefit, the maintenance of income for workers transferred within the company, defining the lower age limit for classification as an adult worker, lengthening the notice required for termination of individual contracts of employment, rules covering leave of absence, calculating overtime pay, scheduling vacations, and conditions for part-time work. Not all these issues were resolved by the agreement that was eventually reached; several were referred back to the parties for further talks. However, they did their bit to confuse and prolong the negotiations. An added complication for the latest wage round came in the form of a new law on working hours, taking effect on 1 January 1971, which provided for a general shortening of the work week from 42½ to 40 hours over the three-year period 1971-73.

However, it appears that the cardinal reason why collective bargaining has tended to result in ever longer and more complicated contract texts is that the central negotiations have come to determine not only the limits to the over-all cost increases but also, increasingly, the way the margin is allocated to various improvements in the contract terms. It is this that reflects the ambition of the central employee organisations to exert a greater influence on wage policy.

The most striking example of this development during the latest wage rounds was the heavy emphasis put by the LO on its " low-wage " claims (i.e. those on behalf of the lower paid). Although these claims have assumed different forms from time to time, they have essentially boiled down to reserving a portion of the over-all margin for a special wage " kitty " to finance wage increases for workers whose hourly earnings fall below a specified amount. The low-wage issue has proved to be one of the big stumbling blocks in the most recent wage rounds. The employers contended that the LO's low-wage demands were too far-reaching, and that the central organisations should not strike bargains which upset the wage structure that had evolved naturally at the local plant level.

Space does not permit going into detail about all the issues arising in connection with the aspirations for " fair shares " voiced during the most recent wage rounds. The simplest approach is to itemise the cost increases envisaged under the latest SAF-LO agreement.

ESTIMATE OF PERCENTAGE COST INCREASES RESULTING FROM THE LATEST SAF-LO AGREEMENT

Cost item	1971	1972	1973
Wage increases:			
Shorter working hours	1.94	3.39	0.92
Wage drift (earnings development guarantee)	3.00	3.20	3.20
Low-wage supplement	1.60	1.50	—
Across-the-board margin	3.00	1.80	1.90
Social costs:			
Old-age pensions	—	—	0.70
Sickness benefit	—	0.40	0.70
Total	9.50	10.30	7.40

The item " shorter working hours " represents the cost of reducing weekly hours of work from 42½ to 40 without loss of earnings.

351

Collective bargaining

The " earnings development guarantee ", which applies to the 1972 and 1973 contract years, means that each industry-wide agreement guarantees an effective wage rate of specified size over and above the negotiated increase. In the absence of any agreement to the contrary between the contracting parties, this guarantee is to be applied on a plant-by-plant basis.

The " low-wage supplement " for 1971 is the estimated cost of raising the wages of employees who earn less than 12.20 kronor per hour by 25 per cent of the difference between that amount and the hourly rate actually earned. The low-wage supplement for 1972 is calculated in the same manner but with an hourly rate of 13.25 kronor as the reference figure.

The " old-age pensions " entry refers to a special retirement pension for manual workers which will be introduced progressively as from 1 July 1973, and which is supplementary to the state pension scheme. The new pension means that manual workers will qualify for retirement benefit as from the age of 65 under conditions that are otherwise comparable with those already in force for white-collar workers.

In regard to " sickness benefit ", the agreement provides that as from 1 September 1972 manual workers will receive certain benefits after the first 30 days of sickness.

Concluding remarks

The latest wage rounds on the Swedish labour market have demonstrated that it is becoming increasingly difficult for the present system of collective bargaining to function satisfactorily. This view commands majority support. A wage round of the type experienced in 1970-71 must not be repeated.

If the latest trends are any guide to what happens in the rest of the 1970s, there is considerable evidence to suggest that the strains on the present bargaining system may become even more severe. There are many observers who feel that the difficulties of reconciling the different wage policy interests on the employee side, as well as of achieving co-ordination on the employer side between the private and public sectors, are so great that direct state intervention in the bargaining process will have to be reckoned with as early as the next wage round in 1973-74. Militating against such a development, however, is the fact that all parties on the Swedish labour market want to preserve the right to bargain freely. One indication that they may yet succeed is that the SAF and the LO have already embarked on direct discussions regarding difficulties that may crop up in the wage round starting later this year.

Recent Trends in Collective Bargaining in the United Kingdom

B. C. ROBERTS [1] and Sheila ROTHWELL [2]

Introduction

UNTIL THE PASSING of the Industrial Relations Act in 1971 it could be claimed that the British system of industrial relations was less regulated by law than that of any other industrialised country. British industrial relations were based primarily on collective bargaining arrangements voluntarily accepted by employers and trade unions without the intervention of the State. Although the State had come to play a much larger role in protecting the economic and social interests of the worker, it had virtually no influence on the procedures and only little more effect on substantive terms and conditions of employment agreed by employers and unions through the collective bargaining process.[3]

In the evidence it gave to the Royal Commission on Trade Unions and Employers' Associations set up in 1965, the Department of Employment listed 500 separate industry-wide negotiating arrangements, including statutory wage-fixing bodies, for manual workers alone. It estimated that approximately 14 million manual workers were covered by these arrangements in 1964—out of a total of 16 million.[4] It was further estimated that out of a total of 7 million non-manual workers some 4 million, mainly employed in the public sector, were covered by collective negotiating machinery. Since that time there has been a substantial expansion of trade union organisation among white-collar workers in the

---

[1] Professor of Industrial Relations, London School of Economics and Political Science.

[2] Research Officer, Department of Industrial Relations, London School of Economics and Political Science.

[3] B. C. Roberts (ed.): *Industrial relations: contemporary problems and perspectives* (London, Methuen, revised edition, 1968).

[4] Total trade union membership in 1970 was 11 million—almost 47 per cent of the total number of employees in the United Kingdom.

private sector and the total covered by collective agreements has greatly increased.[1]

Although minimum wages and certain other terms of employment in a limited number of industries with a low degree of unionisation were set through statutory wages councils, this procedure was essentially an adjunct to the collective bargaining system. The establishment during the past decade of minimum periods of notice through the Contracts of Employment Act [2] and the provision of a statutory redundancy payments scheme were developments which suggested that the collective bargaining system had failed to achieve the standards of protection that were considered essential in a modern State.

The collective bargaining system appeared to be failing in two other important respects which brought about a rising chorus of criticism from wide sections of public opinion, including the press, Parliament and academic experts. Under conditions of full employment collective bargaining continuously produced wage settlements that were highly inflationary. To make matters worse, the structure of union organisation and the attitudes of trade unionists towards technological change restricted adaptation and the rate of economic growth. What gave rise to most criticism, however, was the increase in industrial conflict; by the beginning of the 1970s a level not known since the early 1920s had been reached in terms of the number of strikes and man-days lost.

Inflationary increases in pay had led all governments since the Second World War into prices and incomes policies, but the political difficulties arising from attempts to achieve a policy of central pay and price control in the face of a growing tendency for agreements not to be kept and a steady rise in industrial conflict eventually persuaded the Labour Government to establish the Royal Commission on Trade Unions and Employers' Associations.

The report of the Royal Commission published in 1968 [3] after three years of study and deliberation provided confirmation of the breakdown of the traditional system of industry-wide bargaining and recommended a series of proposals for reform which were based on the hope that they would be acceptable to employers and unions and would also prove to be effective. The Labour Government then in office accepted the Commission's report as a valid analysis of the basic problems, but it was not satisfied that the proposals for reform were adequate. However, the desire of the Government to give the Secretary of State for Employment and Productivity power to impose a compulsory conciliation pause in unconstitutional strikes and to ballot members of a union threatening to go on

---

[1] See *British Journal of Industrial Relations*, Nov. 1972, for various articles on developments in British trade unions.

[2] See ILO: *Legislative Series*, 1963—UK 1.

[3] *Royal Commission on Trade Unions and Employers' Associations 1965-1968: Report* (London, HM Stationery Office, Cmnd. 3623, 1968).

official strike was frustrated by the opposition of the unions and a significant section of the Labour Party. This sequence of events opened the way for the Conservatives, when they were returned to power in 1970, to introduce a root and branch reform of the legal framework of industrial relations through the 1971 Industrial Relations Act.[1]

Factors bringing about change in the bargaining structure

Since the end of the Second World War the structure of the collective bargaining system and the pattern of collective agreements have been changed in a number of important respects. In the early period of collective bargaining in Britain, before the turn of the nineteenth century, collective agreements were generally negotiated on a town, district or regional basis. With the growth of employers' federations and the establishment of national federations of trade unions, towards the end of the nineteenth century agreements began to be negotiated at the national level to cover an entire industry. During the First World War industry-wide agreements, as the basic element in a national system of joint negotiation, were greatly encouraged, and by the end of the war this was the established pattern of collective bargaining.

The Second World War saw the beginning of a process of erosion of industry-wide negotiations which has led to a decline in their significance in favour of agreements negotiated at the level of the plant or enterprise in a large part of the manufacturing and processing industries. The breakdown of the system of industry-wide agreements has been brought about by economic and social changes which have not been confined to the United Kingdom, but their effect has paradoxically been more radical and more disorganising in Britain than in many other countries because of the strength of the established system and the reluctance of national organisations of employers and unions over many years to come to terms with the forces that were reshaping their structure and function.[2]

Influence of full employment

Since the Second World War the demand for labour has been maintained at a level that has kept unemployment below 3 per cent for almost the whole of this period. Only during the past two years has the unemployment level climbed towards 4 per cent and even at this post-war high level it is far below the 13 per cent which was the average of the years between 1920 and 1940. This sustained high level of demand for labour provided a favourable economic and social climate for the development of plant and company bargaining.

---

[1] See ILO: *Legislative Series*, 1971—UK 1.

[2] See A. Flanders: *Management and unions* (London, Faber and Faber, 1970).

Under conditions of mass unemployment the task of the shop steward was largely confined to maintaining trade union membership and endeavouring to prevent employers from undercutting agreements negotiated at the industry level. Full employment has completely altered the bargaining power of the shop stewards and greatly extended their role and function. Shortage of labour made the employer vulnerable to pressure from employees for increases in wages greater than those negotiated nationally.

Effect of union structure

The trend towards plant and company bargaining was encouraged by the structure of the British trade union movement. Unions are for the most part not organised on an industrial basis, but according to occupational categories. Some of the largest and most powerful unions in Britain are " general " in their pattern of membership; that is, they organise irrespective of industrial boundaries or occupational grades.[1]

This pattern of trade union organisation has led to a multiplicity of unions in most enterprises and in both the private and public sectors of employment. Each union is represented by its own shop stewards and is responsible for their credentials, but where, as is normally the case, a joint shop stewards' committee exists, this committee is not subject to the authority or rules of any particular union. In these circumstances a joint shop stewards' committee has considerable freedom of initiative and independence. It is in fact responsible only to itself, and its constituents.

The Royal Commission described the pattern of industrial relations which had developed in Britain as one in which there were two systems. At the national level established procedures existed and worked smoothly; at the enterprise level appropriate procedures were often lacking and the general pattern of behaviour was disorderly. There was no effectively articulated linkage between the two systems at industry and enterprise levels, which were in conflict rather than in harmony.

Growth of unofficial action

It is perhaps not surprising that given this structural deficiency the unofficial strike became an important element in the development of plant and company bargaining. Bargaining units were ill-defined; jurisdiction and lines of authority were confused. Shop stewards discovered not only that they were free to call strikes, but that strikes often led to a rapid solution of problems which either could not be solved in the absence of effective procedures or involved long drawn out struggles often leading to frustration and disappointment.

---

[1] See H. A. Clegg: *The system of industrial relations in Great Britain* (Oxford, Blackwell, second edition, 1972), Ch. 2, for more detailed discussion.

356

Confronted by a growing readiness of shop stewards to take the initiative, national union leaders gradually came to accept the inevitability of this situation. For a period the policy of the unions was to seek to maintain the industry-wide system of agreements which were negotiated between federations of trade unions and federations of employers and to take no responsibility for the additional demands of shop stewards which often immediately followed a national agreement. Frequently the strikes called by the stewards in support of their demands were directed as much against their union leaders as against their employers.

In spite of the fact that many of the strikes called by shop stewards were in breach of union rules, in breach of the procedure agreements to which their unions were a party and also often involved the workers concerned in breaking their individual contract of employment, they were successful. Stewards suffered from no legal liability for their breach of agreements, since these were not legally binding contracts. They were binding only in honour, and when this was cast aside no penalty was incurred. Employers frequently conceded to the stewards the claims they were making as the least costly way to secure a rapid return to work. During the past few years a number of the large unions have decided to recognise the " unofficial " strike as a legitimate action on the part of the stewards, by giving such stoppages retroactive approval. The shift from industry-wide to plant and company bargaining was taken almost to its ultimate by the Amalgamated Union of Engineering Workers (AUEW) when it decided in 1971 to abandon national agreements in favour of local claims made and negotiated by shop stewards, sometimes with, but often without, the assistance of the district officials of the unions concerned. The tactic of the AUEW was to lay down national guidelines which it was confidently believed shop steward negotiators would be able to achieve. In practice the targets fixed by the national committee of the union proved to be completely unrealistic, and widespread failure to achieve them has revived belief in the need to negotiate national agreements on basic pay and hours of work, leaving the stewards free to seek additions according to local circumstances.

The role of the employers

The growth of plant and company bargaining could not have been achieved without the willingness of employers to play their part in this development. The switch in the attitudes of firms in this respect was brought about by changes not only in the economic climate but also in the size and structure of enterprises and in the evolution of management.

As firms have grown larger they have become more conscious of their separate interests and more concerned to develop their own managerial expertise. The role of the personnel officer has been extended in most large companies from responsibility for recruitment and the administration of wage and welfare policies to include also negotiations with unions. The development of specialised industrial relations functions has inevitably brought with it a preference for agreements tailored to meet the particular needs of the enterprise and a growing reluctance to be dependent upon an employers' association.

This change in the policy of management towards plant and company bargaining was encouraged by the example of large American-owned companies. These companies have tended to bring with them attitudes and practices developed in the United States. Many of them were reluctant to join employers' associations and some have been openly anti-union. Most US-owned companies had a more highly developed personnel policy than British companies and they were unwilling to restrict this to the requirements of British employers' associations.[1]

Employers' associations were greatly opposed, until comparatively recently, to the negotiation of separate plant and company agreements, and they did their utmost to prevent their members from making agreements that were in breach of the terms settled for the whole industry. This policy led companies which wished to pioneer new ideas on remuneration and other conditions of employment to resign their membership or face expulsion. Gradually, however, this attitude changed as it became increasingly obvious that it was being honoured more in the breach than in the observance. Some employers' associations are now making special efforts to assist their members to carry out plant and company agreements. In this respect the Chemical Industries Association and the Rubber Manufacturers Association may be cited. Most significant of all, the largest and most powerful employers' association, the Engineering Employers' Federation (EEF), has established an employers' advisory service and a research department to provide member firms faced by union demands with expert advice and information. Although the EEF has had considerable success in bolstering up its members' opposition to extreme demands made on a local basis by the unions, it was compelled to give up its long-cherished national procedure agreement on the refusal of the unions to observe its terms any longer. However, there is reason to believe that both sides see an advantage in having a national disputes procedure, and it is likely that a new procedural agreement will eventually be made. It is necessary to stress that, although plant and company bargaining have become widespread in the private sector of employment, there are some industries, such as electrical contracting, shipbuilding and those which have wages councils, where industry-wide agreements still have an important role.

The existence of an unusually tightly knit employers' association is the main reason why industry-wide agreements remain of importance in the electrical contracting industry. Employers' associations are reasonably

---

[1] J. Gennard and M. D. Steuer: " The industrial relations of foreign owned subsidiaries in the United Kingdom ", in *British Journal of Industrial Relations*, July 1971, pp. 143-159.

well organised in most sections of British industry, but few are as powerful as the Federation of Electrical Contractors, which has been able, unlike most other employers' organisations, to maintain an effective opposition to fragmentary bargaining.

Public service

Each part of the public sector has its own machinery of industrial relations. In the civil service collective bargaining is carried on through Whitley Councils. These are joint bodies on which the unions and employers are represented. Although mainly concerned with problems of remuneration, they cover every aspect of employer-employee relations.[1] Bargaining has been conducted for many years on the principle that the government should be a good employer, but not ahead of the average of good employers. To assist in the application of this doctrine, in the civil service the two sides are provided with the results of regular surveys made by a Civil Service Pay Research Unit.

The information so provided by no means always prevents sharp conflicts between the two sides. A national pay claim for an increase of 15 to 20 per cent made by the Union of Post Office Workers in 1971 resulted in a strike of postal workers which lasted from 20 January until 8 March.[2]

In the local government sector, education and the health service, unions have shown a militancy in negotiations far in excess of what used to be traditional in these sectors of public employment. This rise in the level of conflict and the greater readiness to resort to the threat and use of strikes have been stimulated by a fear of falling behind the pay increases won by manual workers and sharply rising living costs brought about by worsening price inflation.

In Britain it has never been illegal for public servants to go on strike, but it has been an accepted convention that members of the civil service do not use their freedom to cease work collectively as a means of putting pressure on their employer, the State. This tradition has clearly been changing. Although public servants, teachers, nurses and doctors are still reluctant to strike, it has become evident that these middle-class professional men and women are increasingly determined to use their strategic position to secure the standards of remuneration which they believe they are legitimately entitled to enjoy.

Nationalised industries

Each nationalised industry, including the coal, railways, airlines, and gas and electricity industries, has its own machinery of industrial relations,

---

[1] R. Loveridge: *Collective bargaining by national employees in the UK* (Ann Arbor, University of Michigan-Wayne State University, 1971).

[2] The Post Office was changed from a civil service department to a public corporation in 1971, but it is doubtful whether this change was a significant factor in the cause of the strike.

which owes its main characteristics to the structure that existed prior to nationalisation. It was strongly argued and widely believed that nationalisation would transform the pattern of industrial relations, which in some cases, notably mining, had been marked by extreme bitterness. While it could be said that in the mining industry relations between the National Coal Board and the unions are far better than were the relations between the private owners and the unions before nationalisation, they are by no means superior to the state of industrial relations in private industry in general. Experience in the nationalised industries has shown that public ownership has had relatively little effect on industrial relations attitudes. The nature of the industry, its traditions, its technology, the market situation, and current social trends would seem to be far more important determinants of the behaviour of the parties than the fact of public ownership.

Organisation of white-collar employees

Collective bargaining for white-collar employees was until recently more strongly established in the public than in the private sector, where it is only now beginning to spread rapidly. There has been a steady growth in white-collar union membership in the past 25 years, but only since 1968 has it exceeded the rate of increase in white-collar employment. This remarkable increase in white-collar unionism has been the result of economic and social factors; in particular it has been stimulated by the erosion of differentials and the frustration of " established expectations " of salary and career.[1]

Thus the membership of unions such as the Association of Supervisory, Technical and Managerial Staffs and the National Union of Bank Employees has grown rapidly, and the larger general unions, such as the Transport and General Workers' Union and the AUEW, have developed big white-collar sections.

Employees with professional qualifications, such as doctors, engineers, scientists and high-level administrators, have begun to look beyond their traditional professional associations to new bodies ready to bargain collectively on their behalf. These new organisations tend to occupy a middle ground between the traditional unions and the older type of professional association, but it would seem to be only a matter of time before they become fully established as independent trade unions or merge with the older and rapidly expanding white-collar unions.

British employers have often been reluctant to recognise unions seeking to bargain on behalf of their clerical, scientific and administrative staff. This attitude is changing as their staff show an increasing readiness to

---

[1] B. C. Roberts, R. Loveridge and J. Gennard: *Reluctant militants—a study of industrial technicians in the UK* (London, Heinemann Educational Books Ltd., 1972).

join unions and under the pressure of government policy expressed through institutions such as the Commission for Industrial Relations and through the provisions of the new Industrial Relations Act.

The rapid expansion of union membership among non-manual workers has brought a new dynamic to trade union development in Britain, but it has also brought new problems of setting the boundaries of bargaining units for these groups of employees. At present most white-collar workers are in unions affiliated to the Trades Union Congress (TUC), but there are serious conflicts of organisational interest which are giving rise to jurisdictional issues that are proving extremely difficult to resolve.

Changes in the levels and methods of bargaining

Negotiations at the industry level are usually undertaken by permanent national officers of employers' associations and by full-time national officials of the unions. Frequently the representatives of the two sides have met together over many years and built up a certain *modus vivendi*, an understanding of the aims, tactics and limits of the other, which facilitates eventual agreement. Major breakdowns in negotiations have sometimes been due to new members of a negotiating team lacking this knowledge, but more commonly to difficulties arising from the complexity of both trade unions and employers' organisations.

At plant and company level, collective bargaining has developed in the context of industrial relations procedures based on " custom and practice ".[1] While having the virtue of flexibility, the informality of these procedures has been criticised as being " anarchic ", " disorderly " and a prolific source of conflict. However, in recent years there has been a clear trend towards the formalisation of procedures and a more professional approach to the bargaining process.[2]

More firms have been appointing managers with a knowledge of industrial relations problems and with training in this field. Increasingly it is being recognised that industrial relations are as important to business success as production, marketing and finance, and must be accepted as a responsibility of senior management.[3]

Surveys have shown that personnel managers have a strong preference for negotiating on issues arising within an enterprise with their own shop stewards rather than with the national officials of the unions to which

---

[1] William Brown: " A consideration of ' custom and practice ' ", in *British Journal of Industrial Relations*, Mar. 1972, pp. 42-61.

[2] Department of Employment: *The reform of collective bargaining at plant and company level*, Manpower Papers No. 5 (London, HM Stationery Office, 1971).

[3] Idem: *Industrial Relations Code of Practice* (London, HM Stationery Office, 1972), p. 4, para. 2. This code was introduced with the 1971 Industrial Relations Act and it seeks to establish the principles which should serve as the guidelines for good industrial relations practice.

their employees belong.[1] However, where a dispute concerns wages or other items that might have serious cost repercussions, they look for assistance to the employers' association to which they belong. Although the role of the employers' association has been greatly reduced, it still represents an important element of support and guidance, especially for medium-sized and smaller concerns.

On the union side the problem is more difficult. Because of the deeply entrenched pattern of occupational and general unionism in Britain, there is a multiplicity of unions representing different groups of employees in most enterprises. Co-ordination is achieved through the joint shop stewards' committees mentioned earlier, which, since they are not responsible to any union, enjoy a high degree of autonomy. It is common for these committees to conduct negotiations with employers through their own appointed " convenor " or chief steward, who is elected from within the committee. Often only when they are in difficulties or require expert assistance do they ask for the help of district or national offices of one or more of the unions involved. Unions have, however, begun to see the need to service their stewards more efficiently than in the past. There is now widespread provision for giving at least rudimentary training to shop stewards, and some unions and the TUC provide sophisticated courses of advanced training in collective bargaining.

Many recent agreements have given more specific attention to the role and functions of shop stewards or " accredited representatives " of workers and staff, to their number, qualifications and area of representation, and to the facilities, such as office space, use of the telephone and time off, which should be granted to them, although these are not often specified and merely described as " reasonable facilities ". Some companies also agree to help provide training for shop stewards.[2]

It is generally accepted that shop stewards constitute the " employee representatives " on various joint committees, although in some companies other employees may still be members of shop-floor " joint productivity " committees as set up under productivity bargaining or for particular problems. Traditional forms of joint consultation still continue and have even been initiated in some companies where they are seen as providing greater scope for exchange of information and for developing a more co-operative approach. In general, however, joint consultative committees have either become ineffective or their distinction from negotiating committees has withered as unions have extended the scope of collective bargaining.[3]

---

[1] Department of Employment and Productivity: *Workplace industrial relations*, government social survey (London, HM Stationery Office, 1968).

[2] Commission on Industrial Relations: *Facilities afforded to shop stewards*, Report No. 17 (London, HM Stationery Office, Cmnd. 4668, 1971).

[3] For a discussion of joint consultation in Britain, see R. O. Clarke, D. J. Fatchett and B. C. Roberts: *Workers' participation in management in Britain* (London, Heinemann Educational Books Ltd., 1972), pp. 46-54, 72-75, 119.

Term of agreements

During the early 1960s there was a considerable increase in the number of industry-level collective agreements fixing pay increases for a term of years. This type of agreement still exists, but its significance has diminished with the growth of plant and company agreements. There are signs of an emerging pattern of annual negotiations in the larger companies and at industry level in both the private and public sectors. In some cases, under the influence of rapidly rising prices and exceptionally high increases in pay, there have been attempts by shop stewards and their unions to secure advances in wages at even more frequent intervals than a year. It has not been entirely uncommon during the past few years for new pay demands to be made within a few weeks of a pay settlement. One effect of this development has been the tendency for pay negotiations to extend over a longer period as employers have sought to resist compression of the duration of an agreement.

The negotiation of fixed-term agreements is an important break with the traditional type of collective agreement in Britain, concluded for an unspecified term but containing a procedural arrangement for ending the agreement and reopening negotiations on whatever sections either the union or, more rarely, the employer has wished to see changed. This has meant that collective agreements are highly flexible instruments and their terms can be quickly re-negotiated when changes in economic or other circumstances make this desirable. The disadvantage, especially from the point of view of the employer, is that bargaining has been virtually continuous, and this has been a potent factor in the element of wage drift and instability in British industrial relations.[1]

The open-endedness of collective agreements in Britain has been closely related to the absence of a clear distinction between disputes of " rights " and disputes of " interests ". Unlike the situation in continental European countries or North America, all disputes in Britain tend to be disputes of interests, and therefore an issue arising out of the interpretation of a clause in an agreement has traditionally been settled in the last resort by the use of force rather than through the arbitrament of a court or by independent arbitrators [2]

Procedures

Procedures for dealing with disputes arising out of the agreed terms and conditions of employment have traditionally been adopted by each industry. The amount of detail laid down in procedural agreements and the number of stages of discussion within the machinery vary from one

[1] L. C. Hunter and D. J. Robertson: *Economics of wages and labour* (London, Macmillan, 1969).

[2] O. Kahn-Freund: *Labour and the law* (London, Stevens, 1972), p. 58.

industry to another. In most industries workers' complaints are discussed with the foreman in the first instance; then a shop steward may take the issue to higher levels of supervision if satisfaction has not been secured. If the issue is of considerable significance the works committee will be involved and the matter may go to the highest level of management. In the engineering industry, after this domestic procedure was exhausted, a works conference could be arranged which involved full-time union officers and the employers. This second stage, known as the " local conference ", comprised a hearing of the case by regional or district union representatives and employers' association representatives. Finally, if the dispute was still unresolved, it proceeded to a " central conference ", where national union and employers' association representatives were present. If at the final stage there was still failure to agree, both parties were then free to resort to such action as they saw fit, including a strike or lockout. The engineering industry procedure was for many years criticised because of the delays in processing grievances from one stage to the next and because there was no procedure in the final stage which would ensure a specific decision on the issue.

Discussions about a new and more rapid procedure in the engineering industry finally broke down in 1971 over the definition of " management prerogative " in the so-called " status quo " clause. That existing provisions stand until new arrangements are agreed is usually recognised by management as applying to those areas which it has been agreed are the subject of negotiation, but unions argue that any change from an established pattern of work must be subject to negotiation and may not be made without agreement. When the right to make a change is disputed, it is the unions' contention that the employer should observe the " status quo " until agreement is reached. This limitation of managerial freedom is virtually established in printing, coalmining and the docks, and there have been a number of cases where management has been unable to introduce new methods and new technological equipment because agreement could not be reached with the unions concerned. The general trend is, however, towards acceptance of the principle of mutuality, though there is considerable variation in the extent to which management rights are limited in recently negotiated procedural agreements.

The development of plant and company bargaining has brought with it recognition of the need to formalise procedures to deal with discipline, attendance and individual or collective grievances and disputes by clarification of the stages to be gone through and of the parties' rights of representation, consultation and even arbitration in settling problems. Whereas this formalised extension of the scope of bargaining, resulting in written agreements, has so far occurred only in the larger, and particularly in the multi-plant, companies, with the stimulus of the 1971 Industrial Relations Act and Code of Practice it is likely to affect the smaller companies, many of which are already moving towards greater " systematisation " of their procedures.[1] The requirement to inform employees of the person to whom they can apply for the redress of any employment grievance, and in what manner, has led some companies to clarify these arrangements for the first time.

Changes in the content of agreements

In assessing the changing pattern of collective bargaining in the United Kingdom during recent decades, it becomes clear that the development of productivity bargaining, and in this connection the role of the prices and incomes legislation, were of crucial significance.

The first and most famous productivity agreement was negotiated between the Esso Standard Oil Company at Fawley and the Transport and General Workers' Union, together with a number of craft unions.[2] The essential feature was that after prolonged negotiations, in which there was a high degree of shop steward and membership participation within the bargaining unit, it was agreed to make substantial changes in work practices in exchange for substantially higher rates of pay, shorter hours and other improvements in the terms of employment. In short, through this agreement management was able to persuade workers to lift restrictions on manning ratios and to accept a greater degree of flexibility in the way in which work was carried out.

The significance of the Fawley agreements, which were the forerunners of many others, was to show to employers that, by careful managerial planning and control allied to sophisticated techniques of negotiation, great improvements in manpower productivity could be achieved, and to show to the unions and their shop stewards that workplace bargaining, if effectively carried out, could greatly extend the scope of bargaining and yield impressive advances in pay and conditions of employment.

With the establishment in 1965 of a National Board for Prices and Incomes by the newly elected Labour Government, fresh emphasis was placed on productivity as a factor in collective bargaining. Unions and employers were encouraged to negotiate productivity agreements, since the promise of achieving above-average increases in output was accepted as a justification for above-norm pay increases.[3]

From 1 January 1967 to 31 December 1969, 5,185 productivity agreements were registered with the Department of Employment and

---

[1] A. Marsh, E. O. Evans, and P. Garcia: *Workplace industrial relations in engineering* (London, Engineering Employers Federation, 1972).

[2] A. Flanders: *The Fawley productivity agreements* (London, Faber and Faber, 1964).

[3] National Board for Prices and Incomes: *Productivity and pay during the period of severe restraint*, Report No. 23 (London, HM Stationery Office, Cmnd. 3167, 1966); idem: *Productivity agreements*, Report No. 36 (London, HM Stationery Office, Cmnd. 3311, 1967); and idem: *Productivity agreements*, Report No. 123 (London, HM Stationery Office, Cmnd. 4136, 1969).

Productivity. It must be emphasised that by this time the concept of a productivity agreement had been greatly broadened to cover almost any change in work practice, hours of work, wage structure and method of wage payment.[1]

Since the end of the formal incomes policy in 1970, the concept of productivity bargaining, which had often become a rather dubious means of satisfying the incomes policy criteria set by the Government, has given way to a more general concern about the existence of " chaotic pay structures " and the widespread degeneration of long accepted piece-work systems of payment. The reform of company pay policy was greatly encouraged by the reports of the National Board for Prices and Incomes, which examined the problems of pay structures and methods of payment in substantial detail.[2]

More recently, the need to keep pay structures under continuing review has been stressed in the Code of Practice accompanying the 1971 Industrial Relations Act. The question of differentials relating to status, skill or seniority and contradictory concepts of " equity " raise the most difficulties when changes in payment systems are being agreed. Job evaluation was not very widely accepted in Britain until recent years but even now it is mostly applied sectionally as between manual and non-manual workers, and even within these categories, since it is the most powerful groups that are likely to be the most averse to disturbing traditional relativities.

The Code draws attention to the need to ensure that where pay is linked to performance " differences in remuneration should be related to the requirements of the job, which should . . . be assessed in a rational and systematic way in consultation with employee representatives ".[3]

A number of British companies have followed the lead of the electricity supply industry in extending staff status to manual employees. The most important example is Imperial Chemical Industries (ICI), whose " Weekly Staff Agreement " was first introduced in 1969, after a considerable period of preparation and negotiation with the unions. This committed the management to improve the status of employees with annual salaries, paid weekly, on the basis of job-assessment schemes. It guaranteed stability of earnings and its application often involved some form of " job enlargement " and reduction of supervision. By the end of 1971 it had been extended to almost all plants, with considerable success in terms of both job satisfaction and productivity.

---

[1] B. C. Roberts and J. Gennard: " Trends in plant and company bargaining ", in D. J. Robertson and L. C. Hunter (eds.): *Labour market issues of the 1970s* (Edinburgh, Oliver and Boyd, 1970), pp. 31-50.

[2] See, in particular, National Board for Prices and Incomes: *Payment by results systems*, Report No. 65 (London, HM Stationery Office, 1968).

[3] *Industrial Relations Code of Practice*, op. cit., p. 11, para. 38.

Estimates of the proportion of manual employees on incentive schemes would probably remain around the 1950 figure of 40 per cent, as although many firms, in the motor-car industry particularly, are moving away from incentive systems of payment, other employers, such as local government authorities, are introducing them. Moreover, those who are abolishing piece-work systems and moving on to a " measured day-work system " are still using a form of incentive payment; the significant difference lies in the fact that it is work-studied and offers more secure earnings to the employee and more predictable costs and output to the employer.

Traditional union opposition, in many industries, to incentive pay schemes has always been tempered by the unions' desire to widen the scope for increasing their members' earnings and job autonomy. The extent of mutuality in recent agreements over changes in pay systems reflects management recognition of this widening of the scope of bargaining. Some firms have also recognised that changing pay systems is difficult and likely to give rise to conflict, and new dispute procedures have been agreed to meet this difficulty—a measure which is also of significance in illustrating the inextricable linking of substantive change with procedural change at every turn.

With rising unemployment during the past few years, whether resulting from cyclical or structural factors or changes in manpower utilisation via productivity and work-study schemes, fears of redundancy have grown. Management generally reserves the right to decide on labour rundowns, whether permanent or temporary, but various procedure agreements have been signed with unions on the way in which redundancies are to be carried out, although sometimes there has been opposition to this, in principle, by either management or unions. The general " last in, first out " method of selection is usually applied, but unions in Britain have not often attempted to establish hard and fast seniority rules. That has been left to particular circumstances. Large firms have often also agreed to more generous redundancy payments than those stipulated under the Redundancy Payments Act.[1]

It has been accepted in Britain since before the First World War that collective bargaining can give little protection to those categories of workers who for various reasons often cannot be effectively organised. Since 1909 statutory wages councils have in effect settled the terms and conditions of employment for these workers. Elsewhere, collectively bargained terms have been taken as setting a minimum wage standard.[2]

The trade union movement has always included " social justice " among its bargaining aims, but it has not been successful in raising the relative wage level of the lowest paid. Pay settlements have come increasingly to be seen in terms of percentage increases rather than as cash sums,

---

[1] See ILO: *Legislative Series*, 1965—UK 1.

[2] F. J. Bayliss: *British wages councils* (Oxford, Blackwell, 1962).

thus tending to widen rather than narrow money differentials. The TUC has put renewed emphasis on encouraging unions to bargain for higher percentage increases for those workers at the bottom of the scale, but both trade unions and governments have been averse to setting a national minimum, preferring to regard this as a matter for collective bargaining. The National Board for Prices and Incomes found there was no satisfactory definition of low pay.[1]

" Guaranteed week " or " guaranteed earnings " arrangements have also been regarded by government as a matter for collective bargaining, and the recent extension of such arrangements has been partly the result of changes in the qualification period for the payment of certain social security benefits. Public service and white-collar workers have traditionally had greater security of earnings, but otherwise, until recently, guaranteed arrangements were usually negotiated in industries where there were likely to be lay-offs as a result of shortage of supplies, seasonal working or other factors, and they detailed the circumstances when employees would *not* get normal weekly pay. It is likely that two-thirds of employees are now covered by such guarantees expressed in a variety of combinations of money and/or time, with the exceptions ranging from the weather, shortages and strikes to " acts of God "; the operation of the guarantees depends to a greater or lesser extent on management discretion.

The massive increase in the level of retail prices since 1969 has made unions aware that large wage advances can be rapidly eroded. Some industry groups and large companies in banking and insurance, as well as manufacturers, have adopted some form of " wage indexation ", but the majority of workers are not protected in this way. The TUC has urged on the government and employers the wisdom of " threshold " agreements, which would provide for an automatic wage adjustment when the cost of living rose above a certain figure. Support for this principle has been growing, but there is a fear that, contrary to what the TUC believes, cost-of-living pay compensation would add to the inflation, making matters worse rather than better.

British unions in the years since the war have tended to concentrate their efforts on direct pay increases rather than on improvements in hours, holidays or fringe benefits, although there is little statutory regulation of these. Even so, there has been a gradual reduction in the length of the basic week from 45 to 40 hours, and the big unions are now making 35 hours a bargaining aim. A few companies have agreed to greater flexibility in hours of work, and so increases in overtime premiums and/or shift rates have frequently accompanied increases in basic rates as separate features of agreements rather than as adjustments. Moreover, the amount of overtime worked has remained high in most of British industry, partly as

---

[1] National Board for Prices and Incomes: *General problems of low pay*, Report No. 169 (London, HM Stationery Office, Cmnd. 4648, 1971).

a means of achieving a reasonable level of pay.[1] The increased unemployment of 1971-72 marked a slight reduction in the total number of hours worked. Some redundancy agreements have made provision for the reduction of overtime to avoid lay-offs, but most overtime arrangements are not covered by collective agreements: they are a matter for " custom and practice " between supervisors and shop stewards at the workshop level.

Although demands for an extension of the holiday entitlement have taken second place to demands for higher pay, annual holidays have gradually been increasing from two to three weeks and extra days have often been added to public holidays at Christmas or Easter. Some groups have begun to negotiate for four weeks' annual holiday and this has been obtained by non-industrial civil servants and for long-service employees in a growing number of private firms. The payment of average earnings rather than basic rates for holidays has also been the subject of several recent agreements and is likely to be the aim of much future bargaining.

Improved fringe benefits in the form of better sickness payments, pension schemes and insurance plans have featured more prominently in union claims in recent years, but whereas the manual unions have often appeared less willing to press negotiations on these in the last resort (leaving it to the TUC to push for improved government legislation), the white-collar unions have been giving them increasing attention. New state pension plans seem to envisage a more important future role for occupational pension schemes, so that this is likely to become an increasingly important aspect of bargaining at company level.

Pension schemes were among the " terms and conditions " excluded from the scope of the Equal Pay Act of 1970 [2], which makes provision for equal pay for work of equal value and is to come fully into effect in 1975. Equal pay has already been achieved by white-collar workers in most of the public sector, but in general the stages, if any, by which it is introduced are a matter for management decision or collective bargaining.

While women represent over 35 per cent of the labour force in Britain, they generally work shorter hours and are concentrated in the low-paid sectors of manufacturing and notably in wages council industries, such as hotels and catering, laundry and dry cleaning, and retail distribution. Women have not hitherto been highly unionised (although accounting for the greatest proportionate growth in union membership) or of importance in collective bargaining at any level. Since 1970, however, they have obtained larger percentage pay increases than men in most agreements, but over-all in 1971 their rates had only moved from approximately 75 to

---

[1] See National Board for Prices and Incomes: *Hours of work, overtime and shift work*, Report No. 161 (London, HM Stationery Office, 1971); E. G. Whybrew: *Overtime working in Britain*, Royal Commission on Trade Unions and Employers' Associations, Research Paper 9, (London, HM Stationery Office, 1968); and H. Sallis: *Overtime in electricity supply*, Occasional Paper (London, *British Journal of Industrial Relations*, 1970).

[2] See ILO: *Legislative Series*, 1970—UK 1.

82 per cent of men's rates, and high cash differences in the earnings of the two sexes remained. Only a few retail distribution groups have achieved equal pay so far, but most major companies have agreed schemes of gradual implementation. There are signs that this may lead to considerable changes in future patterns of employment, with women facing stiffer competition for jobs or being more rigidly segregated into the lower job-evaluated grades covertly designated as being for " women only ".[1]

There have been signs of a more sophisticated approach to bargaining by both unions and management in recent years in that claims, and replies, at least in certain industries and companies (for example, Ford and ICI in 1971 and local government), have been more carefully worked out and presented. British unions, and likewise employers' associations, have been developing and making greater use of their own research departments and those of universities and consultants. A greater number of British companies have been employing professional personnel managers and working out negotiating aims in a more systematic way, attempting to cost the whole " package " offered and developing a cleared *quid pro quo* approach.

The grounds on which claims for pay increases have been based have obviously varied according to the circumstances of the company, the industry and the national economy. Thus claims based on " equity " and the " cost of living " have come to the fore again in the past year or two of rapid inflation—and particularly in the public sector, where there has been less opportunity for increasing earnings through payment by results schemes or because government pressures to hold back have been stronger. The recent extension of means-tested social security benefits and the incidence of taxation have made unions more aware of the need to be concerned about increasing the real disposable income of their members rather than about simply obtaining higher money wages. Claims presented to the large multinational companies, on the other hand, have shown a greater tendency to stress " ability to pay " or a past or future increase in productivity. This ground was in any case necessary for claims made during the mid-sixties phase of incomes policy, when agreements for pay increases above the norm might subsequently be referred to the National Board for Prices and Incomes for scrutiny. It was also national policy at this period to discourage claims based on " comparability ", but since 1968 the cry for parity—between groups of workers in the same firm, between firms in the same district, between plants of the same company in different regions or even in different countries, as well as between workers in different industries—has become more vociferous as workers' circles of comparison have widened.

---

[1] See N. Seear: " The future employment of women ", in B. C. Roberts and J. H. Smith (eds.): *Manpower policy and employment trends* (London, G. Bell and Sons Ltd., for the London School of Economics and Political Science, 1966), pp. 96-110; and also Department of Employment, Office of Manpower Economics: *Equal pay: first report* (London, HM Stationery Office, 1972).

Moreover, as indicated earlier, claims for further increases have tended to be presented more frequently recently, sometimes almost as soon as one round of collective bargaining is over. However, although there has been some blurring of the edges concerning the " trend-setters ", with the major car firms " leap-frogging " over each other, certain groups, such as the nationalised industries, non-manual civil servants or manual local and central government employees, still tend to follow the leader.

The general bargaining principles on which the strategy of both sides is based have shown some development but inevitably, perhaps, no fundamental alteration over recent years, at least at industry level. At company level, unions have aimed more positively at extending bargaining scope and management has sought to define and preserve " managerial functions ", particularly in respect of the utilisation of manpower, as well as to uphold the principle of " enterprise autonomy ".

Strikes

Collective bargaining as a method of resolving differences of interests inevitably involves the possibility of a strike and trial of strength if agreement is not reached. Whether this factor is overt or covert will depend on the respective tactics and strength of the parties, their appraisal of each other and external influences, particularly the national political and economic climate. The higher the level of bargaining the stronger these influences are likely to be and the higher the level of national involvement. Thus in the pre-war years, when industry-wide bargaining was strong, the " days lost " were chiefly a result of national strikes. In the later 1950s and the 1960s, as increasingly negotiations took place on the " shop floor ", disputes, whether arising from existing agreements or new demands, resulted in a large number of stoppages of fairly short duration not normally involving very many people. Some 95 per cent of these strikes were unofficial; that is, they were in breach of the union rules and of the national agreed procedure. About half concerned wages and over 40 per cent concerned " working arrangements, rules and discipline " and " redundancy, dismissal, suspension, etc." [1] The growth of unofficial strikes has given rise to much public concern, since they are widely believed to be particularly damaging on account of their unpredictability and their deleterious effect on management's willingness to innovate. Their frequency in certain industries crucially important to Britain's balance of payments situation, such as the motor-car industry, shipbuilding, the aircraft industry and port transport, increase their social significance. [2]

---

[1] *Royal Commission on Trade Unions and Employers' Associations 1965-1968: Report*, op. cit., p. 100, paras. 379-380; see also J. Goodman: " Strikes in the United Kingdom ", in *International Labour Review*, May 1967, pp. 465-481; and W. E. J. McCarthy: " The nature of Britain's strike problem ", in *British Journal of Industrial Relations*, July 1970, pp. 224-236.

[2] See Malcom Fisher: *Measurement of labour disputes and their economic effects* (Paris, OECD) (to be published).

The Royal Commission on Trade Unions and Employers' Associations identified the underlying cause of strikes as residing in the conflict between the two systems of industrial relations—the one at plant level, which was informal and disorderly, the other at the national level, which was orderly and systematic, but often less relevant. In its recommendations it argued that the most important part in remedying the problem of unofficial strikes would be played by the reform of collective bargaining at company level [1]; implying that agreements would be kept if they were comprehensive, coherent and relevant to the needs of the situation and if workpeople were involved in their making.

Where there has been this formalisation, however, the widening of the bargaining unit has often meant the broadening of the scope of industrial action in the event of disagreement, and the years 1969-72 have seen an enormous increase in working days lost. This has been the result of a growth in official strikes, rather than of an increase in unofficial activity.[2]

The upsurge in strikes is related to social changes which are world-wide in their significance—a general breakdown of established patterns of authority, expectations of a continually rising standard of living, widening circles of comparison as to what this standard should be, and a determination not to be left behind in the struggle. In Britain the rapid advance of inflation, with its frustration of expectations and adverse effects on the lower paid workers, has been a potent inducement to industrial militancy.

The state machinery of inquiry, conciliation and arbitration, set up mainly under the Conciliation Act, 1896, and the Industrial Courts Act, 1919, worked in the past to the general satisfaction of employers and unions, but the fear that it was being influenced by the Government as an anti-inflationary measure has weakened its credibility with the unions in recent years.[3] Discussions have recently taken place about the possibility of employers and unions setting up a new and " independent " service. There remains some disquiet, however, on the part of the Government and of the general " consumer " interest, lest settlements between employers and unions should be made at the expense of giving a further twist to the inflationary spiral, to the cost of everyone. It remains to be seen whether these initiatives will produce a radically new system of central conciliation and arbitration.[4]

In recent collective agreements several big companies have accepted the need for the final stage of their disputes procedures to include the

---

[1] *Royal Commission on Trade Unions and Employers' Associations 1965-1968: Report*, op. cit., p. 120, para. 454.

[2] For recent strike statistics, see " Stoppages of work due to industrial disputes in 1971 ", in *Department of Employment Gazette* (London, HM Stationery Office), May 1972, pp. 438-446.

[3] Royal Commission on Trade Unions and Employers' Associations: *Written evidence of the Ministry of Labour* (London, HM Stationery Office, 1965).

[4] Since this article was written agreement has been reached by the Confederation of British Industry and the Trades Union Congress on a conciliation and arbitration agreement.

372

possibility of arbitration, although there might be recourse to it only with the agreement of both parties. Most nationalised industries and the public sector already have some final stage of arbitration built into their negotiating machinery as a voluntary procedure, but in many cases this has not been used in the past 25 years.

Of more far-reaching and fundamental importance is whether the Government will be compelled by economic circumstances and the failure of voluntary price and wage restraint to reintroduce some form of statutory prices and pay control.[1] Although the Conservative Government has firmly set its face against this step, there are many experts who believe it will be forced to change its policy by the inability of the unions to restrain their more militant members. In reply to this argument, the Government has pointed to the fact that all statutory attempts to curb collective bargaining by administrative means in democratic countries have failed.[2] To achieve success, it might be necessary to exercise more drastic control over the right to bargain and to strike than has hitherto been acceptable in democratic countries. However, the Government has been compelled by the upsurge of inflation and the need to secure a higher rate of economic growth so as to reduce the level of unemployment to seek through the Confederation of British Industry (CBI) and the TUC a voluntary restraint of price and wage increases.

The influence of the government

Apart from attempting to set an example as a " good employer " in the public sector, the government has traditionally exercised a minimal influence on collective bargaining. Legislation mainly served to establish a legal framework within which collective bargaining could be carried on as freely as possible. In addition, legal protection was gradually extended to cover the basic employment rights and conditions of individual workers, as in the case of the Factory Acts. This type of protection and assistance has been developed considerably in the past few years in the legislation on social security and national insurance, the Contracts of Employment Act, 1963, the Industrial Training Act, 1964, the Redundancy Payments Act, 1965, the Equal Pay Act, 1970, and the dismissals provisions of the Industrial Relations Act, 1971.[3]

In many ways these Acts have dealt with topics inadequately covered in collective bargaining, but there has also, since the fifties, been more government intervention in bargaining through various forms of incomes

---

[1] As this article was going to press, the Government had just ordered a 90-day standstill on wages and prices.

[2] Lloyd Ulman and R. J. Flanagan: *Wage restraint: a study of incomes policies in Western Europe* (Berkeley and Los Angeles, California, University of California Press, 1971).

[3] See K. W. Wedderburn: *The worker and the law* (Harmondsworth, Penguin Books, 2nd edition, 1971).

policy which have sought to control market forces. The agreement of the unions was generally sought, though not always obtained, to these phases of incomes policy and to the setting up of the various tripartite councils, but these measures probably achieved little more than an uneasy temporary accommodation of conflicting interests, from which it would be misleading to draw positive general conclusions. Even the surviving National Economic Development Council, which was set up in 1962 and acts as a forum for closer collaboration between the government and representatives of employers and trade unions in discussing economic policies, has never had more than a tentative role. It only acts in an advisory capacity and this stems largely from the role of Parliament and the relationship of the CBI and the TUC to their members. The fact that they have no formal authority to direct or control the policies of their affiliates and that they have to rely on persuasion has prevented the development of full national tripartite or joint policy making. It has so far remained the government's task to formulate policy and to seek to obtain specific agreement to it on grounds of national emergency, although there is continuing discussion about the possibility of a fuller tripartite system or of voluntary joint agreement to control the level of wages and prices.

One important outcome of the Labour Government's 1964-70 policy was the establishment of the National Board for Prices and Incomes, to which any wage and price increases above the norm could be referred by the government for investigation as to whether they were justified according to various specified criteria. During this period the Board produced 170 reports and, whether or not it reduced inflation, the quality of its methods of investigation and recommendations probably had an educative effect on all the parties. The lessons learnt from the experience of the Board are currently being studied in the event of a similar body being established in the future.[1]

Some of its work in reviewing the pay of top civil servants, doctors, army officers and the judiciary is being continued by the review bodies of the newly created Office of Manpower Economics in the Department of Employment, which has also undertaken other special studies—for example that on equal pay.[2]

The work of the department of the Secretary of State for Employment in the form of its monthly publication of labour, wage and price statistics also exercises a continuing influence on collective bargaining, as do the activities of its central and regional staff of officers, who, when requested,

---

[1] See Allan Fels: *The British Prices and Incomes Board*, University of Cambridge, Department of Applied Economics, Occasional Paper 29 (Cambridge, University Press, 1972); and R. J. Liddle and W. E. J. McCarthy: " The impact of the Prices and Incomes Board on the reform of collective bargaining ", in *British Journal of Industrial Relations*, Nov. 1972.

[2] Department of Employment, Office of Manpower Economics: *Equal pay: first report*, op. cit.

give advice on negotiations and act as conciliators or arbitrators in disputes, according to the wishes of the parties.

The national institution with the greatest potential for influencing collective bargaining is probably, however, the Commission on Industrial Relations (CIR), which was set up in 1969 as a result of the recommendations of the Royal Commission on Trade Unions and Employers' Associations and put on a statutory basis by the Industrial Relations Act of 1971. This body, though appointed and financed by the Government, has an independent role. Its President and the Commissioners direct a staff who investigate and report on specific questions referred to it under the Industrial Relations Act and on issues of broad general importance referred to it by the Secretary of State for Employment.

So far, over 30 reports have been issued by it covering four main areas: procedural reform, recognition problems, collective bargaining problems in particular industries such as shipbuilding, and general topics such as " facilities for shop stewards ". Most of these are in response to questions referred to it by the Government, but the Commission also undertakes some original research. Up to the end of 1971 its membership had included trade unionists and, in most of the matters referred to it, the Commission had been generally successful in obtaining the co-operation of unions and management and their consent to its recommendations. However, since the passing of the Industrial Relations Act, the trade unions, following a policy of non-cooperation with any of the institutions of the Act, have refused to participate in the work of the CIR.

Under the Industrial Relations Act, when a case is referred to it by the National Industrial Relations Court, the CIR has many statutory duties, chiefly as regards procedures for the establishment of " agency shops " or a " special closed shop "; recognition of bargaining units and bargaining agents; conducting a ballot under the emergency procedures to deal with strikes; and making recommendations which may lead to legally enforced procedure agreements.

The Industrial Relations Act, 1971

The controversy surrounding the Industrial Relations Act has adversely affected relations between the Government and the majority of unions in the period 1971-72. The discussion about whether there should not be more legal regulation of industrial relations had been continuing for ten years. It had been argued that unions had become too powerful to be immune any longer from statutory control of their activities, and that industrial disputes were damaging the national interest in an economy which was so precariously balanced and in which industries were becoming increasingly interdependent and at the mercy of strategic groups of workers. Previously, unions had developed their strength by their own efforts through a system of immunities from legal penalties in which, for example, they were free to strike and picket so long as this was in furtherance of an industrial dispute; moreover, by voluntarily registering with the Chief Registrar and submitting their rule books and an annual statement of their financial position, they could obtain tax concessions in respect of their benefit expenditure. After a series of legal cases which stirred up uncertainties about what was or should be the legal position of unions in Britain, after the investigation of the Royal Commission on Trade Unions and Employers' Associations and the publication of its report in 1968, after the publication of the Conservative Party document *Fair deal at work* in 1968 [1], after the Labour Government's proposed legislation described in its White Paper *In place of strife* [2], and its abandonment in the face of trade union opposition, and after the Labour Government's modified Industrial Relations Bill of 1970, there came, finally, the Conservative Government's Industrial Relations Act of 1971.

Following much discussion, it was perhaps not surprising that the Industrial Relations Act should be extremely comprehensive in its 9 parts, 170 sections and 9 schedules. The main purpose of the Act was to strengthen collective bargaining by making employers and unions respect each other's rights and act more responsibly, respectively, towards their employees and members. For the first time workers were given positive rights to belong to a union and take part in its activities and afforded protection against the arbitrary acts of either employers or unions.

The main provisions of the Act on collective bargaining establish new machinery for resolving disputes over claims for recognition or bargaining rights, place new requirements on employers to disclose information to trade unions and employees; and make agreements legally enforceable unless there is written provision to the contrary. In conditions of " national emergency " the Secretary of State for Employment is enabled to apply to the National Industrial Relations Court for an order lasting up to 60 days, restraining industrial action, or for the holding of a ballot to ascertain the workers' wishes in such circumstances. A new concept of " unfair industrial practice " has been introduced, which relates to forms of wrongful industrial action by employers and unions; and a Code of Practice has been established giving practical guidance and laying down standards for promoting good industrial relations. This code is not in itself part of the Act but its provisions are regarded as relevant in establishing rights and are admissible in evidence in proceedings under the Act.

Other important provisions under the Act lay down " guiding principles " for the conduct of workers and employers' organisations and the procedure for their voluntary registration with a new Chief Registrar; this involves scrutiny of their rule books and the fulfilment of various adminis-

---

[1] *Fair deal at work* (London, Conservative Political Centre, 1968).

[2] *In place of strife: a policy for industrial relations* (London, HM Stationery Office, Cmnd. 3888, 1969).

trative and constitutional requirements. Pre-entry closed shop agreements, that is, agreements whereby union membership is made a condition of recruitment for a job, are declared void, but arrangements are included for agreeing to any post-entry " agency shop ", under which non-members may be called upon to pay contributions to the union or to charity.

In addition to the right to belong or not to belong to a union, an employee's rights include those of taking part in all union activities and of complaining against his union. From his employer he has a right to increased information on his terms of employment, longer notice of dismissal and greater compensation in the event of unfair dismissal.

Complaint under the Act is primarily to the industrial tribunals, whose functions have been considerably extended, and to the new National Industrial Relations Court (NIRC). Industrial tribunals were first established on a tripartite basis to deal with issues arising from the Redundancy Payments Act, and under the Industrial Relations Act they will be mainly concerned with questions relating to the rights of individual workers. The NIRC is a new branch of the High Court and its main task will be to determine the issues of collective labour relations arising under the Act.

Since the Act covers the entire gamut of labour law it has only come into force in stages, and most of it has been in operation only since 1 March 1972. After a few months it is too early to make many estimates or predictions on its long-term working. The majority of unions remain strongly opposed to it, but a number of important organisations have decided to remain registered and there is evidence that the Act is supported by the general public, including a very substantial body of trade union members.

Trade union opposition to the Act—maintained since October 1970 when the Bill was first introduced in Parliament—has involved a boycott of the institutions and non-registration. Unregistered " organisations of workers " are not able to make use of many of the provisions of the Act, especially those relating to recognition and bargaining, and are more exposed to liability for unfair industrial actions. Up to the time of writing, so far as is known unions have successfully insisted that every agreement negotiated should include a " non-legally enforceable " clause.

Apart from strongly aroused ideological antagonism to the legislation, the chief grounds of opposition are that the Act, particularly through its registration provisions, limits and makes conditional certain rights previously assumed as won—notably the closed shop agreement and exemption from liability for inducing breach of contract in respect of industrial action. Moreover, the unions believe that the closed shop restriction and the provisions giving members protection against disciplinary action by their unions weaken their strength, at the same time as they are being held more than ever responsible for controlling their members and ensuring their adherence to collective agreements.

377

A second reason for the Act having attracted considerable criticism from the unions in the early stages of its operation was the use of the emergency procedures during a " work to rule " on the railways, when, after a 14-day cooling-off period, a ballot resulted in an overwhelming vote in favour of continued industrial action.

Thirdly, a series of cases brought by small employers in the road haulage and port transport industry against the unfair " blacking " of their goods led eventually to the imprisonment of five dockers' shop stewards for their defiance of court orders to cease the blacking. A House of Lords appeal court decision, which eventually contributed to the release of the persons concerned, made it clear that unions were to be held responsible for the actions of their shop stewards.

Apart from these events, applications to the NIRC for recognition have been made by various white-collar unions. There has also been a steady flow of individual complaints to the industrial tribunals about unfair dismissals and infringement of union membership rights, and in this respect there is greater union satisfaction with the Act, although the unions have refused to permit their officers to serve on the panels of the tribunals.

In the long run the willingness of the unions to come to terms with the Act will depend upon the likelihood of its amendment or repeal. Repeal depends entirely on the election of a Labour Government, but this may not occur for some considerable time. In the meanwhile the introduction of limited amendments and the demonstration by registered unions of the advantages to be gained under the Act may persuade all but the most doctrinaire organisations to register and to use the Act until such time as they can secure its more fundamental revision.

Conclusions

At the moment when Britain is poised on the brink of becoming a member of the European Communities its industrial relations system is in a considerable state of turmoil. However, beneath all the swirl of argument, dissent and uncertainty there are major areas of consensus. Neither employers (except for a very small minority), nor trade unions, nor any of the political parties dispute the fact that collective bargaining is the basic feature of the British industrial relations system. Although the 1971 Industrial Relations Act has given rise to acute controversy and has been seen by the unions as being designed to constrain their freedom and weaken their bargaining power, it was in fact conceived as a necessary means of strengthening the collective bargaining system. Not even the unions would deny that sections of the Act, especially those relating to the recognition of trade unions, protection against unfair dismissal and the provision of information essential to the conduct of collective bargaining should be retained in any future revision of the text.

While it can legitimately be hoped that the Act will contribute towards the development of more systematic collective bargaining at the level of the plant and company, the new legislation will not automatically provide solutions to every industrial relations problem.

One problem to which the Act is designed to provide the possibility of a solution concerns the recognition of unions representing clerical, technical, scientific and managerial staffs. The extension of organisation to these groups and their desire to have their interests protected by collective bargaining have given rise to sharp conflicts between established unions catering primarily for manual workers which wish to extend their boundaries to include non-manual employees, and unions which equally strongly wish to limit their representation to white-collar workers. The problem has been aggravated by the evolution of professional associations and their registration as trade unions seeking bargaining rights for their members. The inter-union conflict endemic in the extension of organisations and collective bargaining has at once been encouraged by the Act and offered a solution through the procedures for which the Act provides.[1]

It has not, however, been customary for trade unions to resolve conflicts over bargaining units and bargaining agents through a quasi-judicial procedure. In the tradition of the British trade union movement such issues have been decided by a power struggle often involving a strike and a bitter conflict that has been settled through the intervention of the TUC or the appointment of a public committee of inquiry. It is going to take time to bring about a reorientation of behaviour and an organisational restructuring that will reduce the element of conflict and smooth the way to a more constructive system of collective bargaining.

One of the most tangled areas of organisational development concerns the articulation of bargaining units at the plant and company level with those which exist on an industry-wide and national basis. Since there is no organic link between shop stewards' committees and the negotiating committees of the federations of unions which conduct negotiations at industry level, there is an extremely difficult problem of co-ordination. Some unions have recently experimented with institutional arrangements giving greater scope for shop steward participation in the formulation of claims and in the ratification of proposed settlements.

Normal practice has been for shop stewards in well-organised plants to use industry-wide agreements as a point of reference rather than as a determining instrument governing the terms and conditions on which their constituents are employed. The drawback of this type of autonomous local bargaining is that it brings benefits to those who happen to be in a strong bargaining position, but leaves the weak to fall behind.

---

[1] Roy Lewis and Geoff Latta: " Bargaining units and bargaining agents ", in *British Journal of Industrial Relations*, Mar. 1972, pp. 84-106.

The attempt by the engineering unions to abandon industry-wide agreements and to rely on the leverage exerted by those capable of winning large plant and company increases proved a failure. After six months the shop stewards had put in claims in 2,493 of the 4,841 member firms, and only 1,472 had actually concluded agreements. In the great majority of cases the improvement achieved in the basic wage rate was no better than the offer made by the Engineering Employers' Federation in 1971, which if it had been accepted would have applied to all the member firms. In these circumstances it became apparent to the unions that they were not succeeding in achieving by plant and company bargaining what they had failed to achieve by national negotiations and that they would be wise to re-open discussions with the EEF.

The 1972 engineering industry agreement, covering some 2½ million employees, establishes minimum time rates, shift premiums, holidays and the length of the working week. All other matters will be the subject of bargaining at the plant and company level. This agreement is a new landmark in contemporary collective bargaining, since it has demonstrated the limitations of plant and company bargaining and enabled the two sides to define clearly what is appropriately negotiated at the national and local levels respectively.

Even more difficult than the articulation of plant, company and industry-wide agreements is the integration of these agreements into an effective national incomes policy. The central framework agreements which are voluntarily negotiated in the Scandinavian countries have aroused much envy over the years. Since neither the CBI nor the TUC has the degree of central authority enjoyed by their Scandinavian counterparts such a policy has never seemed to be practicable. It is, however, remotely possible that in the light of the serious inflation that has occurred in the past two years since the end of the statutory incomes policy, a serious attempt will be made by the CBI and the TUC to establish a jointly agreed framework for the guidance of local and national negotiations.

The proposed national machinery of conciliation due to be formally set up in September 1972 could constitute a first step towards a viable agreement on incomes and prices. The CBI has already shown in its voluntary price restraint policy that it can command the support of its most important constituents if it can demonstrate that there is a real possibility that the unions will act with an equal degree of restraint. Whether the unions will be able to reciprocate probably depends on whether the Government can provide an economic and social climate which will engender a willingness on their part to support a policy of moderation in pay claims.

However, even if the Government is able to satisfy the unions by generating a rate of economic growth that pulls the unemployment level below 3 per cent, the problem which faces the unions is to prevent their militants from making co-operation impossible. To meet this challenge, the unions will have to re-establish the authority of their national leadership; this means that they will have to define afresh, in terms of power and function, the role of shop stewards and plant and company bargaining.

In this respect it is one of the ironies of the industrial relations situation in Britain that the instrument through which this realignment and clarification of the role of leadership at the national and local levels of union organisation might be achieved, namely the 1971 Industrial Relations Act, is boycotted by the unions.

Finally, it is necessary to say a word about the prospect of international collective bargaining. The British trade unions have become very much aware of the existence of multinational corporations during the past two years. The TUC is giving strong support to the demand that multinational corporations should be subject to regulation and control. It has also welcomed the activities of the International Trade Secretariats. It is widely believed that Britain's entry into Europe will make British unions and employers much more aware of standards of employment and work practices there and that this will have an effect on collective bargaining in Britain. Some British unions have given a positive response to the suggestion that there ought to be common standards of employment in the European plants of multinational corporations, although it is generally admitted that it will be some time before a common wage level can be achieved. While it is acknowledged that differences in economic structure, social policy and legal tradition are immense obstacles to harmonisation, it would seem likely that collective bargaining will be extended across the national boundaries of Europe in due course. The fact that in some respects British terms of employment are now below those achieved in the member countries of the European Communities could be a powerful stimulus to British unions to seek parity in these conditions through collective bargaining.

Recent Trends in Collective Bargaining in the United States

Donald E. CULLEN [1]

I. Introduction

A GENERATION AGO in the United States collective bargaining was viewed as an instrument of change by its friends and critics alike. Subsequent events proved that reputation to have been well deserved in most respects. As union membership soared from 3 million workers in the early 1930s to nearly 20 million today, collective bargaining transformed worker-management relations in thousands of American firms— not only by expanding into industries long hostile to unionism, such as the automobile and steel industries, but also by extending the scope of collective agreements far beyond the traditional issues of wage rates and working hours and thus providing new forms of protection to workers and new challenges to employers.

In recent years, however, many critics have charged that American unions have lost their earlier zeal for reform and that today their bargaining activities are more often aimed at preserving rather than attacking the status quo. According to this indictment neither the process nor the structure of bargaining in the United States has shown the flexibility necessary to cope with the problems emerging after the Second World War such as inflation, structural unemployment, the civil rights revolution, the persistence of poverty and the advent of automation. Collective bargaining, it is said, has become part of the very " establishment " it once sought to liberalise.

Viewed in retrospect it is clear that the American system of collective bargaining is indeed far less radical than many had feared (and others had hoped) in the 1930s. Yet, a review of the post-war period will also

[1] Professor, New York State School of Industrial and Labour Relations, Cornell University.

show that this bargaining system is more responsive to change and challenge than some of its critics allege today. And that, in short, is the purpose of this article: to describe *both* the stable and changing aspects of bargaining practices in the United States during the post-war years, and to hazard some prophecies about the future course of this bargaining system.

II. The negotiation process

No one has ever conducted a systematic sampling of the negotiating tactics used in the many thousands of union-management relationships in the United States, but all the evidence available suggests that these tactics have remained basically the same in most relationships in the private sector. Specifically, the orthodox approach to bargaining is still the " haggling " or " horse-trading " one which calls for the parties to demand more (or offer less) in the opening stages than they are actually willing to settle for, after which each probes for the other's " true " position through a series of concessions and trades and bluffs up to the point of final settlement or impasse, when any remaining disagreement is usually resolved by the pressures of an actual or threatened strike.

There is nothing uniquely American about that negotiating style, of course, but it is given a particular form and emphasis by the fact that nearly every collective agreement in the United States has a specified duration (usually of one, two or three years) and a precise expiry date. Unions frequently agree not to strike during the term of any agreement, but they zealously guard their legal right to strike the instant a contract expires. As a consequence, the American negotiator usually knows far ahead of time the date on which bargaining over a new contract will culminate in either an agreement or a strike, and that crucial deadline shapes his tactics from beginning to end, providing him with an inducement to bluff and stall in the early stages of negotiations but also with an incentive to settle as the date of decision draws closer.

Two examples will suggest the extent to which " deadline bargaining " is accepted as the normal mode of negotiating in the United States. In the Labour Management Relations (or Taft-Hartley) Act of 1947 [1] Congress explicitly defined the parties' duty to bargain collectively to mean, among other things, that the party desiring to negotiate new contract terms (usually the union) must serve written notice to this effect upon the other party, must offer to meet with the other party and must continue " in full force and effect, without resorting to strike or lockout, all the terms and conditions of the existing contract for a period of sixty days after such notice is given *or until the expiration date of such contract*, whichever occurs later." [2] In fact, an employer may legally discharge any

---

[1] See ILO: *Legislative Series*, 1947—USA 2.

[2] Section 8 *(d)* (4) of the Labour Management Relations Act (author's italics).

worker who engages in a strike during this sixty-day period. The obvious purpose of these provisions is to require the parties to give negotiations an adequate trial before resorting to direct action, or to ensure that the inevitable strike deadline does not arrive " too soon " in negotiations.

In some cases, however, the same rules may help to prevent the strike deadline from arriving " too late ". Thus, when President Nixon proposed in 1970 that the sixty-day rule of the Taft-Hartley Act be extended to the troubled railroad and airline industries, where a different law (the Railway Labour Act) governs bargaining, his explanation of this proposal was illuminating:

> A labour contract in the railroad or airlines industry presently has no effective termination date. This is true because the right of the parties to engage in a strike or lockout [under the Railway Labour Act] depends on a declaration by the National Mediation Board that the dispute cannot be resolved through mediation. Negotiations can thus drag on for an indeterminate period, far beyond the intended expiration date of the contract, *with no deadlines to motivate serious bargaining.*
>
> I recommend that this unusual procedure be discontinued and that new labour contracts for railroads and airlines be negotiated in the same manner as those for most other industries.[1]

In short, the fixed strike deadline is considered not only an inevitable but often a desirable feature of most bargaining relationships in the United States.

New approaches to bargaining

In spite of its long history and official encouragement, the " orthodox " method of bargaining has often been attacked as an inept and irresponsible way of solving the serious issues at stake in a labour-management negotiation, and for this reason two post-war experiments in bargaining strategy—Boulwarism and continuous bargaining—have excited considerable interest in the United States.

BOULWARISM

Boulwarism is the name given to the General Electric Company's approach to collective bargaining. Initiated in the late 1940s by Lemuel Boulware, a GE executive, this strategy is novel in two respects. At the bargaining table itself the company announces that its first offer will be its full and final offer—i.e. management will offer from the outset everything it is willing to concede in the final contract, rather than starting low and bargaining upwards as the strike deadline approaches. In this way GE seeks to persuade its employees that the company is anxious to deal fairly with them and does not have to be coerced into making a decent offer only at the eleventh hour of negotiations, when union officials

---

[1] Message from President Nixon to Congress proposing legislation on national emergency disputes in the transportation industry, 27 February 1970 (author's italics).

will claim credit for winning what the company was perhaps ready to give from the outset. Second, GE aggressively " sells " its first-and-final offer directly to its employees through a communications programme of extraordinary scope and intensity—letters to the workers' homes, newspaper advertisements, leaflets and so on—reflecting management's belief that union officials will seldom give their members an objective description of a company offer they oppose.

Through most of the 1950s and 1960s Boulwarism rolled up an impressive record at GE: negotiations usually ended on substantially the terms of the company's first offer; union members frequently voted down their officers' requests for strike authorisations; and when a strike was finally launched in 1960 it collapsed in three weeks and the final settlement was again very close to management's first offer. To the supporters of Boulwarism this record demonstrated that management need not always be on the defensive in labour relations, that negotiations can be stripped of much of their hypocritical higgling and haggling, and that workers, if given the facts, will not automatically assume the union is right and management wrong in every dispute. To its many critics, however, GE's tactic of a single firm offer is a take-it-or-leave-it approach to bargaining, its programme of direct communications to workers is an attempt to bypass and undermine the action of union negotiators, and its apparent record of success was due to the fact that unions at GE had been weak and divided for many years.

Recent developments appear to have vindicated the critics of Boulwarism. First, the major unions dealing with GE finally presented a united front in their 1969 negotiations, sustaining a three-month strike without a break in their ranks, and this display of power did indeed move company negotiators to improve upon their initial " firm, fair " offer.[1] Second, in a lengthy litigation ending in 1970 the courts ruled in effect that Boulwarism constitutes bad-faith bargaining and is therefore a violation of the Taft-Hartley Act.[2] Most significant, however, is the fact that few American employers adopted Boulwarism even in the early post-war years when it was widely publicised and seemed to be both legally and successfully practised at GE. The single-offer tactic can easily antagonise workers, and particularly union officials, who are accustomed to the give-

---

[1] GE officials claimed that they only rearranged rather than increased their initial offer in these negotiations. Wages and fringe-benefit packages have become so complex today that it is very difficult for an outsider to judge their cost, but the available evidence strongly suggests that GE did improve its offer under the pressure of the 1969 strike.

[2] More specifically, the National Labour Relations Board ruled that GE's tactics in its 1960 negotiations violated a Taft-Hartley Act provision requiring employers to bargain in good faith with the representatives of their employees. This violation constituted an unfair labour practice subject to a cease-and-desist order from the Board to GE, and this Board order was upheld by the courts upon appeal. The major thrust of the Board and court opinions was to the effect that GE's tactics indicated both a take-it-or-leave-it attitude and a desire to derogate the union. General Electric Co. v. NLRB, 150 NLRB 192 (1964), enforced 418 F2d 736 (2nd Cir. 1969), review denied, 397 US 1059 (1970).

and-take pattern of orthodox bargaining, and apparently most employers decided that this risk of generating added conflict outweighed the possible benefits of following GE's lead.

For all these reasons Boulwarism may soon be only a footnote in American labour history. Its advocates have raised provocative questions about the ethics and efficacy of conventional negotiating tactics, but in practice their alternative technique has failed to win much support from either negotiators or judges.

CONTINUOUS BARGAINING

The other new approach to bargaining has gone by various names—creative or productivity bargaining or the study committee approach—but the most apt term is " continuous bargaining ", to contrast this technique with conventional deadline bargaining. Instead of postponing meaningful negotiations until the last few weeks or even the last few hours before a strike deadline, this system calls for the parties to explore particularly difficult bargaining problems in joint meetings over a long period of time, sometimes throughout the life of a contract.

In the late 1950s many union-management relationships encountered, in many cases for the first time, the complex problems posed by increasing foreign and domestic competition, the advent of automation and persistent unemployment. Negotiators often found it difficult to explore solutions to these new problems in the super-heated atmosphere of the usual bargaining session—described by one negotiator as " a forum where an admission against interest was deadly; where a position once taken was a position to be steadfastly defended; where a movement in the direction of the other party's views was a concession irretrievably made ".[1] Several parties therefore experimented with techniques such as appointing joint study committees, whose membership sometimes included " informed neutrals ", to gather facts about critical problems and to explore alternative solutions over a period of several months or longer; encouraging candour and exploratory thinking in these discussions by agreeing that opinions could be off-the-record and positions could be changed without giving rise to an allegation of bad faith; and in these and other ways minimising the pressure of the strike deadline to the point where sometimes the parties can agree on new contract terms well before the old contract formally expires instead of at the traditional eleventh hour.

Continuous bargaining has scored some spectacular successes in a variety of American industries. In West Coast longshoring, labour and management negotiated on and off for approximately three years before concluding their radical agreement of 1960 that in effect scrapped various featherbedding rules of long standing in exchange for a guaranteed annual

[1] R. Heath Larry: " Steel's Human Relations Committee ", in *Steelways* (New York), Sep. 1963, p. 18.

wage and other job security measures.[1] In basic steel the disastrous 116-day strike of 1959 led to the establishment of a Human Relations Committee of top union and company officials which met frequently in private session and won a large share of the credit for the next two peaceful and moderate contract settlements—one reached well before and one after the expiry date of the previous contract. In the Kaiser Steel Corporation, which split off from the rest of the steel industry in 1959, a committee of union, management and public representatives put three years of study into devising a formula for encouraging technological innovation while offering workers a share of the resulting cost savings, and this formula, with modifications, has been in effect at Kaiser since 1963. Also in 1959 the Armor Company and the two major unions in meat-packing launched a tripartite Automation Committee to study the labour problems arising from the modernisation and centralisation of the company's operations. This committee developed several ideas for cushioning the effects of plant shutdowns, which the parties wrote into their contracts, and also conducted several retraining programmes for displaced Armor workers.[2]

Yet, in spite of these and other successes, continuous bargaining has not spread to the extent hoped for by its many admirers. It was vigorously promoted by the federal Government in 1960 as a possible solution to the work rules problem on the railroads, but a prestigious study committee failed to win a voluntary settlement and Congress finally ordered the issue to be submitted to compulsory arbitration in 1963. In the 1965 election for the presidency of the Steelworkers' Union, the challenger, I. W. Abel, strongly attacked the incumbent, David McDonald, for his support of the Human Relations Committee, charging that the committee's effect had been to turn over much of the bargaining to staff technicians and to freeze out elected officials and the rank and file. There were many other issues in that election, but the fact remains that McDonald did lose, Abel did scrap the Human Relations Committee (but not the Kaiser Committee), and it became clear that any union official who participates in continuous bargaining runs the risk of being accused of over-friendly relations with management. In addition many American employers believe unions have already penetrated too deeply into management prerogatives under orthodox bargaining, and these employers must also have misgivings over anything resembling year-round negotiations with union officials and possibly " outsiders " as well.

---

[1] At the time of preparation of this article, however, a protracted strike stemming from the failure of negotiations over a renewal of this agreement was in progress. Despite their earlier successes, the parties were unable to cope peacefully with the latest innovation on the docks, the containerisation of cargo.

[2] For a good description of these and other examples of continuous bargaining, see James J. Healy (ed.): *Creative collective bargaining* (Englewood Cliffs (New Jersey), Prentice-Hall Inc., 1965). For a detailed study of the Armor experience, see George P. Shultz and Arnold R. Weber: *Strategies for the displaced worker* (New York, Harper & Row, 1966).

In summary, continuous bargaining certainly has brighter prospects than Boulwarism as a new approach to negotiating the labour contract, but it is far too early to declare this technique the wave of the future in American bargaining. Few relationships have tried continuous bargaining across the board—that is, dealing with the entire range of " normal " bargaining issues outside of the context of deadline negotiations; few parties have practised continuous bargaining in respect of even a few issues; and no major relationships have adopted this approach since the resurgence of the economy in the mid-1960s.

Many unions and employers, however, have used a limited version of this technique—setting up a temporary committee to grapple with one specific problem that cannot be easily handled in deadline bargaining, such as revising a complex pension plan or job classification system or working out ways to improve the racial mixture of a company's work-force. These are often " pre-negotiation committees ", set up a few weeks or months before formal bargaining begins and directed at least to map out the factual dimensions of a complex issue for the negotiators if the committee members cannot agree on an actual solution. In addition, the Federal Mediation and Conciliation Service has steadily increased its " preventive mediation " activities, a programme begun in 1962 and ranging from the encouragement of early bargaining and joint, year-around committees to the provision of training for stewards and supervisors.[1]

The post-war record nevertheless demonstrates that the conventional deadline approach to negotiations is remarkably durable and, in spite of its many critics, will continue to be the dominant method of handling most issues at most American bargaining tables.

Strike insurance

Another post-war innovation in bargaining tactics has been the adoption of formal " strike insurance " or " mutual aid " plans by employers in a few American industries. By guaranteeing to cover some part of a participating company's losses during a strike, these plans have several aims: to strengthen a company's hand in negotiations before the strike deadline; to improve its staying power in the event of a strike; and, in most cases, also to protect other companies in the same industry from the " whipsaw "—that is, to prevent a union from winning an over-generous concession when it declares a strike in only one or a few of several competing companies.

The first of these plans appeared in the late 1940s, when the American Newspaper Publishers Association initiated a " suspension insurance " plan that in recent years has covered about 400 newspapers. This plan has all the trappings of insurance: publishers pay a fixed premium to an

---

[1] Each annual report of the US Federal Mediation and Conciliation Service now contains a chapter on the preventive mediation programme.

insurance company for a fixed daily indemnity, with benefits beginning on the eighth day of a strike over issues which (with certain exceptions) the publishers must have offered to submit to arbitration. In 1958 six major airlines entered into a mutual aid pact based on a very different principle, namely that if a strike was declared against one line, the others would pay that line any increased revenue (over costs) they received because of a diversion of passengers or freight. The mechanics of this pact have changed substantially over the years, but the principle of mutual aid (rather than insurance) has been maintained, and the pact now covers all but two of the major American airlines. In railroading, too, nearly every major carrier is now covered by a " service interruption plan ", the first of which was adopted in 1959, combining insurance and mutual aid features to provide benefits equal to the daily fixed costs, up to certain dollar and time limits [1], of a carrier affected by a strike.

Labour unions have bitterly attacked these plans, charging that they encourage bad-faith bargaining and prolonged strikes, but employers argue that strike insurance is simply a management version of the strike benefits that many unions pay to their members. To date, the courts and relevant regulatory agencies have agreed with management and ruled these plans to be legal. To illustrate the stakes involved: in a twelve-day strike in 1960 the Pennsylvania Railroad collected about $7 million in " strike benefits ", and during a month-long airlines strike in 1966 four carriers affected received $44 million from carriers that were not affected.

At about the same time that the railroads and airlines adopted strike insurance in the late 1950s, it was learned that employers in steel and trucking were also exploring the idea, and this led to considerable speculation and controversy over the implications of a trend which, in subsequent years, however, failed to develop. Employers in other industries have flirted with strike insurance proposals from time to time, those in the troubled construction industry providing the latest example, but this technique has not spread significantly beyond the newspaper, airline and railroad industries. As Briggs points out, those three industries share certain " unstable bargaining characteristics "—multiple unionism (aggravated in the airline and railroad industries by rivalry among the unions), a whipsaw strike pattern, and output which cannot be stockpiled prior to a strike, which is sufficiently homogeneous to permit customers to switch firms during a selective strike and which is also such that employer losses cannot be made up after a strike—a set of conditions begging for some kind of employer co-operation but not found in many other American industries.[2]

---

[1] John S. Hirsch, Jr.: " Strike insurance and collective bargaining ", in *Industrial and Labor Relations Review* (Ithaca (New York)), Vol. 22, No. 3, Apr. 1969, pp. 399-415.

[2] Vernon M. Briggs, Jr.: " The strike insurance plan of the railroad industry ", in *Industrial Relations* (Berkeley (California)), Vol. 6, No. 2, Feb. 1967, p. 211.

Also significant, however, is the time span involved. Strike insurance spread to air and rail transport at about the same time that continuous bargaining first appeared in longshoring, meat-packing and steel, and that Boulwarism reached its high-water mark in General Electric. As noted before, the years around 1960 were a difficult time for many bargaining relationships in the United States, as the parties struggled to adjust inflation-born contracts and practices to the harsh environment of the recession which began in 1958 and continued (at least in terms of unemployment) until the Viet-Nam build-up in 1965. The adverse conditions of that period apparently spurred many unions, and more particularly employers, to innovate in their bargaining tactics, some along " hawkish " and others along more " dovish " lines. According to the same line of reasoning, the failure of those innovations to spread much in recent years was probably due in part to the improved state of the American economy in the late 1960s.

Contract rejections

In an unknown but large proportion of negotiations in the United States—probably one half or more—the final step in the negotiation process is the submission of any tentative agreement to the union members for their acceptance or rejection. To many negotiators on both sides of the table, one of the most disturbing trends of recent years has been the apparent rise in the number of cases in which the rank and file have voted down an agreement recommended by their own bargaining committee. When such a rejection is genuine (i.e. not arranged by union officials as a bargaining ploy), it not only raises doubts about whether the union leaders are in touch with their members but it also can put those leaders under great pressure to wring further concessions from an employer who probably thinks he had already gone the " last mile " for an agreement and who certainly does not want to set a precedent of increasing his last offer whenever workers vote it down.

Table I presents the only statistical measurement available of the severity of this problem. Unfortunately this series was not begun until a year or two after mediators and others first noticed an increase in rejections, so there is no way of estimating the " normal " rejection rate in earlier years. Also, the data in table I cover only cases in which federal mediators were actively involved—not only a minority of all negotiations but also presumably the most difficult and conflict-prone—so the percentages shown in that table are believed to be far higher than the percentage of rejections in the bargaining sector as a whole. Many qualified observers nevertheless agree that the rate of contract rejections did increase significantly during the 1960s, even though no one can say by how much.

There is much less agreement on the causes of the increase. The following are among the opinions most frequently advanced: there is a

TABLE I. CONTRACT REJECTIONS IN NEGOTIATIONS
INVOLVING FEDERAL MEDIATORS IN THE UNITED
STATES, 1964-70

Fiscal year	Number of rejections	Percentage of rejections [1]
1964	629	8.7
1965	746	10.0
1966	918	11.7
1967	1 019	14.2
1968	893	11.9
1969	991	12.3
1970	843	11.2

Source: US Federal Mediation and Conciliation Service: *Twenty-third Annual Report, fiscal year 1970* (Washington, DC, 1971), p. 37.

[1] Of all disputes in which federal mediators actually met with the parties in mediation conferences, the percentage in which union membership groups voted down tentative agreements reached by bargaining committees.

generation gap between union leaders and the growing number of young and well-educated members; negotiations have become too centralised to cover the many local issues of concern to workers; labour contracts are now too complex for workers to understand them easily; the Landrum-Griffin Act of 1959, aimed at improving union democracy, went too far in handcuffing union leaders and protecting dissident members; union ratification procedures are often defective in practice, using oral or standing votes instead of secret ballots. Easily the most persuasive analysis, of course, is that the rise in contract rejections is due to the same social forces—if only we knew what they were—that produced the civil rights revolution, women's liberation, student strikes and all the other challenges to the established order and its leaders during the last decade, in the United States and several other countries.

Given this uncertainty over the causes of contract rejections, it is not surprising that there is little agreement on a solution. For example, some persons argue for amending the Taft-Hartley Act so as to require negotiators to have final authority at the bargaining table, thus eliminating ratification votes entirely, while others contend that these votes should be encouraged and the only way to avoid contract rejections is through greater responsiveness of management and union officials to workers' needs.[1]

[1] For more information on this issue, see William E. Simkin: " Refusal to ratify contracts ", in *Industrial and Labor Relations Review* (Ithaca (New York)), Vol. 21, No. 4, July 1968, pp. 518-540; Matthew A. Kelly: " The contract rejection problem: a positive labour-management approach ", in *Labor Law Journal* (Chicago (Illinois)), Vol. 20, No. 7, July 1969, pp. 404-415; and David I. Shair: " The mythology of labour contract rejections ", ibid., Vol. 21, No. 2, Feb. 1970, pp. 88-94.

III. The post-war strike record

Table II presents several measurements of strike activity in the United States since the end of the Second World War.

In a recent study of these and other strike data covering the period 1952-68 Skeels demonstrated that strike activity underwent a secular decline in the United States during that period, a decline which he reasonably interpreted to be the result of " a learning function of the bargaining process " or, stated differently, " the successful institutional accommodation of the parties".[1] Both a cause and an effect of this trend can be seen in the data in table II showing that " union organisation and security " have declined steadily and significantly as a major strike issue since 1946. Issues of principle (rather than of money alone) are notoriously difficult to settle by compromise, and a generation ago a great many American unions and employers were still contesting the basic issues of union recognition and compulsory membership clauses—matters that have subsequently been resolved in most relationships through the passage of time, changes in the law and the " institutional accommodation of the parties ".

Skeels also confirmed the results of other studies, however, that have shown a strong and positive correlation between the business cycle and strike activity in the United States [2], suggesting that American unions still view the strike primarily as a tactical weapon to be used when market conditions promise tangible results at the bargaining table—a view to be expected of " business unions " operating in the context of deadline bargaining. Note in table II that the average duration of strikes, after declining significantly in the 1950s, has returned in recent years to the level of the late 1940s (which was also about the level reached in the turbulent period of the late 1930s). It is clear that the strike continues to play a vigorous role in American labour relations, although only a small percentage of each year's negotiations actually end in a stoppage and the man-days lost by strikers have constituted less than 1 per cent of total working time in every post-war year except 1946.

Table II also shows that, among major strike issues, the decline of " union organisation and security " has been offset by an increase in the relative importance of all the other three categories. It is easy to explain the recent jump in the percentage of strikes called primarily over wages and related matters, for consumer prices increased very sharply during

---

[1] Jack W. Skeels: " Measures of US strike activity ", in *Industrial and Labor Relations Review* (Ithaca (New York)), Vol. 24, No. 4, July 1971, pp. 520 and 525.

[2] Ibid., pp. 522-524. See also Orley Ashenfelter and George E. Johnson: " Bargaining theory, trade unions, and industrial strike activity ", in *American Economic Review* (Menasha (Wisconsin)), Vol. LIX, No. 1, Mar. 1969, pp. 35-49; and Andrew W. Weintraub: " Prosperity versus strikes: an empirical approach ", in *Industrial and Labor Relations Review* (Ithaca (New York)), Vol. 19, No. 2, Jan. 1966, pp. 231-238.

TABLE II. WORK STOPPAGES IN THE UNITED STATES, 1946-70 [1]

Year	Number	Average duration (days) [2]	Workers involved [3]		Major issues involved [4] (percentage of total stoppages)				Percentage occurring during term of agreement [5]
			Number (thousands)	Percentage of total employed	Wages, hours and supplementary benefits	Union organisation and security	Other working conditions	Inter-union or intra-union matters	
1946	4 985	24.2	4 600	10.5	44.9	32.4	17.6	4.9	.
1947	3 693	25.6	2 170	4.7	46.3	29.8	18.8	4.3	.
1948	3 419	21.8	1 960	4.2	50.8	22.8	21.5	3.8	.
1949	3 606	22.5	3 030	6.7	46.6	21.7	25.0	5.8	.
1950	4 843	19.2	2 410	5.1	52.8	19.0	22.0	5.3	.
1951	4 737	17.4	2 220	4.5	44.4	18.7	28.3	6.9	.
1952	5 117	19.6	3 540	7.3	47.9	16.4	26.9	6.5	.
1953	5 091	20.3	2 400	4.7	55.5	14.7	22.3	5.4	.
1954	3 468	22.5	1 530	3.1	49.8	17.0	24.1	7.3	.
1955	4 320	18.5	2 650	5.2	49.9	19.6	22.3	6.9	.
1956	3 825	18.9	1 900	3.6	47.6	20.2	22.5	8.3	.
1957	3 673	19.2	1 390	2.6	47.1	20.4	22.8	8.9	.
1958	3 694	19.7	2 060	3.9	50.8	15.8	23.7	8.7	.
1959	3 708	24.6	1 880	3.3	50.5	17.9	20.5	9.4	.
1960	3 333	23.4	1 320	2.4	47.8	16.2	24.0	9.3	.
1961	3 367	23.7	1 450	2.6	49.4	15.4	23.1	10.8	32.2
1962	3 614	24.6	1 230	2.2	50.5	16.1	22.5	9.7	29.8
1963	3 362	23.0	941	1.1	46.8	15.8	25.2	11.3	35.8
1964	3 655	22.9	1 640	2.7	46.5	15.2	25.2	12.4	36.0
1965	3 963	25.0	1 550	2.5	48.6	15.0	23.2	12.0	34.7
1966	4 405	22.2	1 960	3.0	51.3	13.6	22.7	11.7	36.5
1967	4 595	22.8	2 870	4.3	53.0	12.8	23.6	10.2	33.9
1968	5 045	24.5	2 649	3.8	57.2	10.2	22.6	9.4	31.4
1969	5 700	22.5	2 481	3.5	56.0	10.4	24.3	8.8	34.5
1970	5 600	.	3 300	.					

Source: US Department of Labour, Bureau of Labour Statistics: *Analysis of work stoppages* (a series of annual bulletins) (Washington, DC, US Government Printing Office).

[1] Data refer to all work stoppages that involved six workers or more and lasted a full shift or longer. Data include both strikes and lockouts, but the latter are so rare (and sometimes so difficult to distinguish from a strike) that these statistics are usually accepted as measures of strike activity alone.   [2] Mean average in calendar days. Median duration fluctuated between seven and ten days during this period.   [3] All workers made idle for one shift or longer in establishments directly involved in a stoppage.   [4] For each year, the percentage of all stoppages in which the parties reported the major issue to be as indicated. Figures do not total 100 for each year because of reporting deficiencies. For the definitions used to link issue groups before and after 1961, see US Department of Labour, Bureau of Labour Statistics: *Analysis of work stoppages 1961*, Bulletin No. 1339 (Washington, DC, US Government Printing Office), pp. 41-42.   [5] Negotiation of new agreement not involved. Data not available for the years prior to 1961.

the late 1960s and labour's demand for catch-up wage increases then became the dominant bargaining issue. It is rather surprising, however, that the incidence of strikes over " other working conditions " has remained roughly constant since 1950, for, as noted previously, job security appeared to be the paramount issue in many bargaining relationships during the 1955-65 period. Perhaps this issue was not as crucial in the average relationship as in the headline-catching industries such as steel and longshoring, or perhaps most parties simply resolved the issue peacefully—either because of union reluctance to strike during that recession-marked period or through unpublicised but imaginative compromises such as those reached in the better known cases of continuous bargaining.

Even more surprising at first glance is the increasing share of strikes over " inter-union or intra-union matters ", for the merger in 1955 of the rival union federations, the American Federation of Labour and the Congress of Industrial Organisations, was expected to mute jurisdictional disputes over worker representation. Also, to the extent that disputes over the assignment of work result (as commonly assumed) from workers' fear of a job scarcity, one would expect this strike issue to have dwindled in importance during the prolonged period of prosperity that the American economy has enjoyed since 1940 (even allowing for several post-war recessions). One has to look to the construction industry for the explanation: jurisdictional strikes in the building trades (primarily over the assignment of work and not worker representation) averaged only sixty per year from 1946 through 1949, accounting for about one-third of all " inter-union strikes " in that period; by 1966 through 1969 the construction industry was averaging 400 jurisdictional strikes per year and accounting for more than four-fifths of all such strikes in the country.

Expert opinion is divided over the reasons for this remarkable increase in jurisdictional strikes in construction, just as there is no consensus on the causes of the startling wage increases that many construction unions have won during the past decade. Trade unionists stress their belief that, because of seasonal work and for other reasons, there is still a scarcity of jobs in this industry; employers often charge that the construction unions have created and exploited an artificial shortage of craftsmen; and many outsiders point to the highly decentralised structure of craft bargaining in this industry, which invites considerable inter-union conflict.

Finally, the last column of table II, showing that one out of every three strikes in the United States occurs during the term of an agreement, demands very careful interpretation. It is tempting to use this measurement as a proxy indicator of the incidence of wildcat strikes: there is no direct count of such strikes and most American labour contracts do contain a no-strike clause, which would appear to suggest that most strikes during the life of a contract are violations of the agreement (one meaning of " wildcat ") and that many might also be strikes in defiance

Collective bargaining

of union officials (the other meaning of " wildcat "). But consider these facts:

(1) No-strike clauses frequently provide for exceptions. In 1970, for example, 90 per cent of all major contracts (those covering 5,000 workers or more) contained no-strike clauses, but one-half of those clauses permitted strikes in certain circumstances or over specific issues (such as an issue specifically excluded from grievance arbitration).[1]

(2) The building trades again loom large. Of all strikes called during the term of a contract in the 1960s, about one-third were jurisdictional disputes and nearly 40 per cent occurred in construction—a larger number than in any other industry.[2] Jurisdictional strikes in construction are often (though not always) in violation of no-strike agreements and sometimes in defiance of national union officials, but they seldom occur without the approval of the local business agent.

For these and other reasons, the incidence of strikes during the life of a contract cannot be taken as an indicator of the extent of either illegal or unauthorised strikes in the United States. A purely impressionistic judgment is that the number of strikes in violation of a contract is relatively large but there are very few strikes that occur spontaneously or in defiance of either national or local union officials. (A probable exception is the coal mining industry, in which a large number of strikes during the term of a contract have occurred and internal union affairs have been turbulent in recent years.) It should also be noted that this type of strike is usually limited in scope and duration, accounting in recent years for one-third of all strikes but only about 10 per cent of the man-days lost in strikes.[2]

IV. The structure of bargaining

The available evidence, although mixed and incomplete, supports the prevailing opinion that the bargaining structure in the United States is relatively decentralised.

The Bureau of Labour Statistics has estimated, for example, that in 1968 there were approximately 155,000 collective bargaining agreements in the United States covering a total of about 20 million workers—or an average of only 130 workers per agreement. Other Bureau studies have shown that in 1970, throughout all manufacturing and most non-manu-

---

[1] US Department of Labour, Bureau of Labour Statistics: *Characteristics of agreements covering 5,000 workers or more*, Bulletin 1686 (Washington, DC, US Government Printing Office, 1970), p. 66.

[2] Computed from idem: *Analysis of work stoppages* (a series of annual bulletins) (Washington, DC, US Government Printing Office).

396

facturing industries, there were only 252 contracts that individually covered 5,000 workers or more, and in all industries in 1961 there were only 1,733 contracts (out of an estimated total of 150,000) that covered 1,000 workers or more.[1]

Those figures exaggerate the extent of decentralisation of the American bargaining structure, however. It is true that in 1961 only 1.2 per cent of all contracts covered 1,000 workers or more, but the 1,733 contracts in question accounted for nearly half of the workers covered by all union agreements in the United States in that year. Similarly, the handful of contracts covering 5,000 workers or more accounted for about 20 per cent of total contract coverage in 1970. Also, none of these measurements reflects the important role that pattern-setting bargaining plays within and among many industries and local labour markets.

Another indicator of centralisation is to be found in the identity of the employer signing a labour agreement. This information is not available for most bargaining units, but the study of contracts covering 1,000 or more workers in 1961 showed that a single company was the signer of nearly two out of every three contracts, accounting for slightly more than half of all the workers covered by these major agreements. This indicator can also be misleading, however, for single-employer contracts predominate in the concentrated manufacturing industries like the automobile and steel industries, where one contract can literally cover more than 100,000 workers, and multi-employer bargaining occurs most frequently among small companies in competitive industries, where some contracts are national or regional in scope (as in the coal mining and clothing industries) but others cover only a few dozen craftsmen in one locality (many construction and printing agreements for instance).

In short, there is no accurate measurement of the degree of centralisation of the American bargaining structure, but all of the available evidence attests to the enormous diversity and complexity of that structure.

Attempts to increase centralisation

In view of the difficulties in appraising the structure of bargaining at a given point in time, it is not surprising that no statistical measurement has captured the trends in that structure over time. Weber is undoubtedly correct, however, in his judgment that negotiating units in the United States generally expanded in size and scope between 1935 and the

---

[1] The statistics cited in this and subsequent paragraphs are from *Characteristics of agreements covering 5,000 workers or more*, op. cit. (this study did not cover airlines, railroads or government services, but their inclusion would probably have added no more than another 100 or 200 contracts of the scope described); US Department of Labour, Bureau of Labour Statistics: *Directory of national and international labor unions in the United States, 1969*, Bulletin 1665 (Washington, DC, US Government Printing Office, 1970), p. 79 (for 1968 estimates cited); and idem: *Monthly Labor Review* (Washington, DC, US Government Printing Office), Vol. 85, Oct. 1962, pp. 1136-1144: " Monthly union contracts in the United States, 1961 ".

mid-1950s, and since then the bargaining structure has been in a state of flux, showing conflicting trends towards both centralisation and decentralisation.[1]

Several forces combined to expand bargaining units in earlier years. After a union gained a foothold in a company or industry during the great organising campaigns of the 1930s, it usually attempted to " take wages out of competition " by expanding the scope of the bargaining unit towards the limits of the relevant labour or product markets, and many employers, once organised, also favoured at least some expansion of the bargaining unit as a defence against whipsawing by unions. Certain government policies also encouraged larger units during this period, particularly administrative interpretations of the National Labour Relations Act that often favoured plant-wide over craft units, and during the Second World War several decisions by the Wage Stabilisation Agency to consolidate cases involving firms in the same industry. Some people also argue that there are substantial cost and administrative advantages to handling pension and insurance plans in relatively large units, and therefore the post-war emergence of these " fringe benefits " as important bargaining issues served as one more pressure towards centralising negotiations.

These forces seem to have run their course by the mid-1950s in many, but certainly not in all, relationships. It was not until 1964 that James Hoffa, then President of the Teamsters Union, reached his goal of a national agreement covering 450,000 workers and 1,000 firms in the trucking industry. And it was also in 1964 that the Industrial Union Department of the AFL-CIO created a special division with the primary task of promoting what has become known as coalition or co-ordinated bargaining—the " attempt by a group of local and international unions . . . to bargain with a multi-plant, multi-union employer on a joint basis for all of the employees represented by those unions ".[2]

Multi-union bargaining is not a new tactic in the United States, having been practised particularly by groups of craft unions in railroads and a few other industries for some years and often with the approval of the employers involved. In the 1960s, however, industrial unions attempted to force this type of bargaining upon many large corporations whose employees were represented not by a single dominant union, as in the automobile and steel companies, but rather by different unions in different plants, making it difficult for any one of these unions to mount an effective strike. Most of the target companies vigorously resisted all

---

[1] Arnold R. Weber: " Stability and change in the structure of collective bargaining ", in Lloyd Ulman (ed.): *Challenges to collective bargaining* (Englewood Cliffs (New Jersey), Prentice-Hall, Inc., 1967), pp. 22-36. In discussing structure I have drawn heavily on Weber's excellent article.

[2] William N. Chernish: *Coalition bargaining : a study of union tactics and public policy* (Philadelphia, University of Pennsylvania Press, 1969), p. 3. This is the most comprehensive study yet made of this subject.

demands for company-wide bargaining, leading to a series of legal skirmishes and several strikes, most notably a nine-month stoppage by twenty-six unions in the copper industry in 1967-68 and the three-month strike, noted previously, that fourteen unions launched against General Electric and Boulwarism in 1969-70. To date, labour's drive for coalition bargaining has had a mixed record, often producing generous economic settlements but seldom winning any formal expansion of bargaining units.

On the other hand, there are some relationships in which the employers are pushing for broader bargaining units over union opposition. In the construction industry management feels at such a disadvantage in negotiating with up to eighteen different unions, craft-by-craft and often city-by-city, that the major contractors' association has urged Congress to adopt legislation that would actually *require* coalition bargaining in that industry—that is, a government agency could order a merger of existing units to cover several trades and cities under a single contract. And recently in the printing industry, where the bargaining structure is similar to that in construction, employers tried but failed to instigate multi-union bargaining in New York City, accepted a mediator's proposal (as did the unions) to widen the unit in San Francisco, and fought off a union attempt to splinter a multi-employer unit in Washington, DC.

Finally, if history is any guide, the imposition of wage and price controls in late 1971 provided a significant impetus towards centralised bargaining in the United States. Today's economic and political context is obviously very different from that of the Second World War and the Korean War, and the controls themselves, in their initial formulation, are looser than in those earlier periods. Yet these controls still add up to the need to " clear with Washington " a great many wage and price decisions, providing one more inducement for the locus of decision making to move upwards in many bargaining relationships.

Attempts to decentralise

Those pressures towards more centralisation of bargaining have not gone unchallenged. As noted above, proposals for coalition bargaining have met strong resistance from management in some industries and from labour in others. Also, a few bargaining units have formally decentralised in recent years. In basic steel, disagreement within the management negotiating committee led the Kaiser Corporation to break away from the rest of the industry in 1959, and the company has since continued to bargain separately with the United Steelworkers. In the West Coast pulp and paper industry, on the other hand, it was a worker demand for more local autonomy in bargaining and other matters that led in 1964 to the formation of an independent union which ousted two long-established national unions from their position as bargaining agents in a large, multi-employer unit.

In other cases the formal bargaining unit has remained the same but a decentralisation of power has occurred within the unit. This shift in power has taken a variety of forms:

(1) Whatever the cause may be of the increased rate of contract rejections in recent years, one effect has been to increase the responsiveness of many union negotiators to the opinions of the rank and file.

(2) In several industrial unions skilled workers became increasingly restive during the 1950s and early 1960s, apparently feeling their "minority" interests were being ignored. To allay this discontent, many industrial unions have altered their internal structure to give skilled members a larger voice in bargaining, with two unions (the Auto Workers and Brewery Workers Unions) going so far as to grant craftsmen a right of veto over contract ratification in certain circumstances.

(3) In many multi-plant companies like General Motors, work rules and related issues are handled in local supplements to the company-wide agreement. Thus, when these job security issues became increasingly important in the 1955-65 period, bargaining at the plant level also became more significant in many of the largest units in the country.

(4) In several major relationships in longshoring, agricultural implements and other industries, grievance procedures have buckled under various pressures within the last decade or two, resulting in excessive delays in processing grievances, a large backlog of arbitration cases and often many strikes in violation of the contract. To solve this problem, the parties have adopted a number of techniques aimed at increasing the proportion of grievances settled in the first stages of the appeals system—a most important way of decentralising decision making within a bargaining unit.

On balance, the structure of bargaining in the United States appears to have achieved a certain rough stability. Negotiating units will continue to expand in some relationships and to fragment in others, responding to shifts in the needs and relative power of the parties, but over-all there is no dominant trend towards greater centralisation or decentralisation.

V. The content of agreements

No attempt will be made to catalogue the many changes that have occurred in the terms of American labour-management contracts, but a few trends deserve highlighting in any survey of post-war bargaining practices.

First, the typical collective agreement in the United States—which even twenty or twenty-five years ago was more comprehensive than agreements in many other countries—has continued to expand in length and scope and complexity. Contracts vary greatly in their specific terms, but today in most unionised factories, for example, they explicitly cover the following subjects: the scope of the bargaining unit, contract duration, strikes and lockouts, union security, management rights, grievance procedures, wages (rates, incentive systems, job classification, etc.), work rules, hours of work, discipline and discharge, paid and unpaid leave, employee benefit plans, and the role of seniority in layoffs, promotions and transfers. Most agreements contained provisions covering these general subject areas even in the 1940s, but since then the parties have added specific sub-categories (for instance, the regulation of subcontracting first became a management rights issue in many relationships in the 1955-65 period) and they have also elaborated contract language to meet new problems of administration (seniority clauses, for example, have become exceedingly complex over the years).

The explosive growth in those wage supplements sometimes termed " fringe benefits " also clearly reflects the changing content of collective agreements:

Scarcely four decades ago, compensation for American workers consisted almost entirely of a wage for time worked or units produced.... Today, American employers pay about four-fifths of total compensation as straight-time wages and salaries.... The remaining one-fifth is spent primarily for (1) vacations, holidays, and other types of paid leave; (2) protection against economic hardship resulting from unemployment, retirement, disability, illness, or death of workers or their dependants; and (3) premium pay for overtime, week-end, holiday, or late shift work.[1]

Of all employer expenditures for wage supplements in 1968, only 25 per cent went to social security and similar public programmes; nearly all the rest went to private pension, health, and insurance programmes, vacation and holiday payments, and other benefits not required by law.[2] Collective bargaining was undoubtedly a primary stimulant of this expansion of private benefits, and many American labour contracts now have lengthy and highly technical annexes devoted exclusively to pension and other non-wage programmes.

A second trend in bargaining reflected in the content of agreements has been the decline in conflicts over principle and ideology. As noted earlier in the discussion of post-war strike activity, the parties have reached an institutional accommodation in most established relationships—the union has won a substantial degree of institutional security (more than four out of every five major contracts now require some form of compulsory union membership or dues payment [3]) and both parties

---

[1] Alvin Bauman: " Measuring employee compensation in US industry ", in US Department of Labour, Bureau of Labour Statistics: *Monthly Labor Review* (Washington, DC, US Government Printing Office), Vol. 93, No. 10, Oct. 1970, p. 17.

[2] Ibid., p. 23.

[3] *Characteristics of agreements covering 5,000 workers or more*, op. cit., pp. 12-13. Out of 252 such agreements in 1970, 218 called for the union shop, agency shop, or maintenance of membership, and 184 also provided for the check-off of union dues.

have usually accepted the need for compromise on issues involving " management prerogatives " such as seniority in promotions, the arbitration of grievances, and adjustment to technological change. Disputes certainly continue to occur over these and many related issues, but with less dramatic overtones and therefore a better chance of constructive settlement.

Third, there has been a remarkable shift towards longer-term contracts. The available evidence suggests that agreements of one year's duration accounted for about 70 per cent of all agreements in 1950 but for less than 5 per cent by 1970. On the other hand, the proportion of three-year contracts has apparently soared from around 2 per cent in 1950 to 60 per cent or more today, and another 5 to 10 per cent of contracts now run for longer than three years.[1] This lengthening of contract duration has resulted primarily from the desire of many American employers to minimise some of the costs of collective bargaining and to limit such implications as the enormous amount of management time required to prepare for and conduct major negotiations lasting many weeks and covering many subjects, the turmoil often existing within an organisation during contract talks, the possibility of strike losses in the event of an impasse, and the unpredictability of employment costs subject to annual renegotiation.

Long-term contracts sometimes serve union interests as well, but typically labour believes its risks increase under such contracts and it demands protection in some form—deferred wage and benefit increases spread through the life of the contract, a cost-of-living clause (seldom necessary under a one-year contract), or a wage re-opener (a clause permitting negotiations on wages alone at specified intervals during the life of a contract). It has been estimated, for example, that of 9.4 million workers covered under major agreements in 1972, 3.1 million were due to receive specified wage increases negotiated in an earlier year, 3.6 million were guaranteed both a deferred wage increase and a cost-of-living increase (if consumer prices rose), another 0.7 million were covered by a cost-of-living clause alone, and nearly all the remaining 2.0 million were covered by agreements that either expired in 1972 or provided for wage reopeners.[2]

---

[1] These estimates are drawn from studies of widely differing samples: " Characteristics of 12,000 labour-management contracts ", in US Department of Labour, Bureau of Labour Statistics: *Monthly Labor Review* (Washington, DC, US Government Printing Office), Vol. 73, No. 1, July 1951, pp. 31-35; *Characteristics of agreements covering 5,000 workers or more*, op. cit., p. 6 (see note 3, p. 525, for sample size); and Bureau of National Affairs: *Labor Relations Yearbook, 1969* (Washington, DC), pp. 81-82 (a sample of 400 contracts). For the best study of the implications of this trend, see Joseph W. Garbarino: *Wage policy and long-term contracts* (Washington, DC, Brookings Institution, 1962).

[2] Michael E. Sparrough and Lena W. Bolton: " Calendar of wage increases and negotiations for 1972 ", in US Department of Labour, Bureau of Labour Statistics: *Monthly Labor Review* (Washington, DC, US Government Printing Office), Vol. 95, No. 1, Jan. 1972, pp. 3-8.

VI. The administration of agreements

The American bargaining system has long been noted for its emphasis on the day-to-day administration of contracts, an emphasis which has become even more pronounced since the end of the Second World War.

Under the typical agreement in the United States, the employer retains the authority to initiate action on most aspects of the employment relationship—to assign work, to hire and lay off and promote and discipline employees, and so on—but the worker has access to a multi-stage appeals procedure whenever he believes that a management decision has violated his contractual rights. Most grievances of this kind are settled quickly and informally in the first stage by the worker and his supervisor, often with the aid of a steward or other local union official. Grievances not so resolved can be appealed to successively higher levels of management, with correspondingly higher levels of union officials representing the worker. Finally, in an estimated 90 per cent or more of all relationships, the last stage in the grievance procedure incorporates the following bargain: in return for the union's pledge not to strike during the term of the agreement, the employer agrees that unsettled grievances may be appealed to a private arbitrator, selected and paid jointly by the parties, who has the power to issue a final and binding award that can, if the facts warrant, overturn the management decision under challenge and result, for example, in the reinstatement of a wrongfully discharged worker with back pay or the promotion of a worker passed over by the employer.

The importance of contract enforcement activity in the United States can hardly be exaggerated. In most unionised companies labour and management officials spend far more time on contract administration than on negotiations, and the quality of a bargaining relationship depends heavily upon the manner in which its grievance machinery operates.

This administrative function has become even more significant in most relationships because of certain post-war trends previously described: the increasing scope and complexity of agreements; the decline of ideological disputes (many employers initially resisted grievance arbitration as a threat to their prerogatives); and the shift to long-term contracts (increasing the parties' need for a method of coping with developments not foreseen when the agreement was negotiated). In addition, several post-war decisions by the Supreme Court provided interpretations of the Taft-Hartley Act that strongly encouraged the use of private grievance arbitration [1], to the extent where it has become a major method of dis-

---

[1] See particularly the three 1960 cases known as the " arbitration trilogy ": United Steelworkers of America v. American Manufacturing, 363 US 564; United Steelworkers v. Warrior and Gulf Navigation Co., 363 US 574; and United Steelworkers v. Enterprise Wheel and Car Corp., 363 US 593.

pute settlement in the United States, with hundreds of private neutrals each year issuing literally thousands of decisions, many of which are published by commercial reference services and thereby contribute to a growing " common law " of contract interpretation. (It should be stressed that the arbitration of *new* contract terms remains rare in the United States.)

VII. New sectors of bargaining

After the Second World War the United States became the first nation in which white-collar workers outnumbered blue-collar workers and in which those providing intangible services outnumbered those producing physical goods. Since American unions have historically been concentrated in goods industries and among blue-collar workers, it is relevant to ask how well the bargaining system adjusted to these radical changes in the composition of the labour force.

Although this article is primarily concerned with bargaining trends in private industry, mention must be made of the amazingly rapid spread of collective bargaining within the public sector, for it is there that organised labour has scored its most dramatic success in coping with the " service economy ". In many respects this expansion has closely paralleled that in American private industry in earlier years. The bargaining structure emerging in the public sector is highly decentralised; the unions there are pressing for guarantees of institutional security by way of reaction to what they perceive to be hostile employer and public attitudes; and the scope of bargaining is expanding in spite of the resistance of many employers to demands which they believe to be invasions of management prerogatives (disguised in the public sector as the " sovereignty of the legislature " or the " merit principles of civil service ").

Outside the public sector unions have been less successful in organising workers in service industries and white-collar occupations. The performing arts have been well organised for several decades, however, and in recent years unionism has begun to expand in such diverse areas as hospitals, private colleges and professional sports.

Finally, the recent stirring of bargaining activity in agriculture deserves to be mentioned—if only to point out that, after decades of failure, unionism is at last making some headway among the workers at the very bottom of American society. Even after ten years of intensive activity, however, farm unions have won only a handful of written agreements, and they still face an uphill battle to overcome hostile employers, lack of coverage by the Taft-Hartley Act, and the organising difficulties posed by a migratory labour force.[1]

---

[1] Karen S. Koziara: " Agriculture ", in Seymour L. Wolfbein (ed.): *Emerging sectors of collective bargaining* (Braintree (Massachusetts), D. H. Mark Publishing Company, 1970), pp. 95-128.

VIII. Conclusions

This review of post-war bargaining trends in the United States has concentrated on developments in the structure and process of bargaining, but has not dwelt on the implications of these developments for the economy and public policy. Within that context, the American bargaining system has exhibited a combination of stability and innovation that, by most standards, has effectively served both labour and management.

It is true that deadline bargaining is something less than an ideal problem-solving process, that the bargaining structure is most untidy, with imbalances of power in many relationships, and that the role of collective bargaining remains unsettled in large areas of the services sector, both private and public. Yet this system continues to produce pragmatic compromises in disputes of a type that once appeared to involve irreconcilable differences of principle—compromises that have given literally millions of workers a voice in a growing number of decisions at the bargaining table and an effective procedure for handling grievances at the workplace but that, in most cases, have also preserved a substantial degree of management authority to initiate and innovate.

What, then, of bargaining trends in the United States? For reasons previously noted, it seems safe to predict that deadline bargaining and fixed-term contracts will continue to predominate for many years to come. Also, nearly all observers agree that the scope of bargaining will continue to widen, particularly in the area of fringe benefits, where there appears to be no limit to labour's needs and imagination—and where unions will eventually win a salaried or other guaranteed-income status for many blue-collar employees, a goal already in sight for senior workers in some relationships. There is no evidence, however, that American unions will soon seek or win a voice in many of those price and production and other " basic " management decisions that have so far remained outside the scope of bargaining in most relationships.

But by all odds the most far-reaching change likely to occur in the American bargaining system is further regulation by the federal Government. It is highly significant that the Nixon administration, originally committed to minimising federal intervention in the bargaining process, had by 1971 imposed wage and price controls, proposed major amendments to the Taft-Hartley and Railway Labour Acts to provide more effective remedies (including an ingenious version of compulsory arbitration) for national emergency strikes in transportation, and had also carried the fight against racial discrimination to the point where, particularly in construction and other industries heavily dependent on government purchases, there now is often a third or even fourth party at the bargaining table—government agencies and civil rights groups—putting pressure on unions and managements to alter hiring and apprenticeship and other employment practices of long standing.

This is not the place to debate the merits of these measures—the adequate exploration of which would require at least one article each. I would simply make the point that today there are many forces combining to encourage increased government regulation of collective bargaining in the United States, and few political pressures from either conservatives or liberals for the reduction of such regulation. Thus in the future, as in the past, the nature of this bargaining system will be shaped as much by the choices made by legislators as by those made by the negotiators themselves.

List of works cited
in Part I

Adam, Gérard, Reynaud, Jean-Daniel and Verdier, Jean-Maurice. *La négociation collective en France* (Paris, Les éditions ouvrières, 1972).

Albeda, W. "Recent trends in collective bargaining in the Netherlands", in *International Labour Review,* Vol. 103, No. 3, March 1971. Reprinted in the present volume.

Anderman, Steven D. "Central wage negotiation in Sweden: Recent problems and developments", in *British Journal of Industrial Relations,* Vol. 5, No. 3, November 1967.

Barbash, Jack. "Austrian trade unions and the negotiation of national economic policy", in *British Journal of Industrial Relations,* Vol. 9, No. 3, November 1971.

Beirne, Joseph A. Address printed in Bureau of National Affairs, Inc. (see below).

Blanpain, Roger. "Recent trends in collective bargaining in Belgium", in *International Labour Review,* Vol. 104, Nos. 1-2, July-August 1971. Reprinted in the present volume.

Bok, Derek C., and Dunlop, John T. *Labor and the American community* (New York, Simon and Schuster, 1970).

Brun, André. "Collective agreements in France", in Kahn-Freund (ed.): *Labour relations and the law* (see below).

Bureau of National Affairs, Inc. *Collective bargaining today* (Washington, 1970).

Canada. *Canadian industrial relations,* The report of the Task Force on Labour Relations (Ottawa, Privy Council Office, 1968).

Caples, William G. "Development and problems of bargaining structure in the steel industry", in Weber (ed.): *The structure of collective bargaining* (see below).

—— "The computer's uses and potential in bargaining: A management view", in Siegel (see below).

Carlson, Bo. *Trade unions in Sweden* (Stockholm, Tiden förlag, 1969).

Chamberlain, Neil W., and Kuhn, James W. *Collective bargaining* (New York, McGraw-Hill, 2nd ed., 1965).

Chernish, William N. *Coalition bargaining: A study of union tactics and public policy* (Philadelphia, University of Pennsylvania Press, 1969).

Clegg, Hugh A. *How to run an incomes policy* (London, Heinemann, 1971).

—— *The system of industrial relations in Great Britain* (Oxford, Blackwell, 1970).

Cook, Alice H. "Dual government in unions: A tool for analysis", in *Industrial and Labor Relations Review,* Vol. 15, No. 3, April 1962.

Cooke, John R. Address printed in Bureau of National Affairs, Inc. (see above).

Collective bargaining

Cullen, Donald E. *Negotiating labor-management contracts,* Bulletin 56, New York State School of Industrial and Labor Relations, September 1965.

——— "Recent trends in collective bargaining in the United States", in *International Labour Review,* Vol. 105, No. 6, June 1972. Reprinted in the present volume.

Davey, Harold W. *Contemporary collective bargaining* (Englewood Cliffs, New Jersey, Prentice-Hall, 3rd ed., 1972).

Delamotte, Yves. "Recent collective bargaining trends in France", in *International Labour Review,* Vol. 103, No. 4, April 1971. Reprinted in the present volume.

——— *The social partners face the problems of productivity and employment,* A study in comparative industrial relations (Paris, Organisation for Economic Co-operation and Development, 1971).

Der Österreichischer Gewerkschaftsbund (Vienna, 1970).

"Dismissal procedures — IV: Federal Republic of Germany", in *International Labour Review,* Vol. 80, No. 3, September 1959.

Donovan. See under United Kingdom, Royal Commission on Trade Unions and Employers' Associations.

Dorfman, Herbert. *Labour relations in Norway* (Oslo, Norwegian Joint Committee on International Social Policy, rev. ed., 1966).

Edelman, Murray, and Fleming, R. W. *The politics of wage-price decisions* (Urbana, University of Illinois Press, 1965).

Edgren, Gösta. "Trends of bargaining for remuneration", in Organisation for Economic Co-operation and Development, Manpower and Social Affairs Directorate: *New perspectives in collective bargaining,* Papers prepared for a regional trade union seminar, Paris, 4-7 November 1969.

Erdmann, Ernst-Gerhard. "The Confederation of German Employers' Associations", in ILO: *Role of employers' organisations . . .* (see below).

Fairweather, Owen. Address printed in Bureau of National Affairs, Inc. (see above).

Flanders, Allan. "Collective bargaining: A theoretical analysis", in *British Journal of Industrial Relations,* Vol. 6, No. 1, March 1968.

——— *Management and unions: The theory and reform of industrial relations* (London, Faber, 1970).

——— "The changing character of collective bargaining", in *Employment and Productivity Gazette,* December 1969.

———*The Fawley productivity agreements: A case study of management and collective bargaining* (London, Faber, 1964).

———*Trade unions* (London, Hutchinson, 7th edn., 1968).

Giugni, Gino. "Recent developments in collective bargaining in Italy", in *International Labour Review,* Vol. 91, No. 4, April 1965.

——— "Recent trends in collective bargaining in Italy", in idem, Vol. 104, No. 4, October 1971. Reprinted in the present volume.

Goodman, J. F. B., and Whittingham, T. G. *Shop stewards in British industry* (London, McGraw-Hill, 1969).

Greenberg, David H. "The structure of collective bargaining and some of its determinants", in *Proceedings of the Industrial Relations Research Association,* 1966.

Grunfeld, Cyril. "Australian compulsory arbitration: Appearance and reality", in *British Journal of Industrial Relations,* Vol. 9, No. 3, November 1971.

"Guidelines to better industrial relations in shipbuilding and shiprepairing", in *Department of Employment Gazette* (London), September 1971.

Hamburger, L. "The extension of collective agreements to cover entire trades and industries", in *International Labour Review,* Vol. 40, No. 2, August 1939.

Healey, James J. (ed.). *Creative collective bargaining* (Englewood Cliffs, New Jersey, Prentice-Hall, 1965).

Högberg, Gunnar. "Recent trends in collective bargaining in Sweden", in *International Labour Review,* Vol. 107, No. 3, March 1973. Reprinted in the present volume.

Holmquist, Per G. "The Swedish Employers' Confederation", in ILO: *Role of employers' organisations . . .* (see below).

ILO. *Basic agreements and joint statements on labour-management relations,* Labour-Management Relations Series, No. 38 (Geneva, 1971).

—— *Collective agreements,* Studies and Reports, Series A (Industrial Relations), No. 39 (Geneva, 1936).

—— *Collective bargaining and the challenge of new technology* (Geneva, 1972).

—— *Government services for the improvement of labour-management relations and settlement of disputes in Asia,* An account of the work of the labour-management relations committee, Fifth Asian Regional Conference, Melbourne, 1962, Labour-Management Relations Series, No. 16.

—— *International standards and guiding principles, 1944-1968,* Labour-Management Relations Series, No. 34 (Geneva, 1969).

—— *Participation of workers in decisions within undertakings,* Documents of a technical meeting, Geneva, 20-29 November 1967, Labour-Management Relations Series, No. 33.

—— *Prices, wages and incomes policies in industrialised market economies,* by H. A. Turner and H. Zoeteweij, Studies and Reports, New Series, No. 70 (Geneva, 1966).

—— *Role of employers' organisations in Asian countries,* Record of proceedings of, and documents submitted to, an Asian round table, Tokyo, December 1970, Labour-Management Relations Series, No. 39.

Jensen, Vernon H. "Notes on the beginnings of collective bargaining", in *Industrial and Labor Relations Review,* Vol. 9, No. 2, January 1956.

—— "The process of collective bargaining and the question of its obsolescence", in *Industrial and Labor Relations Review,* Vol. 16, No. 4, July 1963.

Johnston, T. L. *Collective bargaining in Sweden,* A study of the labour market and its institutions (London, Allen and Unwin, 1962).

Kahn-Freund, Otto (ed.). *Labour relations and the law* (London, Stevens, 1965).

—— "Report on the legal status of collective bargaining and collective agreements in Great Britain", in his *Labour relations and the law* (see above).

Kawada, Hisashi. "The Government, industrial relations, and economic development in Japan", in Arthur M. Ross (ed.): *Industrial relations and economic development* (London, Macmillan, 1966).

"Labour dispute and settlement in the United States steel industry", in *International Labour Review,* Vol. 82, No. 1, July 1960.

411

Collective bargaining

Lagasse, André. "The law of collective bargaining and collective agreements in Belgium", in Kahn-Freund (ed.): *Labour relations and the law* (see above).

Lahne, Herbert J. "The intermediate union body in collective bargaining", in *Industrial and Labor Relations Review*, Vol. 6, No. 2, January 1953.

Lerner, Shirley W. "Factory agreements and national bargaining in the British engineering industry", in *International Labour Review*, Vol. 89, No. 1, January 1964.

—— *The impact of technological and economic change on the structure of British trade unions,* paper submitted to the First World Congress of the International Industrial Relations Association, Geneva, 4-8 September 1967 (doc. 1C-67/8-3, mimeographed).

Lester, Richard A. "Reflections on collective bargaining in Britain and Sweden", in *Industrial and Labor Relations Review*, Vol. 10, No. 3, April 1957.

Levenbach, M. G. "The law relating to collective agreements in the Netherlands", in Kahn-Freund (ed.): *Labour relations and the law* (see above).

Levine, Gil. "The coming youth revolt in labour", in *Labour Gazette* (Ottawa), Vol. 71, No. 11, November 1971.

Marcus, Averill G. "The employer's duty to bargain", in *Labor Law Journal,* September 1966.

McCarthy, W. E. J. (ed.). *Industrial relations in Great Britain: A guide for management and unions* (London, Lyon, Grant and Green, 1969).

MacDonald, Robert M. "Collective bargaining in the postwar period", in *Industrial and Labor Relations Review,* Vol. 20, No. 4, July 1967.

Minemura, Teruo. "The role of the Government in industrial relations: An outline", in Japan Institute of Labour: *The changing patterns of industrial conflict* (Tokyo, 1965).

Mitsufuji, Tadashi, and Hagisawa, Kiyohiko. "Recent trends in collective bargaining in Japan", in *International Labour Review,* Vol. 105, No. 2, February 1972. Reprinted in the present volume.

Nieuwenhuysen, J. P., and Norman, N. R. "Wages policy in Australia: Issues and tests", in *British Journal of Industrial Relations,* Vol. 9, No. 3, November 1971.

Noe, Claus. *Gebändigter Klassenkampf: Tarifautonomie in der Bundesrepublik Deutschland* (Berlin, Duncker und Humblot, 1970).

Nousbaum, J. "France", in Organisation for Economic Co-operation and Development, Manpower and Social Affairs Directorate: *Recent trends in collective bargaining,* Supplement to the final report, International management seminar, Castelfusano, 21-24 September 1971.

Pélissier, Jean. *Documents de droit du travail* (Paris, Montchrestien, 1971).

Phelps Brown, E. H. *The growth of British industrial relations* (London, Macmillan, 1959).

Polites, G. "The Australian Council of Employers' Federations", in ILO: *Role of employers' organisations . . .* (see above).

Proksch, Anton. "The Austrian Joint Wage and Price Council", in *International Labour Review,* Vol. 83, No. 3, March 1961.

Quinet, Félix. *Collective bargaining in the Canadian context, with references to collective bargaining in the Public Service of Canada* (Ottawa, 1972; mimeographed), pp. 14-15.

Ramm, Thilo. "Labour courts and grievance settlement in West Germany", in Benjamin Aaron (ed.): *Labour courts and grievance settlement in Western Europe* (Berkeley, University of California Press, 1971).

Reichel, Hans. "Recent trends in collective bargaining in the Federal Republic of Germany", in *International Labour Review,* Vol. 104, No. 6, December 1971. Reprinted in the present volume.

—— "Zwanzig Jahre Tarifvertragsgesetz", in *Bundesarbeitsblatt,* Vol. 20, No. 4, April 1969, p. 195.

Reuther, Walter P. "Labor's role in 1975", in Jack Stieber (ed.): *U.S. industrial relations: The next twenty years* (East Lansing, Michigan State University Press, 1958).

Reynaud, Jean-Daniel. *Les syndicats en France* (Paris, Colin, 2nd ed., 1966).

Rivero, Jean, and Savatier, Jean. *Droit du travail* (Paris, Presses Universitaires de France, 1970).

Roberts, B. C., and Gennard, John. "Trends in plant and company bargaining", in *Scottish Journal of Political Economy,* Vol. 17, No. 2, June 1970.

—— and Rothwell, Sheila. "Recent trends in collective bargaining in the United Kingdom", in *International Labour Review,* Vol. 106, No. 6, December 1972. Reprinted in the present volume.

Ross, Philip. *The government as a source of union power: The role of public policy in collective bargaining* (Providence, Rhode Island, Brown University Press, 1965).

Schregle, Johannes. "Industrial relations in the public sector: An international viewpoint", in Japan Institute of Labour: *The changing patterns of industrial relations in Asian countries,* Proceedings of the Asian regional conference on industrial relations, Tokyo . . ., 1969.

Selekman, Benjamin M. *et al. Problems in labor relations* (New York, McGraw-Hill, 3rd ed., 1964).

Sellier, François. "Les transformations de la négociation collective et de l'organisation syndicale en Italie", in *Sociologie du travail,* April-June 1971.

—— and Tiano, André. *Economie du travail* (Paris, Presses Universitaires de France, 2nd ed., 1970).

Shirai, Taishirô. "The changing pattern of collective bargaining in Japan", in Japan Institute of Labour: *The changing pattern of industrial relations,* Proceedings of the international conference on industrial relations, Tokyo, . . . 1965.

—— "Prices and wages in Japan: Towards an anti-inflationary policy?", in *International Labour Review,* Vol. 103, No. 3, March 1971.

Siegel, Abraham J. (ed.). *The impact of computers on collective bargaining* (Cambridge, Mass., Massachusetts Institute of Technology, 1969).

Simkin, William E. "Refusal to ratify contracts", in *Industrial and Labor Relations Review,* Vol. 21, No. 4, July 1968.

Spitaels, Guy. "Changes in union organization and collective bargaining in Belgium", in B. C. Roberts (ed.): *Industrial relations: Contemporary issues* (London, Macmillan, 1968).

Sturmthal, Adolf F. *Workers' councils* (Cambridge, Massachusetts, Harvard University Press, 1964).

413

Collective bargaining

Summers, Clyde W. "Ratification of agreements", in John T. Dunlop and Neil W. Chamberlain: *Frontiers of collective bargaining* (New York, Harper and Row, 1967).

Suppanz, H., and Robinson, D. *Prices and incomes policy: The Austrian experience* (Paris, Organisation for Economic Co-operation and Development, 1972).

Towy-Evans, M. "The Personnel Management Advisory Service in Great Britain", in *International Labour Review,* Vol. 81, No. 2, February 1960.

Turner and Zoeteweij. See under ILO.

Ulman, Lloyd. *The rise of the national union* (Cambridge, Massachusetts, Harvard University Press, 1955).

—— and Flanagan, Robert J. *Wage restraint: A study of incomes policies in Western Europe* (Berkeley, University of California Press, 1971).

United Kingdom. *Statement on personal incomes, costs and prices, presented by the Prime Minister . . . to Parliament . . .,* Cmd. 7321 (London, HM Stationery Office, 1948).

—— Commission on Industrial Relations. *Facilities afforded to shop stewards,* Report No. 17, Cmd. 4668 (London, HM Stationery Office, 1971).

—— Department of Employment. *The reform of collective bargaining at plant and company level,* Manpower Papers, No. 5 (London, HM Stationery Office, 1971).

—— Ministry of Labour. *Industrial relations handbook,* An account of British institutions and practice relating to the organisation of employers and workers in Great Britain; collective bargaining and joint negotiating machinery; conciliation and arbitration; and statutory regulation of wages in certain industries (London, HM Stationery Office, 3rd ed., 1961).

—— Royal Commission on Trade Unions and Employers' Associations, 1965-1968 (Chairman: Lord Donovan). *Report,* Cmnd. 3623 (London, HM Stationery Office, 1968).

—— —— *Employers' associations,* Research Papers, No. 7 (London, HM Stationery Office, 1967).

United States. *Economic report of the President, transmitted to the Congress, January 1962, together with the annual report of the Council of Economic Advisers* (Washington, Government Printing Office).

—— Bureau of Labor Statistics. *Characteristics of agreements covering 5,000 workers or more,* Bulletin 1686 (Washington, 1970).

—— —— *Directory of national and international labor unions in the United States, 1969* (Washington, 1970).

—— Federal Mediation and Conciliation Service. *Twenty-third annual report, Fiscal year 1970* (Washington, Government Printing Office, 1971).

de Vyver, Frank T. "Employers' organisations in the Australian industrial relations system", in *Journal of Industrial Relations,* Vol. 13, No. 1, March 1971.

Waisglas, H. J., and Craig, Alton W. J. "Collective bargaining perspectives", in *Labour Gazette* (Ottawa), Vol. 68, No. 10, October 1968.

Waline, Pierre. *Cinquante ans de rapports entre patrons et ouvriers en Allemagne, 1918-1968,* Cahiers de la Fondation nationale des sciences politiques, No. 178, Vol. 2: *Depuis 1945: la République fédérale allemande* (Paris, Colin, 1970).

Walker, Kenneth F. *Australian industrial relations systems* (Cambridge, Massachusetts, Harvard University Press, 1970).

414

Walton, Richard E., and McKersie, Robert B. *A behavioral theory of labor negotiations* (New York, McGraw-Hill, 1965).

Webb, Sidney and Beatrice. *Industrial democracy* (London, Longmans, Green, 1902 ed.).

Weber, Arnold R. "Stability and change in the structure of collective bargaining", in Lloyd Ulman (ed.): *Challenges to collective bargaining* (Englewood Cliffs, New Jersey, Prentice-Hall, 1967).

—— (ed.). *The structure of collective bargaining: Problems and perspectives* (Glencoe, Illinois, Free Press, 1961).

Whittingham, T. G., and Towers, B. "Bargaining for change", in *Industrial Relations Journal,* Vol. 3, No. 1, Spring 1972.

Windmuller, John P. *Labor relations in the Netherlands* (Ithaca, New York, Cornell University Press, 1969).

Yerbury, Dianne, and Isaac, J. E. "Recent trends in collective bargaining in Australia", in *International Labour Review,* Vol. 103, No. 5, May 1971. Reprinted in the present volume.

Other ILO Publications

Multinational enterprises and social policy

This volume deals in particular with the effect of multinational enterprises on manpower, the working and living conditions they provide and how industrial relations operate in a multinational framework. The questions covered in the latter respect include the transfer of operations and power relationships, the locus of decision making, adjustment to local policies and practices, the provision of information on the finances of the enterprise, and forms of multinational bargaining and disputes.
ISBN 92-2-101003-1

Social and labour practices of some European-based multinationals in the metal trades

Based on information received in response to a questionnaire sent to the managements of multinational enterprises, workers' organisations, employers' organisations, host country governments and home country governments, this volume concentrates on matters relating to employment and training, wages and basic conditions of work, and labour relations.
ISBN 92-2-101474-6

Multinationals in Western Europe: The industrial relations experience

Based largely on direct interviews held with representatives of employers' and workers' organisations and with government officials, this study compares the industrial relations experience of multinational enterprises in the food and related industries and in the metal industries (with special reference, in the latter case, to the engineering industry and particularly its automobile and electrical-electronics sectors) in six European countries, namely Belgium, France, the Federal Republic of Germany, the Netherlands, Sweden and the United Kingdom. Special attention is paid to such major issues as union recognition, the role of multinational managers in employers' associations in the various countries surveyed, labour problems and union reactions connected with the investment, production and employment policies of multinationals and union and employer experiences and attitudes regarding transnational labour relations.
ISBN 92-2-101476-2

Wages and working conditions in multinational enterprises

This study supplements from a variety of published and unpublished sources the information provided on wages and working conditions by other studies undertaken by the ILO in its current research on multinationals. The comparisons made are between the remuneration, hours of work, holidays and retirement benefits provided for locally recruited personnel by the bulk of foreign-owned firms and by locally owned firms. Although the information available is fragmentary, the conclusions of the study go a little beyond the usual extremely broad generalisations on this subject, which it qualifies by differentiating in particular between developed and developing countries and by industry and size of firm.
ISBN 92-2-101475-4

The impact of multinational enterprises on employment and training

This is a first analysis of the information collected by the ILO on the very controversial issues of the impact of multinational enterprises on employment in developing and industrialised countries respectively, and on the transfer of knowledge to the host countries.
ISBN 92-2-101478-9

Other ILO Publications

International principles and guidelines on social policy for multinational enterprises : Their usefulness and feasibility

The main purpose of this study is to investigate to what extent it might be useful and feasible to establish international principles and guidelines relating to those activities of multinational enterprises that fall within the competence of the ILO. To this end the study examines the relevance to multinational enterprises of existing international labour standards that are geared to implementation within a national rather than an international context, discusses the various domains (industrial relations, employment, etc.) in which principles and guidelines might be devised, and examines the possible forms they might take.

ISBN 92-2-101477-0

Social and labour practices of multinational enterprises in the petroleum industry

This is the result of an attempt by the International Labour Office to gather information from countries in all regions where multinational petroleum companies operate; its coverage is limited, however, to the production and refining sectors, excluding the petrochemicals side of the industry. Although the response to the Office's inquiries addressed to governments and employers' and workers' organisations was much less complete than had been hoped, the replies received tended to corroborate the companies' claim that the petroleum industry generally, and the multinational enterprises in particular, hold a position of leadership at the national and international levels in comparison with other sectors of industry, especially in respect of wages, fringe benefits and other conditions of employment, training and occupational health and safety.

ISBN 92-2-101806-7

Social and labour practices of some US-based multinationals in the metal trades

This study aims to broaden the information base about the impact of multinational enterprises in the social policy field and to determine more clearly the specific problems that might arise in such international operations.

It analyses the information obtained in reply to inquiries relating to six major companies in the metal trades sector with head offices in the United States—namely Caterpillar, John Deere, Ford, General Motors, International Harvester and Otis Elevator—which have manufacturing subsidiaries in North and South America, Europe and Asia (Africa, where such subsidiaries also exist, is not dealt with in this study). The information received from the managements of these companies in the United States, from workers' organisations in the US and in the host countries, from host country governments and from the Government of the United States covers, among other things, reasons for investing abroad, including manpower considerations, employment and training, wages and basic conditions of work, and labour relations.

ISBN 92-2-101840-7

Conciliation in industrial disputes : A practical guide

This guide has been prepared with a view to helping developing countries in their efforts to promote the orderly settlement of industrial disputes through conciliation. Its aim is to meet the needs not only of professional or full-time conciliators but also of industrial relations officers, labour officers or labour inspectors, if conciliation is among their duties, by suggesting forms of behaviour, approaches and attitudes that will enable them to carry out their functions more effectively. The guide is based on contributions prepared by high-level mediators and conciliators from the United Kingdom and the United States as well as on information available to the ILO.

ISBN 92-2-101007-4

Other ILO Publications

Grievance arbitration

Not all industrial disputes are about claims for better conditions than those to which the workers may already be entitled. A large proportion are so-called "grievance disputes", over difficulties in the application of labour legislation, collective agreements or individual contracts of employment. Disputes over the application of collective agreements can often be most easily settled if labour and management agree to submit them to arbitration by an independent, impartial outsider. The present guide, which is a companion volume to *Conciliation in industrial disputes,* is intended to show what sort of grievance-settlement procedure can be introduced in developing countries where changes in the organisation of work, in particular, increase the likelihood of grievance disputes. The guide is based on a draft by Arnold M. Zack, a well known labour arbitrator in the United States.
ISBN 92-2-101722-2

Labour-management relations series

Some titles:

Workers' participation in decisions within undertakings. Summary of discussions of a symposium on workers' participation in decisions within undertakings (Oslo, 20-30 August 1974)

The question of workers' participation in decisions within the undertaking has recently been once more in the public eye in a number of European countries in particular. Developments in that field are being closely monitored by the ILO, which has over the past decade convened a number of meetings to facilitate informed, dispassionate discussion of the subject among experts from a wide variety of countries in various parts of the world. The publication also includes a background paper submitted to the meeting by the ILO.

ISBN 92-2-101452-5

The role of labour law in developing countries. Record of proceedings of, and documents submitted to, a round table (Geneva, 10-14 September, and Selva di Fasano, Italy, 17-19 September 1974)

This round table meeting examined, from the broadest possible angle, the practical connection between labour law in the traditional sense, exclusive of social security, and the development process in the developing countries. The participants whose papers are reproduced were persons holding positions of responsibility in very varied sectors, including workers' and employers' organisations, in Argentina, Bangladesh, Brazil, Egypt, India, Indonesia, Iran, Iraq, Jamaica, Jordan, Kenya, Lebanon, Malaysia, Mexico, Nigeria, Pakistan, Peru, Sierra Leone, Singapore, Sri Lanka, Syria, Trinidad and Tobago, Tunisia and Venezuela.
ISBN 92-2-101287-5

International standards and guiding principles, 1944-1973

This publication makes easily available to those interested in the development of good labour-management relations throughout the world the texts of the main international standards and guiding principles adopted in this field by the ILO in recent years.
ISBN 92-2-101119-4